HUMAN RIGHTS IN EDUCATION, SCIENCE AND CULTURE

Human Rights in Education, Science and Culture

Legal Developments and Challenges

Edited by

YVONNE DONDERS AND VLADIMIR VOLODIN

United Nations
Educational, Scientific and
Cultural Organization

UNESCO Publishing

ASHGATE

The designations employed and the presentation of material throughout this publication do not imply the expression of any opinion whatsoever on the part of UNESCO concerning the legal status of any country, territory, city or area or of its authorities, or the delimitation of its frontiers or boundaries. The authors are responsible for the choice and the presentation of the facts contained in this book and for the opinions expressed therein, which are not necessarily those of UNESCO and do not commit the Organization.

Published jointly by the United Nations Educational, Scientific and Cultural Organization (UNESCO), 7, place de Fontenoy, 75007 Paris, France, and Ashgate Publishing Limited, Gower House, Croft Road, Aldershot, Hampshire, GU11 3HR, United Kingdom / Ashgate Publishing Company, Suite 420, 101 Cherry Street, Burlington, VT 05401-4405, USA.

UNESCO website: http://www.unesco.org

Ashgate website: http://www.ashgate.com

British Library Cataloguing in Publication Data
Human rights in education, science and culture : legal
    developments and challenges
    1. Human rights
    I. Donders, Yvonne II. Volodin, Vladimir III. Unesco
    341.4'8

Library of Congress Cataloging-in-Publication Data
Human rights in education, science, and culture : legal developments and challenges / by Unesco ; edited by Yvonne Donders and Vladimir Volodin.
        p. cm.
    Includes bibliographical references and index.
    ISBN 978-0-7546-7312-5 (alk. paper)
        1. Social rights. 2. Right to education. 3. Cultural policy. 4. Economic policy.
    5. Human rights. I. Donders, Yvonne. II. Volodin, Vladimir. III. Unesco.

    K3240.H8572 2008
    341.4'8--dc22

                                                                                    2007030999

Ashgate   ISBN 978-0-7546-7312-5 (Hbk)
           ISBN 978-0-7546-7313-2 (Pbk)

UNESCO ISBN 978-92-3-104073-3

Printed and bound in Great Britain by MPG Books Ltd, Bodmin, Cornwall.

Contents

About the Authors

Professor Audrey R. Chapman holds the Healey Endowed Chair in Medical Humanities, Law, and Ethics at the University of Connecticut Health Center and is a professor of community medicine. She formerly served as the director of the Science and Human Rights Program at the American Association for the Advancement of Science (AAAS) and as the co-director of the AAAS initiative on Science and Intellectual Property in the Public Interest. She has worked on a wide range of issues related to economic, social and cultural rights in close cooperation with the UN Committee on Economic, Social and Cultural Rights. She also works with the special rapporteur for the right to the highest attainable level of health. She has been involved with several UN-related initiatives to develop indicators and improve the monitoring of economic, social and cultural rights.

Professor Fons Coomans holds the UNESCO Chair in Human Rights and Peace at the Department of International and European Law. He is coordinator and senior researcher at the Centre for Human Rights at the University of Maastricht, and senior researcher at the Netherlands School of Human Rights Research. His fields of research include the international protection of economic, social and cultural rights in general and the right to education and food in particular, as well as international supervisory mechanisms in the field of human rights. He is the coordinator of the courses on economic, social and cultural rights of the European Masters Degree in Human Rights and Democratization in Venice. Presently he teaches bachelor and master courses on human rights at the Faculty of Law of Maastricht University. He is also a consultant for UNESCO, an adviser to the Foodfirst Information and Action Network (FIAN) and a member of the Dutch Section of the International Commission of Jurists (NJCM). His publications include *Extraterritorial Application of Human Rights Treaties* (co-edited with M. Kamminga) (Intersentia 2004); "Reviewing Implementation of Social and Economic Rights: An Assessment of the 'Reasonableness' Test as Developed by the South African Constitutional Court", *Heidelberg Journal of International Law* (2005) 65: 167–96; and "Agrarian Reform as a Human Rights Issue in the Activities of United Nations Human Rights Bodies and Specialised Agencies", *Netherlands Quarterly of Human Rights* (2006) 24: 7–31. He also edited *Justiciability of Economic and Social Rights – Experiences from Domestic Systems* (Intersentia 2006).

Professor Christian Courtis is legal officer economic, social and cultural rights of the International Commission of Jurists in Geneva. He is a former law professor at the University of Buenos Aires Law School and visiting professor at ITAM Law School in Mexico. He coordinates the human rights graduate programme at ITAM and teaches on the law masters programme at the University of Palermo in Buenos Aires. He has been a visiting scholar at Southwestern University and Boalt Hall, University of California-Berkeley School of Law in the United States, and at the universities of Valencia, Sevilla, Carlos III, Castilla-La Mancha and Deusto (Spain), Toulouse-Le Mirail (France), Diego Portales (Chile), ITAM (Mexico) and Nacional Autonoma de Honduras (Honduras). His fields of research include constitutional law, international human rights law, criminal law and criminal justice, economic, social and cultural rights, disability rights and jurisprudence. He is legal consultant for the UN Social Development Agency and the Panamerican Health Organization/World Health Organization.

Yvonne Donders, PhD, is Deputy Director of the Amsterdam Center for International Law (ACIL) of the University of Amsterdam. Her research focuses on economic, social and cultural rights and she teaches international law and human rights. She is former programme specialist in the Division of Human Rights and Struggle against Discrimination of UNESCO's Secretariat in Paris, where her work centred around the implementation of UNESCO's human rights strategy. She was specifically working on research projects with regard to the elaboration of the content, nature of obligations, state of implementation, indicators and justiciability of economic, social and cultural rights. Her PhD is on cultural rights and the right to cultural identity. She is president of the United Nations Association of the Netherlands.

Professor Asbjørn Eide is former director and presently senior fellow of the Norwegian Centre for Human Rights at the University of Oslo. He was previously director of the International Peace Research Institute in Oslo, and secretary-general of the International Peace Research Association. He is the author of numerous books and articles on peace and conflict issues and human rights. He has been Torgny Segerstedt Professor at the University of Gøteborg, Sweden, and is presently visiting professor at the University of Lund. From 1981 to 2003 he was a member of the UN Sub-Commission on Promotion and Protection of Human Rights, and from 1995 to 2004 the chairman of the UN Working Group on the Rights of Minorities. He is presently the president of the Advisory Committee on the Council of Europe's Framework Convention for the Protection of National Minorities.

Professor William A. Schabas is director of the Irish Centre for Human Rights at the National University of Ireland, Galway, where he also holds the chair in human rights law. From 1991 to 2000 he was professor of human rights law and criminal law at the Département des sciences juridiques of the Université du Québec in Montréal, a department he chaired from 1994 to 1998; he now holds the honorary position of *professeur associé* at that institution. He was a senior fellow at the US Institute of Peace in Washington during the academic year 1998–99. In 1998 Professor Schabas was awarded the Bora Laskin Research Fellowship in Human Rights by the Social Sciences and Humanities Research Council of Canada. In May 2002 the president of Sierra Leone appointed Professor Schabas to the country's Truth and Reconciliation Commission, upon the recommendation of Mary Robinson, the UN High Commissioner for Human Rights. Professor Schabas is an officer of the Order of Canada, and a member of the Board of Trustees of the UN Voluntary Fund for Technical Cooperation in Human Rights.

Professor Frans Viljoen is the director of academic programmes at the Centre for Human Rights at the University of Pretoria. He also heads the AIDS and Human Rights Unit at the Centre for the Study of AIDS, based at the same university. He has published and taught internationally on aspects of international law – in particular the African regional human rights system. He is an editor of the *African Human Rights Law Journal* and the African Human Rights Law Reports. He has also acted as consultant for the United Nations, the African Commission on Human and Peoples' Rights, Penal Reform International and the Danish Centre for Human Rights.

Vladimir Volodin is chief of the Human Rights and Gender Equality Section, UNESCO Secretariat, Paris. He graduated from Moscow State University (1970) and the Diplomatic Academy of Moscow (1988). He is a specialist in international law and history. Before joining UNESCO in 1991, he worked in a research institution, in the UN Secretariat in New York and in the Ministry of Foreign Affairs. As a diplomat and international civil servant he took part in a great number of sessions of bodies dealing with human rights, including the Commission on Human Rights and its sub-commission, the Human Rights Council, treaty monitoring bodies, etc. He is the author of articles and editor of several publications, including *A Guide to Human Rights* (UNESCO Publishing, 2003). He contributed to the preparation of a number of works on human rights, including *Human Rights: Questions and Answers* (UNESCO Publishing, 2004) and a three-volume manual on human rights for universities (edited by Janusz Symonides) (UNESCO Publishing and Ashgate, 1998–2003).

List of Acronyms

AAAS	American Association for the Advancement of Science
ACIL	Amsterdam Centre for International Law
ART	anti-retroviral treatment
AU	African Union
CEDAW	Convention on the Elimination of Discrimination against Women
CERD	Convention on the Elimination of All Forms of Racial Discrimination
CESCR	Committee on Economic, Social and Cultural Rights
CRC	Convention on the Rights of the Child
DRC	Democratic Republic of Congo
DPSP	directive principle of state policy
ECHR	European Convention on Human Rights
ECOSOC	Economic and Social Council
EFA	Education for All
FAO	Food and Agriculture Organization of the United Nations
FIAN	Foodfirst Information and Action Network
FOSDEH	Foro Social de Deuda Externa y Desarrollo de Honduras (Honduras Social Forum on External Debt and Development)
FTI	Fast Track Initiative (World Bank)
GNP	gross national product
HAART	highly active antiretroviral therapy
HIPC	heavily indebted poor country
HIPC-II	Enhanced Heavily Indebted Poor Countries Debt Relief Initiative
HRC	Human Rights Committee
IACHR	Inter-American Commission on Human Rights
ICCPR	International Covenant on Civil and Political Rights
ICESCR	International Covenant on Economic, Social and Cultural Rights
ICTs	information and communication technologies
ILO	International Labour Organization
IMF	International Monetary Fund
IVSS	Instituto Venezolano de los Serguros Sociales (Venezuela)
MCO	minimum core obligation
MDG	Millennium Development Goal
MNC	multinational corporation

NGO	non-governmental organization
NJCM	Dutch Section of the International Commission of Jurists
NNPC	Nigerian National Petroleum Company
OAS	Organization of American States
OAU	Organization of African Unity
OHCHR	Office of the United Nations High Commissioner for Human Rights
PRSP	poverty reduction strategy paper
SERAC	Social Economic Rights Action Centre (Nigeria)
STD	sexually transmitted disease
SWRC	Social Work and Research Centre (India)
TAC	Treatment Action Campaign (South Africa)
TLA	timber licensing agreement
TNC	transnational corporation
TRIPS	Agreement on Trade-Related Aspects of Intellectual Property
UDHR	Universal Declaration of Human Rights
UN	United Nations
UNDP	United Nations Development Programme
UNESCO	United Nations Educational, Scientific and Cultural Organization
UNIFEM	United Nations Development Fund for Women
UNITAR	United Nations Institute for Training and Research
UNRISD	United Nations Research Institute for Social Development
UNU	United Nations University
WHO	World Health Organization
WTO	World Trade Organization

Acknowledgements

The editors express their profound gratitude to the authors and would like to thank Pierre Sané, Assistant Director-General for Social and Human Sciences, UNESCO, for the Introduction. The editors also thank their colleagues in the Social and Human Sciences Sector and in particular Konstantinos Tararas and the other members of the Human Rights and Gender Equality Section for their precious advice and assistance in the preparation of this publication. We hope this book will encourage further research, reflection and action with a view to ensuring the enjoyment of all human rights for all.

Foreword

Forty years ago the international community adopted two cornerstone human rights instruments: the International Covenant on Economic, Social and Cultural Rights and the International Covenant on Civil and Political Rights. The covenants transformed into binding standards the provisions proclaimed in the Universal Declaration of Human Rights in 1948. Although both covenants entered into force 30 years ago, in 1976, about 40 state members of the United Nations are still not parties to either one or both. Universal ratification of both instruments thus remains a priority. The main challenge, however, is the implementation of the standards enshrined in the covenants: the codified rights are too frequently neglected or even violated in all parts of the world. This publication, prepared on the occasion of the fortieth anniversary of the covenants (2006), is dedicated to the sixtieth anniversary of the Universal Declaration of Human Rights (2008) as a reminder of the urgent need for more concerted action to make these provisions a reality for all.

The human rights situation at the dawn of the twenty-first century is a cause for serious concern. The world is facing numerous challenges that demand urgent action. Widespread poverty, which is a denial of human dignity, violent conflicts, terrorist acts, environmental degradation and the fragility of human life and health in the face of pandemics and epidemics are only a few. All of these have a detrimental impact on the enjoyment of human rights and create a sense of global instability and insecurity. It is evident that lasting solutions cannot be found without respect for all human rights – civil, cultural, economic, political and social. The interrelation between the promotion and protection of human rights and the building of stable and democratic societies underpins the continuous efforts to reform the UN system.

The concern for a more effective and timely UN response to these threats and challenges prompted the creation of the Human Rights Council in March 2006 in place of the Commission on Human Rights. Vested with a broader mandate and greater flexibility, the Council aspires to strengthen the credibility of UN human rights mechanisms. The council endorsed two new standard-setting instruments – the International Convention for the Protection of All Persons from Enforced Disappearance and the UN Declaration on the Rights of Indigenous Peoples – subsequently adopted by the UN General Assembly in December 2006 and September 2007 respectively. It also renewed the mandate of the working group on the possibility to elaborate an optional protocol to the International Covenant on Economic, Social and Cultural Rights.

In its 60 years of existence, UNESCO has been working to advance human rights without discrimination of any kind. As stipulated in its constitution, the organization is convinced that universal respect for justice, the rule of law and human rights and fundamental freedoms is intimately linked to the maintenance of peace and security. UNESCO has special responsibilities for the rights within its fields of competence, namely education, science, culture and communication. At the same time, it works towards the universal acceptance and observance of *all* human rights through the dissemination of knowledge and the promotion of education on and for human rights. The right to human rights education is now recognized, to a great extent thanks to the efforts of UNESCO, as an integral part of the right to education. The organization also initiates, encourages and supports reflection and dialogue on emerging issues linked with human rights, such as ethics of science and technology, bioethics, cultural diversity, natural disasters and water management.

The UNESCO Strategy on Human Rights, adopted by its General Conference in 2003, defines the organization's main lines of action for the years to come. They include the mainstreaming of human rights into all programmes and activities of UNESCO, human rights education, standard-setting and monitoring, strengthening partnerships and, last but not least, human rights research. The organization's research programme seeks to bridge the gap between research outcomes and policy-making with regard to the rights in UNESCO's fields of competence. In developing policy-oriented human rights research, UNESCO works closely with the academic community, national human rights institutions, research and training centres and non-governmental organizations worldwide. Research draws upon the principles of universality, indivisibility, interdependence, interrelatedness and the equal importance of all human rights. These principles, proclaimed in Vienna in 1993 and reaffirmed by heads of state and government in the final document of the 2005 World Summit, still need confirmation in practice by their daily implementation.

The present publication contains chapters on various issues linked to the implementation of human rights within UNESCO's fields of competence. The chapters provide information on the current status of implementation of these rights, analyse the main obstacles and present good practices. With this publication, UNESCO reaffirms its dedication and commitment to the advancement of human rights.

Vladimir Volodin
Yvonne Donders

Introduction

PIERRE SANÉ

All human rights are universal, indivisible, interdependent and interrelated. They should be treated globally in a fair and equal manner, on the same footing and with the same emphasis. This was the conclusion of the World Conference on Human Rights in Vienna in 1993. The international community had come a long way to reach this conclusion. In 1966 the International Covenant on Economic, Social and Cultural Rights and the International Covenant on Civil and Political Rights were adopted. The very fact that *two* treaties were adopted on the basis of the Universal Declaration of Human Rights reflected the divergence of opinions concerning the different categories of rights. Some states were of the opinion that civil and political rights were "genuine" human rights and should be implemented immediately, while economic, social and cultural rights were considered to be merely goals to be achieved progressively. Other states insisted that the implementation of economic, social and cultural rights is an absolute prerequisite for the implementation of civil and political rights.

Despite this ideological divide, many human rights specialists and defenders have always maintained that all human rights are equally important and intimately linked. They indicated that neglect of any category would be an obstacle to ensure full respect for all human rights for all. This point of view has been progressively accepted by states. At the first International Conference on Human Rights held in Tehran in 1968, representatives of participating states agreed that "since human rights and fundamental freedoms are indivisible, the full realization of civil and political rights without the enjoyment of economic, social and cultural rights is impossible" (Proclamation of Tehran, para. 13).

Notwithstanding this acknowledgement, the preference for one or the other category of human rights persisted. For many years, much time was spent at international meetings on futile discussions concerning which category of rights should be given priority. A major breakthrough was achieved in 1993 when the principles of indivisibility and interdependence were accepted by consensus by the representatives of 171 states participating in the World

Conference in Vienna. Affirming these principles, the conference added: "while the significance of national and regional particularities and various historical, cultural and religious backgrounds must be borne in mind, it is the duty of States, regardless of their political, economic and cultural systems, to promote and protect all human rights and fundamental freedoms" (Vienna Declaration and Programme of Action, Part I, para. 5).

Indeed, human rights are clearly interdependent and interrelated. It is hardly possible to ensure full implementation of someone's political rights without enjoying the right to education. At the same time, how could it be possible to influence the adoption of a policy protecting economic and social rights if people cannot realize their right to vote? How can children truly enjoy their right to education if they do not have adequate food, shelter and health care? Moreover, many human rights can be considered as multidimensional. The right to education could be qualified as a social and a cultural right as well as a civil right. Furthermore, nowadays, with the growing privatization of education, this right is acquiring an important economic dimension. The right to freedom of expression is certainly a civil and a political right. However, it could also be considered as a cultural right.

While the prioritization of one or other category of rights should have disappeared after 1993, this is unfortunately far from true. Certain states still argue that the full implementation of civil and political rights could be realized only after basic economic and social rights are guaranteed. Other states are still convinced that the guarantee of civil and political rights enables the necessary level of implementation of economic and social rights to be attained. Moreover, the point of view is expressed that economic, social and cultural rights are, for some states, "too expensive" to be fully realized.

There is also continuous debate on the justiciability of economic, social and cultural rights and on possible redress in case of their violation, although there is a growing trend to acknowledge both concepts. At the international level, this trend is manifested in the creation by the Commission on Human Rights of a working group to consider the question of the elaboration of an optional protocol to the Covenant on Economic, Social and Cultural Rights, which will allow individuals to complain to an international human rights body in case of alleged violations of the rights stipulated in the covenant. Such a protocol would reinforce the Covenant on Economic, Social and Cultural Rights, putting it on an equal footing with the Covenant on Civil and Political Rights, under which an individual complaints procedure was established long ago.

UNESCO has a clearly articulated human rights mandate. Since its creation, the organization has been working on the basis of the principles of indivisibility and interdependence of all human rights. There are several rights for which UNESCO has a particular responsibility: the right to education, the right to freedom of opinion and expression, including the right to seek, receive and impart information, the right to take part in cultural life and the right to enjoy the benefits of scientific progress and its applications. The organization has contributed to the advancement of human rights by adopting standard-setting instruments and introducing a special procedure for considering complaints about alleged violations of human rights within its competence. Other important contributions by the organization are the dissemination of knowledge about human rights and the recognition of the right to human rights education as an integral part of the right to education.

In order to reaffirm UNESCO's mandate in the field of human rights, its General Conference adopted in October 2003 the UNESCO Strategy on Human Rights. The strategy was extensively discussed with member states, and there were consultations with research and training institutions, the academic community, non-governmental organizations and other UNESCO partners. The Office of the UN High Commissioner for Human Rights and several UN specialized agencies, bodies and programmes also contributed to the preparation of this document. The strategy defines the priorities for UNESCO's human rights activities, including mainstreaming human rights throughout the organization, standard-setting and monitoring, human rights education and, last but not least, human rights research.

UNESCO's human rights research concentrates on problems impeding the full implementation of human rights. The research is also directed to the further elucidation of the content of human rights standards and the exploration of ways to translate these standards into practice. The results of the research should raise the awareness of policy-makers and equip them with knowledge in order to help them to improve policies conducive to the realization of human rights. Research findings should also serve to sensitize and mobilize civil society to advance all human rights for all. Researchers, policy-makers and civil society organizations at national, regional and international levels could make a valuable contribution to the advancement of human rights if they worked closely together.

To encourage such cooperation, UNESCO is setting up regional and subregional research networks. Meetings organized in Latin America and Africa brought together universities, research institutions, national human rights institutions and non-governmental organizations. The meetings identified priority areas of concern in these regions and could become the starting point for the establishment of close cooperation in policy-oriented research on human rights. Similar meetings will be organized in the coming years in other regions. UNESCO is also supporting policy-oriented research on the human rights dimensions of poverty, elucidating its multidimensional nature and emphasizing that freedom from poverty is a human right, a global ethical imperative and a top priority for governments and the international community.

This publication contains chapters reflecting on some of the human rights issues closely related to the work of UNESCO. The publication starts with contributions on general issues, such as the principles of indivisibility and interdependence of all human rights and the application of human rights among private parties. It then addresses specific issues relating to economic, social and cultural rights, such as their justiciability and the development of indicators to measure their implementation. The concluding chapters are devoted to several rights within UNESCO's competence, including the right to education, the right to take part in cultural life and the right to benefit from scientific progress.

The first chapter, prepared by Professor Asbjørn Eide, a well-known human rights expert from Norway, explains the historical background and the meaning of the notions of indivisibility, interdependence and interrelatedness of all human rights. According to the author, indivisibility implies that the state should ensure the comprehensive set of human rights, not just a certain part of them. Interdependence means the synergy between the protection of different rights and the fact that some rights might be limited in order to ensure respect for other rights. Interrelatedness stems from the idea that certain rights, for example academic freedom, are specific applications of a more general right, such as freedom of expression. Eide distinguishes three patterns of interdependence and interrelationship in light of indivisibility: positive, as rights can be mutually reinforcing; negative, as violations or neglect of certain rights can have an impact on others; and the balancing of rights and freedoms of different persons. He applies this theory to the rights within UNESCO's fields of competence and shows clearly that these rights are closely connected in a positive, negative and balanced way to other rights of a civil, cultural, economic, political or social nature. According to the author, the state not only has the obligation to *respect* the freedoms of individuals, but should also *ensure* that individuals are able to enjoy this freedom. In other words, states have negative as well as positive obligations in relation to civil, cultural, economic, political and social rights. Eide emphasizes that "the assumption that civil and political rights are always 'passive' and do not incur costs for the state is wrong; the assumption that economic and social rights always require positive action and are costly is also wrong". Finally, he addresses the obstacles and challenges to these principles and offers possible ways of overcoming them, including the rights-based approach to development and human rights education. The role of international organizations, national human rights institutions and multinational corporations in this regard is also touched upon. The author concludes that, despite the reaffirmation of the principles of indivisibility, interdependence and interrelatedness, much remains to be done to apply them in practice. States should engage themselves actively in the comprehensive and full implementation of the whole set of human rights.

Some claim that only states have obligations concerning human rights and that they therefore do not apply in relations between private parties. Christian

Courtis, legal officer at the International Commission of Jurists argues in his chapter that human rights norms *can* impose duties on private parties. While human rights norms are mainly directed towards states, and states have the main responsibility for their implementation, the duty bearer may well be a private party. Some international human rights standards directly impose duties upon private parties. For example, labour-related rights may impose duties on private employers and certain rights of children may impose duties upon their parents. Some human rights treaties require that states impose duties on private parties. For example, states should prohibit private parties from discrimination against women. Finally, human rights treaties may establish state duties to prevent violations by private parties. For example, children should be protected from possible abuse or violence. While international human rights instruments may, directly or indirectly, impose duties upon private parties, the issue remains that private parties are neither liable nor subject to international jurisdiction. Courtis argues that by incorporating international rules into domestic law, these rules become directly applicable to private parties. However, the international human rights norms should often be further specified in order to make them enforceable. The author concludes by stating that more research is needed to determine how certain rights could be applied among private parties. He considers this all the more relevant in light of the human rights implications of the process of the privatization of services previously provided by the state.

One of the arguments given for differentiating between civil and political rights and economic, social and cultural rights is that the latter are not justiciable. Professor Frans Viljoen, a human rights specialist from South Africa, argues in his chapter, however, that these rights could be justiciable at the national, regional and international levels. He explains justiciability as a claim based on an alleged infringement of a subjective right, which has to be determined by a judicial or quasi-judicial body which, in case a violation is found, is able to find a remedy to redress the violation. This finding should embody an authoritative interpretation of the right and set some form of precedence. Viljoen argues that subjective rights ("the right to …") could be justiciable, while legislative commands ("the state shall …"), which mainly require the adoption of measures, do not give rise to directly enforceable rights. In exploring the ways to determine whether economic, social and cultural rights are justiciable at the national, regional and international levels, the author pays extensive attention to case law, because, as he argues, justiciability depends on whether a judicial or quasi-judicial body considers it amenable to judicial scrutiny. He asserts that the issue of justiciability is often less problematic at the national level, because national legislation tends to be more precisely formulated, overcoming the argument that the norms of economic, social and cultural rights are too vague. At the regional level there is also an increasing trend towards acceptance of the justiciablity of socio-economic rights, or at least some of them. The issue is more challenging at the global level. The Committee on Economic, Social and Cultural Rights in dealing with state reports mainly focuses on the justiciability of these rights at national level. However, by elaborating through its general comments the core content of the rights in the covenant and their corresponding state obligations, the committee indicates that these rights may also be justiciable at the international level. Viljoen addresses several obstacles to the justiciability of economic, social and cultural rights, for example the non-inclusion of these rights in the constitution, lack of clarity of the norms in legislation and lack of expertise of courts or similar bodies. He concludes that most of the problems related to justiciability are overstated and often based on general assertions instead of examining the application of specific rights. The issue of justiciability should first be addressed at the national level, since national legislation remains the most accessible and direct way to make these rights justiciable. The obligations to respect and protect in relation to economic, social and cultural rights are relatively non-controversial. The obligation to fulfil may pose more problems, but, according to the author, these can be overcome. Another conclusion by Viljoen is that lodging a claim on civil and political rights could be a good vehicle to circumvent the issue of the justiciability of economic, social and cultural rights. The author finally concludes that justiciability is not the only way to improve the realization of economic, social and cultural rights. He calls for a recognition of other factors, such as democratization and the role of civil society, which may create a climate favourable to the advancement of economic, social and cultural rights.

The question of developing human rights indicators to assess the level of their implementation has been on the agenda for some time. Audrey Chapman, university professor and human rights activist from the United States, explains in her chapter the issues linked with the development of indicators for monitoring the realization of human rights, especially economic, social and cultural rights. Human rights indicators are important to improve legislation and policies, to identify the actors involved and their obligations and to give early warning of potential violations. Chapman identifies three categories of human rights indicators: structural indicators, which address the institutional, legal and political infrastructure; process indicators, which deal with the activities undertaken to implement human rights; and outcome indicators, which assess the results achieved in the implementation. In order to be valid, human rights indicators have to meet certain criteria. Among others, they need to be objective, feasible, consistently measurable over time and "disaggregatable". The most important dilemma in the development of indicators is the lack of relevant data to meet these criteria. Another dilemma is to find a balance between a sufficient and a manageable number of indicators. From the different meetings organized on the development of indicators, it has become clear that, before developing indicators, the nature, content, scope and immediate core obligations of states need to be defined. Although progress has been made in this regard by the Committee on Economic, Social and Cultural Rights as well as by academics, some rights need to be elaborated upon further and indicators need to be developed. Chapman concludes that UNESCO could play an important role in supporting the efforts to develop indicators for the rights within its competence, including the right to education, the right to take part in cultural life and the right to benefit from scientific progress.

These three rights within UNESCO's competence are addressed in more detail in the following chapters. Professor Fons Coomans, a human rights specialist from the Netherlands, argues that despite the fact that, in theory, the right to education has a solid basis in international law and its content and corresponding obligations have been elaborated, the reality is still very disappointing. Coomans calls the right to education a key right and an empowerment right, because it unlocks the enjoyment of other human rights and enables a person to develop him/herself and contribute to society. Many human rights only obtain substance and meaning when a person is educated. Through this link with other rights, the right to education embodies the unity and interdependence of all human rights. Coomans deals in detail with the scope and content of the right to education. It has a social dimension, which means the right to *receive* an education, and a freedom dimension, which means the right to *choose* an education. An important element is that primary education should be free and compulsory. This implies that no person may be prevented from attending school and that all actors involved must take measures to ensure free and compulsory primary education. The Committee on Economic, Social and Cultural Rights has determined that the four essential features of education are that it should be available, accessible, acceptable and adaptable. Moreover, the committee has elaborated the so-called core content of the right to education – in other words, the fundamental part of the right without which it would lose its essential meaning. Elements of the core content are, for example, the right to have access to education at all levels on a non-discriminatory basis; free and compulsory primary education; special facilities for vulnerable groups; fixed-quality education; free choice of education; and the right of minorities and indigenous peoples to be taught in their mother tongue. Coomans asserts that obstacles to the realization of the right to education could be legal, administrative, financial or political in nature. There is still widespread discrimination against girls and children of minority groups, and the general quality of education is often low. Coomans concludes that states should recognize the human rights perspective of legislation, policies and programmes concerning education. It remains important to clarify vague human rights norms in order to explain to states which obligations they may have in implementing the right to education.

One of the rights that is not well elaborated in the covenants is the right to take part in cultural life. Yvonne Donders, doctor of law and former UNESCO staff member, places this right in the general framework of cultural rights and concludes that, although cultural rights are essential to protect an important part of human dignity, they are the least developed human rights compared to other categories. The author argues that one of the main reasons is that the concept of culture is not easy to define. Moreover, culture is not a fixed and static notion, but dynamic and evolving, and it embraces individual as well as collective aspects. Consequently, any attempt to translate cultural issues in terms of rights is difficult. At the same time, there is a growing trend to consider culture no longer only as a consumer product, but as an expression of the identity of individuals and communities. Cultural rights, including the right to take part in cultural life, should accordingly be considered as more than merely the right to enjoy a cultural product. Donders elaborates the content of the right to take part in cultural life as laid down in the Universal Declaration (Article 27) and the International Covenant on Economic, Social and Cultural Rights (Article 15(1)). She illustrates how the scope of this right has evolved over time. When it was codified, the right was meant to make national culture available and accessible to all people, and culture referred to material aspects, such as art and literature. Over the years, the Committee on Economic, Social and Cultural Rights and academics have broadened the scope of this right to include non-material aspects, such as traditions, language, religion and education. Moreover, taking part in cultural life is more than having access to it. It includes active participation in the decision-making process and being able to contribute actively to culture. Donders asserts that the right to take part in cultural life entails a whole range of issues, some of which are closely linked to other human rights. It concerns rights of creators and transmitters of culture, the right of individuals to contribute and have access to culture and rights related to cultural identity, including education, language and religion. It also concerns the protection of cultural heritage and the establishment and consolidation of cultural institutions, such as museums, libraries and archives. These issues are closely linked to the rights to education and self-determination, as well as the rights to freedom of religion, expression and assembly. This broad approach towards the right to take part in cultural life consequently makes it very difficult to elaborate its core content and the various corresponding state obligations. The author concludes that more analysis and clarification are needed to advance this very important right, which protects an essential part of the well-being of individuals and communities.

One of the very least elaborated human rights, "tucked away at the end of the Universal Declaration of Human Rights", is the right to enjoy the benefits of scientific progress and its applications. Professor William Schabas, director of the Irish Centre for Human Rights, maintains that this right has received very little attention from the international human rights community. At the same time it has gained renewed importance, because of the process of globalization and the apparent tension between this right and the protection of intellectual property, especially in relation to the World Trade Organization and its TRIPS (Trade-Related Aspects of Intellectual Property) agreement. In order to explore the content and scope of the right to benefit from scientific progress, Schabas describes the drafting process of the relevant provisions in the Universal Declaration (Article 27) and the International Covenant on Economic, Social and Cultural Rights (Article 15(1)). He also addresses other documents at the international and regional level containing references to this right. Schabas argues that the right to benefit from scientific progress interacts with other rights, such as the right to health and the right to food. The author points out that in the development of medicine and the production of food, commercial factors are often more decisive in determining research priorities, and thereby scientific progress, than human rights. The right to benefit from scientific progress is also closely related to the right to receive and impart information and thus to the development of new communication and information technologies. Crucially important nowadays, however, is the relationship between the right to benefit from scientific progress and the right to protection of intellectual property. Within the larger debate on the effects of globalization on the promotion and protection of human rights, it is recognized that the trade-related aspects of intellectual property may threaten the realization of human rights. The author finally pays attention to the issue of scientific research devoted to objectives that are inherently harmful for human beings, for example the development of modern weaponry, as well as to possible abuse of scientific progress. Schabas concludes that the issues involved in the promotion and protection of the right to benefit from scientific progress need to be further elucidated.

This volume shows that much progress has been made in the advancement of human rights over the last two decades. The body of international human rights law, which now contains more than 100 binding standard-setting instruments and numerous declarations, recommendations, etc., is a solid basis to ensure the realization of human rights. The priority for the international community should therefore be the reinforcement of human rights implementation and monitoring mechanisms. Moreover, as confirmed by several authors, many issues and rights need to be further elucidated by means of research and reflection. This demands concerted efforts on the part of researchers, policy-makers and intergovernmental and non-governmental organizations. With publications such as this one, and by supporting research networks in different regions of the world, UNESCO wishes to contribute to this ongoing process.

As the founding fathers of the United Nations and UNESCO underlined, universal respect for human rights and fundamental freedoms for all is the very basis of peace, stability and security in the world. This was once again confirmed in the report *In Larger Freedom* by UN Secretary-General Kofi Annan (2005). Respect for human rights is not only a goal in itself; it is a guarantee of a more stable and secure world. A world in which almost half of the population live in conditions of poverty can hardly be considered as stable and secure. A world in which thousands of children are still dying from diseases which can be easily cured by modern medicine can hardly be considered as stable and secure. A world in which women are prevented from realizing their rights can hardly be considered as stable and secure. A world in which people cannot realize their full potential because they are deprived of their rights to education and information can hardly be considered as stable and secure. A world in which people cannot freely express their cultural identity can hardly be considered as stable and secure.

In short, many challenges remain. The sixtieth anniversary of the United Nations and UNESCO should be the starting point to reaffirm what was proclaimed in the UN Charter, namely our faith in the dignity and worth of the human person and in the equal rights of women and men. It should be the starting point to renew our efforts to promote sustainable development and better standards of living in larger freedom, in order to create a more just world, respectful of human rights and fundamental freedoms.

REFERENCE

Annan, Kofi (2005), *In Larger Freedom: Towards Development, Security and Human Rights for All*, Report of the UN Secretary-General, UN Doc. GA A/59/2005, 21 March.

1 Interdependence and Indivisibility of Human Rights

ASBJØRN EIDE

INTRODUCTION

The principle of interdependence, interrelatedness and indivisibility of human rights has been considered fundamental from the very establishment of the United Nations, and is an inherent part of the notion that the rights adopted by the United Nations are universal.

It was already implicit in the UN Charter, adopted in 1945, and is reflected more clearly in the Universal Declaration of Human Rights (UDHR), which can be seen as an authoritative interpretation of the rights intended in the UN Charter. The declaration sets out the list of rights in Articles 3–27, and provides in Article 2 that all the rights listed shall be enjoyed by everyone without discrimination. Article 28 states that everyone has the right to a social and international order in which the rights set out in the declaration can be fully realized.

There is no doubt that the Universal Declaration was conceived as a normative system of interrelated rights, not a menu from which states could pick and choose. The principle of the interdependence and indivisibility of the rights was repeated at the Tehran World Conference on Human Rights in 1968, and in a long string of UN General Assembly resolutions.

Most important for this chapter are the conclusions of the World Conference on Human Rights in 1993. Nearly all independent states were assembled in Vienna for that (second) World Conference on Human Rights, including all major powers and most others, and states that had still been under colonial or imperial rule at the time of the establishment of the United Nations and had therefore not been involved in the adoption of the Universal Declaration of Human Rights. We can therefore see the Vienna Conference as the first global confirmation that the rights in the UDHR were indeed universal. When states from all parts of the world agreed on this, it was because of the broad coverage of rights contained in the declaration. Any effort to limit human rights to a smaller sector of rights undermines the very acceptance of the universality of rights.

Our starting point is therefore the following provision adopted at the World Conference in Vienna:

> All human rights are universal, indivisible, interdependent and interrelated. The international community must treat human rights globally in a fair and equal manner, on the same footing, and with the same emphasis. While the significance of national and religious backgrounds must be borne in mind, it is the duty of States, regardless of their political, economic and cultural systems, to promote and protect all human rights and fundamental freedoms. (Vienna Declaration and Programme of Action, para. 5)

CONCEPTUAL DISCUSSION

"All human rights are universal, indivisible, interdependent and interrelated"

The claim of *universality* has two meanings: first, that the rights are valid and applicable everywhere, in all societies and all cultures in all parts of the world; second, that they should be enjoyed by every human being, without discrimination (by women as well as men, by persons belonging to all racial and religious groups, by citizens and non-citizens, by rich and poor, and so on).

The Vienna statement is that *all* human rights are universal, not just some of them. To support the universality of human rights is to be prepared to embrace the whole system of human rights, to go beyond one's own particular and limited conception derived from the particular history, culture, religion and tradition of one's own society.

The implication is that one cannot on the one hand claim that human rights are universal and at the same time deny the validity of a part of the existing international system of human rights. The reason why human rights could be claimed, in 1948, to be universal was that the list was a product of deliberations over the preceding two years with contributions from different traditions and cultures. In 1948 no society could assert that it had already embraced all the rights listed. The very purpose of proclaiming universal human rights was to go beyond the limited traditions within different societies, to accept a more coherent package of rights which could legitimately be seen as a common aspiration. In the terms of its preamble, the UDHR was proclaimed as a common standard of achievement towards which all nations should move.

It is in this context that the term *indivisible* must be understood, as also expressed in the Vienna Declaration paragraph 5: "The international community must treat human rights globally in a fair and equal manner, on the same footing, and with the same emphasis." This is a message to both the West and the non-West. To claim the universality of inherited civil rights while not embracing the universality of economic and social rights is a challenge to the universality of human rights as such. On the other hand, to claim that economic and social rights should be fulfilled while denying the validity or applicability of civil and political rights is also a direct confrontation with not only the indivisibility but also the universality of human rights.

Indivisibility has two important meanings or implications. First, it is an essential aspect of the claim of universality. We can allege universality of human rights because we have agreed to the comprehensive system of rights. In some cultures and traditions, some of the rights have been part of established customs but others have not; by recognizing the broad package of rights, being the best products of several cultural traditions and/or visions for the future, we accept that we now have a universal system of rights.

The second message in using the term "indivisible" is addressed to the state as the agent of the envisaged social contract within each society. For person A, right X may at a particular point in time be important, but right Y might not be of concern because it is not under threat. For person B, right Y may be of overriding importance, while right X is under the circumstances without interest. The example could be freedom of religion and the right to an adequate standard of living. Person A might be financially comfortable, without any difficulty in ensuring his or her livelihood, but may belong to a religion or faith which is threatened in that particular society. Person B might be out of work or disabled, and therefore in extreme poverty, but may adhere to the dominant religion and be under no threat in that regard. The importance of treating the system of human rights as indivisible is that it requires the state to ensure the implementation of the whole set of rights, even if individuals within the state are concerned only with limited and separate parts of the rights.

This second implication of the claim of indivisibility is therefore that the state should seek to establish and maintain an ideal social contract where the different legitimate concerns of all members of society are taken into account and balanced in a constructive way. The list of human rights can thus be seen as the list of legitimate concerns which should be given the status of rights in the context of policy-making, legislation and administration of a state.

This is also reflected in the words of the Vienna Declaration, quoted above, that "it is the duty of States, regardless of their political, economic and cultural systems, to promote and protect all human rights and fundamental freedoms".

The term *interdependent* can be held to focus on two aspects. One is the synergy for the individual between the protection of two different rights, e.g. the right to education and the right to freedom of expression and participation. The better a person is educated, the more effectively they can make use of their freedom of expression. The right to be free from hunger is a precondition for being able to participate effectively in society. On the other hand, the right to freedom of expression and participation is an important tool in ensuring the right to be free from hunger, though those who have to take action to ensure freedom from hunger are usually not those who suffer from hunger – the latter are physically and often educationally too weak to make headway by themselves.

The second aspect of interdependence can be taken to refer to the balancing requirement which is a common feature in the human rights system. While some rights are absolute in the sense that limitations or derogations cannot be applied (in particular the right to be free from torture and from slavery), most other rights can be limited and in some circumstances must be limited owing to the respect for other rights and for legitimate concerns in society. Under UDHR Article 29(2), persons can be subjected to limitations set by law for the purpose of securing due recognition and respect for the rights and freedoms of others and of meeting the just requirements of morality, public order and the general welfare in a democratic society, but these are the only limitations that can be made. It is closely related to the concern underlying Article 29(1): everyone has duties to the community in which the free and full development of one's personality is possible.

In practice, the scope of some rights not only can but must be balanced to make possible the protection of the enjoyment of other rights by other persons. Freedom of expression must be balanced against protection from hate speech or incitement of terror, which in turn endangers the right to liberty and security of persons.

The term *interrelated* can be held to focus on those situations where some rights are, at least in part, specific applications of more general rights. The right to form and join trade unions is at least in part a specific example of the general freedom of association. The right under the International Covenant on Economic, Social and Cultural Rights Article 15 to "the freedom indispensable for scientific research and creative activity" is in part a specific application of the general freedom of expression, and therefore interrelated with that right, but it is also dependent on the necessary material conditions (adequate standard of living) which make it possible in practice to engage in academic and creative activity, and is therefore interdependent with Article 11 of the covenant.

There is no reason to assume that every human right is interdependent on or interrelated with every other human right. The general claim of the interdependence of or interrelatedness between human rights is valid even if it cannot be shown to apply to every possible pair of rights. The term "indivisible" is intended to ensure that the different legitimate expectations are met by the state and treated as rights.

Patterns of Interdependence and Interrelationship in the Light of Indivisibility

The different rights can relate to each other in at least three different ways: positively, negatively and through balancing.

Positively: Mutual reinforcement

Positive interrelationship between the rights can be mutually reinforcing: the enjoyment of one set of rights as a necessary or desirable condition for the enjoyment of another set, or a necessary component of another right.

Negatively: The impact of violations or neglect of one set, on the other rights

Extensive violations or neglect of one set of rights are likely to have a negative impact on other human rights. Lack of economic and social rights can cause turmoil and disturbances which may give rise to right- or left-wing authoritarian governments. The emergence of fascist and Nazi governments in Europe in the late 1920s and 1930s was deeply affected by the steep rise in unemployment and lack of social security arrangements. Such considerations brought US President Roosevelt to advocate the adoption of an "Economic Bill of Rights". He argued that:

> We have come to the clear realization of the fact that true individual freedom cannot exist without economic security and independence. Necessitous men are not free men. People who are hungry and out of a job are the stuff of which dictatorships are made. (Roosevelt 1944)

Observers have also pointed out that among the major reasons why a number of Latin American countries succumbed to military regimes in the 1970s and 1980s is the deep social cleavage in those countries, the extremely high inequality of income and the difficulty in finding a political consensus to ensure proper economic and social rights for all.

Balancing freedoms and rights of different persons

As pointed out in the discussion of "indivisibility" above, the interrelationship between the protection of different rights for different persons may require limitations to one set of rights in order to make possible the enjoyment of another set of rights. For example, protection against hate speech requires limitations on freedom of speech. Protection of family life or of privacy may also set limits to freedom of information and expression. Protection of security of persons may require limitations to the protection of family life in order to prevent or bring to an end violence against women or children in the home. Protection of the right to health may require restrictions on the freedom of movement of persons carrying contagious diseases.

Avoiding Human Rights Fundamentalism: Partial and Progressive Implementation

While emphasizing the indivisibility of human rights, it is necessary to take into account the qualification made in the Vienna Declaration: "While the significance of national and regional particularities and various historical, cultural and religious backgrounds must be borne in mind, it is the duty of States, regardless of their political, economic and cultural systems, to promote and protect all human rights and fundamental freedoms."

The national and regional particularities and the historical, cultural and religious backgrounds make it difficult for states immediately to embrace fully all human rights in all their dimensions. It is, of course, better to accept for some time a partial implementation while cultural patterns and resource capacity are changed and improved than to insist at all times that all human rights must be immediately implemented, which would be some kind of human rights fundamentalism. It is better that everyone is safeguarded from hunger and has secure shelter even if there is not yet full political freedom, as compared to a situation where there is neither political freedom nor freedom from hunger. Conversely, it is better to have freedom of speech and faith while there are still pockets of hunger than when there exists neither freedom from want nor freedom of speech and faith. Therefore it has to be accepted that there may be transition periods where only some parts of the broad human rights system are implemented. The aim, however, must be to move expeditiously towards a framework where, as emphasized in the Vienna Declaration, states fulfil their duty "regardless of their political, economic and cultural systems, to promote and protect all human rights and fundamental freedoms".

HISTORY AND ORIGIN OF THE BASIC PRINCIPLES OF HUMAN RIGHTS LAW

The World Order Vision in the UN Charter

Human rights became part of international law through the adoption and entry into force of the UN Charter. Until that time, the treatment by the state of its own citizens had in most respects been a matter of purely domestic concern with which the international community – with some exceptions – had no authority to meddle.

The significance of the Universal Declaration and the package of human rights listed therein must be seen in the wider context of the world order as envisaged by the UN Charter. Interdependence and indivisibility must be understood against the wider context of that world order. The purposes of the United Nations, as set out in Article 1 of the UN Charter, are essentially threefold:

- the maintenance of international peace, which includes protection of the territorial integrity of states against external aggression and intervention;
- the development of friendly relations among nations, taking into account the principles of sovereign equality and self-determination of peoples – the latter has led to a comprehensive process of decolonization, which has fundamentally changed the architecture of the international system by vastly increasing the number of sovereign states and dismantling empires of all kinds;
- the achievement of international cooperation in solving international problems of an economic, social, cultural or humanitarian character, including the promotion and encouragement of respect for human rights and fundamental freedoms without distinction as to race, sex, language or religion.

The Role of the State in the UN Order

The UN Charter consolidated the system of nation-states, which had slowly emerged from the time of the Peace of Westphalia, but had been enjoyed only by a limited number of peoples. Thus it can be argued that the UN Charter universalized the system of states which had started as a regional development in parts of Europe and spread to the Americas and a few other places. By 1945 large parts of the world were under colonial or imperial domination. The charter delegitimized any kind of imperial system or "protectorates" by one state over peoples in other parts of the world, through the application of the principle of self-determination and the elimination of the status of non-self-governing territories. It emphasized the sovereign equality of states, large and small. A crucial component in this regard was the prohibition of the use of force against the territorial integrity and political independence of states, except in self-defence. In this sense the charter required peaceful coexistence between all states throughout the world, thus reinforcing the external sovereignty of weak states which could otherwise not have stood up against stronger military powers.

But the content of the internal sovereignty of states was significantly modified as compared to its meaning and sense in the Westphalian system. The modification was a consequence of the introduction of human rights into international law. First, it was made clear that sovereignty remained with the people (the will of the people shall be the basis of the authority of government; the will of the people shall be expressed in periodic and genuine elections …) (UDHR, Article 21). Second, the sovereignty of the people was circumscribed, even in fully democratic states: human rights set limitations on and directions to the exercise of public authority. The freedoms of individuals must be respected and everyone's economic and social rights must be fulfilled, even if this is not what the majority want to do.

The UN Charter also introduced another far-reaching modification in the system of states as compared to the pre-United Nations period: it requires international cooperation in solving international problems of an economic, social, cultural or humanitarian character and in promoting and encouraging respect for human rights. Hence, the charter transformed international law from a law of coexistence between self-contained states to a law of cooperation. This cooperation has during the existence of the United Nations become increasingly comprehensive and demanding.

One of the key instruments to guide that cooperation was the Universal Declaration of Human Rights, which clarified the content of human rights that had been only vaguely referred to in the UN Charter itself. The declaration made it clear that peace and justice can only be built on respect for human rights – its preamble states: "recognition of the inherent dignity and of the equal and unalterable rights of all members of the human family is the foundation of freedom, justice and peace in the world".

Yet like at the time of writing, states weren't free a UDHR was a common aspiration, so too should we see the incompatible notions of peace & justice out of conflict. Whilst hard to reconcile in practice, it is a common aspiration.

The Origin of the Adoption of Universal Human Rights

The reason why, at the end of the Second World War, human rights were made an international concern was twofold: it was due in large measure to "the disregard and contempt for human rights which have resulted in barbarous acts which have outraged the conscience of mankind ...", and also because "the advent of a world in which human beings shall enjoy freedom of speech and belief and freedom from fear and want has been proclaimed as the highest aspiration of the common people" (UDHR, Preamble, para. 2).

This dual purpose – to prevent brutality and repression and to ensure that societies secured to all their inhabitants their basic freedoms and rights, including freedom from want – inspired the drafting of the declaration and its broad content. Human rights – which had been debated during the last three centuries, and parts of which had found their way into the domestic legal order of some states – could no longer be left to the discretion of those holding governmental power. It was felt necessary for the international community to take joint responsibility for the rights of everyone, everywhere in the world.

The UN General Assembly proclaimed the declaration and all the rights listed therein "as a common standard of achievement for all nations and all peoples" (UDHR, Preamble). The Universal Declaration, given its intended worldwide application, was a historical event without precedent in the evolution of global civilization.

What was the historical background to these repeated confirmations, and what does it mean in practice? We now turn to these questions.

The Nation-state and the Evolution of Citizenship

The Universal Declaration was adopted in 1948 as a package of interrelated and interdependent rights which includes and further strengthens elements of 300 years of development. In 1950 T.H. Marshall focused on the historical development in the West of those attributes which were vital to effective "citizenship" (Marshall 1950).[1] He distinguished three stages in this evolution, tracing the formative period in the life of each principal type of rights to a different century and relating it to an evolving concept of citizenship. First, civil rights had been the great achievement of the eighteenth century, laying the foundation of the notion of equality of all members of society before the law. Second, political rights were the principal achievement of the nineteenth century, allowing for increasingly broader participation in the exercise of sovereign power. Third, social rights were the contribution of the twentieth century, making it possible for all members of society to enjoy satisfactory conditions of life.

His description is suggestive of the stages of evolution of human rights. By the 1930s democratic states were increasingly concern with social rights in. The advancement of welfare rights received strong support from both the United States, under the administration of Franklin Delano Roosevelt, and Western Europe. In the United Kingdom, Harold Macmillan of the Conservative Party pleaded in 1933 for social reconstruction and the elimination of poverty, and in 1938 published his paper "The middle way" on this subject. Sir William Beveridge, who chaired the Inter-Departmental Committee on Social Insurance and Allied Services during the Second World War, is credited as being the first to conceptualize social security as a way to ensure basic protection for the whole population, in the 1942 ground-breaking report "Social Insurance and Allied Services". Similar debates were taking place in Latin America. Constitutional debate in India during the final years of colonial rule was deeply affected by similar values, and when India became independent in 1947 it endowed itself with a constitution combining fundamental freedoms with social rights as directive principles. When, after the war, Japan got a new and democratic constitution, it included several fundamental social rights together with civil and political rights (Araki 2002, 215).

Drafting the UDHR: All Human Rights for All

Beyond the nation-state: Human rights for all

The initial impetus for the drafting of the UDHR as well as for the UN Charter came from the United States in 1941. One of the main sources of inspiration was Roosevelt's "four freedoms" speech, his State of the Union Address delivered to the US Congress in January 1941:

> In the future days which we seek to make secure, we look forward to a world founded upon four essential human freedoms. The first is freedom of speech and expression – everywhere in the world. The second is freedom of every person to worship God in his own way – everywhere in the world. The third is freedom from want, which, translated into world terms, means economic understandings which will secure to every nation a healthy peacetime life for its inhabitants – everywhere in the world. The fourth is freedom from fear, which, translated into world terms, means a world-wide reduction of armaments to such a point and in such a thorough fashion that no nation will be in a position to commit an act of physical aggression against any neighbor – anywhere in the world. (Roosevelt 1941)

His vision was endorsed by other Western leaders in the Atlantic Declaration in August 1942, and broadly echoed throughout the world.

Free and equal in dignity and rights: The comprehensive approach

The initial planning of the United Nations as an instrument of post-war world order was pursued within the US administration, influenced to a large extent by the visions contained in the "four freedoms" address. Roosevelt's words had resonated throughout the free world at a time when people in Europe and East Asia were faced with massive brutality and large parts of the world were still under colonial domination.

In 1942 the American Law Institute established a working group which prepared the first draft of what later became the UDHR. The group included participants from different regions and cultures of the world. The draft contained civil, political, economic and social rights side by side.[2] When the UN Secretariat Division on Human Rights under John Humphrey in 1947 prepared the first draft of the UDHR for the Commission on Human Rights, the main text used was that prepared by the American Law Institute (Humphrey 1984, 32).

The idea of the interrelatedness between individual freedoms and economic security and independence underlies the 1944 State of the Union Address by President Roosevelt, who had advocated thereby the adoption of an "Economic Bill of Rights".

In the debate in the Commission on Human Rights, there was broad agreement to include all the components that had emerged during the historical evolution of rights – the civil and the political as well as the economic and social. They were to form building-blocks for the comprehensive system of rights contained in the declaration, to which cultural rights were also added. All were made into a package of rights, in the sense that the different rights were to be interdependent and therefore indivisible.

The List of Rights and Their Relationship

The Universal Declaration starts with the classical civil rights: integrity rights, freedom of action and rights pertaining to fair trial and due process. The integrity rights include the right to life, liberty and security of the person. Torture and maltreatment are prohibited, and so are slavery and forced labour, arbitrary arrest, detention and exile. Freedom of action includes the right to free movement and choice of residence inside the country, the right to leave any country and the right to return to one's own country. It further includes freedom of religion, of expression and information, and of assembly and association.

Most of the integrity rights are absolute in the sense that no derogation is permissible. Freedoms of action, however, can and to some extent must be constrained in order to protect the rights of others. For instance, freedom of expression must be constrained in order to prevent hateful speech.

There cannot be unlimited freedom of action in any society. Indeed, one of the purposes of state formation is to maintain law and order, to ensure that persons do not act towards others in ways which destroy their integrity and freedom or block the measures taken to ensure welfare in society. The state is bound, therefore, to set some restrictions and impose some duties, which is done through penal and other law, and through administrative acts based on law. In order to ensure that penal prosecution and the law on which it is based are compatible with human rights requirements, the right to fair trial and due process is important. The right to a fair trial, as set out in UDHR Article 10, is an essential part of any legal system purporting to be based on the rule of law. Due process requires, *inter alia*, that there are judges competent to interpret the laws and apply them to individual cases, and that these judges are independent of any outside interference as well as impartial *vis-à-vis* the parties concerned.

The UDHR states in Article 21: "the will of the people shall be the basis of authority of the government". This goes beyond the conceptions held by most adherents of the social contract in the eighteenth century, which required only that the government had the consent of the governed, and only a select few were held to be suited to participate in the exercise of authority. Article 21 implies a right for all to participate, directly or through freely chosen representatives, in the exercise of government, and equal rights for all of access to public service. It consolidates, therefore, the notion of freedom with and through participation.

The greatest innovation made by the Universal Declaration is the inclusion of economic, social and cultural rights. Article 22 refers to the economic, social and cultural rights "indispensable for [one's] dignity and the free development of [one's] personality" and to "the right to social security", which entitles everyone to access to welfare state provisions. It precedes five subsequent articles which declare the rights to work (Article 23), to rest and leisure (Article 24), to an adequate standard of living (Article 25), to education (Article 26) and to participate freely in the cultural life of the community (Article 27).

At the core of *social* rights is the right to an adequate standard of living (Article 25). The enjoyment of this right requires, at minimum, that everyone shall enjoy the necessary subsistence rights – adequate food and nutrition, clothing, housing and the necessary conditions of care and health services. Closely related to these rights is the right of families to assistance, briefly mentioned in Article 25 and elaborated in greater detail in subsequent provisions, such as Article 10 of the International Covenant on Economic, Social and Cultural Rights and Article 27 of the International Convention on the Rights of the Child.

In order to enjoy these social rights, there is also a need to enjoy certain *economic* rights. These are the right to property (Article 17), the right to work and other work-related rights (Articles 23 and 24) and the right to social security (Articles 22 and 25).

The combination of economic and social rights serves the dual function of freedom and equality. The right to property, which had a prominent place in the early theory of natural rights, serves as a basis for entitlements which can ensure an adequate standard of living, and is also a basis of independence and, hence, of freedom. But property in the traditional understanding of the word cannot be enjoyed on an equal basis by all. It has to be supplemented, therefore, by the right to work that can provide an income commensurate with an adequate standard of living, and by the right to social security that can supplement, and where necessary fully substitute, insufficient income derived from property or work. The right to work is also a basis of independence, provided the work is freely chosen by the person concerned, that sufficient income is obtained from it and that workers can protect their interests through free trade unions and collective bargaining.

The work-related rights in Article 23 consolidate a development which had started at the beginning of the twentieth century and been promoted through the International Labour Organization (ILO), which was formed in 1919. The right to form and join trade unions ("freedom of association") without interference from the state was included as a basic principle of the constitution of the ILO. It represented a victory over the very restrictive economic liberalism of the nineteenth century, when legislation had prohibited or made redundant all agreements between employers and employees for advancing the latter's wages or working conditions. Of similar importance is the principle included in Article 23 that everyone shall have equal pay for equal work. Lower pay for women was – and still is – a deeply entrenched practice in many societies. By including this principle, the declaration provided a basis for action that in most parts of the world has led to considerable equalization of rates of pay between women and men, though much remains to be done.

The right to social security is essential when a person does not own the necessary property or is not able to secure an adequate standard of living through work owing to unemployment, old age or disability (Articles 22 and 25).

The right to *education* enunciated in Article 26 of the declaration is both a social and a cultural right. The right to education obliges states to develop and maintain a system of schools and other educational institutions in order to provide education to everybody – free of charge, if possible. The obligations of states to promote equality of opportunity and treatment in the matter of education are laid down in greater detail in the UNESCO Convention against Discrimination in Education of 1960. Since education enhances the human capital of society at large, it is one of the few human rights where the individual has a corresponding duty to exercise the right.

Cultural rights, set out in Article 27 of the declaration, accord everyone the right to take part in cultural life; the right to enjoy the benefits of scientific progress and its applications; the right to benefit from the protection of the moral and material interests resulting from any scientific, literary or artistic production of which the beneficiary is the author; and the freedom indispensable for scientific research and creative activity. Cultural rights are closely linked to other rights, such as that to education (Article 26).

One important aspect of cultural rights is the right to preserve the cultural identity of minority groups, which has implications for civil and political as well as for economic and social rights (Stavenhagen 2001). This makes it necessary to distinguish between two approaches to culture: the process-oriented and the system-oriented. The former sees cultural expression as the evolving achievements of artistic and scientific creation. The latter, on the other hand, conceptualizes culture as a coherent, self-contained set of values and symbols "that a specific cultural group reproduces over time and which provides individuals with the required signposts and meanings for behaviour and social relationships in everyday life" (Stavenhagen 2001, 66). From the process-oriented perspective the individual is a producer of culture. From a system-oriented perspective he or she is a product of culture and reproduces it through his or her own activities.

From the Declaration via Standard-setting to Implementation

The substantive drafting of the Universal Declaration was completed by the UN Commission on Human Rights in the spring of 1948 and transmitted to the General Assembly for adoption. The intention of the commission was to move quickly on to the preparation of one or more legally binding conventions to complete the International Bill of Human Rights. The political climate was deteriorating, however. On 25 February 1948 the communist coup in Prague (Czechoslovakia) had confirmed what Winston Churchill had already pointed to in his Fulton speech in March 1946: that the world was about to be divided into two major camps. The Cold War replaced the cooperation of the Allies during the Second World War. It had a deeply chilling effect on further standard-setting in the field of human rights. The socialist countries led by the Soviet Union expressed a strong priority for economic and social rights, though in ways which were not cast in proper human rights terms, and in practice if not in theory those states neglected or violated civil and political rights. The Western countries led by the United States gave priority to civil and political rights, seeking to relegate economic and social rights to the margin. This reciprocal selectivity had a long and harmful effect on the progress of the human rights project which had been started in 1948.

The commission split at an early stage on the question of whether there should be one or two covenants to cover the rights contained in the UDHR. The question was turned over to the UN General Assembly, which, in a resolution adopted in 1950, emphasized the interdependence of all human rights and called on the commission to adopt a single convention.[3] The next year, however, the Western countries were able to reverse the decision of the General Assembly, which now asked the commission to divide the rights in the declaration into two separate covenants, one on civil and political rights and another on economic, social and cultural rights. This was done., and as a consequence it has become a widespread habit to consider the International Bill of Rights as consisting of two distinct categories of human rights.

Fortunately, the climate eased somewhat in the 1960s, making it possible at least verbally to reaffirm the wholeness of the human rights system. In 1966 the General Assembly adopted the International Covenant on Civil and Political Rights (ICCPR) and the International Covenant on Economic, Social and Cultural Rights (ICESCR), but inserted the principle of interdependence and indivisibility in the preambles of both. The language in the preamble of the ICCPR is as follows:

> in accordance with the Universal Declaration of Human Rights, the ideal of free human beings enjoying civil and political freedom and freedom from fear and want can only be achieved if conditions are met whereby everyone may enjoy his civil and political rights, as well as his economic, social and cultural rights ...

Almost identical language was used in the preamble of the ICESCR.[4]

The State as the Main Duty-holder

"Everyone is entitled to all the rights set forth in this Declaration, without distinction of any kind …" (UDHR Article 2). The declaration did not say who was to ensure that those rights were, in fact, assured. It was the underlying assumption that the primary responsibility would be on the state. It was also clear from the word "everyone" that all states should have at least the moral obligation to recognize, respect and protect the rights of everyone within their territory. The states were to be trustees, on behalf of the international community, for the enjoyment of all human rights for those under their power. The more detailed legal obligations in securing the enjoyment of the rights had to be established through legally binding texts subsequently to be adopted, including the two main human rights covenants.

Under ICCPR Article 2, each state party to the covenant undertakes to respect and to ensure to all individuals within its territory and subject to its jurisdiction the rights recognized in the covenant. A similar formulation is used in several other conventions, both regional and global.

Two important points need to be highlighted in this connection. One is that each state is responsible for the human rights of those within its territory and subject to its jurisdiction, and that this responsibility (with some exceptions) covers both citizens and non-citizens provided they are within its territory. The other point is that the task of the state is twofold: to respect and to ensure. The obligation to respect implies a duty not to restrict the recognized freedoms of the individual, while the obligation to ensure the rights implies a duty to protect the enjoyment of those rights against private parties and other non-state actors, and to create conditions under which the rights can effectively be enjoyed.

Article 2 of the ICESCR is somewhat differently formulated. Each state that becomes a party to that covenant undertakes to take steps to the maximum of its available resources with a view to achieving progressively the full realization of the rights recognized in the covenant. Generally, however, the meaning is the same for both covenants: the state shall both respect and ensure the rights, which means that it shall not interfere with the freedoms of individuals to find their own ways to enjoy the economic, social and cultural rights, but will also take the necessary measures to protect and fulfil those rights.

The important point in this connection is to recognize the dual function of the state in regard to human rights: to recognize the freedom of the individual and to ensure the existence of conditions under which that freedom can be enjoyed.

In practice, this will always require balancing acts between different freedoms and different ways to exercise them. The "right of everyone to life, liberty and security of person" (UDHR Article 3) does not only imply that the state shall respect life and liberty, but shall also protect it, which implies various forms of restrictions on the freedom of persons to harm others or block them from enjoying their freedom. The right to enjoy the various rights listed in the human rights instruments without discrimination implies not only a duty of the state not to discriminate, but also to prevent private actors from discriminatory actions which block others from enjoying their rights.

This double task of the state becomes even more comprehensive in the area of economic, social and cultural rights. Human rights in work include the right to form trade unions and bargain collectively, a freedom which must be respected by the state, but human rights in work also include rights to an adequate income, equal pay for equal work and safe and healthy working conditions – all of which to some extent require state regulation and thereby limitations on the freedom of the employer. The right to education is not only a freedom but also a duty, and the state is obliged to take a wide range of measures as set out in both the ICCPR and the Convention on the Rights of the Child. The right to health also implies a combination of respect for freedoms and the duty to protect and to provide.

It is through this combination of the duty to respect and to ensure human rights that their interdependence and indivisibility becomes most clear. States have to take all human rights into consideration when they deal with each one of the rights, otherwise respect for one right could become a violation of another right.

But there is not only a need to balance the rights. There is also the positive interrelationship: ensuring the enjoyment of one set of rights will often increase the possibility of ensuring the enjoyment of another set of rights, a point which will be further elaborated below.

THE JUSTIFICATIONS FOR AND IMPLICATIONS OF THE PRINCIPLE OF INDIVISIBILITY, INTERDEPENDENCE AND INTERRELATEDNESS

The Foundational Concern of Human Rights: Free and Equal in Dignity and Rights

Article 1 of the Universal Declaration proclaims that "all human beings are born free and equal in dignity and rights ...". The language, updated and broadened, originated in the American Declaration of Independence and the French Declaration on the Rights of Man and the Citizen.

Article 1 is the fundamental value basis of human rights. That everyone is born free and equal implies that no distinction can be made on the basis of genetically inherited features such as race or gender, nor on the social position of the parents or their nationality or other factors. More important, however, is that the declaration through the rights listed therein shall ensure that everyone *remains* free and equal in dignity and rights.

Human rights listed in the declaration can be seen as responses to historically known forms of oppression and neglect of conditions of indignity, whether in the form of direct state brutality and oppression, lack of protection by the state against fascist and racist hate-groups or lack of protection of adequate livelihood in the wake of the Industrial Revolution and the social dislocation arising from it. There were many expectations connected with the declaration; all of them, in their own way, justified. While the enormous brutality of the Nazi and fascist states and the terror of Stalin may have been foremost in the minds of the drafters, tackling social justice through a joint responsibility for equal opportunity and adequate safety nets was also a major concern, affected by the miseries of the Great Depression.

Looking closer at the terms of Article 1, where "equality" is paired with "freedom", some discussion is required about these terms and their relationship.

Freedom can be understood in several ways. The first and most widely recognized aspect is freedom from oppression, and it can indeed be argued that a major purpose of human rights is to ensure this freedom. But freedom has much broader meanings. One is to have a wide range of significant options (or opportunities) from which to choose what one wants or what one values highly. Another is to be independent of others in the process of achieving those outcomes. A third, and related, concept is to be free to set one's own values and priorities, and to live by them.

Equality could be understood in the same vein: to have available an equally wide range of significant opportunities as others have; to be equally independent of others in the process of achieving the outcomes; and to be equally free to determine one's own values and priorities.

The content and scope of equality and its relationship to freedom have in the past been highly controversial and a source of deep political cleavage, contributing to the ideological schism and division of Europe which started with the Russian Revolution in 1917 and extended throughout the Cold War. At the ideological level, it took the form of a confrontation between various strands of liberalism on the one hand and Marxism on the other, a confrontation that ended only around 1990. Its ending was due, in no small measure, to the growing acceptance of the broad conception of human rights in the Universal Declaration. This does not mean, however, that controversy over the relationship between equality and freedom is over.

In the decades prior to the adoption of the Universal Declaration, liberal thinking and practice in democratic countries had become socially oriented, moving away from very limited "natural" rights towards a more comprehensive and inclusive conception of freedom and equality. It was this process that culminated in the adoption of the Universal Declaration of Human Rights. It gives *substance* to the principle of equality, which was originally conceived in a much more formal sense. This was achieved partly by adding economic and social rights to the civil and political rights.

The civil rights emphasize in particular the freedoms of individuals in the sense of their personal integrity and their process rights. These are intended as freedoms from interference from the state, but also freedoms from other private parties. The state has therefore not only a duty to respect the civil rights of the individual, but also to protect them, which is one of the main justifications for the existence of the state. The declaration does not endorse atomistic individualism, however: Article 29 points out that the full and free development of any person's personality is possible only when he or she observes his or her duties to the community. The declaration does not make the enjoyment of human rights dependent on the observance of those duties, but makes it clear that the full development of the human being – and of

i.e. we are not totally 'free' - we have some obligation if
we are to develop fully as a human being

a humane society – is possible only when people generally observe their duties to their own community and to society at large.

The negative understanding of freedom held by adherents of extreme liberalism – maximum autonomy of the individual from the community and the state – is alien to the Universal Declaration. Under human rights law as set out in the International Bill of Human Rights, the state as an agent of the national community has positive roles to perform. Responsibility under international law for the realization of human rights rests with the state. To live up to its responsibility the state must shoulder three sets of obligations: to *respect* the freedom of the individual; to *protect* that freedom and other human rights against third parties; and, where required, to *provide* access to welfare covering basic needs such as food, shelter, education and health.

If states are to conform to the requirements of the Universal Declaration and corresponding conventions, they have to take steps, including domestic legislation, to deal with social, economic and cultural rights. In so far as they do take such steps, the protection provided by law must be made without discrimination. Not only should all human rights be enjoyed without discrimination (UDHR Article 2), but any right provided by national law should be enjoyed without unjustified distinctions (ICCPR Article 26; European Convention on Human Rights and Fundamental Freedoms, Protocol 12, Article 1).

States are obliged not only to abstain from discrimination, but increasingly also to prevent discrimination between private parties, which is the main thrust of the Convention on the Elimination of All Forms of Racial Discrimination and the Convention on the Elimination of Discrimination against Women (CEDAW). Common to these conventions is that they take a new step, beyond the two taken previously (equality before the law, and equal protection of, or by, the law). The two new conventions require the *elimination* of discrimination, but open the way for affirmative action, which amounts to a call for the creation of equality by means of law. To fulfil their obligations under these two conventions, states are required to be rather active, and possibly more so than some may find politically acceptable.

Most employment opportunities exist in the private sector. Giving effect to the right to work requires the state, *inter alia*, to prohibit policies of discrimination on the part of private employers. Other examples could be added. The scope of the principle of equality and non-discrimination – and the corresponding obligations of states – with regard to the private sector still remains controversial, however.

Human Rights and Social Integration into a Pluralist Society

Through coherent implementation of the broad range of human rights, a fruitful balance is struck between the respect for the freedom of the creative and entrepreneurial individual whose initiatives and efforts can advance the wealth of nations, and the safeguarding of welfare for all through the realization of economic and social rights. Where only civil rights are respected and economic and social rights neglected, societies are likely to experience strong inequalities, social tension and turmoil, possibly ending up with authoritarian regimes. When, on the other hand, only economic and social issues are pursued through centralized state action while civil freedom and political participation are blocked, creativity is stifled and society is homogenized into boredom.

The combination of civil, political, economic, social and cultural rights guarantees equal opportunity for all but does not stifle creativity.

The latter point is particularly important for the rights of the child. The opportunity for a child to reach a situation in adulthood where it can lead a dignified and creative life should not depend on the failure or success of his/her parents. Children should have equal access to education, health services and adequate food and housing, all of which are dealt with in the International Convention on the Rights of the Child; the convention also covers the right of the child to life, to be protected from physical violence and abuse, to freedom of expression and to freedom of religion and belief. The Convention on the Rights of the Child brings together in one document all aspects of human rights, economic and social as well as civil. It is the most universally ratified of all human rights instruments and thus shows that the vast majority of states endorse the principle of interdependence of all rights.

The combination of individual freedom and economic and social rights, when fully implemented, facilitates social integration in a free society. Through the inclusion of the rights of minorities and the freedom of assembly and association, the broad package of human rights ensures pluralism and the maintenance of the diverse identities of the different groups in society.

Freedom of Self is Linked to the Freedom of Others

Since human rights are for everyone, the freedoms and rights of oneself must take into account the necessary conditions for the enjoyment by others of their rights. The enjoyment of human rights for all implies that one also accepts a set of duties – duties of constraint in the exercise of freedoms, and duties of contribution to facilitate the enjoyment by others of their rights. This is the concern underlying the formulation in UDHR Article 29(1): "Everyone has duties to the community in which alone the free and full development of his personality is possible."

The interconnection between one's own freedom and those of others is one of the main reasons why the normative system of human rights is indivisible and interdependent, in that these rights have to be balanced against each other.

In the human rights instruments adopted by the United Nations, there is otherwise no explicit mention of duties. But it is implicit and sometimes explicit that the state has to adopt and enforce a number of duties, or obligations, in order to ensure in a balanced way human rights for all. It may be duties of omission (constraints) or duties of commission (contributions to be made, actions to be taken). It is explicitly provided in the International Convention on the Elimination of All Forms of Racial Discrimination, Article

4, that states must prohibit and punish certain activities which otherwise would be covered by freedom of expression or association. Such provisions apart, the normal pattern is that states decide for themselves what duties they must impose in order that everyone shall enjoy their human rights, including e.g. taxation to fund the right to education or the right to health services. Underlying the Universal Declaration and the subsequent human rights instruments is the assumption that states will impose such duties as are required. It therefore limits itself to pointing out that, in doing so, "everyone shall be subjected only to such limitations [in the exercise of their rights] as are determined by law solely for the purpose of securing due recognition and respect for the rights and freedoms of others and of meeting the just requirements of morality, public order and the general welfare in a democratic society" (UDHR Article 29(2)).

In assessing what is required to ensure the rights of others and to meet the just requirements of general welfare, it is essential to take into account the interdependence of rights – the economic, social and cultural as well as the civil and political.

A quote from President Roosevelt's famous "four freedoms" address can reflect the thinking about the general welfare in society:

> The basic things expected by our people of their political and economic systems are simple. They are: Equality of opportunity for youth and for others. Jobs for those who can work. Security for those who need it. The ending of special privilege for the few. The preservation of civil liberties for all. The enjoyment of the fruits of scientific progress in a wider and constantly rising standard of living.

> These are the simple, the basic things that must never be lost sight of in the turmoil and unbelievable complexity of our modern world. The inner and abiding strength of our economic and political systems is dependent upon the degree to which they fulfil these expectations. Many subjects connected with our social economy call for immediate improvement. As examples: We should bring more citizens under the coverage of old-age pensions and unemployment insurance. We should widen the opportunities for adequate medical care. We should plan a better system by which persons deserving or needing gainful employment may obtain it. (Roosevelt, 1941)

Freedom from the State and Freedom through the State

From the above, it should be clear that the freedoms which human rights seek to secure have two dimensions of implementation: freedom from the state and freedom through the state. What comes first to mind is freedom from the state: the state shall abstain from torture, from censorship, from arbitrary arrest and detention, from preventing people leaving their country, and many other acts. The state shall respect the freedoms of the individual.

But many freedoms could not be enjoyed unless they were protected or fulfilled by the state. The state is therefore a necessary guarantor for freedoms and rights. The very purpose of having a political unit, a state, is to ensure the enjoyment – on an equal basis – of freedoms and rights. The French Declaration of the Rights of Man and of the Citizen (1789) stated in its Article 2 that "The aim of all political association is the preservation of the natural and imprescriptible rights of man."

At the time of the French declaration the rights listed in Article 2 were "liberty, property, security, and resistance to oppression". Under the Universal Declaration of Human Rights the list is longer and more detailed, but the same principle applies: the aim of political association should be to preserve and protect the rights contained in the Universal Declaration. The "political association" is primarily the state.

The obligations undertaken by states under the normative system of human rights are therefore threefold: the duties to respect the rights and freedoms, to protect them and to fulfil them – by facilitation or provision. This threefold level of obligations applies to all rights, civil and political as well as economic, social and cultural, but there is a difference of emphasis: for civil and political rights the main obligations are to respect and protect the rights; the obligation to fulfil them is less prominent but it does exist, including the duty to establish and fund a legal system consisting of courts and related institutions, and the provision of free legal aid for persons who do not have their own means to be secured due process. The obligations regarding economic, social and cultural rights also start with the obligation of the state to respect the freedom of individuals to find their own ways to secure their own needs, the freedom of workers to form trade unions, the right of parents to set up a private school should they so wish and the right of persons to rely on their own traditional medicine or devices to enjoy the right to health. But the obligation of the state is often to protect the freedom of the persons concerned against third parties – to protect indigenous peoples from encroachment of their land, to protect workers from dangerous working conditions by private employers, to protect the enjoyment of the right to food from those who market adulterated and dangerous food, and so on. The additional third level of obligations – to fulfil the rights by facilitation (making available the necessary educational institutions) or by direct provision (making the education free, at least at the primary level) – is more common in regard to economic and social rights than in regard to civil and political rights. It should not be forgotten, however, that all three levels of obligations apply to both sets of rights, though to different degrees. The assumption that civil and political rights are always "passive" and do not incur costs for the state is wrong; the assumption that economic and social rights always require positive action and are costly is also wrong.

INTERDEPENDENCE IN UNESCO'S AREA OF CONCERN

The constitution of UNESCO provides that its purpose is to contribute to peace and security by promoting collaboration among nations through education, science and culture in order to further universal respect for justice, the rule of law and human rights and fundamental freedoms. The principle of indivisibility, interrelatedness and interdependence manifests itself in numerous ways in UNESCO's work.

Education and the Right to Education

The right to education is a matter of central concern for UNESCO. The right is set out in UDHR Article 26 and ICESCR Article 13. The interdependence with other rights is quite obvious and extensively reflected in UNESCO practice.

Positively: Mutual reinforcement

Education is a precondition for the effective enjoyment and use of other human rights. The enjoyment of many civil and political rights, such as freedom of information, expression, assembly and association, the right to vote and to be elected or the right to equal access to public service, depends on at least a minimum level of education, including literacy. In a complex society every person needs more than a minimum of education in order to be able to participate in economic, social and cultural life.

UDHR Article 26.2 provides that "Education shall be directed to the full development of the human personality and to the strengthening of respect for human rights and fundamental freedoms. It shall promote understanding, tolerance and friendship among all nations, racial or religious groups, and shall further the activities of the United Nations for the maintenance of peace." ICESCR Article 13 paragraph 1 elaborates on the same principles and adds that "education shall enable all persons to participate effectively in a free society".

Education – and the right to education – is therefore a major factor in the promotion of all human rights, civil and political as well as economic, social and cultural.

Negatively: The impact of violations or neglect of one set of rights on other rights

When other human rights are extensively violated, the right to education also suffers. When children do not enjoy their right to adequate food and to be free from hunger, or when their right to housing is neglected, they are unable to benefit fully from education. If teachers are not provided with an income which ensures them an adequate standard of living, their teaching ability and quality suffer. Violations of the freedom of expression and information can seriously weaken the possibility of teachers ensuring an adequate process of education. Repressive military regimes have often targeted educationists at various levels.

Balancing rights

ICESCR Article 13 paragraph 4 seeks to safeguard the liberty of individuals and groups to establish and direct educational institutions. But this freedom must be balanced against the required purpose and quality of education. Private institutions must therefore observe the principles that should guide all education, as set out in the Universal Declaration and ICESCR Article 13 paragraph 1 (quoted above). The state must not allow private education which fosters religious intolerance. It must also prevent educational institutions which are based on theories of superiority on one race or group of one colour or ethnic origin; otherwise it would be in violation of the Convention on the Elimination of All Forms of Racial Discrimination. Similarly, in fulfilling its obligations under CEDAW, including its Article 5, states should not allow educational instruction based on ideas of the superiority or inferiority of one of the sexes or on stereotyped conceptions of the roles of men and women.

Scientific Freedom and the Benefits from the Advancement of Science

Under ICESCR Article 15 paragraph 3, the states parties have undertaken to respect the freedom indispensable for scientific work and creative activity.

Interdependence through mutual reinforcement

Scientific freedom depends on freedom of expression and information, freedom of movement, freedom of assembly and association (links between scientists, scientific gatherings), on the right to education (which is necessary to achieve the level of competence required to engage in scientific endeavours) and on the right to an adequate standard of living which makes it possible to devote time to science without destroying one's livelihood. Freedom of religion and belief, one of the earliest achievements of human rights in the West, was essential for the opening of vast new areas of empirical research based on fundamental reconceptions of nature. Traditional religious doctrines had contained dogmas about the creation of the world and the movement of the earth and the sun; only with greater religious freedom did it become possible to engage in research which in turn made it possible to understand the real processes and dynamics and thereby open up for modern science.

Reciprocally, the existence of academic freedom (both in the civil and the material sense) reinforces other rights, most obviously the right of everyone to benefit from achievements in science and technology. Science benefits the content and quality of education. Social science also contributes to a higher quality in the content of the flow of information and debate which is essential for a constructive democratic process.

Negative links: Reciprocal threats in case of violations

Violations of the freedom of expression and information, and freedom of association and assembly, undermine the freedom indispensable for scientific research. Threats to the political activities of students, sometimes even entailing temporary closures of universities, have in the past seriously weakened the pursuit of science. Violations of the freedom of religion and belief can be highly detrimental. The fate of Giordano Bruno comes to mind, burned at the stake in Rome in 1600 for his theories challenging fundamental doctrines of faith held at that time. He became a symbol to represent the forward-looking, free-thinking type of philosopher and scientist, and scientific martyrdom. In 1664 Pope Alexander VII condemned the idea of heliocentricism in general by explicitly banning "all books which affirm the motion of the earth". Similar repression of scientific discovery and debate, though in other areas, has also occurred in other religions, including Islam.

Balancing rights

The pursuit of scientific activity must be balanced against other rights. The clearest example is the freedom from torture and cruel or inhumane treatment, which requires abstention from certain scientific experiments involving human beings. A number of other issues are on the agenda of the day: the rapid development in biotechnology and genetic engineering has given rise to a strong debate on the ethical and legal consequences of such research, where many human rights can be affected.

UNESCO's work on bioethics is another example of the interrelatedness of human rights and the need to balance different rights. The Universal Declaration on the Human Genome and Human Rights, adopted by UNESCO in 1997, provides several examples. In Article 12(b) it is pointed out that freedom of research is necessary for the progress of knowledge and is part of the freedom of thought, and the applications of research, including applications in biology, genetics and medicine concerning the human genome, shall seek to offer relief from suffering and improve the health of individuals and humankind as a whole. Hence, the positive interrelationship between science and health is reflected in the declaration. On the other hand, it is made clear that freedom of research cannot prevail over other human rights (Article 13), and that practices such as human cloning also have negative consequences, including for the dignity and privacy of persons, and the declaration therefore provides for several limitations on research that have to be respected.

Culture and Cultural Rights

Cultural rights, a major concern for UNESCO, have been given increasing attention in recent years. The core substantive rights of ICESCR Article 15 are the rights of everyone to cultural participation and to benefit from scientific advancements. The supporting rights include academic freedom and authors' right to the moral and material interests arising from their scientific, literary or artistic production. Article 15 also lists two supporting means to achieve the rights: the conservation, development and diffusion of culture, and the benefits of international contact and cooperation in scientific and cultural fields (Marks 2003, 297).

Positively: Mutual reinforcement

Cultural participation is closely connected with freedom of expression (to be able to participate actively) and freedom of information (to be able to benefit from the cultural activities of others).

Important here is also the rights of minorities to preserve and develop their own culture, as provided for in ICCPR Article 27, and in greater detail in the UN Declaration on the Rights of Persons Belonging to National or Ethnic, Religious or Linguistic Minorities. Article 1 of that declaration provides that states shall protect the identities of such minorities and encourage the promotion of that identity. Their identity is expressed by their culture; consequently, their right to preserve and develop that culture is their paramount concern.

In 2001 the UNESCO General Conference adopted the Universal Declaration on Cultural Diversity. Article 1 states: "As a source of exchange, innovation and creativity, cultural diversity is as necessary for humankind as biodiversity is for nature. In this sense, it is the common heritage of humanity and should be affirmed for the benefit of present and future generations." The emphasis on cultural diversity as a source of exchange and innovation reflects its significance in strengthening the rights to education and scientific freedom: learning about the cultures of others generates ideas about other ways to do things and enhances critical thinking which helps to break out of ossified traditions.

Negatively: The impact of violations or neglect of one set of rights on other rights

Defence of cultural diversity is "an ethical imperative, inseparable from respect for human dignity" (Universal Declaration on Cultural Diversity, Article 4). The manifestation of cultural diversity is clearly linked to the enjoyment of other rights mentioned above – freedom of cultural expression, of cultural associations and assemblies, and a number of freedoms related to education. The declaration therefore states that defence of cultural diversity "implies a commitment to human rights and fundamental freedoms, in particular the rights of minorities and indigenous peoples".

Where persons belonging to minorities are denied their right to learn their own language or history, their right to cultural participation is severely limited. Similarly, if they are denied the freedom to form their own associations and have their own assemblies, making it possible for them to organize themselves around their culture, their right to cultural participation is in effect denied. For indigenous peoples, the preservation of their cultural rights also requires preservation and security of the land and resources on which they depend for their way of life.

Balancing freedoms and rights of different persons

Cultural rights must be balanced against other human rights. The defence of cultural diversity cannot be carried out in ways which prejudice the enjoyment by all persons of universally recognized human rights. Cultural diversity can strengthen the implementation of human rights among minorities and indigenous peoples, but it must not weaken the enjoyment of universal human rights, neither for persons who belong to the minority nor for others. In efforts – by states or by minorities – to preserve their traditional culture, their authorities or agencies cannot in the name of cultural diversity adopt measures which interfere with individual human rights. The UNESCO Universal Declaration on Cultural Diversity makes this clear in the final sentence of Article 4: "No one may invoke cultural diversity to infringe upon human rights guaranteed by international law, nor to limit their scope."

Communication and Information

UNESCO has as one of its core missions the promotion of free exchange of ideas and knowledge and maintaining and diffusing knowledge. The UNESCO programme of communication, established in its present form in 1990, provides a good illustration of the interdependence of several human rights.

Positively: Mutual reinforcement

Communication is directly linked to freedom of expression and information. In its contemporary setting it is profoundly affected by the realization of the right to education, and strongly influences the content of education.

The spreading of information and communication technologies (ICTs) has a strong enabling potential for the enjoyment of the rights to education and health. It can also facilitate the realization of other social and economic rights. For global development it is essential to bridge the digital divide and thereby improve the possibility of realizing an adequate standard of living for those currently outside the digital networks.

Harnessing ICTs for education and promotion of the expression of cultural and linguistic diversity through communication and information is of key significance for ensuring the realization of several human rights, showing their close relationship.

Negatively: The impact of violations

Countries that, for political or other reasons, significantly restrict access to information over the Internet, and thereby violate the right to freedom of information, will be unable to reap the full benefit of the opportunities given by modern communications. This will retard their development and thereby also slow down the realization of everyone's right to an adequate standard of living. Development that could be derived from modern information technology will be seriously and negatively affected if there are systematic violations of the freedom of information and academic freedom, or if education is narrow, restrictive and indoctrinating in nature.

Balancing the power of communication with cultural rights and political rights

There is an enormous imbalance in power over the control of the media. Ownership of the media has undergone a radical shift over the last decade, caused by the tremendous change in technology, free flow of investment and free trade in goods and services. There is an unprecedented concentration of media ownership into a few hands, controlling a large part of the media throughout the world. This can negatively affect the exercise of political rights since there is a serious imbalance in the possibility of engaging in political debate. It can also seriously and negatively affect cultural diversity. Steps must therefore be taken to balance the freedom of communication with the ability to exercise political rights and preserve vulnerable cultures. UNESCO's effort to prepare a convention on cultural diversity, drawing on the existing UNESCO Universal Declaration on Cultural Diversity (adopted in 2001), is an important contribution in that regard.

OBSTACLES AND CHALLENGES

Lack of Capability or Lack of Will?

While the Universal Declaration of Human Rights with its comprehensive list of rights was proclaimed "as a common standard of achievement for all peoples and all nations", we know that there are many countries which do not live up to that standard. What are the obstacles? As a simple starting point we might distinguish between situations where the government concerned displays a lack of will, and on the other hand situations where there is a lack of capability to implement some of the rights, even by a well-intentioned government. In practice the distinction is not so simple, as will be shown below.

Lack of Will: Challenge to the Validity or Universality of Some or All Human Rights

Some years ago there was much talk about "Asian values" as being different from those on which human rights are based. The argument by some Asian political leaders was that Asians were much more oriented to collective, community values, while human rights were held to be individualistic in nature. They therefore challenged the universal validity of human rights.

The argument was significantly modified after the adoption of the Vienna Declaration in 1993, when leaders of all countries, including the Asian countries, accepted the consensus formulation: "All human rights are universal, indivisible, interdependent and interrelated. The international community must treat human rights globally in a fair and equal manner, on the same footing, and with the same emphasis."

The problem now is not so much a wholesale rejection of human rights by governments, but a rejection of some of the rights, thus denying indivisibility. Cultural, historical and economic particularities have to be changed, which will take time and will meet resistance by entrenched groups that benefit from existing structures and traditions.

Rejections can be broad or narrower. There was a time when some developing countries argued that civil and political rights could not be implemented until the economic and social conditions had significantly improved. This would in fact mean that one part of the rights was suspended, while economic, social and cultural rights were given at least some formal endorsement by those same countries. This is now quite rare: it is broadly recognized that civil and political rights are also important in the development process, and the Declaration on the Right to Development, Article 6, makes this abundantly clear.

The problem is now rather the opposite: a few countries, while recognizing the validity of civil and political rights, deny the validity of economic and social rights as human rights properly speaking. Evasive language is used, such as the claim that these rights are mere "aspirations". This can at its worst amount to a wholesale rejection of the principle of indivisibility of human rights, and is also in conflict with the consensus adoption of the Vienna Declaration in 1993. Such rejections are associated with some of the more extreme versions of neo-liberal ideologies, the recent versions of *laissez-faire* policies which had wide support in the dominant economic circles during the middle and later part of the nineteenth century in Great Britain and the United States, and which have had a revival in recent years. The ideology opposes an active role of the state in social and economic affairs, claiming that such intervention will negatively affect the economy of the country as a whole. Faced with evidence that such policies lead to vastly increased inequality, the adherents of neo-liberal ideologies either shrug it off based on social Darwinist convictions that societies are best served by the survival of the fittest, or argue that even if some people experience great hardship due to a lack of social prevention of poverty, those who survive will ultimately benefit from a future richer society resulting from the achievements of the most capable and creative.

Obviously such convictions are in stark contrast to the human rights system adopted since the Second World War. Instead of referring to economic and social rights as mere aspirations, attention should be given to the lack of capability for the fully fledged implementation of those rights and to what could be done to improve that capability.

Lack of Capability: The Complexity of the Issue

Even where the government has the will to recognize, as set out in the Vienna Declaration, "the duty of States, regardless of their political, economic and cultural systems, to promote and protect all human rights and fundamental freedoms", it will face a number of cultural, political and material obstacles which weaken its capability to implement the whole range of rights. What appears to be a lack of capability on the side of the government may turn out to be caused by a lack of will within sections of the population, which effectively undermines the well-intentioned efforts of the government.

Sections of the population may persist in maintaining cultural traditions which conflict with human rights, such as the equality of women. Efforts by governments to ensure the right to equality of women – in education, marriage, inheritance and other areas – can face formidable resistance which deprives the government of sufficient authority and legitimacy at the national level to pursue the realization of those rights. Governments which seek to eliminate caste – a particularly serious problem in South Asia – find themselves in difficulties owing to strong cultural and political opposition. Local authorities and the local police are themselves often deeply affected by the traditional culture of discrimination.

Some governments which seek to ensure freedom of religion and combat religious intolerance find themselves confronted with militant groups and often have to back down. Governments seeking to ensure economic and social rights confront opposition from powerful economic groups which, on the basis of a widespread market culture of non-interference by the state, resist the necessary regulation aimed at protecting rights for all; these powerful economic groups refuse to contribute to the common welfare through taxation which is necessary in order to fund the public expenditure required for ensuring health services, public education and basic social security for all.

The second level of obstacles is the inadequate availability of human resources to implement rights. Implementing the right to due process, which shall be enjoyed by everyone without discrimination, requires the existence of a competent, impartial judiciary and a competent set of practising lawyers, operating at costs which are affordable for all. To put in place such institutions and ensure the existence of the necessary human resources, consisting of persons with integrity and with an income sufficient to abstain from corruption, requires not only material resources but also extensive education and training. The same goes for other law enforcement personnel, such as the police, the prison warders and others.

The third level goes to the availability of material resources. Obviously, developing countries have difficulties, even with the best of wills on the part of the government and of the public at large, in ensuring the availability of material resources sufficient to fulfil the right of all to education, to the highest attainable standard of health and to the necessary social security for persons who through no fault of their own are unable to ensure for themselves or their family an adequate standard of living. This, however, is not a reason to dismiss these rights as "aspirations", but rather to proceed immediately with their gradual and progressive realization, recognizing that states have both obligations of conduct and obligations of result in doing so. These correspond to process rights and outcome rights for those who live in the country concerned. The UN Committee on Economic, Social and Cultural Rights has, in a number of so-called general comments, spelled out in detail how these rights are applicable even when the resources are limited. The rights can always be implemented to some degree, and there is a duty to proceed with the greatest possible speed to higher levels of realization as soon as the opportunities are there.[5]

Most countries would, however, be able to ensure at least the core rights within each category. As states move higher up the GNP per capita list, they have less and less excuse to argue that their society as a whole does not have sufficient resources to meet those rights; more probably the problem of lack of resources can then be seen to be a lack of political will by part of the public to assist in making the resources available for public use in line with human rights.

The Fragmentary Approaches Caused by the Functional Subdivision of State Administration

The distinction between "lack of capability" and "lack of will" is probably too simple. In practice, there are conflicting interests inside the state, and there are different functions of the state related to those separate interests. The first problem to be mentioned is that different sets of rights fall under the responsibility of different sectors of the state administration (leaving aside here the legislature, which ideally should have a role to play in regard to the implementation of all human rights, in particular through legislative measures). The more detailed responsibilities will in practice have to be exercised by different ministries or departments. The ministries of justice and/or the interior will have the key roles in regard to many aspects of civil rights implementation, the ministry of labour in many (though not all) labour rights, the ministry of health in many aspects of the right to the highest attainable standard of health, the ministry of education in the right to education, and so on. It should be kept in mind, however, that many rights require complex measures for their comprehensive implementation, and cannot be fully handled by one single ministry at the executive or administrative level.

The main problem for the interdependence of rights is, however, that each ministry is sector-oriented and thus does not fully take into account the relations between other rights and those particular rights for which it has responsibility. Consequently there is a tendency to develop sectoral implementation of particular rights, losing sight of their interdependence.

Conflicting International Institutions and Requirements

An additional problem is caused by conflicting international requirements. There is both increasing international regulation of matters previously left to the discretion of states, and a growing fragmentation of international law. The two fastest-growing sectors of international law during the last half century have been international economic law and international human rights law. Both contain extensive obligations which have to be honoured by states, but those obligations may be conflicting or at odds with each other, particularly with regard to economic and social rights. The different sectors of the state administration often relate to different domestic interest groups, which in turn have links to different international institutions and their different components of international law. People involved in trade and commerce have links to and interest in the WTO and related international law, while people involved in labour relations may have links to the ILO and its conventions and recommendations, which may be somewhat at odds with WTO regulations.

Economic Globalization, Corporations and Privatization: Undermining the Capacity to Ensure Economic, Social and Cultural Rights?

The contemporary processes of globalization have in fundamental ways changed the framework for the implementation of the system of human rights as a whole. The present direction of globalization has been strongly influenced by the neo-liberal ideology mentioned above. In its most problematic forms, this ideology requires privatization of public enterprises, deregulation of the economy, blanket liberalization of trade and industry, massive tax cuts, strict control on labour, reduction of public expenditures, particularly social spending, downsizing of government, expansion of international markets and removal of controls on global financial flows. These have facilitated the enormous growth in the size and reach of multinational corporations, whose power has increased greatly in comparison to the power of states and their governments. In this process, the International Monetary Fund (IMF) and the World Bank have moved to centre stage as guardians of the global economic order, by imposing criteria for credit and grants that are essential to development. During the 1980s and part of the 1990s, those two institutions pursued a rigid neo-liberal approach. One of its most negative aspects, directly relevant to the core concerns of UNESCO, was the World Bank policy to call for the introduction of school fees even at primary school level, in direct conflict with ICESCR Article 13 which requires primary education to be free and compulsory for all. The devastating impact of that policy was revealed by the UN special rapporteur on the right to education (Tomasevski 2003).

Under international law the primary responsibility for human rights continues to rest with the host government. States are required to respect the freedoms and fulfil the rights of their inhabitants. States are never entitled to abdicate from their human rights obligations, be it in the context of international trade regulations, international investment agreements or in any other way. Human rights should hold priority in all such relations.

Problems arise when the authorities of the host state are unwilling or unable to implement all aspects of the internationally recognized human rights. In their quest to encourage investments from abroad, some governments abstain from taking the measures required to implement all human rights, in particular economic and social rights. They establish tax-free havens which eliminate the possibility of raising taxes to ensure social welfare. They prohibit trade union activities. They do not adopt or enforce labour standards as set out in ILO conventions.

In some cases, host states are willing but not able to make the proper decisions for the implementation of human rights, in particular the economic, social and cultural rights, owing to pressure from the outside. This pressure may come from transnational corporations (TNCs), from home governments of the TNCs concerned or from international financial institutions in the context of structural adjustment. Where this is the case, the international monitoring agencies and other human rights bodies must develop an appropriate normative defence against such illegitimate pressures. This has to some extent happened, but so far to a very limited degree.

At the level of the international community, a paradoxical development has taken place during the last decades. On the one hand, the obligations of states have become increasingly detailed, mainly through international human rights law, but the capacity of states to fulfil those obligations has been reduced as a consequence of the marginalization of the role of the state in economic and social fields. On the other hand, international standards of relevance to TNCs have moved in the opposite direction: states provide benefits to the transnationals but no duties to reciprocate. It is in this latter respect that changes are warranted. If globalization is to continue without leading to destructive backlashes and impoverishment of weaker and vulnerable groups, rights and benefits of corporations have to be combined with duties. UDHR Article 29 states that everyone has a duty to the community. For corporations, this must imply that they have duties both to the local community in the area of their operation and to the national society in which they function. The nature and scope of such duties need to be spelled out as part of any future international agreement on investment.

A constructive and corrective relationship between the forces of the market and the powers of the state requires good governance, structured in such a way as to implement human rights optimally. It requires the rule of law, transparency, responsiveness and accountability at national and international levels alike. The responsibility of the World Bank and the IMF for human rights is a matter of some controversy, but recent research shows that such responsibility does exist, at least in the sense that these bodies must respect human rights in their activities (Skogly 2000).

Non-governmental organizations now focus on the social responsibility of corporations, and on means to alter corporate behaviour through public exposure. They have been helped in this endeavour by effective use of communications technology. The international media have responded by running stories about corporate involvement in human rights violations. This has drawn public attention to the activities of the corporations, but so far mainly concerning violations of civil rights.

Globalization is also affected by and contributes to developments in science and technology, communications and, in particular, information processing which have substantially changed the structure of the global system and can have many beneficial consequences for human rights. While during the last two decades they may have had many negative consequences, developments in communications and information processing may, under conditions yet to be worked out, be turned to the advantage of a holistic approach to human rights.

OVERCOMING THE OBSTACLES: THE NEED FOR A RIGHTS-BASED DEVELOPMENT IN THE AGE OF GLOBALIZATION?

While the principle of the indivisibility, interdependence and interrelatedness of human rights has been clearly proclaimed and is based on solid arguments, there are still many obstacles to its full implementation. The greatest challenge is to ensure that economic, social and cultural rights are given the same weight as civil and political rights. What can be done to overcome those obstacles, and who can do it?

Improving Human Rights Capacity by International Cooperation

As previously mentioned, one of the main purposes of the United Nations is to achieve international cooperation in solving international problems of an economic, social, cultural or humanitarian character, and in promoting and encouraging respect for human rights and fundamental freedoms for all. For the implementation of that purpose, the organization shall promote higher standards of living, full employment and conditions of economic and social progress and development. It shall promote solutions to international economic, social, health and related problems, as well as international cultural and educational cooperation, and shall promote universal respect for, and observance of, human rights and fundamental freedoms for all (UN Charter, Article 55). All state members of the United Nations have pledged themselves to take joint and separate action in cooperation with the organization for the achievement of those purposes (UN Charter, Article 56).

Rights-based Development and the Right to Development: Towards a Global Contract?

Under UDHR Article 28, everyone "is entitled to a social and international order in which these rights can be fully realized". ICESCR Article 2(1) requires all states parties "to take steps, individually and through international assistance and co-operation, especially economic and technical, to the maximum of its available resources ...". The Committee on Economic, Social and Cultural Rights observed in its General Comment No. 3 (1990) that the phrase "available resources" refers to both the resources existing within a state and those available from the international community through international cooperation and assistance. Moreover, it noted that the essential role of such cooperation in facilitating the full realization of the relevant rights is further underlined by the specific provisions contained in ICESCR Articles 11, 15, 22 and 23. With respect to Article 22 the committee drew attention, by way of General Comment No. 2 (1990), to some of the opportunities and responsibilities regarding international cooperation. Article 23 specifically identifies "the furnishing of technical assistance", as well as other activities, as being among the means of "international action for the achievement of the rights recognised ...".

The committee noted that, in accordance with Articles 55 and 56 of the UN Charter, with well-established principles of international law and with the provisions of the covenant itself, international cooperation for development and thus for the realization of economic, social and cultural rights is an obligation of all states.[6] It is particularly incumbent upon those states that are in a position to assist others in this regard to honour their commitment. The committee noted in particular the importance of the Declaration on the Right to Development, adopted by the General Assembly in Resolution 41/128 of 4 December 1986, and the need for states parties to take full account of all of the principles recognized therein. It emphasized that in the absence of an active programme of international assistance and cooperation on the part of all those states that are in a position to launch one, the full realization of economic, social and cultural rights will remain an unfulfilled aspiration in many countries.

The Declaration on the Right to Development sets both national and international levels of responsibility for implementation. Its operative Article 3 declares that states have the primary responsibility for creating national and international conditions favourable to the realization of the right to development. States also have the duty to cooperate with each other in ensuring development and eliminating obstacles to it. States should realize their rights and fulfil their duties in such a manner as to promote a new international economic order based on sovereign equality, interdependence, mutual interest and cooperation among all states (Sengupta 1999). Development is described by the declaration as an economic, social, cultural and political process aiming at a constant improvement in the well-being of the population as a whole and of each individual. Its basis should be the individual's active, free and meaningful participation in development and in the fair distribution of its benefits.

With regard to the quest for a social order which assures everyone enjoyment of the rights and freedoms set forth in the Universal Declaration, the Declaration on the Right to Development provides in its Article 8(1) that states shall undertake, at the national level, all necessary measures for the realization of the right to development. They should ensure, *inter alia*, equality of opportunity for all in their access to basic resources, education, health services, food, housing, employment and the fair distribution of income.

Furthermore, with regard to the requirement foreseen in UDHR Article 28 for an international order in which human rights for all can be realized, the Declaration on the Right to Development provides in Article 4 that states have a duty to take steps, individually and collectively, to formulate international development policies with a view to the full realization of the right to development.

An increasing number of UN agencies and other bodies have recognized the necessity of using a human rights framework in guiding their work. This has gone hand in hand with increasing attention to economic and social rights as being of equal value to civil and political rights.

The Human Rights Movement – National and Transnational

During the 1970s and 1980s the human rights movement was – for good reasons – mostly concerned with gross violations of civil and political rights. Nowadays a much more comprehensive approach is taken by most human rights NGOs. While civil rights – freedom from torture, freedom of expression and the others – are still given due attention, human rights organizations are now increasingly concerned about the onslaught on economic, social and cultural rights – on labour rights and the rights to food and water, health care, adequate housing, social security and education. Concern for the implications of increased globalization of the world has increased to such an extent that it is not rare for human rights organizations – including the most traditional among them – to raise the issue as one of fundamental importance to respect for human rights.

Human Rights Education

One of the purposes set by international human rights law for education is to strengthen the recognition and observance of all (other) human rights. This was already envisaged in 1948 when the UN General Assembly proclaimed the Universal Declaration "to the end that every individual and every organ of society, keeping this Declaration constantly in mind, shall strive by teaching and education to promote respect for these rights …" (UDHR, Preamble).

Provisions on human rights education are contained in many international instruments, including UDHR Article 26, ICESCR Article 13, the Convention on the Rights of the Child Article 29, CEDAW Article 10 and the Convention on the Elimination of All Forms of Racial Discrimination Article 7. The importance of human rights education is also underlined by many world conferences, including the Vienna Declaration and Programme of Action paragraphs 33 and 34, and elsewhere.

Human rights education is not only education about human rights instruments, procedures and institutions, but above all about lifelong education, training and information aiming at building a universal culture of human rights. It involves the sharing of knowledge, learning of skills and influencing attitudes in order to strengthen respect for human rights, promoting the full development of the human personality and his or her sense of dignity, the promotion of understanding, tolerance, gender equality and friendship among nations and peoples, enabling all persons to participate actively in a free and democratic society governed by the rule of law, the maintenance of peace and the promotion of socially and ecologically sustainable development.

UNESCO has a prominent role in the promotion of the world programme for human rights education and is therefore strategically well placed to advance the understanding and application of the principle of the indivisibility of all human rights. In collaboration with the UN High Commissioner for Human Rights, UNESCO has presented the plan for the first phase of that programme (2005–2007).[7]

Significantly, the first principle for human rights education activities is to "promote the interdependence, indivisibility and universality of human rights, including civil, political, economic, social and cultural rights and the right to development" (para. 8).

The Role and Impact of the UN Human Rights Bodies and Agencies

Two sets of UN human rights bodies have emerged: the Charter-based and the treaty-based. The main Charter-based bodies were until 2006 the UN Commission on Human Rights, which was the political body dealing with human rights, and its Sub-Commission on the Promotion and Protection of Human Rights, which was its expert advisory body. (In 2006 the commission was replaced by the Human Rights Council, and the sub-commission role is likely to be replaced by another but comparable advisory body.) Within these bodies, the broad range of human rights was addressed, with economic and social rights given increasing attention in recent years. Significant studies have been carried out by the sub-commission on the right to food and the right to housing and more generally on economic and social rights; in the Commission on Human Rights, special rapporteurs have been appointed who have dealt with the situation worldwide concerning the rights to food, education, housing and health, and cross-cutting issues such as human rights and extreme poverty and the impact of the debt crisis on human rights. Cumulatively, a very important body of knowledge has thus been established in these areas.

The treaty bodies, on the other hand, present a more mixed picture. Owing to the fact that in 1951 the United Nations, bowing to Western pressure, decided to divide the rights in the Universal Declaration into two covenants, the treaty-monitoring bodies of those two covenants are naturally bound to monitor only that section of rights which is contained in "their" covenant. The Human Rights Committee monitors the implementation of civil and political rights while the Committee on Economic, Social and Cultural Rights monitors the implementation of those rights, as the name says. The Committee against Torture, naturally, addresses compliance with state obligations to abstain from and prevent torture. But the Committee on the Rights of the Child, the Committee on the Elimination of All Forms of Racial Discrimination and the Committee on the Elimination of Discrimination against Women all address the whole set of rights, since the relevant conventions include economic and social rights as well as civil and political. The same applies to the newly established Committee on the Protection of the Rights of All Migrant Workers and Members of Their Families.

The Office of the High Commissioner for Human Rights has an important integrating role to play and has increasingly done so, in collaboration with UNESCO and other agencies.

The role of the UN specialized agencies and other bodies depends on their respective mandates as well as their receptiveness to human rights in their activities. For UNESCO, the right to education, cultural rights, freedom of expression and scientific freedom, the right to information and the right to benefit from scientific progress are core concerns, including through its work on communication; for the WHO, the central issue is the right of everyone to the highest attainable standard of health; for the FAO, the dominant issue is the right of everyone to be free from hunger and to adequate food. All of these bodies have experienced in their work, however, that their special areas of rights cannot be dealt with in isolation: the right to education or to culture cannot be isolated from the right to freedom of expression and information and many other rights. The same recognition of interdependence has also been made, to varying degrees, by other bodies.

National Human Rights Institutions, National Plans of Action and Governmental Coordination

National human rights institutions have become important in recent years (Kjærum 2003). Under the Paris Principles[8] they should have a broad mandate; this would imply that they should deal with all human rights and therefore be faced with the issues of interdependence and indivisibility. The major issue is whether and to what extent they address economic and social rights. The predominant trend has been to focus on civil rights and take up cases where there are apparent violations of such rights, since violations are more easily detected. But several national institutions in different parts of the world are already on record to address the whole broad range of human rights. These includes the South African Human Rights Commission, the Indian Commission and the Danish Institute for Human Rights.

The World Conference on Human Rights (Vienna, 1993) recommended that each state should consider the desirability of drawing up a national action plan identifying steps whereby that state would improve the promotion and protection of human rights (Vienna Declaration and Plan of Action, para. 71). In this connection, the conference also called for the implementation of strengthened advisory services and technical assistance activities by the then Centre for Human Rights (now the Office of the High Commissioner for Human Rights), in order for states to prepare and implement coherent and comprehensive plans of action for the promotion and protection of human rights.

This can serve as a very useful mechanism to ensure in practice an integrated and systemic implementation of human rights, taking their interdependence fully into account. A number of states have already prepared such plans of action, with somewhat varying contents. As an illustration, one can mention here the plan of action prepared by the government of Norway and endorsed by the parliament.

The plan was prepared in 1999 by the then minister for human rights and development cooperation. It addressed the implementation of all human rights (civil, political, economic, social and cultural), including the rights of the child and prevention of discrimination on the grounds of race and discrimination against women.

In the preparation of the plan, all government departments were involved. Regular meetings were held to identify what responsibilities were held by the different ministries and what steps should be taken by each of them for better implementation of human rights. Where gaps of implementation were identified, special projects or activities were planned and subsequently implemented.

Under the leadership of the minister for human rights and development cooperation, representatives of the different departments held regular meetings after the adoption of the plan in order to assess whether the plan was actually followed up, identifying delays and obstacles and encouraging further progress.

Since the whole range of human rights was covered and the process involved the broad range of executive and administrative institutions, it provided a unique opportunity to understand the interrelationship between the rights. The plan dealt not only with the internal dimension, covering all sectors of the Norwegian government, but also the external dimension, in particular Norwegian human rights policies in multilateral bodies and in development cooperation.

The Role of Multinational Corporations

Multinational corporations play a dominant role in the process of globalization thorough their investments, production and trade. MNCs have been described as the linchpins of the contemporary world economy, and are estimated to account for up to 70 per cent of world trade (Held et al. 1999, 282). A number of measures are required in order to ensure that corporations have a more positive impact on the enjoyment of economic and social rights. The most important task is to strengthen the will and capacity of states to regulate the activities of these corporations to make them compatible with the welfare functions of the state, without blocking their positive functions.

Resulting from extensive criticisms by human rights organizations when corporations have been complicit in human rights violations, some MNCs have started to develop their own voluntary codes of conduct. So far they are mostly expressed in terms of ethics and have yielded limited results in terms of corporate behaviour change. At the international level, much more needs to be done to ensure the compliance of corporations with human rights. A good beginning has been made with the establishment of the "Global Compact" through the initiative of the UN Secretary-General, which seeks to promote corporate citizenship in the world economy by encouraging corporations to comply with human rights, including labour rights, and environmental regulations and to pursue anti-corruption measures.[9]

A more promising initiative was taken by the UN Sub-Commission on the Promotion and Protection of Human Rights, which in 2003 adopted the draft "Norms on the Responsibilities of Transnational Corporations and Other Business Enterprises with Regard to Human Rights".[10] The draft was transferred to the UN Commission on Human Rights, where a variety of views were expressed but no substantial decision was taken before the commission was replaced by the Human Rights Council. Should the council adopt the draft norms, in their present or in revised form, they could serve a dual function: firstly, as a guide to states on the regulations they should impose on corporations operating on their territory, and secondly as a basis for international monitoring of the activities of corporations from a human rights perspective.

Some form of regulation on financial flows is also essential. One proposal is the "Tobin Tax Initiative", consisting of sales taxes on currency trades across borders, originally proposed by James Tobin, a Nobel laureate economist at Yale University. "Tobin taxes" can be enacted domestically by national legislatures, but will require multilateral cooperation to be effectively enforced.

Increased transparency within international financial institutions is essential. These institutions should take seriously the widespread critical assessment of their activities if their policies are to evolve in a credible and balanced manner.

CONCLUSIONS

The United Nations has repeatedly emphasized that the human rights it adopted are universal, indivisible, interdependent and interrelated. This chapter has examined the possible meanings of these terms and the categories of relationships that can exist between them. It has been shown that the justification of the principle of indivisibility can be traced to three major concerns: ensuring that everyone is free and equal in dignity and rights; that human rights should ensure social integration in a pluralist and open society; and that freedom of self is linked to the freedom of others.

Furthermore, it has been shown that freedom not only consists in freedom from abusive state power, but also the protection by the state of freedom from unfair economic systems and from the abuse of private power. The relationships between the rights have wide-ranging practical implications, including in areas of particular concern to UNESCO such as education, science, culture and communication.

Obstacles and challenges to the principle of indivisibility can arise from lack of will or lack of capacity. It is important to avoid human rights fundamentalism and to have an open mind towards the need of societies to take some time in changing their cultural, political and economic systems, but there can be no excuse for states that do not over time try to move towards a comprehensive and full implementation of the whole human rights system, including civil and political as well as economic, social and cultural rights.

To achieve this, measures must be taken on many levels. It requires changes in the focus of academic research and changes in the international environment, including the behaviour and policies of MNCs and the international financial institutions.

The issue of global facilitation of a rights-based development rooted in the indivisibility of human rights raises challenges to human rights scholarship, where predominant attention has been on civil and political rights. This is now changing. What is needed is an improved global dialogue among economists, political scientists, human rights scholars and the wider human rights movement.

Further research in these areas requires a vastly improved flow of information on the impact of globalization on human rights around the world, disaggregated by gender, location, rural versus urban and developed versus developing.

The World Commission on the Social Dimension of Globalization (ILO 2004) has recommended that multilateral organizations should establish joint research programmes to examine objectively the impact of trade on development. This should involve the IMF, the World Bank, the ILO, the UNDP and other relevant UN bodies, as well as the WTO, to explore the coherence of their policies in the light of UDHR Article 28. The UN research organizations, such as the UNRISD, the UNU, UNIFEM and UNITAR, also need to be centrally involved in this research.

Drawing on such research, but turning it into a positive line of action, wide-ranging efforts must be made to pursue a rights-based development which integrates all human rights, fully recognizing their interrelatedness in all their dimensions. UNESCO, in cooperation with the Office of the UN High Commissioner for Human Rights, must clearly have a central role in these efforts. Only through a determined and broad rights-based development will it be possible to achieve the visions of UDHR Article 28: a social and international order in which everyone can enjoy all the rights set out in the declaration.

NOTE ON SOURCES AND LITERATURE

Few authors have examined in depth the issues of the interdependence and interrelatedness of human rights. Two such contributions are listed in the references: Cancado Trindade (1998) and Winston (2000). A broad overview of the drafting of the Universal Declaration of Human Rights and its follow-up is found in Alfredsson and Eide (1999). A more detailed examination of the whole range of economic, social and cultural rights is found in Eide et al. (2001). A similar overview of the rights contained in the UN Covenant on Civil and Political Rights is given in Nowak (1993). There is a vast literature regarding the separate rights, which cannot be listed here.

NOTES

1 The lectures were given in honour of the famous economist Alfred Marshall.
2 The draft is reproduced in the *Annals of the American Academy of Political and Social Science* (1946) 243: 18–26.
3 GA Res. 421(V), 4 December 1950.
4 GA Res. 2200 A(XXI), 16 December 1966, Annex.
5 The general comments of the UN Committee on Economic, Social and Cultural Rights can be found on the website of the UN High Commissioner for Human Rights (www.ochcr.org). Of particular relevance for the discussion are General Comments Nos 3, 9, 11, 12, 14 and 15.

6   HRI/GEN/1/rev.4, General Comment No. 3, p. 12, paras 13 and 14.
7   Set out in UN Doc. A/59/525.
8   Principles relating to the Status of National Institutions (the Paris Principles), adopted by General Assembly A/RES/48/134, 20 December 1993.
9   For further information see www.un.org/Depts/ptd/global.htm.
10   UN Doc. E/CN.4/Sub.2/2003/12/Rev.2, available at http://ap.ohchr.org/documents/dpage_e.aspx?s=58.

REFERENCES

Alfredsson, Gudmundur and Eide, Asbjørn (1999), *The Universal Declaration of Human Rights, A Common Standard of Achievement* (The Hague: Martinus Nijhoff).
Araki, Takashi (2002), *Labor and Employment Law in Japan* (Tokyo: Japan Institute of Labor).
Beveridge, W. (1942), "Social insurance and allied services", Report by Sir William Beveridge, presented to Parliament by Command of His Majesty, November, Cmnd 6404 (London: HMSO).
Cancado Trindade, A. (1998), "The interdependence of all human rights – Obstacles and challenges to their implementation", *International Social Science Journal*, 158: 513–23.
Eide, A., Krause, C. and Rosas, A. (eds) (2001), *Economic, Social and Cultural Rights: A Textbook*, 2nd edition (The Hague: Martinus Nijhoff).
Held, David, McGrew, Anthony G., Goldblatt, David and Perraton, Jonathan (1999), *Global Transformations: Politics, Economics and Culture* (Stanford: Polity Press/ Stanford University Press
Humphrey, J.P. (1984), *Human Rights and the United Nations: A Great Adventure* (Sydney: Oceania Publications).
ILO (2004), *World Commission on the Social Dimension of Globalization* (Geneva: International Labour Organization).
Kjaerum, M. (2003), "National human rights institutions implementing human rights", in M. Bergsmo (ed.), *Human Rights and Criminal Justice for the Downtrodden: Essays in Honour of Asbjørn Eide* (Leiden: Martinus Nijhoff).
Macmillan, H. (1938), "The middle way", *Economic Journal*, 48:191, 551–4.
Marks, S. (2003), "Defining cultural rights", in M. Bergsmo (ed.), *Human Rights and Criminal Justice for the Downtrodden: Essays in Honour of Asbjørn Eide* (Leiden: Martinus Nijhoff), pp. 293–324.
Marshall, T.H. (1950), *Citizenship and Social Class and Other Essays* (Cambridge: Cambridge University Press).
Nowak, M. (1993), *UN Covenant on Civil and Political Rights (CCPR) Commentary* (Kehl: N.P. Engel).
Roosevelt, F.D. (1941), "State of the Union Address 1941", available at www.gutenberg. org/dirs/etext04/sufdr11.txt.
—— (1944), "State of the Union Address 1944", available at www.gutenberg.org/dirs/ etext04/sufdr11.txt.
Skogly, S. (2000), "The position of the World Bank and the International Monetary Fund in the human rights field", in Raija Hanski and Suksi Markku (eds), *An Introduction to the International Protection of Human Rights* (Åbo: Institute for Human Rights, Åbo Akademi).
Sengupta, A. (1999), "Realizing the right to development", *Development and Change* 31: 3.
Stavenhagen, R. (2001), "Cultural rights and universal human rights", in A. Eide, C. Krause and A. Rosas (eds), *Economic, Social and Cultural Rights: A Textbook*, 2nd edition (The Hague: Martinus Nijhoff).

Tomasevski, Katarina (2003), *Education Denied. Costs and Remedies* (London: Zed Books).

Winston, M. (2000), "Indivisibility and interdependence of human rights", *University of Nebraska Human Rights and Human Diversity Monograph Series* 2:1 (Lincoln: University of Nebraska).

2 The Justiciability of Socio-economic and Cultural Rights: Experience and Problems

FRANS VILJOEN

INTRODUCTION

This chapter investigates to what extent "economic, social and cultural rights" are justiciable at the national and international (global and regional) levels. To chart the terrain, reliance is placed on concrete examples of the potential and actual justiciability of these rights in national legislation and international treaties, as well as in national and international case law. The scope of this study makes an exhaustive overview impossible; rather, as a country- and institution-based inventory, it aims to illustrate general trends, problems and possibilities. By illuminating the "experience" of states in which justiciability has been accepted, the study aims to provide a response to the perceived "obstacles" raised in countries where socio-economic rights are formally provided for, but not accorded justiciability.

Defining Social, Economic and Cultural Rights

Suggesting that somehow the essence of social, economic and cultural rights is self-evident, much academic writing on the topic never finds it necessary to define these rights. This may be so because these fixed categories are not relevant or useful when one is confronted with facts in a particular *context*, giving rise to questions about the state obligation inferred from a right, rather than when classifying a right with relation to its *content*.

An attempt at conceptual clarification is usually further constrained owing to the conflation of the "social", the "economic" and the "cultural". Sometimes the "social" and "economic" are kept separate, sometimes they are combined as "socio-economic". Mostly, "cultural" is tagged along, without paying much attention to its peculiarities.

"Social rights" have been defined as referring to rights "with regard to relationships in society" (Victor Condé 2004, 241), such as the right to family, to special protection for children and the elderly and to form trade unions. "Economic rights" are defined as rights "whose purpose is to assure that human beings have the ability to obtain and maintain a minimum decent standard of living consistent with human dignity" (ibid., 55). Examples are the rights to food, health care, work, social security and to form trade unions. This distinction between "social" and "economic" rights, which is based on differences in the content of the right covered, is not relevant in the context of justiciability. In any event, a division into these categories is by no means watertight, as the right to form trade unions most clearly demonstrates. In so far as these categories give rise to shared concerns, most importantly the perception that they are programmatic and that their realization requires resource allocation (or at least greater allocation than other rights), the term "socio-economic right" is used in this study.[1] The concept also includes the right to education, not only because it may properly be included in the definition of both "social" and "economic" rights as set out above, but also because it is closely associated with the concerns raised below in respect of socio-economic rights.

Rights traditionally categorized as civil and political in nature may have a hidden socio-economic character, or may be interpreted to realize socio-economic benefits and needs, thus enhancing socio-economic rights. Although it may be argued that on closer inspection at least some of the traditional civil and political rights *are* indeed at least partly socio-economic[2] or have social or economic implications, these rights are not treated as socio-economic rights here. Even if "civil and political" rights such as the right to life may provide a normative basis to secure socio-economic benefits,[3] such an approach does not convert for example the right to life into a socio-economic right. Deriving a state obligation to fulfil is contingent upon discretionary judicial activism. While conceding the important role that the expansive interpretation of "civil and political" rights can play in securing socio-economic benefits, the emphasis in this chapter falls on those "socio-economic rights" in respect of which states have unequivocally committed themselves.

Delineating cultural rights is complex, in part because of the different understandings one may have of "culture". However "culture" is defined, a distinction may be drawn between "cultural rights" as referring to rights of a "cultural" nature, such as the right to education, and "right to culture" as a right to develop or participate in the cultural life of a community. For the purposes of this study, the term "cultural rights" is understood as being intertwined with Article 15 of the International Convention on Economic, Social and Cultural Rights (ICESCR), which protects the right to participate in cultural life, to enjoy the benefits of scientific progress and to benefit from scientific, literary and artistic production. "Cultural rights" can also be understood as an umbrella concept under which is included all the rights that serve to protect aspects of culture, such as the right to freedom of religion and freedom of expression. Although it is difficult to argue that a broad "right to cultural identity" is justiciable, respect for cultural identity is an animating principle that guides the interpretation of any right *in a cultural context* (Donders 2002, 331). When other rights are made justiciable in respect of cultural claims, the "right to cultural identity" indirectly becomes justiciable. For the purposes of this study, however, "cultural rights" are defined more or less with reference to ICESCR Article 15, rather than more expansively.

In summary, the concept of "socio-economic rights", as it is used here, excludes "civil and political" rights, such as the right to life, in respect of which there is little controversy as to justiciability.

Justiciability

Calling the dispute about a right "justiciable" implies something about the *claim* (or petition), about the *setting* in which it may be resolved and about the *consequences* of successfully invoking it. The claim (or petition) must be based on the alleged infringement of a subjective right (invoked by an individual or collectively). This claim has to be determined by a court or other tribunal or judicial body, or by a quasi-judicial body sharing the main features of a court.[4] If a violation of the subjective right is found, a court (or quasi-judicial body) must be able to find a remedy to redress the violation,[5] even in the form of a recommendation, and the finding should set a form of precedent or at least embody an authoritative interpretation of that right (Arambulo 1999, 55). The remedy is based on some form of "judicial review", usually of executive conduct or legislation, and may include a declaratory order, an invalidation or suspension of a law, or constitutional damages. As South African experiences indicate, the remedy may often be directed at a change to national law and practice rather than at satisfying the subjective interests of an individual.

In this study, this definition of "justiciability" is used to apply to both national and international levels; to do otherwise runs the risk of compounding the conceptual confusion that already exists. Craven (1995, 16) takes issue with making justiciability at the international level dependent on the existence of a legal remedy, because in his view international human rights law also functions as an "appeal to the adjustment of national law and practice" to address inadequate national law even when there are no "specific international remedies open to the individual". The present author's view is that it is incorrect to equate the gravitational pull of international human rights law on national law, in the absence of available remedies, with justiciability. Craven's approach seems to depart from a misunderstanding of the difference between justiciability and legal validity. The "appeal" of international law is derived from the legal validity of international human rights law: the gravitational pull or "appeal" follows upon ratification of a treaty. Ratification of an international human rights treaty places a legal obligation on states to ensure that its legal system mirrors the treaty. But ratification, as such, does not give rise to a claim based on a subjective right leading to a remedy.

Restricting the concept to the strictly judicial and related settings does not negate or minimize the other possible forms of "review" that may also constitute "justiciability" in a broader sense. Such a narrower definition, as is adopted here, poses a greater challenge in making out a case that socio-economic rights are justiciable, as most criticism of justiciability is usually directed at the judicial setting.

"Justiciability" should be distinguished from the implementation of a court's decision. Once a remedy has been ordered, it needs to be implemented or "realized". Courts retain a role to "enforce" the remedy contained in the decision should it not be implemented. All rights that have been made justiciable are not enforced. The lack of enforcement at the international level has led some to question the justiciability of rights at that level. But implementation or enforcement is different from justiciability.[6] Enforcement at the international level is indeed much weaker than at the national level – at the national level a court's enforcement order is backed up by domestic institutional force. At the international level, enforcement primarily takes the form of mobilizing shame, but may exceptionally be bolstered by more concrete measures such as economic sanctions or the threat of institutional expulsion. Although this study concerns itself primarily with "justiciability", if the South African experience is anything to go by, an acceptance that socio-economic rights are justiciable is soon followed by concerns for more effective implementation and enforcement. The intimate linkage between justiciability and enforcement is undeniable. Criticism was directed at the South African Constitutional Court's decision in *Grootboom CC* for not retaining the court's supervisory role and for making the order only declaratory (Pillay 2002; *East London Traditional Local Council*).

This study follows the taxonomy devised by Shue (1980), in terms of which justiciability is dependent on the obligation of states in respect of a particular right, rather than exclusively on the nature of the right. The obligations of states in respect of all rights are at three levels: "respect", "protect" and "fulfil". States must *respect* rights by refraining from interfering with the enjoyment of these rights, for example by not evicting people who have nowhere to go. This obligation is understood to be "negative", in that it does not require government intrusion or resource allocation. States must *protect* bearers of rights from intrusions by third parties, by way of legislating or adopting other measures, for instance by prohibiting exploitative child labour. States have to *fulfil* rights when they are required to take positive measures to ensure the direct enjoyment of a right, for example by building and equipping clinics and providing medication. A fourth category, to "promote" rights, has subsequently been devised (van Hoof 1984, 106). This obligation requires a state to enable people to exercise rights over a longer term, for instance by education and awareness-raising. This study focuses on the first three obligations.

Some authors have underlined that the concept of justiciability is deceptive, and that its meaning is contingent upon assumptions about the role of the judiciary (Scott and Macklem 1992, 17). In this study, "justiciability" is regarded as contingent, inevitably, on the judiciary, but also on the nature of the state obligation arising from the specific right that is at stake.

EXPERIENCES AT THE NATIONAL LEVEL

An effort is made to include experiences from a diverse range of countries in different parts of the world. One of the 11 countries surveyed here is from Africa (South Africa), three are from Europe (the Czech Republic, Finland and Latvia), one from North America (Canada), two from South America (Colombia and Venezuela) and three from Asia (Fiji, India and the Philippines).[7] This choice has been guided by the availability of material, important or trend-setting developments and the ideal of global representativity. Before discussing some developments in these countries, a typology of ways in which justiciable socio-economic and cultural rights may feature domestically is attempted.

A Typology of Domestic Justiciability

Legislation

Socio-economic rights may be justiciable as legal provisions in the positive law of a particular country. As a relatively accessible source of possible redress or a remedy, domestic legislation provides an important first port of call for the realization of socio-economic or cultural rights. Not all legislation dealing with socio-economic benefits will give rise to justiciable rights as understood here. A distinction may usefully be drawn between subjective rights (such as "the right to ...") and legislative commands (such as "The minister shall ...") embodied in legislation (De Wet 1996, 32). A breach of the former entitles the individual to approach a court directly, without further legislative action being required, for a remedy. The latter, such as a legislated duty on states to adopt a housing scheme, does not give rise to a directly enforceable right, but rather requires the adoption of (mostly legislative) measures by the government. Legislative commands (just like constitutional commands) may, however, also be the basis of a review of a governmental policy or programme.

An example of justiciable socio-economic subjective rights provisions in national law is the South African Extension of Security of Tenure Act (Act 62 of 1997), which provides for the subjective right of the occupier of land on which he/she resided and which he/she used on or after 4 February 1997 to "have the right to reside on and use" that land and "to have access to such services as had been agreed upon with the owner or person in charge, whether expressly or tacitly" (s. 6(1)). Under certain conditions, an occupier "shall have the right to security of tenure", to "receive bona fide visitors at reasonable times and for reasonable periods", to "family life in accordance with the culture of that family", "not to be denied or deprived of access to water" and "not to be denied or deprived of access to educational or health services" (s. 6(2)(a)–(e)). In addition to these socio-economic rights, the important cultural right to "visit and maintain family graves on land which belongs to another person" is also recognized (s. 6(4)).[8]

The adoption of socio-economic legislation does not depend on the existence of similar provisions in the national constitution (or in international law binding on the state). In the Canadian case of *Gosselin v Quebec (Attorney General)*, Arbour J remarked that although it is "desirable" that economic and social rights should be entrenched in a charter of rights, it is "not essential to recognition of those rights in positive law" (para. 431). Social law, she continued, had "in fact developed in Quebec well before the enactment of the Quebec Charter" (ibid.). However, national law may give more precise embodiment to vague constitutional guarantees.[9] National law on these topics may also be delinked from binding international law obligations, as is demonstrated by the fact that South Africa has signed, but did not become a state party to, the ICESCR.

Failure effectively to implement relevant legislation and disputes about the content of statutory provisions introduce the role of the national judiciary. Even if rights are relatively clearly formulated, disputes about their content may still arise. A number of cases demonstrate that activist courts may use constitutional provisions to invigorate impasses about the implementation of statutes. In *Bandhua Mukti Morcha v India* the Indian Supreme Court underlined the importance of national legislation to secure socio-economic rights. The court remarked that although workers' rights under the directive principles of state policy are not "enforceable in a court of law", to the extent that guarantees of working conditions have been provided for in statute, courts may be approached to "ensure observance of such legislation" (p. 103). In this respect, the court highlighted the connection between ordinary legislation and constitutional provisions: government failure to implement legislation may amount to a violation of the constitution – in the particular case, the right to life (ibid.). In *Nontembiso v The Member of the Executive Council of the Department of Welfare, Eastern Cape*, a provincial government failed timely and effectively to apply social security legislation, prompting persistent judicial intervention: "For the past few years there has been a persistent and huge problem with the administration of social grants in this province. The failure in proper administration has led to the situation where the courts have become the primary mechanisms for ensuring accountability in the public administration of social grants" (p. 429, para. 5).

Constitutional inclusion

The constitutional inclusion of socio-economic rights comes in two main forms – as part of a bill of rights or chapter on fundamental rights, and as directive principles of state policy (DPSPs). In the first form, the justiciability of socio-economic rights is usually accepted; at least in principle, in the second, they are not justiciable as such, but serve as a guide to the executive or legislature,[10] or as a guide for the interpretation of the constitution and other laws.[11] In principle, a bill of rights contains subjective rights, while

DPSPs contain objective legal norms that still need to be converted into subjective claims.

Given the dearth of jurisprudence giving effect to socio-economic rights, it may come as a surprise how many national constitutions provide for at least some socio-economic or cultural rights. Latin American constitutions stand out in their inclusion of such provisions. For example, most Latin American constitutions make extensive provision for socio-economic rights, in particular the right to basic education, the right to form trade unions and other worker's rights.[12] Even on the African continent, mostly associated with serious socio-economic deprivation, there are only a handful of states, notably Botswana, Nigeria and Tunisia, which do not explicitly guarantee any socio-economic or cultural rights.[13] Comprehensive protection of socio-economic rights is found in all four "colonial" legal traditions imposed on and received in Africa. Despite the unequal levels of constitutional inclusion, some rights, in particular the rights to education and to form trade unions, are almost universally provided for in African constitutions.[14] Although these rights are, on their face and on paper, made justiciable, few cases dealing with claims based on socio-economic or cultural rights have been brought to and decided by courts in most of these countries.

A number of constitutions, among them those of India, Ireland, Ghana, Namibia, Nigeria, Uganda and Zimbabwe, include socio-economic and cultural rights as part of DPSPs. Among these, the Ghanaian constitution, and to a lesser extent that of Uganda, dispel the oppositional dichotomy that is often posited between constitutionalized socio-economic and cultural rights on the one hand, and DPSPs on the other, by including a DPSP dealing with "economic", "social" and "cultural objectives" in the same document, next to clearly justiciable socio-economic and cultural fundamental rights.[15]

Despite the importance of national legislation, there are sound reasons for the constitutionalization of socio-economic rights. Constitutional norms are superior to and may invalidate or correct national legislation or executive conduct, if required. Constitutional provisions may also be employed as guides to the interpretation of statutory provisions.[16] In the South African case of *Residents of Bon Vista Mansions v Southern Metropolitan Council*, residents of a block of flats approached the High Court for an interdict to restore the water supply to the flats, disconnected by the local authority. Under the Water Services Act (Act 108 of 1997), water supply to a person may not be discontinued if that person proves that he or she is unable to pay for basic services. Referring to the obligation of the government to "respect" existing access to water, on the basis of section 27(1)(a) of the constitution, the court held that the act of disconnecting the water supply constituted a prima facie violation of that right, in that it deprived the applicants of existing access. The court's decision to grant the interdict is based on the right of access to water and the relevant section of the Water Services Act. A similar result could arguably have been obtained without reference to the constitution, but the court's interpretation was reinforced by invoking a constitutionalized socio-economic right.

International human rights often form part of the domestic constitutional order. Regarding the relationship between international and national norms, a distinction is usually drawn between the monist and dualist traditions. Increasingly, though, it has become clear that this traditional distinction is less than helpful, veiling the question whether international human rights provisions are "justiciable" – that is, whether they may be invoked as the basis for a remedy before domestic courts. In this regard, some legal systems use the notion of "self-executing" provisions of treaties, meaning that some treaty provisions are justiciable before national courts without any domestication or enabling legislation. In theory, at least, "self-executing" provisions may be invoked in the national legal arena without any further legislative action.

Case law

In practice, the justiciability of a right depends on whether a court (or similar body) regards a particular right as amenable to judicial scrutiny. A survey of case law is therefore crucial in any discussion about justiciability. International standards, the constitution and legislation may be invoked before courts. In many of its concluding observations, the ICESCR Committee underlined the importance of the practical application of social, economic and cultural rights, as reflected in case law. Case law may deal with the violation of subjective rights found in national legislation, or result from the invocation of constitutionalized guarantees. Especially in Latin America, the AIDS pandemic has had a role in bringing to life the constitutionalized right to health and social security. Increasingly, from the late 1990s, Latin American courts declared these rights to be justiciable in order to ensure access to anti-retroviral treatment (ART). This trend is reflected not only in the case law of Colombia and Venezuela, discussed below, but also in other states in the region, such as Argentina, Brazil, Costa Rica and El Salvador.[17] While these decisions concern ART for all HIV-positive persons, the other case relevant to AIDS, the South African *TAC* case, discussed below, relates to the narrower issue of prevention of transmission from mother to child.

Despite the jurisprudential growth on access to ART as a justiciable claim, courts seldom rely on or refer to foreign case law in their decisions. This omission may be attributed to the fact that courts are dealing with this issue more or less simultaneously, to a lack of accessibility of decisions, to linguistic differences and to distinguishable legal frameworks. The survey below aims at highlighting the commonalities in approaches and providing an inventory from which courts may draw inspiration – not only on the right to health, but on other socio-economic rights as well.

Canada

Even before the Canadian Charter of Rights and Freedoms was adopted, the province of Quebec included a chapter on economic and social rights in its charter, the Quebec Charter of Rights. Adopted in 1976, the justiciability of these rights only became a pertinent issue some years later, as discussed below. Owing to the absence of any explicit provision on socio-economic rights in the Canadian Charter, the courts have – perhaps understandably – been hesitant to develop a social justice jurisprudence. As far as the socio-economic implications of charter rights are concerned, most developments have been based on the equality provision in the charter, and are often found in minority judgments.

Section 15 of the Canadian Charter provides for equality "before and under the law" and for the right to equal protection and benefit of the law. Although the Canadian Charter does not include economic or social rights, "economic prejudices or benefits" are not irrelevant, especially when they arise as consequences of discrimination or distinctions that "offend inherent human dignity" (*Egan v Canada*, L'Heureux-Dubé J dissenting, p. 37). In *Schachter* the issue was the constitutionality of unemployment insurance legislation granting adoptive parents, but not natural parents, unemployment benefits to care for a new child. In this case a violation was found, but the Supreme Court refused to order that the equality guarantee be "read into" the existing legislation, opting instead for a declaration of invalidity and a suspension thereof. The court grappled with the role of budgetary constraints in constitutional adjudication. Lamer CJC drew the following important distinction: budgetary considerations "cannot be used to justify a violation" (p. 20) under the general limitations clause (s. 1 of the Canadian Charter), but such considerations are clearly relevant in determining an appropriate remedy ("what action should be taken") once a finding of unconstitutionality has been made (ibid.).

In a subsequent decision, in *Egan v Canada*, a majority of the court found that the exclusion of a homosexual partner from the benefit of "spousal allowance" under the Old Age Security Act did not violate section 15 of the Canadian Charter.[18] The application represents an attempt to ensure that a social benefit already granted to the majority of the population be extended to an excluded group (gay and lesbian partners) on the basis of the non-discrimination clause (s. 15). The financial and budgetary implications of such an extension of benefits featured in the judgments of Sopinka J and Iacobucci J.

Agreeing with the majority, Sopinka J applied the two-phased approach to constitutional decision-making (the *Oakes* approach). Although the non-extension of a spousal allowance on the basis of sexual orientation constitutes a violation of section 15, in his view this limitation is "saved" under section 1 of the charter because it "is not realistic for the courts to assume that there are unlimited funds to address the needs of all" (p. 99). Relying on previous case law, Sopinka J explained that it is legitimate for the government "to make choices between disadvantaged groups", and that it must be allowed some leeway to take incremental measures (ibid.). Because he was satisfied that the legislation addressed the situation of those in greatest need, it met constitutional muster (p. 101).

Taking issue with Sopinka J, Iacobucci J, harking back to the approach set out in *Schachter*, expressed the view that financial concerns ought to inform remedies but should not serve to "legitimize discriminatory conduct" (p. 158). In his own words:

Permitting discrimination to be justified on account of [...] the need for governmental "incrementalism" introduces [an] unprecedented and potentially indefinable [criterion] into S. 1 analysis. It also permits S. 1 to be used in an unduly deferential manner well beyond anything found in the prior jurisprudence of this Court. The very real possibility emerges that the government will always be able to uphold legislation that selectively and discriminatorily allocates resources. This would undercut the values of the *Charter* and belittle its purpose. (*Egan v Canada*, pp. 157–8)

A similar challenge was lodged in *Eldridge v British Columbia (Attorney General)*. Again based on section 15, the constitutional complaint was directed at the failure of hospitals to provide sign-language interpreters. As miscommunication between hearing-impaired persons and their doctors may lead to misdiagnosis, the court found a substantial impairment of the right to non-discrimination. The government invoked the cost of such a service to justify the violation under section 1 of the charter. However, as the estimated cost of providing sign-language interpretation for the whole of the state (British Columbia) was only C$150,000, or "approximately 0.0025 per cent of the provincial health care budget at the time" (p. 230), the court found that the government "has manifestly failed to demonstrate that it had a reasonable basis for concluding that a total denial of medical interpretation services for the deaf constituted a minimum impairment of their rights" (p. 229).

In *Gosselin v Quebec (Attorney General)* [2002] the Canadian courts had an opportunity to deal again with the socio-economic implications of section 15, and also section 7 of the Canadian Charter, which guarantees the right to "security of the person". The facts of the case were as follows. Under the 1984 Social Aid Act, the amount of welfare benefit payable to persons under the age of 30 was set at about a third of the amount payable to those of 30 years and older. Gosselin brought a class action, contesting the constitutional validity of the relevant legislation.

The first question before the courts was whether section 7 includes the economic capacity to satisfy basic human needs. The majority adopted a static and restrictive interpretation of the ambit of the right to "security of the person". Based on the dominant strand of existing jurisprudence, the majority viewed section 7 as being aimed at protecting life, liberty and personal security in the context of the justice system and its administration. Four judges dissented. Arbour J, dissenting, adopting a textual, purposive and contextual interpretation of the right, found that section 7 also contains a "positive dimension". She took the view that "Freedom from state interference with bodily or psychological integrity is of little consolation to those who, like the claimants in this case, are faced with a daily struggle to meet their most basic bodily and psychological needs. To them, such a purely negative right to security of the person is essentially meaningless: theirs is a world in which the primary threats to security of the person come not from others, but from their own dire circumstances" (para. 375). Accordingly, the legislative scheme violates section 7 and is not saved by section 1. In the course of her judgment, Arbour J took issue with the argument that an expansive interpretation of section 7 is inappropriate as it would lead to the court prescribing to other branches of government how to allocate resources. In her view the case raised a different issue, namely whether the state is under a positive obligation to provide basic means of subsistence to those who cannot provide it themselves.

A further issue in *Gosselin* was whether the legislative scheme violated section 45 of the Quebec Charter, which provides that: "Every person in need has a right, for himself and his family, to measures of financial assistance and to social measures provided for by law, susceptible of ensuring such person an acceptable standard of living." Dissenting from the view of the majority in the Court of Appeal that section 45 only guarantees the right of access without discrimination in respect of measures that already exist in law, Robert J remarked that it is "erroneous to see socio-economic rights as second-class rights devoid of binding force and not subject to legal recourse".[19] Agreeing with Robert J, and dissenting with the majority in the Supreme Court, L'Heureux-Dubé J subscribed to the view that section 45 "includes, at the very least, the right of every person in need to receive what Canadian society objectively considers sufficient means to provide the basic necessities of life" (*Gosselin*, para. 148). The majority accept that section 45 "purports to create a right", and that even if it cannot be used to invalidate laws or claim damages, it entitles individuals to approach the courts for a declaratory order (para. 96). However, the majority of Supreme Court judges, following a rather literalist approach based on the use of the word "measures" and the phrase "susceptible to ensuring", found that the adequacy of the state's social assistance measures is not a subject of judicial review.

One section in the Canadian Charter, section 23, provides for the right of linguistic minorities to mother-tongue instruction at primary and secondary levels. A number of cases illustrate that this right has been made justiciable without controversy. In *Mahe v Alberta* the Canadian Supreme Court found that although parents of francophone children do not have the right to an independent francophone school board, they must be guaranteed a number of representatives on the school board. In a subsequent case, *Reference re Public Schools Act (Manitoba) s 79(3), (4) and (7)*, the court confirmed that the right in section 23 includes the right to education in a distinct physical setting and the right of parents to participate in the management and control of schools. Parents of a group of francophone children applied on the basis of the same section to have a separate education facility established in a town on Prince Edward Island (*Arsenault-Cameron v Prince Edward Island*). The court rejected the province's arguments as to pedagogical and financial considerations, and found the refusal to allow the establishment of the school to be unconstitutional.

Colombia

The 1991 constitution of Colombia provides for the right to health care (Article 49) and for the supremacy of international human rights norms ratified by the state (Article 93). Article 49 provides as follows:

Public health and environmental protection are public services for which the State is responsible. All individuals are guaranteed access to services that promote, protect, and rehabilitate public health. ... It is the responsibility of the State to organize, direct, and regulate the delivery of health services and of environmental protection to the population in accordance with the principles of efficiency, universality, and cooperation, and to establish policies for the provision of health services by private entities and to exercise supervision and control over them. ... The law will determine the limits within which basic care for all the people will be free of charge and mandatory.

Article 93 gives international human rights treaties and agreements ratified by the Congress priority over domestic law. It further states that "the rights and duties mentioned in this Charter will be interpreted in accordance with international treaties on human rights ratified by Colombia". In Chapter 5, concerning the social purpose of the state and the public services, priorities in budgetary allocation are stipulated. Article 366 provides as follows:

The general welfare and improvement of the population quality of life are social purposes of the State. A basic objective of the State's activity will be to address unsatisfied public health, educational, environmental, and potable water needs. For this purpose, public social expenditures will have priority over any other allocation in the plans and budgets of the nation and of the territorial entities.

In *Tutela*, a case "concerning the rights of sick persons/AIDS patients", the claimant, who suffered from AIDS, applied for an order compelling the director of a hospital to "arrange for the immediate provision of the necessary services which would tend to protect his life and restore his health". This claim was based on the above-mentioned provisions, in particular the right of access to health services. The claimant, who is indigent, was initially treated free of charge (in San Jorge), but, due to rejection by family members, went to live with his mother in the town of Caldi. There, the costs of medical consultations, tests and medicines were not covered. After some intervention he obtained treatment, but still remained responsible for some of the cost. The Constitutional Court found in his favour and granted an order as requested.

As far as the state's argument about a lack of resources is concerned, the court noted that the important public purpose of preventing and containing AIDS cannot be made subservient to resource constraints. Highlighting the important interest at stake, namely the struggle against AIDS as a fatal disease, the court noted as follows:

The cost of services, although not irrelevant to the allocation of scarce medical resources, cannot be, in the struggle against a transmittable and fatal disease, the determining factor in the rendering of medical care. Although integral service is not without its costs, the collection of payment must be subordinate to the provision of services. The denial of tests, treatment or consultation unless they are paid for, or unless payment is judicially guaranteed, is contrary to the *ordre public* objective of preventing and containing an epidemic.

However, applying the prescriptions of Article 366, the court goes much further, by highlighting the requirement that the state budget satisfies society's basic needs:

The Constitutional norms regarding budgetary issues give priority to social spending above any other appropriations (Const. Art. 350), and their application is mandatory in the plans and budgets of the Nation as well as regional entities. With a view to meeting the population's needs in health, education, sanitation and potable water (Const. Art. 366), the framers of the Constitution opted to recognize a hierarchy of public spending priorities and subordinated the constitutionality of the respective budgetary laws to the principle of social spending. ... On the other hand, the Constitution establishes that every person has a duty to contribute to the financing of the State's spending and investments (Const. Art. 95-9). Correlatively, it is the taxpayer's right that the income received by the treasury be applied with priority above any other purpose to the satisfaction of society's basic needs, so as to prevent a deficit of resources in, among other sectors, the health sector, which might alter and endanger the taxpayer's life and property.

Czech Republic

The Charter of Fundamental Rights and Basic Freedoms features in the constitutional order of the post-communist Czech Republic.[20] The charter contains a chapter on the rights "of national and ethnic minorities", and one dealing expansively with socio-economic and cultural rights. The latter chapter includes the "right to the protection of ... health", education and the legal protection of the right "to the fruits of one's creative intellectual work" (as a legislative or constitutional command, rather than a subjective right).

After considering the initial report of the Czech Republic, the ICESCR Committee adopted a concluding observation regretting that "the Covenant has not been given full effect in the State party's legal order and that most of the rights contained in the Covenant are not justiciable in the domestic legal order, in particular, the right to adequate housing, which the State party considers as a merely 'declaratory non-entitlement right'".[21]

Under Czech legislation,[22] citizens enjoy the right to education free of charge in elementary and secondary government schools. The right to education can be secured in exchange for payment in private or religious schools. Under a subsequent regulation,[23] students or their parents pay for educational materials owned and used by the students, with the exception of materials that the state provides to students in the first year of elementary school, to the value of 200 Czech crowns per student. It further provides that textbooks for elementary school are lent to the students free of charge, but they do not become their property. In secondary schools the students buy their own textbooks, which then become their property.

A constitutional complaint was brought to the Czech Constitutional Court, alleging that the regulation, which essentially requires students to pay for their own textbooks, violates Article 33(2) of the Czech Charter of Fundamental Rights and Basic Freedoms, which guarantees to all citizens the right to elementary and secondary school education free of charge, as well as a similar provision in the Convention on the Rights of the Child,[24] which has been domesticated through legislation.[25]

The court implicitly accepted that the right to free education is justiciable and imposes a duty to "fulfil" on the state when it observed that the right to education "free of charge unquestionably means that the State shall bear the costs of establishing schools and school facilities, of their operation and maintenance". The matter then turns on the interpretation of this right, and the extent of the obligation to "fulfil": is the state obliged to provide free textbooks as well? Finding that the regulation does not restrict or substantially affect the right to education free of charge, the court concluded that "the provision on the degree to which the government provides free textbooks, teaching texts, and basic school materials cannot be placed under the heading of the right to education free of charge".[26] By narrowly construing the right, some of the important financial implications of the right to education have been defined out of the scope of the right (see also Sajo 2004, 55).

Fiji

The constitution of the Republic of the Fiji Islands, adopted in 1997, has a justiciable Bill of Rights but makes little provision for economic, social or cultural rights. Exceptions are the often-recognized right to strike and undertake collective bargaining, and the right to basic education, as well as the right to maintain schools on the basis of culture (Articles 33 and 39).

In a case decided by the High Court of Fiji,[27] the court interpreted the "civil and political" right guaranteeing humane treatment as including the right not to be deprived of food. In the process of interpretation, the court relied on the more explicit right to adequate food provided for in a treaty ratified by Fiji.

As a result of being convicted for escaping from prison, the prisoner was sentenced to a further six months' imprisonment. In addition, his food rations were reduced for two weeks. This reduction was allowed for under a provision of the Prisons Act. On his behalf, it was contended that the provision conflicts with Article 25(1) of the constitution, which provides that every person has a right *inter alia* to freedom from disproportionately severe treatment or punishment or cruel, inhumane and degrading treatment.

Interpreting Article 25(1) broadly and purposively, the court found that the provision of the Prison Act violates Article 25 and declared it null and void. Referring to the right to human dignity proclaimed by the preamble to the constitution, the court remarked:

> Food is a basic necessity for daily sustenance. To reduce rations as a form of punishment is in principle an offensive concept. The amount is unimportant. The very idea that the State would use a necessity of life to punish proscribed behaviour and thereby devalue prisoners' lives is intrinsically unacceptable.

In arriving at this conclusion, the court also made reference to Article 11(1) of the ICESCR, which guarantees the right to "adequate food". Although Fiji's ratification of the ICESCR did not give rise to a "mandatory obligation", the court noted that the deprivation of food as a means of control ran contrary to the "spirit" of the ICECSR.

Finland

Nordic countries, and in particular Finland, have been at the forefront of including statutory subjective rights containing socio-economic rights. Scheinen (1995, 61) points to Acts of Parliament that provide, among others, for the right to municipal day-care for small children and the right to social assistance. In a case brought before the Finnish courts, an unemployed person alleged that the municipality failed in its duty to provide him with a six-month employment possibility.[28] Basing its decision on statutory provisions, the Finnish Supreme Court found in the unemployed person's favour. Section 18(3) of the Employment Act (Act 275 of 1987) provides that the municipality was obliged to arrange an opportunity to work for six months in respect of a long-term unemployed person if other efforts to employ the person have failed. The court observed as follows: "The objective of the norms on the right of long-term unemployed persons to an arranged job was not merely to promote employment in general but explicitly to guarantee to a person qualifying as a long-term unemployed under the Employment Act, an individual right to an arranged job." As it had refused an eligible person such a job, the court ordered the municipality to pay the unemployed person compensation.

India

The Indian constitution contains a chapter (Part III) on "Fundamental Rights", comprising mainly "civil and political" rights that are enforceable in the High and Supreme Courts. In a separate chapter (Part IV), social and economic rights are included as "Directive Principles of State Policy".[29] In the constitutional design, the DPSPs had to be taken into account by the executive and legislative branches of government, but were not "enforceable by any court" (Article 37). Socio-economic rights and interests were thus provided for as DPSPs. These include the right to an "adequate means to livelihood" (Article 39), and the rights to work, education and "public assistance in case of unemployment" (Article 41).[30] The exclusion of social and economic rights from the chapter on "Fundamental Rights" and the conceptual wall between rights and DPSPs posed an obstacle to the justiciability of socio-economic rights. Under the heading "Cultural and Educational Rights", a limited number of rights in this category are provided for, such as the right to converse in a language that is distinct in a territory (Article 29(1)), and the right of minorities to establish educational institutions of their choice (Article 30(1)).

Initially, the courts adhered to this duality. Subsequently, though, especially following the introduction of a state of emergency by Prime Minister Indira Ghandi in 1975, the courts took on a more activist stance (Baxi 1980). The Indian Supreme Court held that fundamental rights and DPSPs are complementary because "what was fundamental in the governance of the country could be no less significant than that which was fundamental in the life of an individual" (*Kesavananda Bharati v State of Kerala*).

Two cases dealing with the right to education illustrate how, in the 1990s, the Indian Supreme Court steered a course between making DPSPs "real" and not collapsing Part IV into Part III. *Mohini Jain v State of Karnataka* argued the constitutionality of a state law setting a much higher admittance fee for "non-government" students, compared to "government students", at private medical colleges in that state (1861, para. 1). It was argued that the difference in fees is justified on the basis that "government" students are "meritorious" (1862, para. 4), while others are not. The court found that although the "right to education" is not a "fundamental right" in Part III, the "Constitution made it obligatory for the State to provide education for its citizens" (1863, para. 7), based on a cumulative reading of the right to life and DPSPs such as the right to education. Emphasizing the indivisibility of rights, the court observed:

> The fundamental rights guaranteed under Part III of the Constitution of India including the right to freedom of speech and expression and other rights under Art. 19 cannot be appreciated and fully enjoyed unless a citizen is educated and is conscious of his individualistic dignity ... The "right to education", therefore, is concomitant to the fundamental rights enshrined under Part III of the Constitution. The State is under a constitutional mandate to provide educational institutions at all levels for the benefit of the citizens. The educational institutions must function to the best advantage of the citizens. Opportunity to acquire education cannot be confined to the richer section of the society. (*Mohini Jain v State of Karnataka*, paras 13 and 14)

In *Unni Krishnan J P v State of Andhra Pradesh* the court went one step further, holding that the DPSP, which calls upon the state to "provide, within a period of ten years from the commencement of this Constitution, for free and compulsory education for all children" up to 14 (Article 45), had matured into a fundamental right (p. 735). The obligation of the state is to "provide educational facilities" to citizens "within its economic capacity and development" (p. 737). However, the court added that this conclusion does not transfer Article 41 (the right to education) from Part IV to Part III – the court is "merely relying upon Article 41 to illustrate the context of the right to education flowing from Article 21" (the right to life) (ibid.).

The Indian Supreme Court has interpreted civil and political rights, in particular the right to life, necessarily to imply an array of social and economic benefits and, sometimes, rights. Departing from the premise that all rights are indivisible and interdependent, the Supreme Court derived the right to health and the right to emergency medical treatment (*Paschim Banga Khet Majoor Samity v State of West Bengal*), the protection of the health and strength of workers and women (*Bandhua Mukti Morcha v India*, pp. 811–12) and the right to a livelihood (*Olga Tellis v Bombay Municipal Corporation*) from the right to life.

In one of these cases (*Samity*, p. 102), a man fell off a train and sustained serious head injuries that required immediate medical attention. He was referred from one government hospital to another, but was not treated either due to a lack of vacant beds or because the hospital lacked the necessary facilities for surgery. Eventually he was admitted and treated at a private hospital, where he personally incurred the costs. The Supreme Court found that the failure of the public hospitals violated his right to life because the preservation of human life is of "paramount importance" and because the government hospitals "run by the State and the Medical Officers employed therein are duty bound to extend medical assistance for preserving human life" (para. 9). An amount of compensation was awarded. To ensure that such an incident does not recur, the court ordered further remedial measures. In arriving at an appropriate order, the court relied on the findings of a government-appointed enquiry committee. Among other measures, this order required that a central communications facility be established to ensure immediate treatment at an appropriate hospital, that the facilities at district level be upgraded to enable them to deal with similar emergencies, and that ambulances be appropriately equipped to deal with similar situations.

The court was not unmindful that financial resources are needed to ensure compliance with its order. However, the court underlined that "it cannot be ignored that it is the constitutional obligation of the State to provide adequate medical services to the people. Whatever is necessary for this purpose has to be done." The court had held that the constitutional duty to provide free legal aid cannot be undone by the lack of resources (*Khatri (II) v State of Bihar*). A similar approach is even more pertinent "in the matter of discharge of constitutional obligation of the State to provide medical aid to preserve human life" (para. 16 of the *Khatri* judgment).

Latvia

Latvia's 1922 constitution, incorporating amendments up to 2003, contains a justiciable Bill of Rights.[31] A number of socio-economic rights are provided for, including the rights to social security and to education. As for cultural rights, the constitution provides for persons belonging to ethnic minorities to "have the right to preserve and develop their language and their ethnic and cultural identity" (Article 114).

In an application to the Constitutional Court, the constitutionality of social security legislation was placed in dispute (Case No. 2000-08-0109). The relevant provision states that an employee is socially insured only if compulsory premiums have been paid for him or her. The obligation to pay the premiums falls on the employer. The applicants argued that the refusal or inability of the employer to pay the premium and the inability of the state to do its duty to ensure the collection of these payments should not lead to unfavourable consequences for the employee. In particular, the contention was that the provision violates Article 109 of the constitution, as well as Articles 9 (the right to social security) and 11(1) (the right to an adequate standard of living) of the ICESCR.

Article 109 of the Latvian constitution provides to everyone the right to social guarantees for old age, work disability, unemployment and other cases determined by law. "Thus", the Constitutional Court observed, "in Latvia the right to social security has a constitutional value." The court notes that the right is granted "without any exceptions", and "independently from payment or not payment of different compulsory premiums". To guarantee the rights of persons to social insurance, payment shall not be connected with whether other persons have or have not performed their duties, as the relevant law envisaged. The court held that, as "some social rights are included in the fundamental law, the State cannot relinquish them", and added that these rights "do not have just a declarative nature". Having thus clearly established the justiciability of the right to social security, the Latvian Constitutional Court decided that the contested legal provision violates Article 109 of the constitution and declared it "null and void" to the extent of its inconsistency.

Although the application also invoked the ICESCR, the court did not base its decision on its provisions. The court noted that "in international instruments social rights are formulated as universal obligations of the States, letting the State itself choose the way of implementing those rights". However, with reference to the Limburg Principles, the court further took note that "viewpoints on the legal nature and binding force have advanced" since the entry into force of the ICESCR. As far as domestic measures under the ICESCR are concerned, the court observed that they must be "undertaken to reach the objective, shall be implemented in a reasonably short time after the Pact has taken effect in a Member State and that every Member State has the obligation of securing implementation of the most essential liabilities at least on the basic level".

The Philippines

The 1987 constitution of the Philippines contains a Bill of Rights and a Declaration of Principles and State Policies. In terms of Article VIII, section 1 of the constitution, "Judicial power includes the duty of the courts of justice to settle actual controversies involving rights which are legally enforceable ..."

In *Minors Oposa v Fulgencio S Factoran* the Philippine Supreme Court had to decide a class suit brought by a number of minor petitioners representing "their generation as well as generations yet unborn" for the cancelling of all existing timber licensing agreements (TLAs) issued by the government. Their claim was directed at preventing irreparable damage to the Philippine rainforests.

On the government's behalf, it was argued that the claim does not constitute a valid cause of action as it does not allege the violation of a specific right. Rejecting this contention, the court held that the complaint "focuses on one specific fundamental legal right – the right to a balanced and healthful ecology" in section 16, read together with the right to health (s. 15). The fact that both these rights are to be found in the Declaration of Principles and State Policies, and not in the Bill of Rights, did not in the court's view present an obstacle to their justiciability:

> While the right to a balanced and healthful ecology is to be found under the Declaration of Principles and State Policies and not under the Bill of Rights, it does not follow that it is less important than any of the civil and political rights enumerated in the latter. Such a right belongs to a different category of rights

altogether for it concerns nothing less than self-preservation and self-perpetuation – aptly and fittingly stressed by the petitioners – the advancement of which may even be said to predate all governments and constitutions. As a matter of fact, these basic rights need not even be written in the Constitution for they are assumed to exist from the inception of humankind. (*Minors Oposa*, p. 187)

Having established the justiciability of these rights, the court infers an obligation to "respect" on the state ("the correlative duty to refrain from impairing the environment"). On the government's behalf, it was further argued that the "question of whether logging should be permitted in the country is a political question which should be properly addressed to the executive or legislative branches of Government". Emphasizing that "the political question doctrine is no longer the insurmountable obstacle to the exercise of judicial power or the impenetrable shield that protects executive and legislative actions from judicial inquiry or review", the court rejected this objection as well.

Although the case was not finalized, because the timber licence grantees needed to be "impleaded", the court found that the cause of action reveals a prima facie violation of rights. The rights under sections 15 and 16 imply the "judicious management of the country's forests. Without such forests, the ecological or environmental balance would be irreversibly disrupted." The court therefore ordered that the lower court's decision, dismissing the claim, be set aside and that the petitioners be allowed to "implead as defendants the holders or grantees of the questioned timber licence agreements".

The case highlights at least three important points. The court's finding demonstrates that the inclusion of rights as DPSPs does not present an insurmountable obstacle to the effective application (or justiciability) of those rights. The case further illustrates the collective invocation of rights other than civil and political rights in the form of a class action. Lastly, it lends support to the notion that rights are interrelated. The right to a liveable environment, sometimes regarded as a "third-generation" right, is here involved with a "second-generation" right, the right to health. Cumulatively, these rights implicitly serve to uphold the right to cultural heritage, as the rainforests are the "habitat of indigenous Philippine cultures, which have existed, endured and flourished since time immemorial".

South Africa

Preceding the negotiations for a democratic, rights-based South African constitution, some debate occurred about the inclusion of socio-economic rights in such a document. Concerned about tilting the scale too far in favour of "an ill conceived rights discourse" that will erode meaningful public participation, Davis (1992, 489–90) favoured the "recognition of social and economic demands in the form of directive principles". Emphasizing judicial review in a negative form, restricted to striking down what could not be justified as sincere or rational, Mureinik (1992, 174) opted for the inclusion of these rights as justiciable, but only to the extent that judges would "review expenditure by some other branch of government".

A limited number of socio-economic and cultural rights were included in the interim constitution: some worker's rights (s. 27), the right to "acquire and hold rights in property" (s. 28(1)) and the right to education (s. 32). An example of a cultural right provided for is the right to language and culture (s. 31). During the limited lifetime of the interim constitution, a final constitution had to be drafted in conformity with 34 constitutional principles contained in the interim constitution. This process being completed, the Constitutional Court had to "certify" that the final text was in compliance with the 34 principles. At these hearings, the argument was raised but rejected that socio-economic rights are not justiciable and that their inclusion in the final constitution would violate the principle of the separation of powers. The Constitutional Court concluded that it was "of the view that these rights are, at least to some extent, justiciable" (*Second Certification* judgment, para. 78). As a consequence, the final constitution saw the inclusion of the right of access to housing, health care, sufficient food and water, social security and basic education.

Since the Constitutional Court had thus unequivocally settled that these socio-economic rights are justiciable, there was no need to reopen or to elaborate on this issue in later cases. What had to be determined, in the terminology of the court, was the "enforcement" of these rights (*Grootboom v Oostenberg Municipality*; *Grootboom CC* case, para. 20; *TAC* case, paras 23 and 25). In the three cases before the court the issue was whether "the measures adopted by the government ... fell short of its obligation under the Constitution" (see, for example, *TAC*, para. 25) – in other words, whether the measures adopted were reasonable. The court made it clear that the "enforcement" of a right is "difficult" and needs to be "explored on a case-by-case basis" (*Grootboom CC*, para. 22).

Textual differences in laws are important. The main difference lies between those rights that are formulated as "rights to ..." and those that are formulated as "rights of access to ...". Compare, on the one hand, the right of children to "basic nutrition, shelter, basic health care services and social services" (1996 Constitution, s. 28(1)(c)) or the right "to basic education" (s. 29(1)(a)) with the right of "access to adequate housing" or "access to health care services" (ss. 26(1) and 27(1)(a)), on the other.

Included in the first category, for example, is the right of detained and sentenced persons to "conditions of detention that are consistent with human dignity, including at least exercise and the provision, at state expense, of adequate accommodation, nutrition, reading material and medical treatment" (s. 35(2)(e)). In *Van Biljon v Minister of Correctional Services* HIV-positive prisoners approached the court for an order entitling them, on the basis of their right to "adequate medical treatment", to anti-retroviral treatment.

The second category of rights, the "indirect" or "access" rights, has been the subject of three major Constitutional Court judgments, in which the court accepted that the state is obliged to comply with its positive (or "fulfilment") obligations under sections 26 and 27 of the constitution.

In the first of these, *Soombramoney v Minister of Health (KwaZulu-Natal)*, the applicant, who suffered from chronic renal failure, applied for a order enabling him to benefit from a renal dialysis programme offered at the provincial hospital. It was accepted that he was in the final stage of the disease, that his prognosis was not good, and that the treatment would prolong his life but would not reverse his condition. It was argued on behalf of the applicant that the matter fell to be decided under section 27(3) of the constitution, which provides that no one may be refused emergency medical treatment. The court found that his condition did not call for "emergency medical treatment", as it resulted from an ongoing state of affairs and did not require immediate remedial treatment. A distinction was also drawn between the facts of the case and that of the Indian case of *Samity*, discussed above.

Having decided that the matter had to be determined on the basis of section 27(2), which provides for the right of access to medical treatment within "the available resources" of the state, the court then proceeded to test the reasonableness of the government programme. The programme functioned according to guidelines, which are aimed at "curing patients, and not simply to maintaining them in a chronically ill condition" (para. 25). In this respect, the court made reference to the fact that there are many more patients suffering from chronic renal failure than there are dialysis machines to treat them, and that the Department of Health in KwaZulu-Natal did not have sufficient funds to cover the cost of the services that were being provided to the public. The court also underlined the need to defer to "political organs" in decisions about the allocation of resources (para. 29). Consequently, the court found that the guidelines and their application to Mr Soobramoney were reasonable.

In *Government of the Republic of South Africa and Others v Grootboom and Others*, a number of applicants living under "intolerable conditions" approached the court alleging that the housing programme violated section 26, which allows for the right of access to housing. Although the government had a plan for the progressive realization of the right to housing and major achievements had been attained, it was contended that there was a major flaw in the programme in that it did not make reasonable provision for those in the most dire need of housing – those with no roof over their heads and no access to land. Referring to section 26(2), the Constitutional Court devised a "reasonableness test", observing that the question is "whether the legislative and other measures taken by the state are reasonable. A court considering reasonableness will not enquire whether other more desirable or favourable measures could have been adopted, or whether public money could have been better spent. The question would be whether the measures that have been adopted are reasonable ..." (para. 41).

On the facts of the particular case, the Constitutional Court held that the exclusion of a significant segment of society from the national programme cannot be said to be reasonable. In this respect, the government cannot rely on statistical advances in the realization of the right: "If the measures, though statistically successful, fail to respond to the needs of those most desperate, they may not pass the test" (para. 44). Analysing the national programme, the court found that it "falls short of obligations imposed upon national government to the extent that it fails to recognize that the state must provide for relief for those in desperate need" (para. 66). Finding that the relevant programme "fell short of the obligations imposed upon the state by section 26(2) in that it failed to provide for any form of relief to those desperately in need of access to housing" (para. 95), the court made a declaratory order that the government must adopt, implement and supervise measures that address effectively the situation of those most desperately in need of housing. At the time of the court proceedings, the relevant authorities had formulated a plan that "on the face of it" met the government's obligations. Alluding to the important distinction but inextricable link between justiciability, emanating in a court order, and effective implementation, the court observed that the formulation of a programme and its implementation must both meet the reasonableness requirement (para. 42).

HIV/AIDS has had a serious impact on South Africa, with the prevalence of HIV among pregnant mothers standing at 28 per cent in 2003 (Makubaldo et al. 2003). One way of curbing the spread of HIV is to minimize mother-to-child transmission by providing the mother and newly born child with a single dose of Nevirapine. The manufacturers of this drug supplied it to South Africa free of charge. In *Minister of Health and Others v Treatment Action Campaign and Others* (the *TAC* case), the TAC approached the Constitutional Court on two issues. First, the TAC argued that the government-imposed exclusion of the use of Nevirapine from public hospitals and clinics other than research and training sites violated the constitution. Second, the TAC contended that the national programme of mother-to-child prevention for HIV did not meet constitutional muster in that it was restricted to certain sites and did not set out a time-frame for the programme's "roll-out".

On the first issue, what was at stake is the government's obligation to "respect" the right of access to health care. The court found that the inflexible restriction on the use of Nevirapine was unconstitutional. Deciding the second issue, and accepting that the right of access to health-care services is clearly justiciable, the court framed the question as "whether the applicants have shown that the measures adopted by the government to provide access to health care services for HIV-positive mothers and their newborn babies fall short of its obligations under the Constitution" (para. 25). The court accepted that section 27 does not entitle everyone access even to a "core" service immediately (para. 35). Nonetheless, the court had to determine whether the current programme met the "reasonableness" test. Finding that it did not, the court ordered the government to "extend the testing and counseling facilities at hospitals and clinics throughout the public health sector to facilitate and expedite the use of Nevirapine for the purpose of reducing the risk of mother-to-child transmission of HIV" (para. 135). The resource implications relate mostly to the provision of counselling, as the drug itself was available free of charge.

The case of *Laerskool Middelburg v Departmentshoof, Mpumalanga* illustrates the different kinds of issues involved when applying cultural rights. At stake was the right to government schooling in one's mother tongue, also guaranteed in the Bill of Rights. It was contended that a school's single-language admission policy (of requiring competence in Afrikaans) discriminated unfairly against learners who preferred the majority language of instruction, English. The High Court held that blanket prohibition on all schools to operate as single-medium institutions, without having regard to questions of practicality, violates section 29(2). In the court's view, a claim to single-medium education is best understood as a claim to emotional, cultural, religious and social-psychological security. However, such a right was subordinate to the right of everyone to education, and had to make way where there was a clearly proven need in another community. The court therefore concluded that, as long as a dual-medium school was properly run, the right to education in the language of choice was not compromised.

Venezuela

Under the 1999 constitution of the Bolivarian Republic of Venezuela, the rights to health and social security are dealt with in detail (Articles 83 and 86, respectively). The Venezuelan courts have been called upon to determine whether the failure by the state to provide anti-retroviral drugs to persons not covered under the national "social security" system violates the constitution.

In *Cruz Bermudez v Ministerio de Sanidad y Asistencia Social* (discussed in UNAIDS and Canadian HIV/AIDS Legal Network 2006, 64), on an application by 170 persons living with HIV who were in need of anti-retroviral drugs, the Supreme Court held that the failure to supply the necessary drugs violated, *inter alia*, the right to health. Requiring the government to supply the drugs, the court not only ordered the relevant ministry to seek the required resources, but extended the remedy to all those in a similar situation as the specific litigants. In *Glenda Lopez v Instituto Venezolano de los Seguros Sociales* (IVSS), and a number of further decisions, the Constitutional Chamber of the Venezuelan Supreme Court established that a person registered with the IVSS (the national social security agency), meeting the legal requirements for social security, who has been diagnosed with HIV/AIDS and who has applied for ART is entitled to the treatment.

These decisions are based on the rights to life, to health, to liberty and security of the person, to non-discrimination and to social security. By ordering the IVSS to provide anti-retroviral medication to those registered for social security to whom it has been prescribed, the court's order also reverberated beyond the confines of the particular dispute.

EXPERIENCES AT THE INTERNATIONAL LEVEL

International experience pertaining to the justiciability of social, economic and cultural rights is dealt with separately at the regional and global (UN) levels.

Regional Level

European system

The substantive basis of the European human rights system, functioning under the auspices of the Council of Europe, is the European Convention on Human Rights and the European Social Charter.

When the European Convention was promulgated soon after the Second World War, the priority was to accomplish a document as soon as possible in order to get a bulwark for democracy up and running. As a consequence, the convention only contains rights about which general consensus existed at the time and only exceptionally provides for a right of a social or economic nature, namely the right to form and join trade unions, as part of the right to freedom of peaceful assembly and freedom of association (Article 11).

This provision is clearly justiciable. Legislation in the United Kingdom that offered more favourable conditions of employment to employees agreeing not to be represented by trade unions caused a number of employees to approach the European Court of Human Rights, alleging a violation of Article 11 (*Wilson, National Union of Journalists and Others v United Kingdom*). The court found that, although the legislation did not involve a "direct intervention by the State" (para. 41), by "permitting employers to use financial incentives to induce employees to surrender important union rights, the respondent State has failed in its positive obligation to secure the enjoyment of the rights under Article 11 of the Convention" (para. 48). This finding should be interpreted as imposing an obligation on states to "protect" the right to "form and join trade unions" by taking positive measure to ensure that employers do not use indirect means of creating obstacles to the effective realization of that right.

Subsequent "protocols" have extended the substantive content of the convention. Through the first of these, Protocol No. 1, the convention was extended to include the right to education. In the case *Relating to Certain Aspects of the Law on the Use of Languages in Education in Belgium* (the *Belgian Linguistic* case) the European Court of Human Rights was confronted with the interpretation of Article 2 of Protocol 1 to the European Convention. The first sentence of this article contains a negative formulation of the right to education: "No person shall be denied the right to education." Despite this negative formulation, the court observed that the language still indicates that a "right" exists. However, this formulation does not entail a state obligation to "fulfil" the right by *establishing* an education system of a specific kind, but only requires states to guarantee those in its state can "avail themselves of the means of instruction *existing at a given time*" (para. 3 of the court's "interpretation", emphasis added). Other aspects, such as the "official recognition of the studies" completed, are also included under this right (para. 4).

The second sentence of Article 2 provides as follows:

> No person shall be denied the right to education. In the exercise of any functions which it assumes in relation to education and to teaching, the State shall respect

the right of parents to ensure such education and teaching in conformity with their own religious and philosophical convictions.

As the wording indicates, the obligation on states is to "respect" a right that is here categorized as a "cultural right".[32] This is also the interpretation adopted by the court: "This provision by itself in no way guarantees either a right to education or a personal right of parents relating to the education of their children: its object is essentially that of protecting the individual against arbitrary interference by the public authorities in his private or family life" (para. 7). In the *Belgian Linguistic* case the court (by eight votes to seven) found that this provision was violated because Belgian legislation differentiated between the rights of Dutch-speaking and French-speaking parents to choose the education of their children. Access to French-speaking schools in some predominantly Dutch-speaking suburbs in Brussels was refused to children who did not live in those suburbs. With respect to Dutch-speaking schools in those same suburbs, such a rule did not apply. The decision is based on the principle of non-discrimination, guaranteed in Article 14 of the convention, read with Article 2: "The … right of access to existing schools is not … secured to everyone without distinction on the ground, in particular, of language" (para. 32).

Initially, then, socio-economic rights received scant attention in the European system. Some years after the adoption of the European Convention, in 1961, the European Social Charter was adopted. It has subsequently been amended, most recently taking the form of the Revised European Social Charter.[33] Like its predecessors, implementation of the rights in the Revised Social Charter primarily takes the form of state reporting to the European Committee of Social Rights. In 1995 an additional protocol to the European Social Charter, providing for a collective complaints system, was adopted.[34] This system elevates rights at the regional level to clearly justiciable guarantees. However, there are some limitations – acceptance of the complaints mechanism is optional,[35] and NGOs and labour organizations need to be granted participatory status before they may bring complaints (Articles 1 and 2 of the additional protocol). Justiciability is eroded, as a political organ, the Committee of Ministers, remains the final decision-making body. By 30 April 2006 32 complaints had been submitted under the additional protocol. Of these, three were declared inadmissible, 26 had been finalized on the merits (17 leading to findings of violation, and nine to findings of no violation) and three had been declared admissible but awaited decisions.[36]

Under both the European Social Charter and the Revised European Social Charter, member states may select from a menu of rights those that they consider binding. Of the 31 rights in the Revised European Social Charter, states have to accept at least 16 (Article 1). This minimum has to include at least six from among the "core rights": the rights to work, organize, collective bargaining, protection of young people, families, social security, assistance to migrant workers and equal opportunities. From this list, it would appear that the system is primarily focused on the rights of workers, and it seems that the charter does not deal with cultural rights.

Two examples are given of the justiciability of the Social Charter. In a complaint brought against Portugal (*International Commission of Jurists v Portugal*), it was contended that notwithstanding the statutory provisions adopted and the measures taken by Portugal to prohibit child labour and ensure that this rule is enforced, a large number of children under the age of 15 years continue to work illegally in many economic sectors. In particular, it was alleged that the Labour Inspectorate, which is the principal body for supervising compliance with the legislation on child labour, is not performing its functions effectively. Recalling that "the aim and purpose of the Charter, being a human rights protection instrument, is to protect rights not merely theoretically, but also in fact" (para. 32 of the finding), the European Committee of Social Rights emphasized that legislation needs to be "effectively applied and rigorously supervised" (ibid.). Although there had been a progressive reduction of child labour in recent years, the "problem has not been resolved", mainly due to inadequate supervision and monitoring by the Labour Inspectorate (para. 40). The committee therefore found a violation of Article 7(1), which sets 15 as the minimum age of employment. In what could be construed as a veiled attempt to contest the justiciability of the right, a dissenting committee member criticized the majority for their "static and narrow concept of 'legality'", which ignores the "natural and unavoidable viscosity of social changes, and the need to take account of the dynamic aspect of social problems" (para. 3 of the opinion of Mr Bruto Da Costa).

In a subsequent case, *Autism-Europe v France*, the European Committee of Social Rights found France in violation of the Social Charter on the basis that the "proportion of children with autism being educated in either general or specialist schools is much lower than in the case of other children" and that there is "chronic shortage of care and support facilities for autistic adults" (para. 54 of the finding). In arriving at this conclusion, the committee took into account not only the complexities and expenses involved, but also "the impact that their choices will have for groups with heightened vulnerabilities as well as for other persons affected including, especially, their families on whom falls the heaviest burden in the event of institutional shortcomings" (para. 53). Resource constraints do not free the state from its obligation to achieve the objectives of the charter within a reasonable time, with measurable progress and to an extent consistent with the maximum use of available resources.

Inter-American system

The founding document of the human rights system in the Americas, the American Declaration of the Rights and Duties of Man, integrates social, economic and cultural rights with civil and political rights.[37] Adopted by the Organization of American States (OAS) at its Ninth Conference in Bogotá, Colombia, in 1948, this document pre-dates and served as a precedent for the Universal Declaration of Human Rights. Although the American Declaration does not have a binding status, the Inter-American Commission has used it as a substantive basis to develop its reporting and petition procedure for all OAS member states. Initially, at least, civil and political rights were prioritized in the commission's work (Craven 1998, 289).

The conversion of the non-binding standards into a binding treaty, the American Convention on Human Rights, saw economic, social and cultural rights being reduced to a single provision (Article 26). Following the dichotomy of the ICESCR/ICCPR, the American Convention distinguishes civil and political rights from economic, social and cultural rights by placing them in two separate chapters, and categorizing the second group, in Article 26, under the heading "progressive development".[38] In terms of the convention, petitions in which a violation of any of the rights is alleged may be directed to the Inter-American Commission. Despite the fact that no complaint related to socio-economic rights has been decided on the merits, Article 26 of the American Convention has served as a basis for far-reaching precautionary measures ordering governments to provide ART to avoid the death of petitioners.

To some extent, socio-economic rights also feature in reports resulting from country studies. This situation led Craven (1998, 319) to conclude that "Unless the Commission puts itself in the position whereby putative violations of economic, social and cultural rights are brought before it, many of its pronouncements in this regard will remain at an abstract level and be devoid of real significance." No case dealing with these rights in the convention has as yet been considered by the Inter-American Court of Human Rights.

Realizing that there is a lacuna in respect of justiciable socio-economic and cultural rights, the Inter-American Commission began discussing strategies to improve the implementation of these rights. In a draft protocol, the commission foresaw a number of substantive provisions, a system of state reporting and a right of petition in respect of a limited number of rights (ibid., 308). In its "observations" on the draft, the Inter-American Court supported the proposal that not all, but at least some, economic, social and cultural rights could be considered to be "jurisdictionally enforceable".

The eventual Additional Protocol to the American Convention in the Area of Economic, Social and Cultural Rights (the Protocol of San Salvador) mirrors most of the provisions in the ICESCR.[39] It provides for state reports in respect of all rights (Article 19(1)–(5)), but only two rights (the right to join and organize trade unions, Article 8(1)(a), and the right to education, Article 13) are made subject to individual petition to the commission or court. In this respect the protocol relies on the European Convention, in which these two provisions are included as justiciable rights. In *Cortez v El Salvador*, Jorge Odir Miranda Cortez and 26 other HIV-infected petitioners submitted a claim to the Inter-American Commission alleging that the refusal of El Salvador to provide triple therapy medication to them constitutes a violation of numerous convention provisions as well as Article 10 of the Protocol of San Salvador.[40] Although the Inter-American Commission declared the Article 10 allegation inadmissible *ratione materiae*, the commission observed that it "can consider" the Protocol of San Salvador "in the interpretation of other applicable provisions" (para. 36).

The adoption of the Protocol of San Salvador may represent "a considerable advance in terms of the potential of the system" (Craven 1998, 321), but it is likely to have only limited effect in ensuring the justiciability of socio-economic rights in the Americas. Only 13 OAS member states have so far ratified the protocol. Only one case based on the protocol has yet reached court (*Baena Ricardo et al (270 Workers) v Panama*). The court declared the case, dealing with the dismissal of 270 trade union members for staging a walk-out, inadmissible because the respondent state, Panama, had not ratified the protocol at the time of the violations (para. 99).

Before the adoption of the Protocol of San Salvador, none of the inter-American human rights instruments provided for a right to participate in or benefit from culture. In this context, the Inter-American Commission dealt with a number of cases in which cultural rights were either implicitly or explicitly invoked. In these cases, cultural rights are closely interconnected with the complexity of "indigenous peoples" and communal land rights – issues that are not explored here. In the *Yanomami* case against Brazil, violations of, *inter alia*, the rights to life, equality, property and health of the Brazilian Yanomami Indians were alleged. The complaint arose from the exploitation of minerals in their ancestral lands, leading to the building of a highway and the influx of miners and prospectors. This caused the displacement of the Yanomami. Finding that Brazil had failed adequately to "protect" the Yanomami, the Inter-American Commission recognized their right to cultural identity. It used the concept as a "broad collective value including land rights, but also the right to life, health and residence" (Donders 2002, 236).

The Inter-American Commission invoked ICCPR Article 27, even though the ICCPR had not been ratified by Brazil, and held that "international law in its present state ... recognizes the right of ethnic groups to special protection on their use of their own language, for the practice of their own religion, and, in general, for all those characteristics necessary for the preservation of their cultural identity" (*Yanomami*, para. 7 of finding). Donders (2002, 234) concludes that the case demonstrates that the right to cultural identity, though not explicitly provided for, is "protected as a value by several other human rights". It should be noted that the commission based its finding of violation on rights in the American Declaration, which does not include the right to cultural identity ("Resolution" part of finding, para. 1).

African human rights system

The African regional human rights system, which functions under the African Union (AU) (previously the Organization of African Unity – OAU), is composed primarily of the Charter on Human and Peoples' Rights,[41] but also includes other treaties such as the African Charter on the Rights and Welfare of the Child and the Protocol to the African Charter on the Rights of Women in Africa.

With its adoption in 1981, the African Charter on Human and Peoples' Rights became the first regional human rights instrument to contain a relatively comprehensive list of justiciable socio-economic rights. Its preamble affirms the interdependence of civil, political, economic and social rights, as well as the importance of cultural rights. Relying on the ICESCR, an initial draft of the charter differentiated the implementation of socio-economic rights from that of other rights.[42] In the final document all rights are included in one chapter, and no distinction is made in respect of their realization.

Socio-economic rights in the charter include the right to education (Article 17(1)), the right to the "best attainable state of physical and mental health" (Article 16(1)) and the right to "work under equitable and satisfactory conditions" (Article 15). Despite the profound deficits in the realization of these rights on the continent, very few of the more than 300 cases submitted to the African Commission allege state violations of any of these rights.

Initially, some infringement of socio-economic rights has been invoked as part of and in the context of the violation of civil and political rights. In *Free Legal Assistance Group and Others v Zaire*, for example, the commission found the Mobutu regime responsible for serious and massive violations of the charter. The finding is based on widespread arbitrary arrests, torture, extrajudicial killings and unfair trials in Zaire (now the Democratic Republic of Congo – DRC) between 1989 and 1993. Finding a violation of the right to health, the commission observed: "The failure of the government to provide basic services such as safe drinking water and electricity and the shortage of medicine … constitute a violation …" (para. 47). This single sentence illustrates the tersely reasoned approach of the commission's initial jurisprudence, and invites some uncertainty, such as whether this statement only applies to detainees.[43] The statement also contains a clear finding of violation on the basis of a socio-economic right, and seems to impose an obligation to "fulfil" on the state.

A complaint about environmental degradation by the Nigerian National Petroleum Company (NNPC), a Nigerian state oil company, and military operations against dissidents in Ogoniland, Nigeria, led to the commission's most far-reaching finding on this issue, the *Social Economic Rights Action Centre* (SERAC) case.[44] In the finding, the commission distinguished (para. 44) between the obligations on governments to respect, protect, promote and fulfil *all rights* (both civil and political and social and economic). In its conclusion, the commission reiterated that it "will apply any of the diverse rights contained in the African Charter", and that "no right in the African Charter cannot be made effective" (para. 68). These statements, and the rest of the reasoning, underscore the justiciability of and a commitment to implement and enforce socio-economic rights. In the particular circumstances of the case, the commission found that Nigeria had not met the "minimum expectations" (ibid.) of the charter. In respect of the right to health, the government violated its "non-interventionist" (para. 52) obligation not to carry out or sponsor practices, policies and laws. Departing from the interdependence of rights, the commission "read into" the charter two socio-economic rights – the rights to food and to shelter. Finding violations of these implied rights, the commission again does not find or explore the obligation of governments to "fulfil".

Some pronouncements of the African Commission in *Purohit and Moore v The Gambia* are clearer in placing an obligation to fulfil on governments.

A complaint was brought to the African Commission alleging *inter alia* that the conditions under which patients were detained for reasons of mental health in a public health facility in the Gambia violated the right to health in the African Charter. In its interpretation of Article 16(1), the African Commission highlighted that provision is made not just for "attainable standards", but the highest attainable standards of health care (para. 82), and that the enjoyment of the right to health is vitally linked "to all aspects of a person's life and well-being, and is crucial to the realisation of all the other fundamental human rights and freedoms" (para. 80). According to the commission, the right to health includes the right to health facilities and access to goods and services. In the commission's view, the state has the obligation to take "concrete and targeted steps", while "taking full advantage of its available resources" to ensure that the right is realized "without discrimination of any kind" (para. 84). Because the Gambian legislative scheme lacked "therapeutic objectives as well as *provision of matching resources* and programmes of treatment of persons with mental disabilities" (para. 83, emphasis added), it gave rise to a violation of Article 16. The commission therefore recommended that the Gambian state should provide "adequate medical and material care for persons suffering from mental health problems in the territory of The Gambia". It should be inferred from the case that "care" requires the provision of adequate resources.

After the entry into force of the protocol establishing it in 2004, the African Court on Human and Peoples' Rights was set up in 2006. In the main, the African Court will strengthen the protective mandate of the African Commission through the adoption of unequivocally binding judgments. Thus, the unqualified wording of the social, economic and cultural rights in the charter (that is, not making their application conditional on resources or "progressive realization") becomes all the more crucial, as the court is mandated to find violations and order remedies to rectify them. In this process, the court may be expected to take into account the African Commission's findings, although it is not bound to follow those findings. Even so, as explained above, in the author's view the commission has not clarified the obligation on states to "fulfil" these rights.

In fact, the African Court may go much further than expanding on the "fulfilment" of the relevant rights *under the charter* by entertaining claims based on social, economic and cultural rights *not* provided for in the charter. This is so because the Protocol to the African Charter on the Establishment of an African Court on Human and Peoples' Rights expands the substantive jurisdictional scope of the court beyond that of the commission (which is limited to the charter) to "any other human rights instruments ratified by the States" concerned (Article 7). Most states in Africa have ratified the ICESCR; thus for these states, rights not explicitly included in the charter but in the ICESCR – such as the right to an adequate standard of living (ICESCR Article 11(1)) or to social security (Article 9) – are seemingly justiciable before the court.

A word of caution should be raised in this context. A very small minority of cases are, as matters stand at present, likely to be based on the expanded substantive jurisdictional scope of the court; the majority of cases will still proceed first to the commission. Such cases are limited, under the commission's mandate, to the substance of the African Charter. When that case is referred to the court, it may be argued that the substantive scope of the case has already been "fixed". Even if a more expansive interpretation of its protocol may allow the court to "apply" a broader array of instruments, this "broadening" will not enable the *submission, ab initio*, of a case on those expanded grounds. Only when a state has made an optional declaration to accept the right of individuals (and NGOs) to bypass the commission (under Article 34(6) of the Court Protocol), enabling them to submit cases *directly* to the African Court, can cases be instituted on the basis of the expanded material jurisdiction of the court. So far, only one state (Burkina Faso) has made such a declaration.

The substantive scope of the court's adjudication will include the African Charter on the Rights and Welfare of the Child, which provides in more clarity for some socio-economic rights.[45] The court's jurisdiction extends to the Protocol to the African Charter on the Rights of Women in Africa, since its entry into force on 25 November 2005. Numerous socio-economic and cultural rights are included in this protocol. An awareness of the complexities of judicialization appears from the way in which the protocol deals with, for example, the right to health. Women are granted specific "rights", all implying state obligations to respect and protect.[46] States have obligations of fulfilment, for example to "provide adequate, affordable and accessible health services", in respect of which there are no explicit rights bearers (Article 14(2)). As far as culture is concerned, women have "the right to live in a positive cultural context and to participate at all levels in the determination of cultural policies" (Article 17).

Some uncertainty still exists, though, because the African Court is in the process of being merged with the Court of Justice, provided for under the AU Constitutive Act.[47] Initially conceived as two separate institutions, the AU Assembly decided that the two courts have to be fused into a single African Court of Justice and Human Rights. Although a revised protocol is still being finalized, it is unlikely that the complementary relationship between the new court and the African Commission will be altered, or that the substantive jurisdiction of the merged court will be affected.

United Nations

As its title indicates, the ICESCR is the UN instrument most clearly directed at the subject matter of this study. In their interpretation of other UN human rights treaties, such as the International Covenant on Civil and Political Rights (ICCPR) and the Convention on the Elimination of All Forms of Racial Discrimination (CERD), the relevant treaty bodies have also explored the socio-economic potential of these instruments. These treaty experiences, as well as that under the UNESCO complaints system, are briefly surveyed.

International Covenant on Economic, Social and Cultural Rights

When the Universal Declaration of Human Rights was adopted in 1948, a comprehensive list of social, economic and cultural rights was included. They are, *inter alia*, the right to work (Article 23(1)), the right to social security (Article 22), the right to education (Article 25(1)) and the right to participate freely in the cultural life of the community (Article 26(1)). Although some of the rights in the Universal Declaration have crystallized into binding rules of customary international law, it is generally accepted that the socio-economic (and cultural) rights are of a non-binding nature, as they are part of a hortatory or declaratory instrument. Their inclusion in the Universal Declaration may be important for purposes of identifying a universally agreed standard and for lobbying and persuasion, but they are not justiciable.

In subsequent efforts to convert these non-binding standards into a legally binding covenant, the UN General Assembly initially called for the adoption of a single "covenant", including a "clear expression of economic, social and cultural rights".[48] After some vigorous debates, *inter alia* about the legal "enforceability" of this "category" of rights, the General Assembly (on a recommendation from its Third Committee) reversed its initial stance and called for the adoption of two separate instruments. The major difference between the two, the eventual ICCPR and the ICESCR, lies in the nature of state obligations and in their implementation. The rights in the ICESCR are qualified by Article 2, which requires states to "undertake steps ... to the maximum of its available resources, with a view to achieving progressively the full realization of the rights". No such qualification was inserted into the ICCPR, thus underscoring the difference in the obligation of states.

The ICCPR also provides for a treaty-monitoring body, the Human Rights Committee, mandated to examine state reports and consider individual (and inter-state) communications if states have ratified the First Optional Protocol or have accepted the competence under Article 41 of the ICCPR. Although the ICESCR also provides for state reporting, the treaty does not establish a treaty-monitoring body, leaving the fate of reports in the discretion of ECOSOC and other UN specialized agencies (Craven 1995, 21). The possibility of allowing the Human Rights Committee to deal with petitions under the ICESCR was resisted, mainly owing to the view that economic, social and cultural rights were "programmatic" – that is, non-justiciable (Craven 1995, 35). In 1985 ECOSOC eventually established the Committee on Economic, Social and Cultural Rights (CESCR), mandated to examine state reports (Resolution 1985/17).

Over the years the CESCR engaged in discussions about the possibility of an optional protocol to the ICESCR, similar to the (First) Optional Protocol to the ICCPR allowing for individual petitions. In 1992 the committee formally proposed that such an instrument should be adopted. From the outset, the nature of the rights in the ICESCR was again a bone of contention, with views differing about whether all rights could be the subject of petitions or only some, and if so, which ones (Craven 1995, 99; Arambulo 1999, 173–346). Craven (1995, 101) summarized the main reason for the inability to make progress on the adoption of an optional protocol as follows: "The principal argument against the creation of a petition system relating to economic, social and cultural rights has been, and remains, the idea that they are essentially non-justiciable." More specifically, it was argued that the CESCR would not be able to make concrete findings about "programmes" – for example it would be impossible to determine if the rate of progress in a particular instance had been sufficient (ibid.).

In 1993 the Vienna World Conference on Human Rights, in its Declaration and Programme of Action, encouraged the Commission on Human Rights, in cooperation with the CESCR, "to continue the examination of Optional Protocols" (para. 75) to the ICESCR. The Commission on Human Rights called for, and ECOSOC in 2002 endorsed, the establishment of an open-ended working group "with a view to considering options regarding the elaboration of an optional protocol"[49] to the ICESCR. In a recent report of this working group, the chairperson-rapporteur notes the lack of consensus on whether to start drafting such a protocol, but requested the renewal of the working group's mandate.[50]

Meanwhile, the CESCR elaborated upon the nature of state obligations, highlighting that appropriate implementation measures include "the provision of judicial remedies with respect to rights which may, in accordance with the national legal system, be considered justiciable" (General Comment No. 3, para. 5). As far as legislation embodying covenant rights are concerned, states should report "as to whether such laws create any right of action on behalf of individuals or groups" – in other words, if they are (indirectly) justiciable (ibid., para. 6). As far as covenant provisions that have been constitutionalized or "incorporated directly into national law" are concerned, states should report about "the extent to which these rights are considered to be justiciable" (ibid.). Although these comments illustrate an acceptance by the committee of the justiciability of covenant rights *at the national level*, they do not translate into a conclusion that these rights are equally justiciable *at the international level*.

However, the CESCR has elaborated other concepts that indicate the covenant rights may be justiciable even at the international level (that is, if the committee were mandated to deal with petitions). One such concept is that of minimum core obligations. It is, according to the committee, incumbent upon every state to ensure the satisfaction of "at the very least, minimum essential levels of each of the rights" (ibid., para. 10). Another concept that seems to be justiciable at the international level is the adoption of "deliberately retrogressive measures" (ibid., para. 9). The obligation of states to meet their responsibilities in relation to international cooperation also seems capable of being subjected to a direct pronouncement on compliance.[51] In its General Comment No. 14 on the right to health, the committee recognizes that some rights impose obligations "of immediate effect" (para. 30), such as the guarantee against discriminatory exercise of covenant rights and the obligation to "take steps" (at least *some* steps, in other words).[52] By postulating state obligations to "respect", the committee also enshrined obligations that are justiciable at both national and international levels, for example by "refraining from denying ... equal access for all persons" (ibid., para. 34; see also para. 35).

In its General Comment No. 9 on domestic implementation, the CESCR lamented the fact that the assumption is often made that "judicial remedies for violations" are not essential in respect of covenant rights, and added: "While the general approach of each legal system needs to be taken into account, there is no Covenant right which could not, in the great majority of systems, be considered to possess at least some significant justiciable dimensions" (para. 10).

In its concluding observations adopted after examining state reports, the committee has reinforced the importance of the justiciability of covenant rights. In its observations in 2004 after the initial report of Kuwait, for example, the CESCR concluded: "The Committee urges the State party to ensure that economic, social and cultural rights are incorporated into domestic legislation and made justiciable. The Committee points out that, irrespective of the system whereby international law is incorporated in the domestic legal order, following ratification of an international instrument, the State party is under an obligation to comply with it and to give it full effect in its domestic legal order" (E/C.12/1/Add.98, para 27). It is not satisfactory that states allege glibly that the covenant is "generally reflected in domestic law" (ibid., para. 7).

International Covenant on Civil and Political Rights

In an important finding against the Netherlands, the Human Rights Committee (HRC) illustrates how the optional complaints mechanism under the ICCPR may become a vehicle for the protection of socio-economic rights (Communication 182/1984, *Zwaan-de Vries v Netherlands*). Section 13(1) of the Dutch Unemployment Benefits Act required a married woman, in order to receive unemployment benefits, to prove that she was a "breadwinner". A similar condition did not exist in respect of married men (and unmarried men and women). Mrs Zwaan-de Vries, a married woman, contended that this provision violated Article 26 of the ICCPR, which guarantees to everyone, without discrimination, equal protection of the law.

In its defence, the Dutch government raised two arguments that relate to justiciability. First, it argued that as the right to social security (of which unemployment benefits form part) is enshrined in the ICESCR and not in the ICCPR, the state's obligations to realize that right are qualified by Article 2(1) of the ICESCR. Applying that standard, the state contended that a "process of gradual realization to the maximum of available resources is well on its way in the Netherlands" and that remaining elements of discrimination in the realization of the rights "are being and will be gradually eliminated" (para. 4.1 of the HRC's opinion). Second, as for the possible application of Article 26 to the rights to social security, the government argued that Article 26 can only be invoked in the sphere of civil and political rights.

Rejecting the first argument, the HRC found that the question to be determined is not whether social security "should be progressively established in the Netherlands", but whether the legislation that already provides for social security violates Article 26 (ibid., para. 12.4). In other words, Article 26 gives rise to an obligation to *extend the fulfilment of the right* to meet the standard of non-discrimination. In respect of the second contention, the HRC by implication embraced the argument by the author of the communication that the view of the Dutch courts and Parliament is that Article 26 applies to "areas otherwise not covered by the Covenant" (ibid., para. 9.2), including the right to social security. On the facts, the HRC found a violation of Article 26, thus establishing unequivocally that the non-discrimination guarantee in the ICCPR can serve as a means for the protection of social and economic rights not contained in the ICCPR, but in the ICESCR.

Article 27 of the ICCPR has been used to enforce the right to culture. Article 27 provides: "In those States in which ethnic, religious or linguistic minorities exist, persons belonging to such minorities shall not be denied the right, in community with the other members of their group, to enjoy their own culture, to profess and practise their own religion, or to use their own language."

Section 14 of the Canadian Indian Act provides that "[an Indian] woman who is a member of a band ceases to be a member of that band if she marries a person who is not a member of that band". As such, she loses the right to the use and benefits, in common with other members of the band, of the land allotted to the band. Sandra Lovelace, born and registered as a Masileet Indian, lost her membership of her "band" as a consequence of marrying a non-Indian and also the right to reside on a reserve allocated to the band. When her marriage broke down, she wanted to return to her band, but she could not in terms of the Indian Act claim a legal right to reside where she wished to, on the Tobique Reserve, which is also where her band resides. The Human Rights Committee found that, although the right to live on a reserve is not as such guaranteed by Article 27, the right of Sandra Lovelace to access to her native culture and language "in community with the other members" of her group, had in fact been and continued to be interfered with, because there is no place outside the Tobique Reserve where such a community exists (Communication 24/1977, *Sandra Lovelace v Canada*, para. 15). The HRC then concluded that the statutory restrictions, as applied to the specific case, are not reasonably and objectively justified, and constitute a violation of Article 27 (ibid., paras 16 and 19). It should be noted, though, that the HRC stopped short of finding that the particular provisions of the Indian Act violate Article 27.

The Convention on the Elimination of All Forms of Racial Discrimination

The CERD is the first UN human rights instrument to make rights justiciable by way of a system of individual "communications" to be considered by a treaty body consisting of independent experts sitting as a quasi-judicial institution – the CERD Committee. However, the acceptance of this possibility is optional (under CERD Article 14), and by 31 June 2006 it was accepted by only 45 states.

In the main, the CERD prohibits all forms of racial discrimination. This clearly implies an obligation on states to "respect" the right of non-discrimination and to "protect" against instances of discrimination. In Article 5(d) specific reference is made to "economic, social and cultural rights". The obligation placed on states parties is to guarantee the right to equality to everyone in the enjoyment of those rights, which include the rights to work and to housing. As the committee held that these rights are not justiciable (*Diop v Senegal*, para. 6.4), social and economic rights had to be asserted indirectly, making use of other rights under the CERD, such as the right to effective remedies or the right to free movement.

In *Diop v France* the CERD Committee had to consider whether an allegation by a Senegalese national, who was refused work as a lawyer in Nice, amounts to a violation of the CERD. Under the subheading "economic, social and cultural rights", CERD Article 5(e)(i) provides that states undertake to guarantee without any form of discrimination to everyone the right "to work, to free choice of employment ...". Linking the socio-economic guarantees to the non-discrimination injunction in CERD Article 5 confirms that the state obligation arising from Article 5 is one to "respect" and "protect", rather than to "fulfil". This is not the way the CERD Committee saw the matter. Finding that no right had been violated, the committee observed: "As to the alleged violation of Article 5(e) of the Convention and of the right to a family life, the Committee notes that the rights protected by Article 5(e) are of programmatic character, subject to progressive implementation" (para. 6.4). This seems to be a misreading of the CERD. The committee then continued: "It is not within the Committee's mandate to see to it that these rights are established; rather, it is the Committee's task to monitor the implementation of these rights, once they have been granted on equal terms. Insofar as the author's complaint is based on Article 5(e) of the Convention, the Committee considers it to be ill-founded" (ibid.). These remarks fly in the face of the fact that the right to choose employment freely is generally granted, allowing for its "monitoring", and contradicts the more general obligation under CERD Article 2(1)(d) to "prohibit and bring to an end, by all appropriate means, including legislation ... racial discrimination ...".

In its General Recommendation No. 20[53] the committee confirmed this view, but further clarified that it has a role to play in the application of this provision:

> Article 5 of the Convention contains the obligation of States Parties to guarantee the enjoyment of civil, political, economic, social and cultural rights and freedoms without racial discrimination ... Article 5 of the Convention, apart from requiring a guarantee that the exercise of human rights shall be free from racial discrimination, does not of itself create civil, political, economic, social or cultural rights, but assumes the existence and recognition of these rights. The Convention obliges States to prohibit and eliminate racial discrimination in the enjoyment of such human rights. (General Recommendation No. 20, para. 1)

A non-Danish citizen who was denied a loan by a Danish bank approached the CERD Committee for a remedy (*Habassi v Denmark*). The CERD does not provide for a right to financial credit; and in any event the complaint was not directed at an obligation to "fulfil" such a right, but at the failure of the government (in the form of its prosecutorial and police services) to investigate properly whether the bank's general policy not to approve loans to non-Danish citizens amounted to racial discrimination. Finding that "nationality is not the most appropriate requisite when investigating a person's will or capacity to reimburse a loan" (para. 9.3), the committee found that the author was denied an effective remedy within the meaning of CERD Article 6 in connection with Article 2(d) (para. 10). In its recommendation as to an appropriate remedy, the committee goes much further than the individual case, by recommending that "the State party take measures to counteract racial discrimination in the loan market" (para. 11). Also, in *Koptova v Slovak Republic*, the specific social, economic and cultural rights guaranteed under the CERD were not invoked, but the petition nonetheless resulted indirectly in the acceptance of the right to a minimum form of housing.

UNESCO system

Alongside the procedures laid down in UNESCO conventions, in 1978 the executive board of UNESCO laid down a confidential procedure for the examination of complaints received by the organization concerning alleged violations of human rights in its fields of competence, namely education, science, culture and information.[54]

The rights falling under UNESCO's competence are the right to education (Article 26 of the Universal Declaration of Human Rights), the right to share in scientific advancement and the right to participate freely in cultural life (Article 27), as well as the right to information, including freedom of opinion and expression (Article 19). Of necessity, these rights may imply the exercise of others, such as the right to freedom of thought, conscience and religion and the right to freedom of assembly and association for the purposes of activities connected with education, science, culture and information (Articles 18 and 20).

Since the UNESCO Committee on Conventions and Recommendations is not an international tribunal, it endeavours to resolve problems in a spirit of international cooperation and mutual understanding. In search of an amicable solution, the committee works in strictest confidentiality, which is seen as vital to the success of its action. The problem with engaging in an analysis of the "case law" under this procedure is the wall of silence insulating these findings from public scrutiny. As far as conclusions may be drawn from the "results" of the application of UNESCO's complaints procedure, the relevant rights are understood to impose mainly a duty to respect. Of the 300 communications settled between 1978 and 2001, the majority of cases led to the complainant being "released/acquitted" (UNESCO 2002). Authorizations to leave or return to a particular state account for a major proportion of the settled cases. This information tends to indicate that cultural rights, at least in this context, mainly come into play when freedom has been deprived or movement restricted, thereby invoking the government's obligation to "respect".

PROBLEMS AND OBSTACLES: PERCEIVED AND REAL

At the National Level

It is argued here that the lack of justiciability often lies in the fact that, although the relevant rights are provided for under domestic legislation and in the national constitution, these rights are not accessed or invoked in practice, rendering the legal guarantees meaningless. The cause of such a state of affairs may often be ascribed to the lack of efficiency or legitimacy of the legal system as a whole, and of court structures in particular. If the formal legal system is too remote, alien or complex, and approaching a court is too burdensome and too costly, legal guarantees in general, and socio-economic and cultural rights specifically, will remain a dream or ideal. Even if these obstacles are overcome, potentially justiciable claims are often simply not invoked owing to perceptions about their lack of justiciability or, when they are made, these claims are stifled. Seven of the most pronounced stifling remarks are now assessed in light of the country experiences outlined above.

"There are no justiciable socio-economic rights in the national legal order"

It may be assumed that the most obvious bar to the judicial protection of socio-economic rights is the non-inclusion of such rights in the constitution, or their inclusion in the form of non-justiciable DPSPs.[55]

While these factors certainly pose obstacles, they are by no means conclusive. Such a view gives insufficient weight to the domestic dimension of justiciability, by way of the invocation and judicial application of domestically legislated norms. It further neglects the extent to which the overview shows that, through expansive interpretation, civil and political rights have become vehicles for the realization of socio-economic rights and benefits. It also presumes a firewall between rights and DPSPs, something which the experience in at least the Philippines and India contradicts. In sum, experience shows that one of the determinative factors in ensuring justiciability is an independent and activist judiciary that does not pay absolute deference to the executive and legislature.

In similar vein, it may be argued that international norms in treaties that have been ratified but not domesticated are not as such justiciable in the national legal order. The survey here confirms this argument. Domestic judicial "reference" to international norms serves to guide the interpretation of national law, including constitutional guarantees, rather than as the basis for a subjective right. This insight further reinforces the importance of the national legal order integrating international standards into national legislation and the constitution.

"There are inherent differences between socio-economic rights and civil and political rights"

It has been argued that the nature of socio-economic rights is different from that of civil and political rights. The first category imposes positive obligations on states and therefore has resource implications, it is contended, while the second category contains negative rights, without resource implications, as it only requires states to restrain themselves. This has led to a widely invoked view that the first category provides for "programmatic" rights, which are not immediately (or "really") justiciable.

As others before her, Arbour J of the Canadian Supreme Court unmasked the falseness of this dichotomy:

> As a theory of the Charter as a whole, any claim that only negative rights are constitutionally recognised is of course patently defective. The rights to vote (section 3), to trial within a reasonable time (s 11(b)), to be presumed innocent (s 11(d)), to trial by jury in certain cases (s 11(f)), to an interpreter in penal proceedings (s 14), and minority language education rights (s 23) to name but some, all impose positive obligations of performance on the state and are therefore best viewed as positive rights (at least in part). By finding that the state has a positive obligation in certain cases to ensure that its labour legislation is properly inclusive, this Court has also found there to be a positive dimension to the s 2(d) right to associate (*Dunmore v Ontario (Attorney General)* [2001] 3 SCR 1016; [2001] SCC 94). (*Gosselin v Quebec (Attorney General)* (2002-12-19) SCC)

Recently, a comprehensive overview of positive obligations imposed on states under the European Convention appeared (Mowbray 2004). These obligations are derived from a wide array of civil and political rights, and include varying obligations, such as the positive duty to investigate killings[56] and to provide free legal assistance to indigent criminal defendants.[57]

Two concrete case law examples bear out this contention. The Supreme Court of India remarked in respect of the right to legal aid: "In the context of the constitutional obligation to provide free legal aid to a poor accused this Court has held that the State cannot avoid its constitutional obligation in that regard on account of financial constraints. (See *Khatri (II) v State of Bihar*, (1981) 1 SCC 627 at p. 631: (AIR 1981 SC 928 at p. 931)." The South African case of *August v Electoral Commission* illustrates that a classical civil and political right, the right to vote, also has resource implications. Prisoners were not formally excluded from voting in the 1998 elections. However, prior to the election the Electoral Commission did not make any arrangements enabling prisoners to register and vote. In a case brought on behalf of some prisoners, the Constitutional Court held that such omissions would disenfranchise prisoners. As the right to vote "by its very nature imposes positive obligations upon the legislature and the executive" (para. 16), the state has the obligation to "take reasonable steps to create the opportunity to enable eligible prisoners to register and vote" (para. 22).

An all-or-nothing approach also does not take cognizance of the nuanced obligations of states along the three-level taxonomy of "respect", "protect" and "fulfil". All rights, of whatever nature, may give rise to at least some aspect of any of these obligations. An example is the right to basic education, which requires the state to respect (by not excluding children on discriminatory grounds), to protect (by imposing a fine on parents who do not ensure that their children go to school) and to fulfil (by constructing school buildings and paying teachers).

In this discussion, especially, the injudicious bundling together of cultural rights with socio-economic rights is foregrounded. While most socio-economic rights imply the potential of an obligation to fulfil, this aspect is much less pronounced when it comes to the rights to take part in cultural life and to scientific and creative freedom. Most aspects of cultural rights do not require resources, and may thus be categorized as negative rights. This aspect perhaps accounts for the relative success of the UNESCO procedure for collective complaints.

"Socio-economic rights cannot be made justiciable due to resource constraints"

States almost invariably point to the resource implications of decisions dealing with socio-economic rights. Judges also often make reference to the difficulty of resource constraints. At the level of "practical reality", these concerns relate to the perceived or real inability of the state to make resources available to address the situation occasioning violations. It has been argued that legal rights are meaningless in a context of resource constraints, as the magic wand of justiciability cannot with one sweep undo the deeply entrenched effects of poverty, mismanagement, colonial rule, international trade and global economic inequalities, or the disproportionate burdens of debt and disease.

It is certainly correct to say that insisting on the justiciability of socio-economic rights under conditions of widespread poverty or famine is far-fetched, if not perverse. However, a distinction may be drawn between justiciability and implementation or enforcement, arguing that the lack of implementation does not negate the inherent justiciability of the relevant rights. It may mean that rights are not implemented, or enforced, due to weaknesses in the domestic legal system. But this concern illustrates that justiciability presupposes a certain level of economic stability.

In any event, few of the cases discussed here expect states to "fulfil" the right in question. When courts did find such an obligation, for example in the Colombian AIDS case, they tend to rely *narrowly* on a *broad national consensus* as set out in the constitution. In that particular case, the subjective right of access to health is bolstered by an objective constitutional norm requiring the state to prioritize social spending, including on health-care services, above other spending, particularly when the social spending is directed at preventing and dealing with a fatal disease. Court decisions on such matters are mostly anchored in the constitution (as in Colombia and South Africa), but may also be the result of an activist and creative expansion of the constitution (as in the case of India).

One should avoid a tendency to be blinded by adversarial circumstance, to the extent that one loses sight of the different state obligations arising from justiciability. Even where socio-economic and cultural rights are not "fulfilled", there is room left to ensure that these rights are at least "protected" and "respected". When the inclusion of socio-economic rights in the South African Bill of Rights was contested during the drafting process (*Certification of the Amended Text* case), the Constitutional Court rejected similar concerns on several grounds. First, the court emphasized that, at "the very minimum, socio-economic rights can be negatively protected from improper invasion" (para. 78), thus underscoring the state's duty to "respect" and "protect". Second, the court relied on the similarities between civil and political rights on the one hand, and socio-economic rights on the other, as far as budgetary implications are concerned. It held that many of the civil and political rights entrenched in the proposed constitution "will give rise to similar budgetary implications without compromising their justiciability. The fact that socio-economic rights will almost inevitably give rise to such implications does not seem to us to be a bar to their justiciability" (ibid.).

Faced with an obligation to fulfil and resource constraints, courts have devised a few approaches or techniques to address some of the mentioned concerns.

Courts have invoked a degree of deference. Mostly not negating the importance and implications of resource allocation, courts have emphasized that it is not in their domain to prescribe budgetary allocations or priorities. By conceding that available resources are not irrelevant, courts show that they do not close their eyes to the realities within which they operate, and that they are mindful of their own legitimacy. When orders impact on budgetary allocation, they do so indirectly, and do not take the form of orders directing budgetary allocation as such (Lieberberg 2005).

However, courts have held that resources do not trump the constitution. This is especially so because in none of the cases was the argument that there are no resources available – the issue is rather *how* these resources should be prioritized, and *who* bears the responsibility for that prioritization. A number of South African cases illustrate that adverse findings against states are sometimes based on the lack of financial data or other evidence provided by the state (see *Khosa*, para. 18; *Van Biljon*, para. 58). If the state is obliged under the constitution to adhere to a certain duty, the courts have not hesitated to hold that they are not only entitled, but constitutionally mandated, to review the steps taken (see e.g. *Samity*, at 2432). In this respect, they apply judicial review of the programme or steps, adopting a standard of reasonableness. If these are not reasonable, there is a violation. Resources may be a factor in the review of reasonableness, but cannot trump all other considerations. In this process, courts find legitimacy in the constitutional text. A strict interpretation of the right of access to health may entail that existing benefits are extended to everyone. On the basis of the subjective right of access to health care, the South African courts devised a reasonableness standard of review of government programmes, requiring at least minimum core entitlements to those most in need of them. The same subjective right, read with an objective legal norm (or constitutional command), resulted in a more far-reaching obligation on the Colombian government: to provide non-existing benefits (treatment and medication), derived from the constitutional command obliging the Colombian government to prioritize social spending (including spending on health) above other priorities, especially in respect of curbing and preventing fatal disease.

Resource availability determines the nature and extent of the appropriate review. By its very nature, a court views matters retrospectively – that is, the measures that have been taken are reviewed. By applying a reasonableness standard, courts determine whether measures comply with constitutional standards. In this process they may be guided by minimum threshold requirements, in respect of which a resource defence is irrelevant, as illustrated in *Grootboom* and some remarks by Canadian judges.

In directing them to the future, by ordering a remedy, courts concede that resources are relevant, though. A "way out" has been to account for resources when determining an appropriate remedy. Canadian courts have held that resource constraints cannot serve to justify a violation, but that they take on a renewed prominence when a remedy is to be tailored. In the *TAC* case the court made an order with respect to the roll-out of Nevirapine, which did not have far-reaching resource implications, at least as far as the medication – which was provided free of charge – was concerned. The remedial order did have financial implications in respect of the extension of testing and counselling facilities, but did not extend to the provision of alternatives to breast milk (*TAC*, para. 128; Cottrell and Ghai 2004, 78). Still, courts have been reluctant to be too prescriptive in the exact nature of the remedy to be adopted. When it comes to resource allocation and budgetary priorities, there are always a number of options that could be followed (see e.g. *Eldridge* para. 96). It is left to legislatures and the executive to determine the exact steps required, as long as they meet the standard required by the constitution.

An aspect that has received some academic attention,[58] but has not served as the basis for any court decision under review here, is a cost-benefit analysis of the resources allocated towards realizing a socio-economic right. Is it the unquestionable benefit of having an educated populace that has convinced most states to accept, at least in principle, that the right to basic education is justiciable? This aspect was raised, but did not serve as the basis of the court's decision, in the *TAC* case. Part of the evidence before the court indicated that making state resources available (by proving access to medication) in the present would lead to savings in medical care costs in the future (para. 116).

"Making socio-economic rights justiciable threatens the separation of powers doctrine"

Courts are also faced with the dilemma of democratic legitimacy and allegations that they intrude on the spheres of decision-making reserved for or better dealt with by the legislature and executive, thus threatening the principle of separation of powers. As an unelected branch, the judiciary should be wary of usurping the competences or power of legitimately elected parliaments and executives. Couched in different terms, courts are accused of dealing with matters that are "too political", thus detracting "from the efficiency of the legal process" (Cottrell and Ghai 2004, 89).

The CESCR has given the following guidance to domestic courts:

> It is sometimes suggested that matters involving the allocation of resources should be left to the political authorities rather than the courts. While the

respective competences of the various branches of government must be respected, it is appropriate to acknowledge that courts are generally already involved in a considerable range of matters that have important resource implications. The adoption of a rigid classification of economic, social and cultural rights which puts them, by definition, beyond the reach of the courts would thus be arbitrary and incompatible with the principle that the two sets of human rights are indivisible and interdependent. It would also drastically curtail the capacity of the courts to protect the rights of the most vulnerable and disadvantaged groups in society. (General Comment No. 9, para. 10)

Responding to similar arguments, the South African Constitutional Court held:

It is true that the inclusion of socio-economic rights may result in courts making orders which have direct implications for budgetary matters. However, even when a court enforces civil and political rights such as equality, freedom of speech and the right to a fair trial, the order it makes will often have such implications. A court may require the provision of legal aid, or the extension of state benefits to a class of people who formerly were not beneficiaries of such benefits. In our view it cannot be said that by including socio-economic rights within a bill of rights, a task is conferred upon the courts so different from that ordinarily conferred upon them by a bill of rights that it results in a breach of the separation of powers. (*Ex Parte Chairperson of the Constitutional Assembly*, para. 77)

In her dissent in *Gosselin*, Arbour J conceded that legislatures are better suited than courts to address policy matters, given that they have the express mandate of the taxpayers as well as the benefits of extensive debate and consultation. She drew a distinction (para. 330) between a rights-based claim posing the question "whether the state is under a positive obligation to provide basic means of subsistence to those who cannot provide for themselves" (which is justiciable) and "questions of how much the state should spend, and in what manner" (which are not justiciable). She concluded:

The role of courts as interpreters of the *Charter* and guardians of its fundamental freedoms against legislative or administrative infringements by the state requires them to adjudicate such rights-based claims. One can in principle answer the question of whether a *Charter* right exists – in this case, to a level of welfare sufficient to meet one's basic needs – without addressing how much expenditure by the state is necessary in order to secure that right. It is only the latter question that is, properly speaking, non-justiciable. (*Gosselin*, para. 330)

She conceded that "in practice it will often be the case that merely knowing whether the right exists is of little assistance to the claimant. For, unless we also know what is required, or how much expenditure is needed, in order to safeguard the right, it will usually be difficult to know whether the right has been violated" (ibid., para. 331). In that particular case, however, that difficulty did not arise, because the state had already established the level of welfare sufficient to meet one's basic needs.

"Socio-economic rights are too vaguely formulated to serve as justiciable rights"

It is often argued that the justiciability of socio-economic (and cultural) rights is undermined because of the lack of precision with which these rights are formulated. Among the consequences of vaguely formulated provisions are that potential right bearers may not know what they can rely on, duty bearers (mostly states) do not know what is required of them, and courts may be uneasy about their role.

This argument assumes that civil and political rights are all formulated with precision, and that their application does not give rise to similar problems or uncertainties. However, concepts such as "unfair", "undue", "reasonable", "inhuman", "degrading" and "dignity", closely linked to civil and political rights in many national constitutions, belie this argument.

It could be argued that the exclusion of socio-economic rights from constitutions and the dearth of a body of case law (in the form of domestic or foreign precedents) are significant causes of the lack of precision about the content and scope of these rights. It is difficult to gainsay that precision about all rights, including civil and political rights, only emerges gradually, through their application on a case-by-case basis. In fact, the survey of cases here demonstrates attempts of national courts to do exactly that.

These cases also illustrate that the argument about vagueness cannot be generalized. Indeed, problems about lack of precision are determined more by the nature of the state obligation involved than the nature of the right at stake. If the obligation is to "respect" or "protect", vagueness is less problematic, irrespective of the "category" of the right. For example, an eviction of illegal occupiers of land without regard to where they will be evicted to infringes on the right of access to adequate housing, and gives rise to a violation of the obligation to "respect", thus giving a nebulous right precise content in a given situation.[59] These obligations are often more closely linked to remedies with which courts are familiar, such as interdicts. With regard to the duty to "fulfil", the programmatic and non-immediate implications of socio-economic rights are more pronounced – but the same applies to similar obligations arising from civil and political rights. Regarding the obligation to fulfil socio-economic rights, some courts have interpreted their role not as one of filling the right with precise content, but as applying a reasonableness standard of review. Even in respect of these obligations, the courts have relatively exact guidelines: states may be required to take at least *some* immediate action towards the realization of a right; states may be required not to adopt retrogressive measures reversing gains in respect of the fulfilment of the right; or states may be required to ensure that a core entitlement, for example the rights of those in the most desperate circumstances, is ensured.

Once again, the importance of domestic legislation is evident. The problem of imprecision is less pronounced when socio-economic guarantees are contained in specific legislation which serves as a basis for their judicialization in case of executive non-compliance.

As far as the domestic application of international norms is concerned, a distinction is usually drawn between self-executing provisions, which impose clear obligations capable of immediate application, and non-self-executing provisions, which do not. Responding to the view that justiciability of the rights in the ICESCR is particularly problematic owing to their vagueness, the CESCR observed:

> Similarly, judicial training should take full account of the justiciability of the Covenant. It is especially important to avoid any a priori assumption that the norms should be considered to be non-self-executing. In fact, many of them are stated in terms which are at least as clear and specific as those in other human rights treaties, the provisions of which are regularly deemed by courts to be self-executing. (General Comment No. 9, para. 11) These observations underscore that the extent to which socio-economic (and other) rights become justiciable domestically depends primarily on the place allowed for these international norms by the national constitutional order.

"Courts are inappropriate forums to determine matters of a socio-economic nature"

Courts are considered to be inappropriate forums owing to the inherent unsuitability of judges, linked to their lack of expertise and skills in matters pertaining to social and economic rights such as developmental issues or budgetary allocations. In addition, concerns have been raised about their ideological position, deriving from their membership of a conservative ruling élite implicated in upholding societal power relations.

While it is true that judges may lack skills and expertise when it comes to resource allocation, the Indian experience in particular shows how courts can overcome this by relying on expert bodies. In the *Samity* case, for example, the Indian Supreme Court relied on a governmental enquiry committee. In other cases the court appointed a panel of experts to advise it (see e.g. *T. N. Godavaram Tirumulkpad*). Violations of social and economic rights, especially systematic and programmatic violations, may require evidence that is different from that usually tendered in courts. "Brandeis briefs", setting out evidence about social facts, came to be accepted by courts,[60] and are also useful in this context. Generally, courts have accepted and relied on evidence by experts, such as medical evidence and statistical information (*TAC*, para. 90).

While the ideological position of judges has in some instances, such as in the case of the Czech Republic, and in jurisdictions not canvassed here, obstructed the justiciability of socio-economic (and other) rights,[61] cases from countries as diverse as Colombia, India, Latvia, the Philippines and South Africa demonstrate that these considerations are not a universal impediment.

"Courts are inappropriate to deal with collective claims, which are often the most effective way of invoking socio-economic rights"

It may be argued that socio-economic and cultural rights are logically linked to collective rather than individual claims. Courts are not best positioned to deal with such collective claims, it is further argued. When individuals bring inherently collective claims, the problems are not removed. On the contrary, the setting of an individual case may be inappropriate to deal with matters of a much broader and more general scope, and an individual remedy may lead to inequalities in respect of many others directly or indirectly affected by the issue before the court. The Venezuelan experience illustrates that this "problem" may be overcome.

As far as the objection is procedural in nature, a response is that some legal systems allow for class actions. Even if a case comes to a court based on an individual violation, the claim could point clearly to the collective concerns. One or more judicial decisions on an individual basis "will be a warning sign to the political branches in regard to a generalized situation of failure to comply with obligations in matters relevant to public policy" (Abramovitch and Courtis, quoted in Goldman et al. 2001, 551). Addressing this concern, courts may weigh an individual claim to health care against broader claims to available resources, as was done in *Soobramoney*. The Colombian Constitutional Court also followed such an approach in a case where the discharge of a stable but irreversible patient was opposed on the grounds that the discharge would violate the right of access to health-care services: the court found that the rational and equitable use of resources requires that hospital beds should be occupied by patients whose state of health was expected to improve.[62] In cases dealing with the right of access to housing, South African courts found that the state is constitutionally required to address the situation of the litigants, who are among the most desperate, even though that would prioritize them above the general group on "waiting lists" for housing.[63] This finding departs from the premise that the constitution imposes minimum core entitlements, as well as broader guidelines for progressive realization.

In so far as the government is required to adapt its housing programme, the order in *Grootboom CC* reaches beyond the situation of the specific group of litigants. The finding in the *TAC* case goes a step further, in that it requires the government to implement a national programme with a much broader scope. In fact, in *TAC* the individual litigants are absorbed into the collective claim, and all stand to benefit equally from the court's order.

At the International level

Although there may be differences in the problems pertaining to justiciability at the regional and global levels, the problems are broadly similar and are treated under one heading. Some problems raised above also apply here, but are not canvassed again. It has in particular been argued that the interpretation of resource-dependent standards cannot be the same for all countries party to these treaties, thus inevitably leading to uncertainty about how distinctions will be drawn and justified, and giving rise to different interpretations (and levels of justiciability) in states at different levels of development (see e.g. Dennis and Stewart 2004). The introduction of the core content of rights seems to feed into this concern by raising the fear that mostly developing countries will be found in "violation" of the duty to fulfil the core of socio-economic rights, as most developed countries have already progressed beyond the minimum threshold. Other arguments are linked to those about resource allocation and the separation of powers, discussed with respect to the national level. These arguments underscore the sovereignty of the (executive and legislative branches of the) state. Such concerns become more pronounced at the international level, where the court or quasi-judicial tribunal is institutionally delinked from the state apparatus, mostly geographically removed, and comprising judges or members who are not nationals and cannot be expected to have detailed knowledge of or insight into local conditions. In response, reference could be made to the doctrine of the margin of appreciation, and the reluctance of international bodies to replace local judgments with their own. International adjudicatory bodies are, however, concerned with a global standard that applies equally to all states, based on the voluntary acceptance of the state to become bound under international law (*pacta sunt servanda*).

CONCLUSION

Socio-economic guarantees should no longer remain dead letters, as they often do. As this study demonstrates, problems or obstacles raised concerning the justiciability of socio-economic and cultural rights are mostly overstated, and are often based on generalized assertions rather than on the application of specific rights in specific contexts. If this survey shows one thing, it is that one cannot generalize or make absolute claims about the justiciability of these rights.

The study also shows that, in the main (and as far as generalization allows), cultural rights do not pose the obstacles that are usually raised in respect of the justiciability of socio-economic rights. As they predominantly give rise to the obligation to respect and protect, the controversial issues surrounding "fulfilment" do not enter the debate.

The non-inclusion of justiciable socio-economic and cultural rights in the constitutional order of a state is not a bar to the judicial application of these rights. Indian and Philippine cases illustrate how DPSPs can be (and have been) converted to justiciable guarantees. Many other cases demonstrate how civil and political rights, in particular the rights to life and to non-discrimination[64] and due process (or fair trial) clauses, may serve as a basis to guarantee social and economic benefits or interests. Strictly speaking, the application of these rights does not provide support for the justiciability of socio-economic rights, standing alone. In such instances, it is the *interpretation of a civil and political right* that gives rise to the realization of a social or economic benefit. Stated differently, the *implication of a finding based on a justiciable civil or political right* is that a socio-economic right is guaranteed. However, the "integrated" approach and the self-standing justiciability of socio-economic rights aim at realizing the same result – the advancement and protection of people's socio-economic situation.

It should be kept in mind that national legislation may contain rights independent of constitutional guarantees. National legislation remains the most accessible and direct way of making rights justiciable, even if these rights are included in the constitution.[65] Given its relatively precise content and intimate link to a legitimate national consensus, legislation circumvents most of the obstacles raised about justiciability, such as "separation of powers" and "vagueness" arguments. By enacting socio-economic guarantees as subjective rights (perhaps reinforced by legislative commands), justiciable socio-economic rights will minimize the potential for a "deficit in democracy and accountability".[66] Increasing domestic legislative assertion of socio-economic rights (especially as subjective rights, but also as legislative commands) will underscore the justiciability of these rights and contribute to filling the jurisprudential void surrounding their interpretation. The inventory of cases in this chapter reveals the neglected potential for jurisprudential cross-fertilization.

The role of the judiciary is more pronounced when it comes to applying the constitution. Even though a (judicial) decision of unconstitutionality may serve as a rebuke to the legislature and executive, courts are understandably reluctant to usurp the role of these other two branches. As far as constitutionalized socio-economic guarantees are concerned, most obstacles to justiciability are overcome when a state obligation to respect or protect is implied. In fact, the study's main conclusion is that all socio-economic and cultural rights are justiciable in so far as the right implies a duty to respect and protect. What is expected for courts to do with regard to these duties is not dissimilar from the application of civil and political rights. The study abounds with examples of courts doing just that. Although cultural rights may also imply positive action, the obligations imposed by those under review here are mostly to respect and protect. A common characteristic of these cases is that they deal with individual-focused remedial action, rather than institutional programmatic reform.

Although all rights are justiciable, the extent or degree of justiciability varies from context to context. When a particular socio-economic right implies a positive obligation to fulfil, there may be some problems about justiciability. This does not detract from the justiciability of a particular right, especially in the light of the fact that there is no hierarchy in terms of which the duty to fulfil is prioritized at the pinnacle of a triad. Judgments discussed in this chapter provide examples of a great degree of sensitivity for these problems and show how courts have adopted strategies to overcome associated issues, including an acceptance that socio-economic rights can often not be realized "immediately" (see e.g. *Grootboom CC*, para. 94), by emphasizing their role as a last resort to which those in the most dire need can turn, and by taking resource constraints into account when devising remedies.

The reluctance to incorporate socio-economic (and cultural) rights into international human rights treaties is strongly motivated by perceptions about problems associated with justiciability. By grappling with this notion, the main contribution of the ICESCR has been to encourage and give guidance about justiciability at the national level. The aim of international law is in any event not to replace protection at the national level. Even when socio-economic rights in international treaties (especially the ICESCR) have been made self-executing at the national level, courts have been reluctant to give "direct effect" to them.[67] Courts have mainly made "reference" to international treaties as interpretative guides (see e.g. the *Fiji* case discussed above, and *Grootboom CC*, paras 28–31). In so far as they include socio-economic rights, international human rights treaties do not subscribe to wholesale justiciability; rather, selective justiciability is preferred. This approach has its roots in the European Convention and its protocol, which guarantee only two socio-economic rights, namely the rights to unionize and to education. The very same rights are the only ones that became justiciable under amendments to the American Convention. In a minority of European states the scope of socio-economic rights has been extended, but even these new instruments, at least to some extent, depart from a premise of domestic selection rather than one uniform standard.

The same principle of selectivity applies at the national level as well. In general, a national agreement is not aimed at destabilizing the status quo. The pervasive inclusion of the rights to unionize and to education illustrates that point. States are prepared to adhere to an obligation to protect and respect, but fulfilment is problematic. Inclusion of guarantees tends to confirm the existence of guarantees at the national level, and mostly only allows for their restrictive extension. Based on what the internal consensus in the form of a constitution allows, a number of constitutions have accepted state obligations to fulfil. Judicial interpretation of this obligation is constrained primarily by constitutional provisions, as cases in Colombia and South Africa illustrate.

There is, in conclusion, a need to go beyond justiciability to acknowledge all the other factors that impact on the realization of socio-economic and cultural rights. Although courts may be an important mechanism to address issues of poverty and social vulnerability, such efforts can never be dependent entirely on courts. Ensuring justiciability of socio-economic (and cultural) rights at the national and international levels is but one method in a multifaceted approach in which other means, such as non-judicial monitoring,[68] "naming and shaming", democratic struggles and the role of civil society, are perhaps more important. These strategies should not be seen as mutually exclusive, but rather as reinforcing each other. Civil society and social struggles may be directed towards ensuring a national climate that will accept the justiciability of these rights through legislation and constitutionalization, and litigation may strengthen the efforts of civil societies to improve societies (see e.g. *TAC*, para. 126).

ACKNOWLEDGEMENTS

My thanks to Danie Brand, who commented on an earlier draft, and to research assistance by Lilian Chenwi and Orazukile Ugochukwu. Inaccuracies remain my own.

NOTES

1   Scott and Macklem (1992) also categorize these rights together under the heading "social rights".

2   See Gutto (1999), arguing that the guarantee against discrimination is really "also a core socio-economic right".

3   See for example Bhagwati J in *Francis Coralie Mullin*, para. 7: "the right to life includes the right to live with human dignity and all that goes along with it, namely, the bare necessities of life such as adequate nutrition, clothing and shelter over the head and facilities for reading, writing and expressing oneself ...".

4   See e.g. Vierdag (1987, 78): violations are justiciable if they "can be judged to have occurred, or to be occurring, by courts of law or similar bodies".

5   See e.g. Vierdag (1987, 78): justiciable claims are "able to afford redress: the violation will consist of actions or omissions by officials or private persons which can be cancelled, rectified, declared void, or lead to the payment of compensation for damage".

6   See Arambulo (1995, 57), who distinguishes between a court decision that a right is subjected to judicial scrutiny (justiciability) and a decision that the "right can actually be executed and put into effect".

7   For a recent development in the last region, see "Conclusions and recommendations of the colloquium and workshop for judges and lawyers on the justiciability of economic, social and cultural rights in the Pacific region", Suva, Fiji, 1–3 June 2006.

8   The case of *Nkosi v Bührmann* deals with the question whether an occupier has the right to bury a deceased family member on the farm he occupies. The court found that these provisions did not extend to include a right to bury family members. The legislature subsequently intervened by adding Section 6(2)(dA) to Act 62 of 1997 guaranteeing explicitly the right of an occupier to bury a family member who was residing on the occupied land.

9   See e.g. *Port Elizabeth Municipality v Various Occupiers* 2004, where the provisions on eviction in the Prevention of Illegal Eviction from and Occupation of Land Act 19 of 1998 mirror those of s. 26(3) of the constitution, and both were invoked.

10 See e.g. Article 45 of the Irish constitution, which stipulates that the principles of social policy are intended as general guidelines for the legislature; and Article 37 of the Indian constitution, which calls the DPSPs fundamental in the "governance of the country" and "in making laws".

11 See e.g. the "National Objectives and Directive Principles of State Policy", following the preamble of the 1995 Uganda constitution.

12 See e.g. Article 19 of the constitution of Chile; Articles 56, 67 and 70 of the constitution of Colombia; Articles 60, 61 and 78 of the constitution of Costa Rica; Articles 71, 74, 94 and 100 of the constitution of Guatemala; Articles 57, 70 and 71 of the constitution of Uruguay.

13 For reprinted versions of the human rights provisions of all African states, see Heyns (2004); see also e.g. Chirwa (2005).

14 See e.g. Article 53 of the 1976 constitution of Algeria; Article 27 of the 1991 Benin constitution; the preamble of the Cameroon constitution; Article 77 of the 1992 Cape Verde constitution; Article 23 of the constitution of the Democratic Republic of Congo; Article 18 of the Egyptian constitution; Article 25 of the 1994 Malawi constitution; Article 20 of the Namibian constitution; Article 8 of the 2001 Senegalese constitution; and Article 30 of the 1995 Ugandan constitution.

15 See e.g. Articles 24–26 of the present constitution of Ghana, which entered into force in 1993.

16 See e.g. Article 43(2) of the Fiji constitution: "In interpreting the provisions of this Chapter, the courts must promote the values that underlie a democratic society based on freedom and equality and must, if relevant, have regard to public international law applicable to the protection of the rights set out in this Chapter."

17 See generally Ely Yamin (2003), and on Brazil specifically see *Diná Rosa Vieira v Município de Porto Alegre*, in which the Brazilian Supreme Court finds that Article 196 of the constitution, guaranteeing the right to health, entitles persons with HIV to suitable medication and medical care at state expense.

18 The Act requires a "spouse" to be a person of the "opposite sex".

19 Court of Appeal, at 440–2, quoted by L'Heureux-Dubé in Ghai and Cottrell at 48.

20 Act 2/1993 Sb, adopted 16 December 1992.

21 Para. XX, E/C.12/1/Add.76 (Concluding Observations/Comments) 05/06/2002.

22 Act No. 29/1984 Sb on the System of Basic and Secondary Schools (the Education Act), s. 4 para. 1.

23 Regulation No. 15/1994 Sb on the Provision Free of Charge of Textbooks, Teaching Texts, and Basic School Materials.

24 CRC Article 28(2)(a) and (b). Article 28(2)(a) deals with free primary education, while 28(2)(b) obliges states to "encourage" secondary education and take appropriate measures such as free education and "offering financial assistance in case of need".

25 Promulgated under No. 104/1991 Sb.

26 Part II of the judgment.

27 *Taito Rarasea v State*, from 2002 *Interights Commonwealth Human Rights Law* in the Interights database.

28 For a brief discussion and excerpts from the judgment, see the updated version of Scheinen (1995) quoted in Goldman et al. (2001, 575–6).

29 Although all the DPSPs are framed as obligations on the state ("The State shall …"), a few formulations refer to "rights", such as Article 39(a) (the right to an adequate means of livelihood) and Article 41 (the rights to work, to education and to public assistance).

30 See also Article 45, which provides for the principle of free and compulsory education for children up to 14 years old (within a period of ten years after commencement of the constitution).

31 Article 89 states: "The State shall recognise and protect fundamental human rights in accordance with this Constitution, laws and international agreements binding upon Latvia."

32 See also *Kjeldsen, Busk Madsen and Pedersen v Denmark*, where an application was brought on the basis of Article 2 of Protocol No. 1, alleging that sex education violated Article 2 when read with Articles 8, 9 and 14 of the European Convention (privacy, religious freedom and equality rights).

33 Strasbourg 3.V. 1996 (opened for signature in 1996, entered into force 1999).

34 It entered into force in 1998, after five states had ratified it (Article 14 of the additional protocol).

35 By 30 August 2004 11 member states of the Council of Europe (Belgium, Croatia, Cyprus, Finland, France, Greece, Ireland, Italy, Norway, Portugal and Sweden) had ratified the protocol.

36 See www.coe.int/T/E/Human%5FRights/Esc.

37 See e.g. Article XI, the right to presentation of health and well-being; Article XII, the right to education; Article XIII, the right to benefits of culture; Article XIV, the right to work and to fair remuneration.

38 Article 26 of the Convention places an obligation on states to "undertake to adopt measures … with a view to achieving progressively" unspecified "economic, social, educational, scientific and cultural standards".

39 Signed in El Salvador, 17 November 1988; entered into force 16 November 1999 after ratification by 11 OAS member states.

40 Article 10(1) reads: "1. Everyone shall have the right to health, understood to mean the enjoyment of the highest level of physical, mental and social well-being.

41 See, on socio-economic rights in the African Charter, Odinkalu (2001). See also Seminar on Social, Economic and Cultural Rights in the African Charter (2005).

42 See the M'Baye draft African Charter on Human and Peoples' Rights (reprinted in Heyns 1999, 65–77), which divides the content of the charter into different chapters, one on socio-economic rights and one on civil and political rights, and imposes an obligation on states to submit reports on the first but not the second of these chapters.

43 See also *Huri-Laws v Nigeria*, para. 41. However, the sentence contains the seeds of the "implied rights" doctrine, upon which the commission elaborated later by "reading in" the "safe drinking water and electricity" as part of the right to health.

44 For a discussion of the case see Coomans (2003).

45 The African Charter on the Rights and Welfare of the Child delineates the right of the child to health by providing for clear state obligations, such as the reduction of child mortality rates.

46 See e.g. Article 14(1), providing for the right to "control their fertility", "the right to decide whether to have children, the number of children and the spacing of children" and the "the right to choose any method of contraception".

47 When the AU Assembly met in July 2004, and without any debate, it mandated a dramatic departure from the previous AU position by deciding that "the African Court on Human and Peoples' Rights and the Court of Justice should be integrated into one Court" (Assembly/AU/Dec.45 (III), para. 4). As of 31 July 2006, the process of elaborating this protocol was still under way.

48 GA Res. 421 (V), Sec. E (4 December 1950), quoted in Craven (1995, 18).

49 ECOSOC Dec. 2002/254 of 25 July 2002.

50 UN Doc. E/CN.4/2004/44, dated 15 March 2004, para. 76.

51 Under ICESCR Articles11, 15, 22 and 23.

52 Under ICESCR Article 2(1), emphasis added.

53 Non-discriminatory implementation of rights and freedoms (Article 5), of 15 March 1996.

54 104 EX/Decision 3.3 of the executive board. See in general Marks (1992).

55 Here, as below, the criticisms are not linked to a specific author or judgment, but are generally derived from the literature – see e.g. Arambulo (1999, 1–97); Dennis and Stewart (2004).

56 *Kelly v UK* (where the violation was based on the right to life); see Mowbray (2004, 30).

57 *Artico v Italy* (where the violation was based on the right to a fair trial).

58 In their study on the cost of HIV prevention and treatment interventions in South Africa, Geffen et al. (2003) conclude: "Highly active antiretroviral therapy (HAART) is expensive, but the *net* costs to government are significantly lower than the direct costs of providing HAART. This is so because people on HAART experience fewer opportunistic infections ..." (thus in the long term saving the state on hospital costs).

59 See e.g. the South African cases of *City of Cape Town v The Various Occupiers of the Road Reserve of Appelate parallel to Sheffield Road in Phillipi* and *Baartman and Others v Port Elizabeth Municipality*, discussed by Budlender (2004, 34–5).

60 This mechanism, known in the United States and Canada, is named after the first person to submit such a brief, in *Muller v Oregon*.

61 As happened in the USA, in *Lochner v New York* and immediately thereafter. In *Lochner* the US Supreme Court held in violation of the Fourteenth Amendment (right to property and due process) the New York statute prescribing a maximum of 60 hours for weekly employment as a baker, holding that the statute, motivated by concerns for the right to health, excessively limits freedom of contract.

62 For a discussion of the case (Decision No. T-527 of 10 November 1993) see Toebes (1999, 226–7).
63 See e.g. *Port Elizabeth Municipality v Various Occupiers* (judgment of 1 October 2004), where the government raised the defence that by not evicting the occupiers, they would be "jumping the queue" (para. 3). The defence was rejected, as the government had made no effort to address the position of those to be evicted prior to eviction (para. 57).
64 It should be borne in mind that there are perils involved in using equality as the yardstick for socio-economic benefits: "once social justice is equated with or measured in terms of equality, the central problem cannot be anything but relative inequality, and the ultimate goal cannot be anything but relative equality" (Van der Walt 2004, 176), rather than addressing absolute poverty or deprivation.
65 See e.g. Article 196 of the Brazilian 1988 constitution and Law 931/96. The first provides in general terms that health "is the right of all" and the government must make "social and economic policies aimed at reducing the risk of illness and other maladies", while the latter provides in much detail that persons infected with HIV and ill with AIDS must receive all necessary treatment at state expense, with an explicit indication of which government department is responsible for financing the law's implementation.
66 For the argument about democratic deficit, see e.g. Cottrell and Ghai (2004, 88).
67 See e.g. the discussion about the position in the Netherlands in Toebes (1999, 194–200).
68 See, for an example at the national level, the role of the South African Human Rights Commission in monitoring the realization of socio-economic rights (s. 184(3) of the South African constitution).

REFERENCES

Arambulo, Kitty (1999), *Strengthening the Supervision of the International Covenent on Economic, Social and Cultural Rights: Theoretical and Practical Aspects* (Antwerp: Intersentia-Hart).
Baxi, Upendra (1980), "The post-emergency Supreme Court: A populist quest for legitimation", in *The Indian Supreme Court and Politics* (Lucknow: Eastern Books, 1972).
Budlender, Geoff (2004), "A Canadian perspective on economic and social rights", in Yash Ghai and Jill Cottrell (eds), *Economic, Social and Cultural Rights in Practice: The Role of Judges in Implementing Economic, Social and Cultural Rights* (London: Interights), pp. 34–59.
Chirwa, D. M. (2005), "A full loaf is better than half: The constitutional protection of economic, social and cultural rights in Malawi", *Journal of African Law*, 49: 207–41.
Coomans, Fons (2003), "The *Ogoni* case before the African Commission on Human and Peoples' Rights", *International and Comparative Law Quarterly*, 52: 749–60.
Cottrell, Jill and Ghai, Yash (2004), "The role of the courts in the protection of economic, social and cultural rights", in Yash Ghai and Jill Cottrell (eds), *Economic, Social and Cultural Rights in Practice: The Role of Judges in Implementing Economic, Social and Cultural Rights* (London: Interights), pp. 58–89.
Craven, Matthew (1995), *The International Covenant on Economic, Social and Cultural Rights: A Perspective on its Development* (Oxford: Clarendon).
_____ (1998), "The protection of economic, social and cultural rights under the inter-American system of human rights", in David J. Harris and Stephen Livingstone (eds), *The Inter-American System of Human Rights* (Oxford: Clarendon).

Davis, D. (1992), "The case against the inclusion of socio-economic demands in a bill of rights as directive principles", *South African Journal on Human Rights*, 8: 475–90.

De Wet, Erika (1996), *The Constitutional Enforceability of Economic and Social Rights* (Durban: Butterworths).

Dennis, Michael J. and Stewart, David P. (2004), "Justiciability of economic, social, and cultural rights: Should there be an international complaints mechanism to adjudicate the rights to food, water, housing, and health?", *American Journal of International Law*, 98:3, 462–515.

Donders, Yvonne M. (2002), *Towards a Right to Cultural Identity?* (Antwerp: Intersentia).

Ely Yamin, E. (2003), "Not just a tragedy: Access to medications as a right under international law", *Boston University International Law Journal*, 21: 325–71.

Geffen, Nathan, Nattrass, Nicoli and Raubenheimer, Chris (2003), "The cost of HIV prevention and treatment interventions in South Africa", Working Paper No. 28, Centre for Social Science Research, University of Cape Town, available at www.uct.ac.za/depts/cssr/pubs.html.

Goldman, Robert Kogod, Grossman, Claudio M., Martin, Claudia and Rodriguez-Pinzon, Diego (2001), *The International Dimension of Human Rights: A Guide for Application in Domestic Law* (Washington, DC: Inter-American Development Bank).

Gutto, Shadrack B.O. (1998), "Beyond justiciability: Challenges of implementing/enforcing socio-economic rights in South Africa", *Buffalo Human Rights Law Review*, 4: 89–91.

Heyns, Christof (ed.) (1999), *Human Rights Law in Africa* (The Hague: Kluwer Law International).

_____ (ed.) (2004), *Human Rights Law in Africa*, Vol. 2 (Leiden: Martinus Nijhoff).

Lieberberg, S. (2005), "The interpretation of socio-economic rights", in M. Chaskalson, J. Kentridge, J. Klaaren, G. Marcus, D. Spitz and S. Woolman (eds), *Constitutional Law of South Africa* (Cape Town: Juta Law Publishers), pp. 32.1–32.9.

Makubaldo, L., Netshidzivhani, P., Mahlasdela, L. and Plessis, R. (eds) (2003), *National HIV and Syphilis Antenatal Sero-Prevalence Survey in South Africa 2003*. Health Systems Research, Research Coordination and Epidemiology, Department of Health, South Africa.

Marks, Stephen P. (1992), "The complaints procedure of the United Nations Educational, Scientific and Cultural Organization", in Hurst Hannum (ed.), *Guide to International Human Rights Practice* (Philadelphia, PA: University of Pennsylvania Press), pp. 86–98.

Mowbray, A.R. (2004), *The Development of Positive Obligations Under the European Convention on Human Rights by the European Court of Human Rights* (Oxford: Hart).

Mureinik, E. (1992), "Beyond a charter of luxuries: Economic rights in the constitution", *South African Journal on Human Rights*, 8: 464–74.

Odinkalu, C. A. (2001), "Analysis of paralysis or paralysis by analysis? Implementing economic, social, and cultural rights under the African Charter on Human and Peoples' Rights", *Human Rights Quarterly*, 23: 327–69.

Pillay, K. (2002), "Implementing *Grootboom*: Supervision needed", *Economic and Social Rights Review*, 3:1, 13–14.

Sajo, Andras (2004), "Implementing welfare in Eastern Europe after communism", in Yash Ghai and Jill Cottrell (eds), *Economic, Social and Cultural Rights in Practice: The Role of Judges in Implementing Economic, Social and Cultural Rights* (London: Interights), pp. 50–7.

Scheinen, Martin (1995), "Economic and social rights as legal rights", in Asbjørn Eide, Catherina Krause and Allan Rosas (eds), *Economic, Social and Cultural Rights: A Textbook* (Dordrecht: Martinus Nijhoff), pp. 41–62.

Scott, Craig and Macklem, Patrick (1992), "Constitutional ropes of sand or justiciable guarantees? Social rights in a new South African Constitution", *University of Pennsylvania Law Review*, 141:1, 1–148.

Seminar on Social, Economic and Cultural Rights in the African Charter (2005), "Statement from seminar on social, economic and cultural rights in the African Charter", *African Human Rights Law Journal*, 5: 182–93.

Shue, H. (1980), *Basic Rights: Subsistence, Affluence and US Foreign Policy* (Princeton, NJ: Princeton University Press).

Toebes, Brigit C.A. (1999), *The Right to Health as a Human Right in International Law* (Antwerp: Intersentia-Hart).

UNAIDS and Canadian HIV/AIDS Legal Network (2006), *Courting Rights: Case Studies in Litigating the Human Rights of People Living with HIV* (Geneva: UNAIDS Best Practice Collection).

UNESCO (2002), *UNESCO's Procedure for Dealing with Alleged Violations of Human Rights* (Paris: UNESCO, Office of International Standards and Legal Affairs), available at http://portal.unesco.org/en/file_download.php/cf69cf5cdd6f47d99f6 906491d7701a7Booklet+CR.pdf.

Van der Walt, A. (2004), "South African reading of Frank Michelman's theory of social justice", in Henk Botha, Andre Van der Walt and Johan Van der Walt (eds), *Rights and Democracy* (Stellenbosch: Sun Press), pp. 163–211.

van Hoof, G.J.H. (1984), "The legal nature of economic, social and cultural rights: A rebuttal of some traditional views", in P. Alston and K. Tomasevski (eds), *The Right to Food* (Utrecht: Martinus Nijhoff).

Victor Condé, H. (2004), *A Handbook of International Human Rights Terminology* (Lincoln: University of Nebraska).

Vierdag, E. (1987), "The legal nature of the rights granted by the International Covenant on Economic, Social and Cultural Rights", in *Netherlands Yearbook of International Law*, 9: 69–78

CASE LAW

African Commission on Human and Peoples' Rights

Free Legal Assistance Group and Others v Zaire (2000) AHRLR 74 (ACHPR 1995).

Huri-Laws v Nigeria (2000) AHRLR 273 (ACHPR 2000).

Malawi African Association and Others v Mauritania (2000) AHRLR 149 (ACHPR 2000).

Purohit and Moore v The Gambia, Communication 241/2001, Sixteenth Activity Report of the African Commission, 2002–2003, Annex VII.

The Social Economic Rights Action Centre and Another v Nigeria, Communication 155/96, Fifteenth Activity Report of the African Commission.

Brazil

Diná Rosa Vieira v Município de Porto Alegre, Supreme Federal Tribunal, 12 September 2000, Agr. No recurso extraordinário N. 271.286-8 Rio Grande do Sul, on file with author.

Canada

Arsenault-Cameron v Prince Edward Island (2000) 70 CRR (2nd) 1.
Egan v Canada [1985] 2 SCR 513, (1995) 29 CRR (2nd) 79.
Eldridge v British Columbia (Attorney General) (1997) 46 CRR (2nd) 189.
Gosselin v Quebec (Attorney General) [2002] 2 SCR 429, 2002 SCC 84.
Mahe v Alberta (1990) 1 SCR 342.
R v Oakes (1986) 19 CCR; 24 CCC (3rd) 321.
Reference re Public School Act (Manitoba) s 79(3), (4) and (7) 1993 14 CRR (2nd) 74.
Schachter v Canada (1992) 10 CRR (2nd) 1.

Czech Republic

Pl. US 25/1994 (School Materials Decision), available (in English) at http://test.
concourt.cz/angl_verze/doc/p-25-94.html.
(1997) 4 East European case Reporter of Constitutional law (EECRCC) 6.

Colombia

Tutela No. T-505/92, 22 August 1992.

Committee on the Elimination of Racial Discrimination

Communication 2/1989, CERD/C/39/D/2/1989, 18 March 1991.
Diop v France, Communication 2/1989, CERD/C/39/D/2/1989, 18 March 1991.
Habassi v Denmark CERD/C/54/10/1997, 6 April 1999.
Koptova v Slovak Republic, Communication 13/1998, CERD/C/57/D/13/1998, 1
November 2000.

Commonwealth

Taito Rarasea v State [2000] ICHRL 29 (12 May 2000).

European system

Artico v Italy ECHR Ser. A No. 37 (1980).
Autism-Europe v France, Complaint No. 13/2002.
Belgian Linguistic case, ECHR Ser. A 6, judgment of 23 July 1968.
International Commission of Jurists v Portugal, Complaint 1/1998.
Kelly v UK, ECHR, 4 May 2001.
Kjeldsen, Busk Madsen and Pedersen v Denmark (1976) 1 EHRR 711.
Wilson, National Union of Journalists and Others v United Kingdom, applications 30668/96,
30671/96 and 30678/96, judgment of 2 July 2002.

Human Rights Committee

Communication 24/1977, *Sandra Lovelace v Canada*, CCPR/C/13/D/24/1977, 30 July 1981.
Communication 182/1984, *Zwaan-de Vries v Netherlands*, CCPR/C/29/D/182/1984, 9 April 1987.

India

Bandhua Mukti Morcha v Union of India [1984] 2 SCR 67.
Francis Coralie Mullin v Union Territory of Delhi AIR 1981 SC 746.
Kesavananda Bharati v State of Kerala (1973) 4 SCC 225.
Khatri (II) v State of Bihar (1981) 1 SCC 627; (1981) AIR (SC) 928.
Mohini Jain v State of Karnataka (1992) AIR 1861 (SC).
Olga Tellis v Bombay Municipal Corporation (1985) 3 SCC 545.
Paschim Banga Khet Majoor Samity v State of West Bengal (1996) 4 SCC 37; (1996) AIR (SC) 2426.
T. N. Godavaram Tirumulkpad v Union of India (2000) 6 SCC 413.
Unni Kkrishnan J P v State of Andhra Pradesh (1993) 1 SCC 645 (SC).

Inter-American system

Baena Ricardo et al (270 Workers) v Panama (Merits), IACtHR, 2 February 2001, Ser. C, No. 72.
Jorge Odir Miranda Cortez v El Salvador, IA Comm HR, 7 March 2001, Report 29/01.
Yanomami v Brazil, Case 7615, Resolution 12/85, 5 March 1985, OAS Doc. OEA/Ser. 1/V/II. 66, Rev. 1.

Latvia

Constitutional Court of the Republic of Latvia, Case No. 2000-08-0109.

Philippines

Minors Oposa v Fulgencio S Factoran, Jr (in his capacity as Secretary of the Department of Environment and Natural Resources) 33 ILM (1994) 173.

South Africa

August v Electoral Commission 1999 (3) SA 1 (CC).
Certification of the Amended Text of the Constitution of the Republic of South Africa, 1996 (Second Certification judgment) 1997 (2) SA 97 (CC).
City of Cape Town v Rudolph and Others [2003] 3 All SA 517 (C).
East London Traditional Local Council v Member of the Executive Council of the Province of the Eastern Cape for Health and others [2000] 4 All SA 443 (Ck).

Ex Parte Chairperson of the Constitutional Assembly: In re Certification of the Constitution of the Republic of South Africa, 1996.
Government of the Republic of South Africa and Others v Grootboom and Others 2000 (11) BCLR 1169 (CC); [2000] 10 BHRC 84 (CC) (*Grootboom CC* case).
Grootboom v Oostenberg Municipality 2000 (3) BCLR 277 (C).
In the case of In Re The School Education Bill of 1995 (Gauteng) 1996 (4) BCLR 537 (CC).
Khosa and Others v Minister of Social Development and Others and Saleta Mahlaule and Another v Minister of Social Development and Others (CCT 13/03, judgment of 4 March 2004).
Laerskool Middelburg v Departmentshoof, Mpumalanga 2003 (4) SA 160 (T).
Local Council v Member of the Executive Council of the Province of the Eastern Cape for Health and others [2000] 4 All SA 433 (Ck).
Minister of Health and Others v Treatment Action Campaign and Others (no. 2) 2002 (5) SA 721 (CC).
Nkosi v Bührmann 2002 (6) BCLR 574 (SCA).
Nontembiso v The Member of the Executive Council of the Department of Welfare, Eastern Cape 2004 JDR 429 (SE).
Port Elizabeth Municipality v Various Occupiers 2004 (12) BCLR 1268 (CC).
Residents of Bon Vista Mansions v Southern Metropolitan Council 2002 (6) BCLR 625 (W).
Soombramoney v Minister of Health (KwaZulu-Natal) 1997 (12) BCLR 1696; [1997] 4 BHRC 308 (CC).
Van Biljon v Minister of Correctional Services 1997 (2) SACR 50 (C); 1997 (6) BCLR 789 (C).

United States

Lochner v New York 198 US 45 (1905).
Muller v Oregon 208 US 412, 28 SCt 324 (1908).

Venezuela

Cruz del Valle Bermudez v Ministerio de Sanidad y Asistencia Social [Ministry of Health and Social Assistance], Supreme Court of Justice of Venezuela, Decision 916, 15 July 1999.
Glenda Lopez v Instituto Venezolano de los Seguros Sociales, Supreme Court of Venezuela (Constitutional Chamber), judgment of 6 April 2001.

3 Development of Indicators for Economic, Social and Cultural Rights: The Rights to Education, Participation in Cultural Life and Access to the Benefits of Science

AUDREY R. CHAPMAN

INTRODUCTION

There has been increasing awareness in recent years that the development of indicators is central to developing the capacity for monitoring economic, social and cultural rights and evaluating the performance of countries in implementing these rights. Effective monitoring requires the systematic collection and analysis of appropriate data. The determination of which data are relevant requires translating the abstract legal norms in which various human rights covenants are framed into operational standards. This process involves conceptualizing specific enumerated rights, for example the right to education, and developing standards by which to measure implementation or identify violations of state obligations. These standards or indicators, some of which will be based on statistical data, can then provide yardsticks to assess compliance. For more than ten years human rights advocates, special rapporteurs and UN treaty-monitoring bodies have acknowledged the need for indicators. Nevertheless, the UN human rights system has been slow in responding. This chapter outlines some of the problems and reviews the status of efforts to formulate indicators, particularly for the rights relevant to UNESCO: the rights to education, to enjoy the benefits of scientific progress and its applications and to take part in cultural life.

REQUIREMENTS OF HUMAN RIGHTS INDICATORS

An indicator is an instrument or tool for evaluation, a yardstick to measure results and to assess realization of desired levels of performance in a sustained and objective way.[1] A human rights indicator may be defined as "a piece of information used in measuring the extent to which a legal right is being fulfilled or enjoyed in a given situation" (Green 2001). Indicators may be based on quantitative or qualitative information. They may measure inputs to realizing specific human rights as well as outcomes or the degree to which the human rights are being enjoyed.

There is general agreement in the literature that rights-based indicators differ from other types of indicators, such as the statistical indicators used by specialized agencies to measure economic and social development. Statistical indicators may overlap with rights indicators, but the two are not synonymous. Therefore, at a minimum, use of existing statistical indicators to evaluate human rights compliance requires screening to determine their appropriateness and reanalysis from a human rights perspective (United Nations 1993, paras 170–71).

The *Human Development Report 2000* (UNDP 2000) recognizes that while human development indicators and human rights indicators have some common features, they also have significant differences. It identifies three contrasts in their approach.

- *Conceptual foundation.* Human development indicators assess the status of people's capabilities. Human rights indicators evaluate whether people are living with dignity and freedom, and the extent to which critical actors, usually states, have fulfilled their obligations to establish and uphold just social arrangements to enable their residents to do so (UNDP 2000, 91). In human rights terminology, what is key is for indicators to provide ways to assess whether states are respecting, protecting and fulfilling the rights enumerated in the International Covenant on Economic, Social and Cultural Rights (ICESCR). To be in compliance with the obligation to respect requires that the state refrains from undertaking actions, policies or laws that contravene the standards set out in the ICESCR. The obligation to protect requires the state to take all necessary measures to safeguard persons within their jurisdiction from infringements of their rights by third parties. Obligations to fulfil entail taking all necessary steps to ensure that the benefits specified in the rights are being met and that access to them is being made secure for all.
- *Focus of attention.* While both types of indicators focus on human outcomes and inputs so as to draw attention to unacceptable disparities

and suffering, human rights indicators also need to cover the policies and practice of legal and administrative entities and the conduct of public officials (ibid.). Or to put this distinction in another way, inputs are far more important to human rights analysis. In fact, some human rights specialists, including this author, argue that state parties to the covenant primarily have an obligation of conduct (inputs) rather than an obligation of result (outputs). An obligation of conduct refers to the minimum conditions a government has to fulfil to be in compliance with its obligations under the ICESCR. This latter emphasis has the advantage of highlighting policy priorities and implementation, both of which are under the control of state parties, rather than outputs or results, which reflect a confluence of factors, including the availability of resources.

- *Additional information.* A human rights assessment requires a wider range of data than a development analysis and has greater need for the data to be disaggregated by a variety of variables, such as gender, ethnicity, race, religion, nationality and social origin (ibid.). While a human rights framework begins with the principle of universality, human rights assessment focuses primarily on the status of the most disadvantaged and vulnerable communities. Because a human right is a universal entitlement, its implementation is measured particularly by the degree to which it benefits and empowers those who hitherto have been among the human rights "have-nots" (Chapman 1994, 153). National averages, even breakdowns in regional or urban-rural data, often camouflage wide disparities in the extent to which specific groups in the population are reliably enjoying their human rights.

Human rights indicators may be categorized in several ways. The approach suggested by Paul Hunt, the UN special rapporteur for the right of everyone to enjoy the highest attainable standard of physical and mental health, while initially proposed with application to the right to health, has subsequently been adopted for other economic, social and cultural rights as well. He distinguishes between three types of indicators: structural, process and outcome (Hunt 2003).

- *Structural indicators* address whether or not the infrastructure is in place that is considered necessary for, or conducive to, the realization of a specific right. Specifically, structural indicators evaluate whether a country has established the institutions, constitutional provisions, laws and policies that are required. Most structural indicators are qualitative in nature and therefore not based on statistical data. Many can be answered by a simple yes or no.
- *Process indicators* assess the degree to which activities that are necessary to attain specific rights-related objectives are being implemented, and the progress of these activities over time. The types and amounts of governmental inputs are one important kind of process indicator. Process indicators are variable and require statistical data.

- *Outcome indicators* assess the status of the population's enjoyment of a right. They show the "facts" and measure the results achieved. Many of the Millennium Development Goal indicators, for example, are outcome indicators. Like process indicators, outcome indicators are variable and require statistical data.

Indicators have a variety of potential applications. According to the UN *Human Development Report* (UNDP 2000, 89), human rights indicators offer a tool for the following:

- making better policies and monitoring progress;
- identifying the unintended impacts of laws, policies and practices;
- determining which actors are having an impact on the realization or non-realization of rights;
- revealing whether the obligations of these actors are being met;
- giving early warning of potential violations so as to enable prompt preventive action;
- enhancing social consensus on difficult trade-offs required in the face of resource constraints;
- exposing issues that have been neglected or silenced.

Like other types of indicators, human rights indicators have to meet specific standards to be valid. There is general consensus (e.g. International Commission of Jurists 2002, 6) that indicators should be:

- *valid* – measure what they purport to measure;
- *objective* – achieve similar results when applied in comparable situations;
- *sensitive* – susceptible to social changes in certain situations;
- *specific* – accurately reflect social change only in relation to particular situations;
- *user friendly*;
- *feasible* – they must acquire data without undue effort and/or expense.

For the purposes of human rights monitoring, indicators should also be:

- *policy relevant* – capable of measuring policy inputs and influencing policy decisions;
- *consistently measurable over time* – capable of demonstrating progress over time towards target realization;
- *capable of disaggregation* – allowing for a special focus on certain groups or issues, e.g. the effects on vulnerable or marginalized populations (ibid.).

Of the criteria noted above, three are particularly important for human rights indicators: feasibility, consistent measurability over time and the ability to disaggregate. All three, however, are problematic to achieve.

Feasibility refers to having data available to fit the requirements of specific indicators. The dilemma is that the types of data available and their quality and reliability, particularly in developing countries, often do not match the requirements identified above. Data-collection systems in developing countries often lack the capacity to collect a wide range of good-quality and reliable data. Therefore in developing indicators there is a kind of chicken-and-egg dilemma: should the indicators be based on the data available in most countries, or should the indicators become the basis of efforts to improve the statistical data-collection systems in countries with limited infrastructures for doing so?

The disaggregation of data is a central requirement for human rights monitoring. Human rights particularly focus on the status and condition of vulnerable and disadvantaged groups and communities. Typically human rights treaty-monitoring bodies require country reports to provide process and outcome data that are disaggregated on a variety of grounds: sex, ethnicity and geographic areas, particularly urban and rural breakdowns. Again, this principle, while central to human rights monitoring, may meet serious data limitations. Countries with weak data-collection systems may not have the necessary disaggregated data available. Moreover, countries that do collect data on disaggregated bases may be reluctant to make the data available to human rights monitors because doing so may reveal serious inadequacies in realizing the human rights of vulnerable and disadvantaged groups, perhaps even to the point of constituting a form of discrimination. In contrast, highly aggregated data, such as country averages, can camouflage these differentials. The unavailability of disaggregated data may therefore require either undertaking small-scale targeted research studies to evaluate the status of vulnerable communities or choosing indicators that are particularly sensitive to the condition of these communities.

The importance of having indicators with data that are consistently measurable over time reflects the standard of "progressive realization" specified in the ICESCR. The concept of progressive realization reflected the drafters' recognition that most states parties would not be able to achieve the full realization of all economic, social and cultural rights immediately upon ratification of the ICESCR, or even in a short period of time. Therefore the language of the covenant mandates states parties:

> to take steps, individually and through international assistance and cooperation, especially economic and technical, to the maximum of its available resources, with a view to achieving progressively the full realization of the rights recognized in the present Covenant by all appropriate means, including particularly the adoption of legislative measures. (Article 2(2)[2])

This standard differs considerably from the requirement specified in Article 2 of the International Covenant on Civil and Political Rights, which imposes an immediate obligation to respect and ensure implementation of all enumerated rights.[3]

While the language of "progressive realization" introduces an element of flexibility, reflecting the difficulties of any country achieving the immediate and full realization of these rights, it is not meant to eliminate states parties' obligations to move as expeditiously and effectively as possible towards fulfilment of these rights. According to a series of general comments adopted by the UN Committee on Economic, Social and Cultural Rights, the treaty-monitoring body that oversees implementation of the covenant, any deliberately retrogressive measures with regard to economic, social and cultural rights constitute a violation of states' duties.

Evaluating progressive realization, however, imposes difficult demands. It requires using a stable series of indicators backed by access to appropriate good-quality statistical data, preferably disaggregated in a number of categories, including gender, race, geographic region and linguistic group, that are collected in an identical manner over several periods in time. Otherwise it is not possible to assess trends. Obviously, these requirements may be difficult to fulfil.

Yet another issue is the number of indicators to develop and apply for purposes of human rights monitoring. Each human right usually has many different components and dimensions. Moreover, to assess fully the realization of specific human rights requires a variety of different kinds of indicators. As noted above, there are three types of human rights indicators: structural indicators to evaluate whether the requisite institutions, laws and policies are in place; process indicators to measure the degree to which inputs and activities that are necessary to attain specific rights-related objectives are being implemented; and outcome indicators to reveal the status of the population's enjoyment of a right. Given the need to disaggregate the data and put them into time series, it can get complicated and onerous very quickly.

Then there is the related issue of whether indicators should be applicable to all countries, regardless of their level of development and geographic location, or whether specific sets of indicators more targeted to conditions in specific countries should be used. In principle, all states parties have similar obligations, especially to realize the core obligations of specific rights. Nevertheless, at least on some items, for example indicators that measure steps taken to preserve culture or assure cultural participation, the contexts vary considerably.

Eibe Riedel, currently the vice chair of the Committee on Economic, Social and Cultural Rights, has put forward the notion of a "toolbox" of indicators for each right (cited in Roaf et al. 2005, 5). The toolbox would consist of a relatively limited set of indicators applicable across countries. To these core indicators, additional sets of indicators addressing variable contexts and situations could be added.

This notion of a "toolbox" sets the goal for a relatively small number of indicators for each right, and in principle it would be an advantage to work with fewer indicators, especially if the principle of disaggregation of data is followed. Nevertheless, trial efforts to develop rights-based indicators have found it difficult to attain this goal, especially when such initiatives have attempted to identify the three types of indicators (structural, process and outcome) noted above. This raises yet another critical issue: the balance between a sufficient number of indicators to measure performance and the limitations of having a manageable set of indicators, particularly for human rights monitoring bodies overseeing a wide range of rights.

Special Rapporteur and the 1993 Expert Seminar on the Use of Indicators

Obstacles to monitoring

Until recently the implementation and monitoring of the rights articulated in the ICESCR, as well as the development of indicators for that purpose, have been hampered by a series of conceptual and methodological difficulties. A lack of intellectual clarity as to the definition and scope of these rights constituted a serious problem for virtually all the rights.[4] Challenges are presented by the different nature of economic, social and cultural rights; the vagueness of many of the norms; the absence of national institutions specifically committed to their promotion as rights; and the range of information required in order to monitor compliance effectively. In contrast with civil and political rights, the rights contained in the covenant, with the exception of the cluster of labour-related rights, are not grounded in historically based bodies of domestic or international jurisprudence. Most of these rights were first recognized in the Universal Declaration of Human Rights and then given greater specificity in the covenant. Additionally, the international community has had fewer opportunities for systematic norm clarification.

Appointment of a special rapporteur

Attempting to circumvent some of these problems, the Sub-Commission on the Prevention of Discrimination and Protection of Minorities and the Human Rights Commission appointed Danilo Türk as a special rapporteur in 1988 with a mandate to prepare a study of the problems, policies and practical strategies relating to the more effective realization of economic, social and cultural rights. In several of his reports the special rapporteur discussed the potential use of economic and social indicators for clarifying the content of the rights as well as assessing progress in their realization. According to Türk, indicators can provide a quantifiable measurement device of direct relevance to the array of economic, social and cultural rights; a means of measuring the progressive realization of these rights over time; and a method for determining difficulties or problems encountered by states in fulfilling the rights. In addition, he anticipated that indicators would be able to assist with the development of the "core contents" of these rights and offer yardsticks whereby countries could compare their progress with other countries (Türk 1990). He therefore recommended that the United Nations convene a seminar for discussion of appropriate indicators to measure achievements in the progressive realization of economic, social and cultural rights so as to offer an opportunity for a broad exchange of views among experts.

In January 1993 the UN Centre for Human Rights (now the Office of the High Commissioner for Human Rights) convened such an expert seminar, for which this author served as the rapporteur. It included a variety of experts on a wide range of rights from academic, activist, governmental and UN agency backgrounds. After extensive review of the understanding of economic, social and cultural rights, the members of the seminar concluded that, far from being a short-cut to defining and monitoring these rights, human rights indicators require the conceptualization of the scope of each of the enumerated rights and the related obligations of states parties. The seminar therefore concluded that additional work was needed in particular to:

- clarify the nature, scope and contents of specific rights enumerated in the covenant;
- define more precisely the content of the specific rights, including the immediate core obligations of states parties to ensure the satisfaction of, at the very least, minimum essential levels of each of these rights;
- identify the immediate steps to be taken by states parties to facilitate compliance with their legal obligations towards the full realization of these rights, including the duty to ensure respect for minimum subsistence rights for all (United Nations 1993, para. 159).

In addition, members of the seminar recommended that there is a need to improve evaluation and monitoring of progressive realization, identify and address violations, institute improved cooperation within the UN system, facilitate the participation of non-governmental organizations and affected communities in each of the tasks outlined above, and apply scientific statistical methodologies (ibid., para. 181).

Benchmarks

In view of the difficulties in developing indicators for monitoring economic, social and cultural rights, some experts have proposed formulating national benchmarks instead. While there is some inconsistency in the human rights literature, benchmarks and indicators usually refer to different approaches in evaluating progress towards implementation of rights. Human rights indicators measure human rights observation or enjoyment in absolute terms: in theory the same indicators would apply to all countries. In contrast, national benchmarks generally refer to targets established by particular governments, and therefore vary from country to country. The primary use of benchmarks is to offer a tool to assess the performance of states in reaching goals they have set for themselves within a particular interval of time as part of the process of fulfilling their obligations.

Paul Hunt, a law professor who served as a member of the UN Committee on Economic, Social and Cultural Rights and is currently appointed as the special rapporteur for the right to health, wrote a background paper for the committee (Hunt 1998) dealing with indicators and benchmarks, in which he proposes a multi-step process.

(1)   The first step would be the development of a set of ten or so key indicators agreed to by all treaty bodies and specialized UN agencies for a specific right. Wherever appropriate, each right would be disaggregated.
(2)   A state party would set appropriate levels or benchmarks for each indicator, and by extension for each of the rights being monitored. In doing so the committee could ask the specific state party to report on its current rate for each benchmark and set an appropriate rate or benchmark for five years' time. If a state party's projected benchmark appears to be overly modest, the committee could ask for an explanation and revision, and if the state party refuses to set a more appropriate goal, the committee could set a more appropriate benchmark. NGOs may want even more ambitious ones. These benchmarks would vary with time and differ among states parties.
(3)   Once generated, the benchmarks could be used by all interested parties, including NGOs, to monitor that particular state's progress during the next five years, and at the end of the five-year period state parties would report to the committee using the agreed indicators. Consistent with its monitoring role, the committee would evaluate and comment on the state's progress, including making recommendations for improving performance. The committee would also ask the state party to identify new and most likely more advanced benchmarks for the next five-year period.
(4)   The committee would then monitor how these benchmarks have been met when it reviews the reports of states parties. If the benchmarks have been reached, the committee would commend the state and set new benchmarks. If the state has failed, the committee would seek to find out whether it was due to unavoidable circumstances or neglect. If it turns out to be the latter, the state can be accused of violating the covenant (ibid., p. 7).

This proposal was incorporated in the committee's General Comment No. 14 (paras 57–8) on the right to the highest attainable standard of health, which recommends that benchmarks be used as an additional tool along with agreed-upon sets of indicators using the process outlined in the paper.

Millennium Development Goals

In September 2000 the UN General Assembly adopted the Millennium Development Goals (MDGs) as a framework for a partnership between developed and developing countries with the goal of reducing poverty in all forms and promoting development.[5] The MDGs consist of eight goals, each of which has a number of associated targets, usually to be achieved by 2015, with linked indicators to measure progress. Two of the goals are related to education: Goal 2 is to achieve universal primary education; Goal 3 is to promote gender equality and empower women, including a target to eliminate gender disparity in primary and secondary education, preferably by 2005 and at all levels by 2015. Although there are no goals specifically addressing science or culture, Goal 8, to create a global partnership for development, includes targets related to making available the benefits of new technologies, such as access to affordable drugs and information and communication technologies.

There are 48 agreed indicators to measure progress towards these goals (www.developmentgoals.org/goals.htm), including the following of relevance to UNESCO-related rights:

- net enrolment ratio in primary schools;
- proportion of pupils starting grade 1 who reach grade 5;
- literacy rate of 15–24-year-olds;
- ratio of girls to boys in primary, secondary and tertiary education;
- ratio of literacy of women to men, 15–24 years old;
- proportion of population with access to affordable essential drugs on a sustainable basis;
- telephone lines and cellular subscribers per 100 population;
- personal computers in use per 100 population.

It is important to note, however, that neither the MDG initiative nor its associated indicators is based on a human rights approach. As noted above, there is a considerable difference between human rights and development indicators, and the MDGs are intended to be the latter. A 2002 joint statement by the UN Committee on Economic, Social and Cultural Rights and the UN Commission on Human Rights' special rapporteurs on economic, social and cultural rights identified this oversight and noted the potential contributions a comprehensive human rights approach could make in developing strategies to realize the MDGs and in the formulation of the corresponding indicators to measure progress.

Briefly, the MDGs do not address human rights principles and values, such as raising the level of empowerment and participation of individuals and affirming the accountability of various stakeholders. Unlike human rights indicators, the MDGs focus exclusively on outcomes and do not deal with the policy, legal or institutional requirements. Nor do they consider associated inputs. Because the indicators do not specify the need for disaggregation in reporting and analysis, it would be possible for states to make significant progress towards the goals without improving the status of disadvantaged communities. To show progress they might in fact focus on improving the profile of other groups that are easier to reach. Nevertheless, the MDGs offer the prospect of improving the situation of the world's poorest countries, and the indicators will provide important outcome data that can be applied for human rights purposes.

STATUS OF EFFORTS TO DEVELOP INDICATORS FOR MONITORING ECONOMIC, SOCIAL AND CULTURAL RIGHTS

As noted above, the conceptualization of the nature, scope and contents of the rights enumerated in the covenant is a prerequisite for developing indicators and monitoring strategies. Over the years since the 1993 expert seminar there has been some significant progress in this regard. In 1995 the Committee on Economic, Social and Cultural Rights adopted its first general comment conceptualizing the content and states parties' obligations for an enumerated right, the right to adequate housing. In the next ten years this was followed by general comments on the rights to food, education, health, water, intellectual property and work. In addition, the Commission on Human Rights has appointed special rapporteurs to address several of the rights, among them the rights to housing, education and health. There have also been significant contributions to this process of conceptualization by non-governmental organizations and experts.

Despite these advances, however, there has not been comparable progress in developing indicators or benchmarks for monitoring these rights. For example, while the general comments dealing with education and health articulate the need to formulate indicators for the purposes of monitoring, neither identifies specific indicators for the right in question.

One reason for this lack of progress in developing indicators has been the failure of the UN system to implement a key recommendation made by the 1993 expert seminar. To achieve the various objectives outlined in its report, the seminar recommended that the UN Centre for Human Rights (now the Office of the High Commissioner for Human Rights) convene a series of expert seminars focused on specific economic, social and cultural rights. It envisioned that each of the right-specific seminars would include experts on the right, representatives of specialized agencies, chairpersons of treaty-monitoring bodies and relevant NGOs (Committee on Economic, Social and Cultural Rights/Commission on Human Rights 2002, para. 202). Taking up this call, the Commission on Human Rights adopted a series of resolutions requesting that the United Nations sponsor such seminars (see, for example, Commission on Human Rights 1994, 1996). The Committee on Economic, Social and Cultural Rights has also been keen to hold these seminars.

The Office of the High Commissioner for Human Rights did sponsor a 1998 round-table discussion on benchmarks for the realization of economic, social and cultural rights. Like the 1993 expert seminar, however, the round-table was more a discussion of the need for and characteristics of benchmarks. It did not have the time or the appropriate representation to begin the task of developing either benchmarks or indicators.

Another reason for the delay has been the lack of an agreed conceptual framework for human rights indicators. Recently there has been progress in developing such. A meeting of experts co-sponsored by the Office of the High Commissioner for Human Rights, held in March 2005 at Abo Akademi University in Turku, Finland, reviewed existing work on human rights indicators with a view to assessing its usefulness for UN human rights treaty bodies in assessing compliance (see www.abo.fi/instut/imr->seminars). Following that meeting, a new UN expert working group on indicators was established by the Office of the High Commissioner for Human Rights. The chairs of the UN human rights treaty-monitoring bodies requested that this working group develop a conceptual framework for indicators applicable to all types of human rights, civil and political as well as economic, social

And it did

and cultural, and asked that the working group have a proposal and sample indicators ready for its June 2006 meeting.[6]

At its initial meeting in August 2005 the members of the working group, which include this author, agreed on a conceptual framework applicable to all human rights. The approach consisted of first identifying a limited number of characteristic attributes for each human right for which indicators were to be elaborated, followed by the selection of a configuration of structural, process and outcome indicators as initially proposed by Paul Hunt with reference to the right to health (Office of the High Commissioner for Human Rights 2005). The framework was subsequently refined at its March 2006 meeting, along with the development of sample indicators for four rights, two economic and social and two civil and political (Office of the High Commissioner for Human Rights 2006). None of the UNESCO-related rights was addressed, but the right to education was designated as one of several rights to be next considered. *& it has been.*

Right to Education

The right to education is one of the most affirmed economic, social and cultural rights. There are provisions recognizing the right in the Universal Declaration on Human Rights (1948) and a series of human rights instruments based on the Universal Declaration: the ICESCR, the International Convention on the Elimination of All Forms of Racial Discrimination (1965), the Convention on the Elimination of All Forms of Discrimination against Women (1979) and the Convention on the Rights of the Child (1989). The right to education is also dealt with in such documents at the UNESCO Convention against Discrimination in Education (1960), the ILO Convention Concerning Indigenous and Tribal Peoples (1989) and regional human rights instruments, including the American Declaration of the Rights and Duties of Man (1948) and the African Charter on Human and Peoples' Rights (1986).

There has also been considerable progress in specifying the content and scope of the right and the concomitant obligations of states parties. The Committee on Economic, Social and Cultural Rights has adopted two general comments. General Comment No. 11 (Committee on Economic, Social and Cultural Rights 1999a) addresses the requirement set by Article 14 of the covenant that countries which have not been able to secure compulsory primary education, free of charge at the time of ratification, undertake within two years of becoming states parties to work out and adopt a detailed plan of action for its progressive implementation within a reasonable number of years. The committee then followed up later in the same year with another general comment dealing with the provisions of Article 13 on the right to education (Committee on Economic, Social and Cultural Rights 1999b). There has also been considerable jurisprudence on this right in national courts.

In 1999 the Commission on Human Rights appointed Katerina Tomasevski as the first UN special rapporteur on the right to education; in 2004 she was replaced by Vernor Munoz Villalobos. Like other special rapporteurs, the role has involved efforts to conceptualize the right, conducting human rights missions to individual countries to assess problems and prospects, investigating alleged violations of the right to education and promoting rights-based education at all levels. The existence of a special rapporteur has the additional advantage of providing a focal point for advocates and monitors of the right.

Specific provisions of the right to education

Article 26 of the Universal Declaration on Human Rights (1948)[7] specifies three principles that have framed the normative content of the right to education in subsequent human rights instruments based on the declaration: everyone has the right to education, and therefore education should be free and compulsory at least in the elementary stages and higher forms of education should be equally accessible to all on the basis of merit; education should be directed to the full development of the human personality and strengthening of respect for human rights and fundamental freedoms; and parents have a prior right to choose the kind of education given to their children.

The most extensive enumeration of the right to education occurs in the ICESCR. Like the Universal Declaration, Article 13(1) states that education shall be directed to the full development of the human personality and sense of dignity and shall strengthen respect for human rights and fundamental freedoms. Article 13(2) of the covenant stipulates that:

(a)   primary education shall be compulsory and free to all;
(b)   secondary education in its various forms shall be made generally available and accessible, in particular by the progressive introduction of free education;
(c)   higher education shall also be made equally accessible to all, in particular by the progressive introduction of free education;
(d)   fundamental education shall be encouraged for those persons who have not received or completed primary education;
(e)   the development of a system of education at all levels shall be actively pursued, and the material conditions of the teaching staff shall be continuously improved.

Article 13(3) reiterates the principle set forth in the Universal Declaration that parents or legal guardians should have the right to choose educational institutions other than those established by the government, provided they conform to the minimum educational standards laid down or approved by the state.

Article 14 further enforces the need for free and compulsory education. It goes beyond the standard of "progressive realization" of the right to education to direct that each country which at the time of becoming a state party to the ICESCR has not achieved universal primary education has two years to work out and adopt a detailed plan of action to achieve this goal within a reasonable number of years.

Article 10 of the Convention on the Elimination of All Forms of Discrimination against Women[8] directs states parties to take all appropriate measures required to eliminate discrimination against women and ensure them equal opportunities in the field of education. It identifies in particular the need to ensure the basis of equality between women and men in relation to career and vocational guidance; access to educational establishments at all levels; and access to the same curricula, examinations, teaching staff with the same qualifications and school buildings with the same standard of equipment. It also mentions the obligation to eliminate stereotypical concepts of gender roles at all levels and forms of education. This article specifies as well that states parties should conduct initiatives to address the reduction of female drop-out rates and organize programmes for girls and women who have left school prematurely.

The Convention on the Rights of the Child[9] has two articles devoted to the right to education. Like the ICESCR, Article 38 makes primary education compulsory and free; encourages the development of different forms of secondary education and specifies that they should be available and accessible to every child, and to that end recommends that states introduce free education and offer financial assistance in case of need; and states that higher education should also be accessible to all. Article 38 goes beyond the ICESCR in that it directs states parties to take measures to encourage regular attendance at schools and reduce the drop-out rate. It also mentions the importance of promoting and encouraging international cooperation in matters relating to education, specifically in relation to the needs of developing countries. Article 39 repeats several of the principles enunciated in the Universal Declaration and the ICESCR about the purpose of education. It explains that the education of a child should be directed to fostering the child's fullest potential, developing respect for human rights and fundamental freedoms and preparing the child for responsible life in a free society.

Efforts to develop indicators have lagged behind other work on this right. The Committee on Economic, Social and Cultural Rights made a tentative decision to begin work on indicators with this right, but the expert seminar it hoped to organize has never taken place.

1999 World University Service-International/AAAS seminar

In 1999 the World University Service-International (an organization which no longer exists), with the support of the Science and Human Rights Program of the American Association for the Advancement of Science (AAAS),[10] organized a one-day seminar to discuss and begin to develop indicators to monitor the progressive realization of the right to education (World University Service-International 1999). The seminar was seen as a preliminary effort to model a process, identify some of the issues that would need to be resolved, determine criteria to use in selecting indicators and possibly to choose a set of provisional indicators. Workshop participants included members and staff of the Committee on Economic, Social and Cultural Rights, along with representatives of relevant specialized agencies and NGOs and a few academics knowledgeable about this subject matter.

In the seminar/workshop participants decided the following criteria should be used in selecting indicators: feasibility of obtaining good-quality disaggregated data, simplicity, comparability, verifiability, affordability, relevance and extent to which a proposed indicator was keyed to the contents of the right in the ICESCR. According to the participants, the most important disaggregators were gender, urban/rural, ethnic group, income level and age. They also noted the need to distinguish between attendance in public and private educational institutions. In addition, the workshop participants expressed the desirability of having a set of common indicators agreed upon by all treaty bodies and the specialized UN agencies in order to have a common language currency in which to discuss the right to education (ibid.).

The workshop identified and discussed a list of existing and proposed indicators, specifically the core indicators adopted by the Education for All Forum 1996 Mid-decade Review meeting in Amman, Jordan, to measure progress towards the targets set at the World Conference on Education for All in Jomtien, Thailand, in 1990. It then chose ten provisional sets of indicators to stimulate further discussion without consideration of the availability of the data:

- literacy rate disaggregated by gender, urban/rural breakdown, ethnic group and age;
- net enrolment rate disaggregated by gender, urban/rural breakdown and ethnic group, with separate data for primary, secondary and tertiary levels of education;
- percentage of cohort reaching grade 5 or completing primary education, with data disaggregated by gender, urban/rural location and ethnic group;
- pupil/teacher ratio for primary, secondary and tertiary education, with breakdowns for public and private education in urban and rural areas;
- required level of teacher training, percentage of teachers who have reached it and composition of teaching, with each disaggregated by gender and ethnic group and data for primary, secondary and tertiary levels of education;
- percentage of government expenditure spent on education and expenditure per pupil, with data disaggregated by urban/rural location and for each level of education;
- percentage of households who need to travel more than a specified amount of time by car, bus or foot to reach the nearest educational centre;
- cost of education for each family, including direct (fees) and indirect costs;
- salaries of teachers in comparison with other professions, disaggregated by gender and urban/rural location for each level of the educational system and further broken down by public and private education (ibid.).[11]

Obviously, this initiative should be seen as very preliminary. For one thing it does not identify any structural indicators. For another it is not based on an assessment of data available. In addition, these indicators do not cover all of the components of the right to education as outlined in the ICESCR.

Special rapporteur for the right to education

Katarina Tomasevski identified the need to develop rights-based indicators as part of the process of operationalizing the right to education in several of her reports. She also expressed concern with the inadequacy of statistical data for use with the indicators. Recognizing that statistical averages camouflage gender, racial, ethnic, linguistic and religious fault-lines, which are crucial from a human rights perspective, she emphasized the need for disaggregation of data (Commission on Human Rights 2002, para. 27). In her January 2003 report she particularly noted the inadequacy of statistics based on the internationally prohibited ground of discrimination (Commission on Human Rights 2003, para. 22). To be able to promote the global priority for eliminating gender disparity in education by the year 2005, she recommended prioritizing quantitative and qualitative data related to gender disparities in education so as to create a foundation for assessing progress (ibid., para. 25).

To portray the complexity of state obligations related to the right to education, particularly at a primary school level, she proposed a 4-A scheme: availability – ensuring that primary schools are available for all children; accessibility – ensuring access to public schools, most importantly in accordance with the existing prohibition of discrimination; acceptability – respect for parental freedom to have their children educated in conformity with their religious, moral or philosophical convictions; and adaptability – making the knowledge, skills and values imparted respectful of local cultures and appropriate to the evolving needs of the society (Commission on Human Rights 1999, paras 51–74).

In her 2002 report the special rapporteur translated the 4-A scheme into a menu for rights-based indicators (Table 3.1).

This conceptualization of how the 4-As could be monitored is a useful intermediary step, but it does not identify indicators *per se*. Instead it identifies the topics for which indicators should be formulated. Some of these would be feasible and others quite difficult to translate into indicators.

South African Human Rights Commission

The 1996 South African constitution includes a Bill of Rights that contains an extensive commitment to social and economic rights, including recognizing the right to education. To support the implementation of these rights, the constitution establishes the national Human Rights Commission and assigns it a mandate to promote, monitor and assess the observance of human rights in South Africa. It specifically tasks the commission with the responsibility for requiring relevant organs of state to provide it with information on the measures they have taken towards the realization of these rights on a regular basis.[12] This has given rise to perhaps the most comprehensive and significant national effort to monitor social and economic rights, including attention to the use of indicators for this purpose.

To fulfil its mandate the Human Rights Commission has developed a series of reporting protocols, which have been periodically revised. These have been distributed to national, regional and some parastatal agencies. The commission has used the data collected along with supplementary information to write detailed reports on the status of the realization of these rights. The 2003–2004 report, the latest available at the time of writing, was the commission's sixth on the implementation of social and economic rights.[13]

The issue of what types of data should be collected in this process and how detailed the reporting protocols should be has been a subject of some controversy within South Africa.[14] The first set of monitoring protocols focused on clearly defined and limited information: the impact of past discriminatory policies and practices; the understanding by government departments of the obligation imposed on them by the socio-economic rights in the constitution; the policies, laws and programmes planned or in place to implement the socio-economic rights; and the existence of information and monitoring systems by which the implementation of social and economic rights could be tracked (Brand and Liebenberg 2000). Subsequently the protocols were much expanded, relying on the advice of a Canadian expert on statistical indicators. The new format requested far more data from government departments. The various protocols have had both narrative portions and indicators. In developing the protocols, however, there was insufficient consultation with government departments and South African academic experts. Nor did the commission conduct a careful analysis of what kinds of statistical data were available when drafting the protocols.

The South African experience shows the difficulties in finding a balance in the development of protocols that elicit sufficient information to be able to assess the status of a particular human right without being so comprehensive that the system breaks down. Had the protocols elicited the data requested, the commission would have been hard pressed to analyse them all, especially if it tried to do so on a disaggregated basis. But instead many departments have not regularly provided the data as requested, possibly because some of the updated comprehensive data were not available. The various reports written by the commission note the difficulties in collecting the data, and the commission has also occasionally resorted to subpoenaing uncooperative departments and ministries.

A review of the education protocols used for the 2003–2004 report provides a greater sense of the strengths and weaknesses of the South African approach.[15] There were two different instruments: one on general education, covering from early childhood development through secondary school; the second focused on the right to further education and training, specifically grades 10–12, training colleges and universities. Both protocols are quite lengthy and detailed, and combine open-ended narrative sections with others more oriented towards indicators.

Table 3.1   Translating the 4-A scheme into rights-based indicators

Availability	Correspondence between *profile of intake and input* Correspondence between *budgetary allocations* and human rights obligations Governmental supervision of *educational institutions* to ensure minimum standards and foster inclusion Professional educators *Parental choice of education* for their children	*Profile* to include disaggregation by all internationally prohibited grounds of discrimination *Budgetary allocations* at central and local levels should correspond to guarantee of free and compulsory education for all children up to minimum age for employment and progressive realization of right to education Licensing, supervision and funding of *educational institutions* should correspond to human rights law, including objective of enhancing *all-inclusive education* Status of *professional educators* should correspond to their internationally recognized rights and trade union freedoms Recognition and enforcement of *parental choice* should conform to international human rights law
Accessibility	*Compulsory education*: elimination of all obstacles to access to education for all school-aged children *Post-compulsory education*: non-discriminatory access and affordability	Elimination of *obstacles*: legal and administrative; direct, indirect and opportunity costs of education; transportation Identification of obstacles regarding *post-compulsory education* corresponding to internationally prohibited grounds of discrimination Review of access to post-compulsory education by criterion of *affordability* in accordance with international human rights law
Acceptability	*Minimum standards* *Teaching process* *Learning process*	*Minimum standards* for quality, safety and environmental health should be enforced Human rights law should guide *teaching process*, especially purpose, contents and methods of instruction, academic freedom and discipline *Learning process* requires elimination of barriers, such as poverty-induced obstacles, language of instruction, ability/disability
Adaptability	*Concordance of age-determined rights* *Out-of-school education* for categories who cannot access educational institutions Safeguarding *human rights through education* by adapting education to enjoyment of all human rights	*Concordance* between school-leaving age and minimum age for employment, marriage, military recruitment, criminal responsibility *Out-of-school education* for children and young people deprived of their liberty, refugees, internally displaced people, working children, nomadic communities *Impact of education on all human rights* to be assessed by indices such as graduate unemployment or increasing racism among school-leavers

Source: Annual report of the special rapporteur on the right to education, E/CN.4.2002/60, para. 28, available at www.hri.ca/fortherecord2002/documentation/commission/e-cn4-2002-60.htm.

On the positive side, the general education protocol seeks to focus on vulnerable groups, which is very important for human rights analysis. But this term is used very broadly to refer to 21 different groups, some of them quite large – for example persons living in rural areas and informal settlements. It is also unlikely that educational records are maintained in such a way that some, perhaps most, of the members of these groups can be identified.

The narrative portion of the protocol is very broad and open-ended, always a problem in trying to assess progressive realization without sufficient interpretive guidance. It requests information on the key programmes and sub-programmes to realize the right and asks specifically for such detailed data as key objectives, the political and legal mandate, the key strategic plan targets, the budget allocation, key implementation difficulties, actual expenditures and audited expenditures. It goes on to elicit the assessment of outcomes in terms of the constitutional obligations to respect, protect and fulfil the right, leaving the request open-ended and not explaining how these terms specifically apply to the right to education. Then there is a section on the key challenges faced.

The indicators portion of the protocol is also very detailed. There are general indicators on the literacy rate for children and adults and the number of school-aged children who are not attending school. The protocol requests data for each level of education and training programme on the enrolment statistics by a variety of categories of students: numbers of learners from previously disadvantaged groups, homeless learners, those with disabilities and students from informal settlements and in farm schools. It also has many items seeking to elicit specifics of the school infrastructure and equipment: numbers of schools with buildings in a state of disrepair, with a shortage of classrooms and textbooks, without electricity, telephones and adequate toilet facilities, without access to libraries and recreational and sporting facilities. Yet another concern is the number of students residing beyond a five-kilometre radius. There are also sections on budgetary expenditures, and the results of monitoring and evaluation. Many of these indicators are frequently used for educational administrative data as well.

Colombian system for monitoring and evaluating public policy related to the right to education

Recently, the Office of the Ombudsman of Colombia developed a system for monitoring and evaluating public policy in furtherance of the right to education. It is one of a series of initiatives in that country to encourage national, departmental and municipal bodies responsible for devising and implementing public policies to be more oriented toward the effective observance of economic, social and cultural rights (Pérez 2004). The Colombian monitoring and evaluations system involves three phases of work.

The first phase consists in establishing the nature and normative scope of the right to education and the corresponding obligations of the state. In doing so for the right to education, the Office of the Ombudsman drew on international human rights instruments ratified by Colombia, the general comments of the Committee on Economic, Social and Cultural Rights, the observations of the UN special rapporteur on the right to education, the 1991 Colombian constitution and the jurisprudence of its Constitutional Court.

Following an analysis of existing public educational policies and the functions and responsibilities of the different national bodies and levels of authority, the second phase consists in developing a measurement tool comprising questions and indicators for monitoring and evaluating the right to education.

The third phase involves applying the measurement tool and then drafting a report setting out the main achievements and shortcomings of public policies to ensure the effective realization of the right to education, and offering recommendations aimed at better achieving that goal (ibid.).

There is not the space available in this chapter to undertake a comprehensive analysis of this measurement tool, but a few points should be made. Like the work of the South African Human Rights Commission, the Colombian initiative represents a significant effort to date to measure the right to education. There is much in the instrument to commend it as a potential model. Nevertheless, there are some limitations from a human rights perspective. One is that the tool seems to have multiple functions. The concept of the right to education sometimes appears to get submerged in broader concerns with educational development.

The tool merges administrative data on educational status and the evaluation of public educational policies with data more specifically focused on the right to education. For example, one of its goals is to assess whether the education system meets the minimum educational standards established by the state. While a worthwhile objective, this goal is not necessarily rights-oriented. Another is to measure whether there are continually improving material conditions for members of the teaching profession in order to ensure that they receive domestically competitive salaries. Again, such a legitimate concern of educational administrators is not a component of the right to education.

The length and comprehensiveness of this tool are daunting. The measurement tool comprises five parts, several of which are quite detailed. Parts I and II are to be answered by all administrative levels, while the remaining three are specific to a particular administrative level (central government, department or municipal and district – although some questions overlap between the levels). In parts III–V the right to education is broken into a series of subcategories, which are themselves broken into three parts: obligations to be fulfilled immediately; obligations to be filled progressively; and obligations to individuals and population groups requiring special protection. Therefore the use of the instrument may be unwieldy for both the collection of data and their ongoing analysis, particularly if the goal is to assess disadvantaged groups' progressive realization of the right to education.

Yet another limitation is that the Colombian measurement tool does not conform to the threefold categories proposed initially by Paul Hunt and then adopted by the Office of the High Commissioner for Human Rights' expert working group on human rights indicators. Because the Human Rights Ombudsman's office is aware of the legal provisions and institutional infrastructure, there is little in the tool that can be considered to be structural indicators.

In addition, not all of the questions and the data they seek to elicit can be considered to be true indicators. In many cases they approach areas or categories of concern rather than clearly demarcated ways to measure these topics.

Candidate indicators utilizing the OHCHR framework

This author has recently drafted a set of candidate indicators for the right to education using the conceptual framework adopted by the OHCHR expert working group. The indicators are based on the interpretation of the right to education in General Comment No. 13 (Committee on Economic, Social and Cultural Rights 1999b), and made use of previous work on rights-based education indicators by the Colombian Ombudsman and the South African Human Rights Commission. The indicators are included in an appendix to this chapter.

The process of developing the indicators has underscored some of the dilemmas noted in the discussion above on developing rights-based indicators. Although the indicators proposed do not exhaustively cover all dimensions of the right, for example the 4-A scheme is omitted, there are undoubtedly still too many to use for human rights monitoring, especially if the measurement is to be appropriately disaggregated. It is also questionable whether poor countries would have good-quality data available for many of these indicators. Nevertheless, the candidate indicators offer a model of how the three-category framework could be applied to the right to education.

The Right to Take Part in Cultural Life

Article 15(1) of the ICESCR recognizes the right of everyone to take part in cultural life. Several other international instruments mention culture, cultural development and cultural life. Article 2 of the ICESCR recognizes the right of all peoples to dispose freely of their natural wealth and resources based on the principle of mutual benefit. References to the right to participate in cultural life and pursue cultural development also appear in the UN Charter, the UNESCO Constitution, UNESCO's Declaration on the Principles of International Cultural Co-operation, the Convention on the Rights of the Child, the Convention on the Elimination of All Forms of Discrimination against Women and the International Convention on the Elimination of All Forms of Racial Discrimination. At the regional level there are provisions in the American Declaration on the Rights and Duties of Man and the Additional Protocol to the American Convention on Human Rights that echo the language of the Universal Declaration and the ICESCR. And on the national level, many states have incorporated aspects of cultural rights into their constitutions.

Lack of conceptualization

As noted above, a clear conceptualization of a right is a prerequisite to developing indicators. To date, however, there is little agreement as to how to interpret the content of the right to take part in cultural life as enumerated in Article 15(1)(a) of the ICESCR or the resultant obligations on states parties. Cultural rights have been aptly characterized as "undeveloped". Part of the problem is that culture is difficult to translate into legal terms (Donders 2004). Another major issue is the difficulty of defining what we mean by cultural rights and cultural life. Issues of culture, cultural values and cultural rights are often complex and frequently touch on politically sensitive and contested issues (Hansen 2002). In addition, initiatives to deal with cultural rights do not necessarily use a human rights approach.

There are a number of unresolved issues surrounding the right to cultural life. One is the relationship between the narrowly defined right to take part in cultural life enumerated in the ICESCR and the broad group of rights that have a link with culture, such as freedom of thought, conscience and religion (ICCPR Article 18) and the right to education (ICESCR Article 13). A second issue is the interrelationship of the right to take part in cultural life with the other components of Article 15. A third question is the extent to which the right to participate in culture is an individual or a collective right. Traditionally, human rights are considered to be vested in individuals, but many aspects of culture are collective in nature and can only exist when practised by members of a community. A fourth is whether it is feasible to adopt an approach to culture which, consistent with a rights approach, would apply equally to everyone in all societies. Yet another is the conflict between universal human rights standards and cultural relativism, or more specifically how to deal with the dimensions of traditional cultures that are inconsistent with human rights principles.

In 2001 the Committee on Economic, Social and Cultural Rights initiated a process to draft a general comment on the right to take part in culture, in partnership with a group of academics and NGOs. Subsequently, the committee's process was supplanted by an initiative organized by the Interarts Foundation. Working in collaboration with the Universal Forum of Cultures 2004 and UNESCO, the Interarts Foundation organized a series of regional seminars on the theme of cultural rights and cultural indicators of human development. The seminars took place in Amman, Jordan, Maputo, Mozambique, and Sao Paolo, Brazil, in 2004. In theory these seminars were a continuation of the committee's process, but in reality the definition of culture and the goals of these seminars differed so greatly that they bore little relation to the committee's work. Culture was understood within the framework of the Interarts Foundation seminars as an instrument of good governance, integration and socialization to promote the development and well-being of societies. One of the main intentions of the seminars was to submit specific and viable proposals concerning the subjects to the Universal Forum of Cultures, Barcelona, 2004.[16]

The Right to the Benefits of Scientific Progress

The first paragraph of Article 27 of the Universal Declaration states that "Everyone has the right freely to participate in the cultural life of the community, to enjoy the arts and to share in scientific advancement and its benefits." The second paragraph of Article 27 adds another provision: "Everyone has the right to the protection of the moral and material interests resulting from any scientific, literary or artistic production of which he is the author."

The language in Article 15 of the ICESCR builds on but also differs from the Universal Declaration in a number of ways. Much like the Universal Declaration, the first paragraph recognizes three rights – the right of everyone:

(a)   to take part in cultural life;
(b)   to enjoy the benefits of scientific progress and its applications;
(c)   to benefit from the protection of the moral and material interests resulting from any scientific, literary or artistic production of which he is the author.

The responsibilities of states parties to achieve these rights are outlined in paragraphs 2–4:

(2)   The steps to be taken by the States Parties to the present Covenant to achieve the full realization of this right shall include those necessary for the conservation, the development and the diffusion of science and culture.
(3)   The States Parties to the present Covenant undertake to respect the freedom indispensable for scientific research and creative activity.
(4)   The States Parties to the present Covenant recognize the benefits to be derived from the encouragement and development of international contacts and cooperation in the scientific and cultural fields.

The three provisions of ICESCR Article 15 were viewed by drafters as intrinsically related to one another. Three major human rights instruments – the Universal Declaration, the American Declaration and the Covenant – enumerate these rights as components of a single article.

Limited availability of resources for conceptualizing the content of Article 15(1b)2–4

As noted, conceptualizing the scope and limitations of a right and the concomitant obligations of a state party is a prerequisite of developing indicators. There have been few efforts to conceptualize the provisions of Article 15 relating to the development of science. The Committee on Economic, Social and Cultural Rights has not held a day of general discussion on the portions of the article relating to science and technology. Nor has it initiated a process to draft a general comment to clarify the normative content.

There have also been few efforts by other groups to conceptualize this right. During the 1970s the Secretary-General (secretariat) and specialized agencies prepared a number of substantive reports on scientific and technological developments and their impact on human rights for presentation to the General Assembly and the Commission on Human Rights, but these studies did not result in standard-setting. Also in the mid-1970s socialist countries took the initiative and developed the Declaration on the Use of Scientific and Technological Progress in the Interests of Peace and for the Benefit of Mankind.[17] While this declaration was approved by the General Assembly, many Western countries decided to abstain because of the references to "liberation movements" in the text. As an action of the General Assembly it is not legally binding.

The 1975 Declaration on the Use of Scientific and Technological Progress includes the following provisions:

> All States shall take appropriate measures to prevent the use of scientific and technological developments, particularly by the State organs, to limit or interfere with the enjoyment of the human rights and fundamental freedoms of the individual as enshrined in the Universal Declaration of Human Rights, the International Covenants on Human Rights and other relevant international instruments. (Article 2)

> All States shall take measures to extend the benefits of science and technology to all strata of the population and to protect them, both socially and materially, from possible harmful effects of the misuse of scientific and technological developments, including their misuse to infringe upon the rights of the individual or of the group, particularly with regard to respect for privacy and the protection of the human personality and its physical and intellectual integrity. (Article 6)

> All States shall take effective measures, including legislative measures, to prevent and preclude the utilization of scientific and technological achievements to the detriment of human rights and fundamental freedoms and the dignity of the human person. (Article 8)

One of the few sources attempting to flesh out the human right to the benefits of science is a chapter written by Richard Claude in a volume dealing with core obligations of economic, social and cultural rights (Claude 2002). Two dimensions of core obligations that Claude mentions are setting priorities for governmental policy relating to science and creating a regulatory framework. He also makes a pioneering effort to identify violations of this right. However, the chapter has limited relevance for the purposes of developing indicators because it focuses more on scientists' rights and scientific freedom issues than rights to the benefits of science.

In a paper written for a 1998 panel discussion organized by the World Intellectual Property Organization in collaboration with the Office of the High Commissioner for Human Rights (Chapman 1999), the author proposed that the right of everyone to enjoy the benefits of scientific progress and its applications has three central components:

- right of access to beneficial scientific and technological developments;

- a right of choice in determining priorities and making decisions about major scientific and technological developments to receive public support;
- a right to be protected from possible harmful effects of scientific and technological development, on both individual and collective levels.

As interpreted through a human rights lens, a right of access at a minimum entails that the freedom and opportunity to benefit from scientific and technical advancement be broadly diffused within a nation "without discrimination of any kind as to race, colour, sex, language, religion, political or other opinion, national or social origin, property, birth or other status" (ICESCR Article 2(2)). It also requires governments "to ensure the equal right of men and women to the enjoyment" of the benefits (ICESCR Article 3). These obligations have also been interpreted as requiring both negative measures to prevent discrimination and positive "affirmative action" type initiatives to compensate for past discrimination (Alston 1991, 47). To fulfil these requirements, the Committee on Economic, Social and Cultural Rights places considerable emphasis on the realization of the human rights of women, minorities, the poor and other disadvantaged groups both in its reporting guidelines and in its review of state party reports.

What, then, does this mean for interpreting the right to benefit from scientific advances? It certainly imposes a different standard from the current tendency to favour the interests of large corporations or to promote the abstract principle of scientific competitiveness. A human rights approach establishes a requirement for the state to undertake a very rigorous and disaggregated analysis of the likely impact of specific innovations and to utilize these data to assure non-discrimination in the end result. When making choices and decisions, it calls for particular sensitivity to the effect on those groups whose welfare tends to be absent from the calculus of decision-making about scientific developments: the poor, the disadvantaged, racial, ethnic and linguistic minorities, women and rural residents. Consequently, in undertaking these determinations, the status of the middle class, the comforts that are likely to accrue to the affluent or the potential profits to investors count for much less than improving the status of the vulnerable and bringing them up to mainstream standards.

CONCLUSION

The establishment of an agreed framework and methodology for developing human rights indicators through the efforts of the expert working group on human rights indicators of the Office of the High Commissioner for Human Rights represents an important achievement. It fulfils a requirement and hopefully will provide an incentive to other bodies to formulate candidate indicators for specific rights, to field-test these indicators and to disseminate them. The absence of other current initiatives relating to the rights to participation in cultural life and the benefits of science provides UNESCO with a particular opportunity to make an important contribution to conceptualizing the content and sponsoring the development of indicators.

NOTES

1   This definition is adapted from Kapoor (1996).
2   International Covenant on Economic, Social and Cultural Rights, adopted 16 December 1966, 993 UNTS 3 (entered into force 3 January 1976), GA Res. 2200 (XXI), 21 UN GAOR Supp. (No. 16), p. 49, UN Doc. A/6316 (1966).
3   International Covenant on Civil and Political Rights, adopted 16 December 1966, 999 UNTS 171, GA Res. 2200 (XXI), 21 UN GAOR Supp. (No. 16), p. 52, UN Doc. A/6316 (1966).
4   See for example the perspective of the first chair of the Committee on Economic, Social and Cultural Rights, Philip Alston (1987).
5   Millennium Development Goals (MDGs), available at http://mdgs.un.org/unsd/mdg/default.aspx
6   Seventeenth Joint Meeting of the Chairpersons of UN Human Rights Treaty Monitoring Bodies, June 2005, Geneva, Doc. A/60/278, para. 9.
7   Universal Declaration of Human Rights, adopted and proclaimed by the UN General Assembly on 10 December 1948, GA Res. 217 A (III).
8   Convention on the Elimination of All Forms of Discrimination against Women, adopted 18 December 1979, GA Res. 34/180, 32 UN GAOR Supp. (No. 46), p. 193, UN. Doc. A/34/36 (1980), entered into force 3 September 1981.
9   Convention on the Rights of the Child, adopted 20 November 1989, GA Res. 44/25, 44 UN GAOR Supp. (No. 49), p. 165, UN Doc. A/44/736 (1989), entered into force 2 September 1980.
10 This author was then the director of the program and in that role co-organized the workshop.
11 The workshop participants did not include four EFA indicators: intake rates; repetition rates; percentage of pupils mastering a nationally defined basic learning competencies; and literacy gender parity index.
12 Constitution of the Republic of South Africa, para. 184, available at www.polity.org/za/html/govdocs/constitution/saconst.html.
13 The reports are available on the South Africa Human Rights Commission website (www.sahrc.org.za), along with the protocols used to collect data.
14 This author has been present over the years at some of the meetings of the Human Rights Commission with NGOs, academics and representatives of government departments at which this topic has been discussed. See also Klaaren (2005).
15 Available at www.sahrc.org.za/protocols-2003_2004.htm.
16 See the final report of the International Forum on Diversity and Cultural Rights, Sao Paolo, Brazil, 31 March – 2 April 2004.
17 Declaration on the Use of Scientific and Technological Progress in the Interests of Peace and for the Benefit of Mankind, proclaimed by UN General Assembly on 10 November 1975, GA Res. 3384.

REFERENCES

Alston, Philip (1987), "Out of the abyss: The challenges confronting the new UN Committee on Economic, Social and Cultural Rights", *Human Rights Quarterly* 9: 332–81.

—— (1991), "The International Covenant on Economic, Social and Cultural Rights", in *Manual on Human Rights Reporting*, UN Doc. HR/PUB/91/1.

Brand, Danie and Liebenberg, Sandra (2000), "The Second Economic and Social Rights Report", *ESR Review*, 2:4, available at www.communitylawcentre.org.za/ser/esr2000.

Chapman, Audrey R. (1994), "A human rights approach to health care reform", in Audrey R. Chapman (ed.), *Health Care Reform: A Human Rights Approach* (Washington, DC: Georgetown University Press).

—— (1999), "A human rights perspective on intellectual property, scientific progress, and access to the benefits of science", in *Intellectual Property and Human Rights* (Geneva: World Intellectual Property Organization), pp. 127–68.

Claude, Richard Pierre (2002), "Scientists' rights and the human right to the benefits of science", in Audrey R. Chapman and Sage Russell (eds), *Core Obligations: Building a Framework for Economic, Social and Cultural Rights* (Antwerp: Intersentia), pp. 247–77.

Commission on Human Rights (1994), "Question of the realization in all countries of the economic, social and cultural rights contained in the Universal Declaration of Human Rights and in the International Covenant on Economic, Social and Cultural Rights, and study of the special problems which the developing countries face in their efforts to achieve these human rights", 1 March, 1994/20, E/CN.4/1994.

—— (1996), "Question of the realization in all countries of the economic, social and cultural rights contained in the Universal Declaration of Human Rights, and study of special problems which the developing countries face in their efforts to achieve these rights", 11 April, E/CN.4/1996, 1996/11.

—— (1999), "Preliminary report of the special rapporteur on the right to education, Ms. Katarina Tomasevski, submitted in accordance with Commission on Human Rights resolution 1998/33", CHR Fifty-fifth session, 13 January, E/CN.4/1999/49.

—— (2002), "Annual report of the special rapporteur on the right to education, Katarina Tomasevski, submitted pursuant to Commission on Human Rights resolution 2001/29", CHR Fifty-eighth session, E/CN.4/2002/60.

—— (2003), "The right to education, report of the special rapporteur, Katarina Tomasevski, submitted pursuant to Commission on Human Rights resolution 2002/23", CHR Fifty-ninth session, 21 January, E/CN.4/2003/9.

Committee on Economic, Social and Cultural Rights (1999a), "General Comment No. 11: Plans of action for primary education (Article 14 of the Covenant)", CESCR Twentieth session, Geneva, 10 May, E/C.12/1999/4.

—— (1999b), "General Comment No. 13: The right to education (Article 13 of the Covenant)", CESCR Twenty-first session, Geneva, 8 December, E/C.12/1999/10.

—— (2000), "General Comment No. 14: The right to the highest attainable standard of health", CESCR Twenty-second session, Geneva, 11 August, E/C.12/2000/4.

Committee on Economic, Social and Cultural Rights/Commission on Human Rights (2002), "The Millennium Development Goals and economic, social and cultural rights", joint statement by UN Committee on Economic, Social and Cultural Rights and UN Commission on Human Rights' special rapporteurs on economic, social and cultural rights, Geneva, 29 November.

Donders, Yvonne (2004), "Towards a right to cultural identity in international human rights law", paper presented at International Forum on Diversity and Cultural Rights, Sao Paolo, Brazil, 31 March – 2 April, paras 43–5.

Green, Maria (2001), "What we talk about when we talk about indicators: Current approaches to human rights measurement", *Human Rights Quarterly*, 23:4, 1062–97.

Hansen, Stephen A. (2002), "The right to take part in cultural life: Toward defining minimum core obligations related to Article 15(1)(a) of the International Covenant on Economic, Social and Cultural Rights", in Audrey R. Chapman and Sage Russell (eds), *Core Obligations: Building a Framework for Economic, Social and Cultural Rights* (Antwerp: Intersentia), pp. 282–3.

Hunt, Paul (1998), "State obligations, indicators, benchmarks and the right to education", background paper for Committee on Economic, Social and Cultural Rights, June, available at www.unhchr.ch/tbs/doc.nsf/(Symbol)/3e83f2a145015575802566ab0051ce4e?Opendocument.

Hunt, Paul (2003), *Interim Report of the Special Rapporteur of the Commission on Human Rights on the Right of Everyone to Enjoy the Highest Attainable Standard of Physical and Mental Health*, UN General Assembly, Fifty-eighth session, Agenda item 117(c), 10 October, available at http://daccessdds.un.org/doc/UNDOC/GEN/N04/543/38/PDF/N0454338.pdf?OpenElement, pp. 14–29.

International Commission of Jurists (2002), "Economic, social and cultural rights in practice: The right to health", report of 11 April Parallel Meeting, Geneva.

Kapoor, Ilan (1996), *Indicators for Programming in Human Rights and Democratic Development: A Preliminary Study* (Quebec: Political and Social Policies Division, Canadian International Development Agency).

Klaaren, Jonathan (2005), "A second look at the South African Human Rights Commission, access to information, and the promotion of socioeconomic rights", *Human Rights Quarterly*, 27: 539–61.

Office of the High Commissioner for Human Rights (2005), "Indicators for monitoring compliance – Conclusions and recommendations", expert consultation, 29 August (Geneva: Office of the High Commissioner for Human Rights).

—— (2006), "Indicators for monitoring compliance – Conclusions and recommendations", second expert consultation, March (Geneva: Office of the High Commissioner for Human Rights).

Pérez, Luis Eduardo (2004) *System for Monitoring and Evaluating Public Educational Policy in Furtherance of the Right to Education* (Bogotá: Office of the Ombudsman of Colombia).

Roaf, Virginia, Khalfan, Ashfaq and Langford, Malcolm (2005), "Monitoring implementation of the right to water: A framework for developing indicators", based on proceedings of a workshop Brot für die Welt (Bread for the World), October 2004, organized by the Heinrich Böll Foundation and the Centre on Housing Rights and Evictions, Centre on Housing Rights and Evictions Global Issue Papers No. 14, March.

Türk, Danilo (1990), *The New International Economic Order and the Promotion of Human Rights: Realization of Economic, Social and Cultural Rights*, report by special rapporteur, Sub-Commission on Prevention of Discrimination and Protection of Minorities, Forty-second Session, Provisional Agenda Item 7, para. 96. UN Doc. E/CN.4/Sub.2/1990/19.

UNDP (2000), *Human Development Report 2000: Human Rights and Human Development* (New York and Oxford: Oxford University Press).

United Nations (1993), *Report of the Seminar on Appropriate Indicators to Measure Achievements in the Progressive Realization of Economic, Social and Cultural Rights*, World Conference on Human Rights, UN Doc. A/CONF.157/PC/73.

World University Service-International (1999), *Report of the Workshop on Indicators to Monitor the Progressive Realisation of the Right to Education*, 9 May (Geneva: World University Service-International).

APPENDIX: CANDIDATE INDICATORS FOR THE RIGHT TO EDUCATION

Structural Indicators

Structure

Which levels of the political system have responsibilities for the provision of education:
  (a) National (yes/no)
  (b) Regional, state, or provincial level (yes/no)
  (c) Local, town, or municipal level (yes/no)

Constitutional provisions

Does the country's Constitution include education as a right? (yes/no)

If so,
  (a) is the provision of universal education a directive principle of state policy? (yes/no)
  (b) is the right to education an entitlement? (yes/no)
    • for universal primary education? (yes/no)
    • for universal secondary education? (yes/no)
  (c) Does the Constitution specify the right of access to education without discrimination? (yes/no)
  (d) Does the Constitution recognize the right of adults who have not received of completed the whole period of their primary education to a basic education? (yes/no)

Legislation

Does the state have legislation expressly recognizing the right to education? (yes/no)

Does the legislation recognize the right of children to a place in primary school? (yes/no)

Is there legislation making primary education compulsory? (yes/no)

If there is legislation making education compulsory, specify the ages and/or number of years:
  • Compulsory beginning at age _____
  • Compulsory ending at age _____
  • Compulsory for _____ number of years

Is there legislation making primary education free to all? (yes/no)
Is there legislation expressly prohibiting local governments or schools from charging supplementary fees for:

(a) Books? (yes/no)
(b) School supplies? (yes/no)
(c) Construction or maintenance of school buildings? (yes/no)
(d) Teacher's salaries? (yes/no)

Is there legislation providing for the right of access to public educational institutions and programmes on a non-discriminatory basis? (yes/no)

Is there legislation expressly prohibiting any form of discrimination for students on the basis of
(a) Sex? (yes/no)
(b) Race or colour? (yes/no)
(c) Language? (yes/no)
(d) Religion? (yes/no)
(e) Political or other opinion? (yes/no)
(f) National or social origin? (yes/no)
(g) Financial resources? (yes/no)

Is there legislation expressly prohibiting discrimination in the recruitment and promotion of teachers on the basis of
(a) Sex? (yes/no)
(b) Race or colour? (yes/no)
(c) Language? (yes/no)
(d) Religion? (yes/no)
(e) Political or other opinion? (yes/no)
(f) National or social origin? (yes/no)
(g) Financial resources? (yes/no)

Is there legislation recognizing the right of handicapped persons with disabilities to education? (yes/no)
• If so, does the legislation make provision for the necessary equipment and support to enable handicapped students to attend school? (yes/no)

Is there legislation prohibiting early marriages (below the age of 16) that would interfere with school attendance? (yes/no)

Is there legislation restricting child labour to encourage children to attend school? (yes/no)

Private schooling

Is there legislation expressly recognizing the liberty of individuals and groups to establish and direct educational institutions, subject to the requirement that the education given in such institutions shall conform to such minimum standards as may be laid down by the state? (yes/no)

Is there legislation expressly recognizing the right of parents and, when applicable, legal guardians to choose for their children schools, other than those established by the public authorities, which conform to the minimum educational standards as may be laid down or approved by the state? (yes/no)

Is there legislation expressly recognizing the right of parents and, when applicable, legal guardians to ensure the religious and moral education of children in conformity with their own convictions? (yes/no)

Treaty ratification

Has the state ratified the following international treaties:
  (a) ICESCR? (yes/no)
  (b) CRC? (yes/no)
  (c) CEDAW? (yes/no)
  (d) ICERD? (yes/no)

Has the state ratified any regional human rights instruments recognizing the right to education? (yes/no)

National strategy and plan of action

Does the state have a policy to protect girls' access to education by ensuring that third parties, including parents and employers, do not prevent girls from going to school? (yes/no)

Does the state have a national educational strategy and plan of action? (yes/no)
  (a) Does the national educational strategy include a timeline for achieving the goals? (yes/some/no)
  (b) Does the national educational strategy have a monitoring mechanism for assessing the attainment of the goals? (yes/some/no)

If yes, does the national educational strategy and plan of action expressly include the goals of
  (a) Universal, compulsory, and free primary education? (yes/no/not relevant because already achieved the goal)
  (b) Progressive introduction of free secondary education (yes/no/not relevant because already achieved the goal)

Gender issues

Have public policy measures been taken to
  (a) Remove gender bias from primary education primers? (yes/no)
  (b) Remove gender bias from teachers' educational strategies? (yes/no)
  (c) Remove gender bias in terms of male and female roles in school? (yes/no)
  (d) Remove gender bias in terms of gender-targeted optional subject? (yes/no)
  (e) Train teachers in gender issues? (yes/no)

Are there opportunities for pregnant girls to continue their education? (yes/no)

Curriculum

Does the state establish minimal standards regulating the curriculum and the quality of study programmes and educational methods? (yes/no)
    (a) If so, are these national standards for the entire country? (yes/no)
    (b) Or are the standards set by provincial, regional, state and/or municipal governments? (yes/no)

Is there an inspection system to monitor and evaluate the quality and content of education? (yes/no)

Does the official curriculum include human rights education and/or values, such as respect for human dignity, non-discrimination and equal status before the law
    (a) In primary school? (yes/no)
    (b) In secondary school? (yes/no)

Does the official curriculum include units on the constitution and democracy? (yes/no)
    (a) In primary school? (yes/no)
    (b) In secondary school? (yes/no)

Is there legislation mandating respect in the educational system for the culture and religious practices of various groups and communities in the society? (yes/no)

Human rights institutions

Does the state have human rights institutions (commission or ombudsperson) mandated to monitor the right to education?

If yes, does the human rights institution collect data and issue regular reports on the status of the achievement of the right to education? (yes/irregularly/no)

Participation

Does the state have a mechanism to consult representatives of teachers and parents in the formation of educational policy, other than normal political institutions, at the
    (a) National level? (yes/no)
    (b) Provincial, state or regional level? (yes/some/no)
    (c) Local level? (yes/some/no)

Process Indicators

Basic financial context

Percentage of GDP devoted to education
  (a) Total all sources
  (b) Public sources
  (c) Private sources

Percentage of budget allocated overall to education by
  (a) National government
  (b) Regional, state, or provincial governments
    • Regional government by name
    • Regional government by name
    • Regional government by name
  (c) Local governments

Percentage of national budget allocated to
  (a) Primary education
  (b) Secondary education
  (c) Vocational training
  (d) Higher education
  (e) Teacher training
  (f) Special disbursements to improve the gender balance
  (g) Targeted aid to poor localities and areas of the country

Percentage of total spending by regional, state or provincial governments allocated to
  (a) Primary education
  (b) Secondary education
  (c) Vocational training
  (d) Higher education
  (e) Teacher training
  (f) Special disbursements to improve the gender balance
  (g) Targeted aid to poor localities and areas of the country

Percentage of each region, state or provincial government – listed by name – allocated to
  (a) Primary education
  (b) Secondary education
  (c) Vocational training
  (d) Higher education
  (e) Teacher training
  (f) Special disbursements to improve the gender balance
  (g) Targeted aid to poor localities and areas of the country

Percentage of total spending by local governments allocated to
  (a) Primary education
  (b) Secondary education

(c) Vocational training
(d) Higher education
(e) Teacher training
(f) Special disbursements to improve the gender balance
(g) Targeted aid to schools serving poor and vulnerable groups

Amount of educational funding received from foreign bilateral and multilateral funding sources:
(a) Total amount for most recent year _____
(b) Percentage of total public educational budget _____

Was there overspending by more than 10 per cent of the amount allocated for education in the last fiscal year by the
(a) National government? (yes/no)
(b) Provincial, regional or state governments? (yes/some/no)
   • If some or yes, by how much cumulatively? _____
   • If some or yes, list the provinces, regional or state government in ascending order of overspending:

_____
_____
_____

Was there underspending by more than 10 per cent of the amount allocated for education in the last fiscal year for which data are available by the
(a) National government? (yes/no)
   • If yes, by how much? _____
(b) Provincial, regional or state governments/ (yes/some/no)
   • If some or yes, by how much cumulatively? _____
   • If some or yes, list the provinces, regional or state governments in ascending order of underspending:

_____
_____
_____

Charges payable in public education

Specify whether or not there are charges for each of the following components in public primary education
(a) Enrolment fees (yes/no)
(b) Tuition fees (yes/n
(c) Uniforms (yes/no)
(d) Schools supplies and educational materials (yes/no)
(e) School meals (yes/no)
(f) School transport (yes/no)

Total average cost per year per family for a student in a public primary school _____

Is there a special funding system to ensure access to primary education for students from the following population groups:

(a) Low income groups
(b) Female students
(c) Persons with disabilities
(d) Displaced persons
(e) Groups living in dispersed rural areas

Specify whether or not there are charges for each of the following components in public secondary education:
(a) Enrolment fees (yes/no)
(b) Tuition fees (yes/no)
(c) Uniforms (yes/no)
(d) School supplies and educational materials (yes/no)
(e) School meals (yes/no)
(f) School transport (yes/no)

Total average cost per year per family for a student in a public secondary school _____

Is there a special funding system to ensure access to secondary education for students from the following population groups:
(a) Low income groups? (yes/no)
(b) Female students? (yes/no)
(c) Persons with disabilities? (yes/no)
(d) Displaced persons? (yes/no)

School facilities

Primary schools (infrastructure)	*Total*	*Rural*	*Urban*	*Private*	*Public*
Total number of schools					
Number of schools with buildings in a state of disrepair					
Number of schools that have a shortage of classrooms					
Number of schools with inadequate textbooks					
Number of schools with no water within walking distance					
Number of schools with lack of access to sanitary facilities					
Number of schools with no electricity					
Number of schools with no telephones					
Number of schools with inadequate toilet facilities					
Number of schools with lack of access to library facilities					

Secondary schools (infrastructure)	Total	Rural	Urban	Private	Public
Number of schools with buildings in a state of disrepair					
Number of schools with inadequate textbooks					
Number of schools with no water within walking distance					
Number of schools with no electricity					
Number of schools with inadequate toilet facilities					
Number of schools with lack of access to computers					
Number of schools with lack of access to library facilities					
Number of schools with lack of access to recreational and sporting facilities					

Physical accessibility

Percentage of children having to travel more than 1 kilometre to reach primary school
   (a) Nationally
   (b) In rural areas
   (c) In urban areas

Monitoring

Does the national government collect data adequate to evaluate performance under the strategy/national action plan, particularly in relation to vulnerable groups? (yes/no)
   (a) Through educational statistics collected through school reporting? (yes/no)
   (b) Through national household surveys? (yes/no)
   (c) Through national census surveys? (yes/no)

Are data collected at the primary level that disaggregate on the basis of students'
   (a) Age? (yes/no)
   (b) Sex? (yes/no)
   (c) Urban/rural location? (yes/no)
   (d) Income of family? (yes/no)
   (e) Linguistic or ethnic group? (yes/no)
   (f) Disabilities? (yes/no)

Are data collected at the secondary level that disaggregate on the basis of students'
   (a) Age? (yes/no)

(b) Sex? (yes/no)
(c) Urban/rural location? (yes/no)
(d) Income of family? (yes/no)
(e) Linguistic or ethnic group? (yes/no)
(f) Disabilities? (yes/no)

Are data collected at the higher education level that disaggregate on the basis of students'
(a) Age? (yes/no)
(b) Sex? (yes/no)
(c) Urban/rural background? (yes/no)
(d) Income of family? (yes/no)
(e) Linguistic or ethnic group? (yes/no)
(f) Disabilities? (yes/no)

Are reports issued annually analysing these data that cover trends at the
(a) National level? (yes/no/sometimes)
(b) State/regional or provincial levels? (yes/no/some)

Are disaggregated data publicly available related to
(a) Primary education? (yes/no/some)
(b) Secondary education? (yes/no/some)
(c) Higher education? (yes/no/some)

Reporting

Number of reports the state has submitted to the UN treaty-based bodies monitoring the following treaties that include the status of the right to education
(a) ICESCR
(b) CRC
(c) CEDAW
(d) ICERD

Participation

Did the state consult with a wide range of representatives of the following groups in the past year about issues relating to formulating, implementing and/or monitoring national educational policy:
(a) Non-governmental organizations? (yes/no/some)
(b) Educational professional organizations? (yes/no/some)
(c) Local governments? (yes/no/some)
(d) Community leaders? (yes/no/some)
(e) Representatives of vulnerable groups? (yes/no/some)
(f) Private sector? (yes/no/some)

In the past year, did the state disseminate information on its educational policies and relevant educational data to
(a) Non-governmental organizations? (yes/no/some)

(b) Educational professional organizations? (yes/no/some)
(c) Local governments? (yes/no/some)
(d) Community leaders? (yes/no/some)
(e) Representatives of vulnerable groups? (yes/no/some)
(f) Private sector? (yes/no/some)

Teacher availability and qualifications

Number of years of education for primary school teachers to meet certification requirements
(a) for lower primary school teaching _____ years
(b) for upper primary school teaching _____ years
(c) for lower secondary school teaching _____ years
(d) for upper secondary school teaching _____ years

Percentage of teachers meeting the minimum certification requirements:
(a) in lower primary school classes (grades 1–3)
  • in urban areas _____
  • in rural areas _____
(b) in upper primary school classes (grades 4 and above)
  • in urban areas _____
  • in rural areas _____
(c) in lower secondary school teaching (first three years)
  • in urban areas _____
  • in rural areas _____
(d) in upper secondary school teaching (fourth year and above)
  • in urban areas _____
  • in rural areas _____

What is the learner/educator ratio
(a) in lower primary school classes (grades 1–3)
  • in urban areas?
  • in rural areas?
  • in public schools?
  • in private schools?
(b) in upper primary school classes (fourth year and above)
  • in urban areas?
  • in rural areas?
  • in public schools?
  • in private schools?
(c) in lower secondary school teaching (first three years)
  • in urban areas?
  • in rural areas?
  • in public schools?
  • in private schools?
(d) in upper secondary school teaching (fourth year and above)
  • in urban areas?
  • in rural areas?

- in public schools?
- in private schools?

What is the percentage of public schools with a sufficient number of qualified teachers
  (a) primary schools
  - in urban areas?
  - in rural areas?
  - in sex-segregated schools catering to girls?
  (b) secondary schools
  - in urban areas?
  - in rural areas?
  - in sex-segregated schools catering to girls?

Complaints and court cases

Number of administrative complaints that considered educational rights in the last five years regarding:
  (a) Availability or accessibility of primary education
  (b) Funding of primary education
  (c) Availability or accessibility of secondary education
  (d) Accessibility of higher education
  (e) Discrimination issues
  (f) Registration or closing of private schools
  (g) Parents' rights to ensure the religious and moral education of their children in conformity with their own convictions

Number of court cases that considered educational rights in the last five years regarding:
  (a) Availability or accessibility of primary education
  (b) Funding of primary education
  (c) Availability or accessibility of secondary education
  (d) Accessibility of higher education
  (e) Discrimination issues
  (f) Registration or closing of private schools
  (g) Parents' right to ensure the religious and moral education of their children in conformity with their own convictions

Number of complaints filed in the past five years regarding:
  (a) Availability or accessibility of secondary education
  (b) Funding of secondary education
  (c) Availability or accessibility of secondary education
  (d) Accessibility of higher education
  (e) Discrimination issues
  (f) Registration or closing of private schools
  (g) Parents' rights to ensure the religious and moral education of their children in conformity with their own convictions

Number of court cases filed in the past five years regarding
  (a) Availability or accessibility of secondary education
  (b) Funding of secondary education
  (c) Availability or accessibility of secondary education
  (d) Accessibility of higher education
  (e) Discrimination issues
  (f) Registration or closing of private schools
  (g) Parents' rights to ensure the religious and moral education of their children in conformity with their own convictions

School registrations

Number of schools that the government has refused to register in the past year
  (a) primary schools
  (b) secondary schools
  (c) vocational schools
  (d) institutions of higher learning

School closings

Number of schools that the government has temporarily closed in the past year
  (a) primary schools
  (b) secondary schools
  (c) vocational schools
  (d) institutions of higher learning

Number of schools that the government has permanently closed in the past year
  (a) primary schools
  (b) secondary schools
  (c) vocational schools
  (d) institutions of higher learning

Outcome Indicators

Literacy rate

Literacy rate		Urban		Rural	
	Total	Female	Male	Female	Male
Age 12–18					
Age 19 and over					

School attendance

(a) percentage of eligible children of primary school age attending school (net enrolment ratio)
- total
- females
- males
- in urban areas
- in rural areas
- among low income groups
- with disabilities
- by provinces/states with full listing

(b) percentage of total primary school population who are older than the official primary school age
- total
- in urban areas
- in rural areas
- by provinces/states with full listing

(c) percentage of total students in primary school who are enrolled in private schools
- total
- in urban areas
- in rural areas
- by states/provinces with full listing

(d) percentage of eligible children of secondary school age who attend secondary school
- total
- females
- males
- in urban areas
- in rural areas
- by states/provinces with full listing

(e) percentage of total students in secondary school who are enrolled in private schools
- total
- in urban areas
- in rural areas
- by states/provinces with full listing

(f) percentage of total students in primary school attending single-sex institutions
- total
- in urban areas
- in rural areas
- by states/provinces with full listing

(g) percentage of total students in secondary school attending single-sex institutions
  - total
  - in urban areas
  - in rural areas
  - females
  - males
  - by states/provinces with full listing

Educational attainment

Percentage of children entering primary school who complete the full number of years prescribed for the primary school cycle:
  (a) total
  (b) urban
  (c) rural
  (d) females
  (e) males
  (f) by states/provinces with full listing

Percentage of primary school leavers who pass the primary school leaving exam if one is given:
  (a) total
  (b) urban
  (c) rural
  (d) females
  (e) males
  (f) by states/provinces with full listing

Percentage of number of primary school leavers who enter secondary school
  (a) total
  (b) urban
  (c) rural
  (d) females
  (e) males
  (f) by states/provinces with full listing

Percentage of secondary school students in their final year who pass the requisite examinations
  (a) total
  (b) urban
  (c) rural
  (d) females
  (e) males
  (f) by states/provinces with full listing

4 The Applicability of Human Rights Between Private Parties

CHRISTIAN COURTIS

INTRODUCTION

One of the main features of the notion of "human rights" is that they generate duties for states. On this basis, a widespread scholarly position claims that human rights impose duties *only* on states, and thus are not applicable in relations between private parties.[1] The aim of this chapter is critically to discuss this idea, suggesting arguments that may lead to the opposite conclusion.

The chapter will claim that the idea that human rights are not applicable between private parties is exaggerated and wrong. The basis for the mistake is the confusion between several normative levels that should be distinguished: once those distinctions are made, and within the proper boundaries, there is no theoretical inconvenience in sustaining that human rights norms can also impose duties on private parties and be the ground for legal claims between them.

SOME DIVERGENCES BETWEEN LEGAL DOCTRINE AND LEGAL TEXTS

A simple but useful distinction may help to clarify the problem under examination. The notion of "legal duty" or "legal obligation" is related to the conduct imposed by a legal norm – a mandate or a prohibition. The notion of "liability" or "legal responsibility" is related to the sanction imposed by a legal norm for failure to comply with a legal duty (Kelsen 1979, 129–38). While there is usually coincidence between the passive subject of the legal duty – the person whose conduct is a matter of prohibition or mandate – and the passive subject of a sanction – the person who has to bear the sanction – this is not always the case. In domestic law, for example, parents may be liable for their children's conduct, employers may be liable for their employees' conduct, shareholders may be liable for their partners' or the enterprise managers' conduct, etc.

The first aspect that it is important to analyse to understand the idea that human rights cannot impose duties on private parties is linked to the privileged source of the notion of human rights – that is, international law. While in the domestic constitutional law tradition, rights, which are granted a special level of protection, are often called "fundamental rights" or "constitutional rights", the label "human rights" has mainly derived from international law, at least since the proclamation of the Universal Declaration of Human Rights in 1948.[2] The growing task of recognition and codification of a number of rights considered inherent to the human condition, and thus universal, has developed under the label of "international human rights law". However, it is useful to point out that, in spite of the pre-eminence of the international law sources, the label is not completely alien to domestic law, and there are many examples of its usage in domestic legislation and institutions.[3] It is important to underscore here that the name "human rights" is mainly used – in both international and domestic law – to refer to rights included in international norms.

It is thus important to acknowledge that, due to the history and the present configuration of international law, states are its privileged subjects (see, generally, Barberis 1984). This principle, which still governs international law to a great extent, has some exceptions – the most notorious being international criminal law, where individuals are subjected to duties and liable for violations of international norms (Ambos and Karayan 1999; Blanc Altemir 1990; Fernández Flores 1991; Gil-Gil 1999; Gómez Guillamón 1999). But the rule continues to be that, beyond other passive subjects of international law – such as international organizations – the state still bears most of the duties and is mainly responsible for non-compliance with international norms.[4]

Beyond establishing lists of rights in favour of human beings, international human rights instruments design mechanisms and monitoring bodies to assess states' compliance with their duties in this field. It is clear that, before those bodies, liability is placed upon states that have ratified the respective treaties.[5] In this sense, and leaving aside the limited but important exception of international criminal law, stating that human rights norms are directed to states and not to private parties is correct – but relatively trivial. It means that private parties are not subject to international human rights treaty-monitoring bodies, and thus are not passive subjects of international law sanctions. The question does not seem to pose major difficulties.

Nevertheless, this argument does not exhaust the matter at all. Saying that international norms mainly impose duties on states only informs us about a central feature of modern international law. However, in order to be able to understand fully the matter at stake, we need to take a more detailed look to the content of international norms which enshrine human rights. If one takes the time to review the concrete content of the catalogue of human rights included in international norms, the panorama one faces is surely more complex than could have been inferred from naively assuming that international law only imposes duties on states. To do this, it is necessary to analyse the concrete configuration of the rights established in international human rights instruments, their structure, their content, the duties that emanate from them and their active and passive subjects – that is, the legal positions designated by those rights. Once this exercise is completed, the normative span appears more varied than under the initial assumption.

To begin with, it is relatively common to find human rights treaty norms which establish rights whose passive subject is a private party. Many examples could illustrate this statement.

Duties Imposed on Private Parties

It seems evident that those clauses of the International Covenant on Economic, Social and Cultural Rights which establish labour-related rights do not only refer to cases where the state is the employer: they include cases where the employer is a private party. Take, for example, the right to fair wages and equal remuneration for work of equal value, in particular between men and women (Article 7, para. a.1), safe and healthy working conditions (Article 7, para. b) and rest, leisure and reasonable limitation of working hours and periodic holidays with pay, as well as remuneration for public holidays (Article 7, para. d): these clauses are obviously meant to impose duties on both public and private employers.

The Inter-American Court of Human Rights (2003) plainly confirmed this idea in its Advisory Opinion OC-18/03, required by the Mexican government. In that advisory opinion, requested to clarify the rights of undocumented migrant workers, the Inter-American Court strongly states that the fundamental labour rights of migrant workers derived from international law should be respected by both the state and private employers. The court argued that:

> In an employment relationship regulated by private law, the obligation to respect human rights between individuals should be taken into consideration. That is, the positive obligation of the State to ensure the effectiveness of the protected human rights gives rise to effects in relation to third parties (erga omnes). This obligation has been developed in legal writings, and particularly by the *Drittwirkung* theory, according to which fundamental rights must be respected by both the public authorities and by individuals with regard to other individuals. (Ibid., para. 1406)[6]

In this way, the obligation to respect and ensure human rights, which normally has effects on the relations between the state and the individuals subject to its jurisdiction, also has effects on relations between individuals. As regards this advisory opinion, the said effects of the obligation to respect human rights in relations between individuals are defined in the context of the private employment relationship, under which the employer must respect the human rights of his workers (ibid., para. 146).

> In labor relations, employers must protect and respect the rights of workers, whether these relations occur in the public or private sector. The obligation to respect the human rights of migrant workers has a direct effect on any type of

employment relationship, when the State is the employer, when the employer is a third party, and when the employer is a natural or legal person. (Ibid., para. 151)

Moving even further, the court considers that the prohibition of discrimination is a *jus cogens* duty, and thus is applicable both to states – whether or not they have ratified human rights treaties – and to individuals. The court says that:

> Finally [...], the contents of the preceding paragraphs are applicable to all the OAS Member States. The effects of the fundamental principle of equality and non-discrimination encompass all States, precisely because this principle, which belongs to the realm of *jus cogens* and is of a peremptory character, entails obligations *erga omnes* of protection that bind all States and give rise to effects with regard to third parties, including individuals. (Ibid., para. 110[7])

One can offer further examples of this point. Article 14 of the American Convention on Human Rights includes, in the following terms, the right to reply or make a correction:

> 1. Anyone injured by inaccurate or offensive statements or ideas disseminated to the public in general by a legally regulated medium of communication has the right to reply or to make a correction using the same communications outlet, under such conditions as the law may establish.

> 2. The correction or reply shall not in any case remit other legal liabilities that may have been incurred.

> 3. For the effective protection of honor and reputation, every publisher, and every newspaper, motion picture, radio, and television company, shall have a person responsible who is not protected by immunities or special privileges.

It seems obvious that this clause does not only refer to state-owned media, but *mainly* to private media. The three sections of the article impose duties on both public and private media, and establish guarantees in favour of the individual aggrieved by the inaccurate or offensive information.

Article 25 paragraph 1, termed "Right to Judicial Protection", offers another interesting example. According to this clause,

> Everyone has the right to simple and prompt recourse, or any other effective recourse, to a competent court or tribunal for protection against acts that violate his fundamental rights recognized by the constitution or laws of the state concerned or by this Convention, even though such violation may have been committed by persons acting in the course of their official duties.

Several comments could be made here. First, the clause grants a cause of action against violations of fundamental rights recognized by the constitution of the state party, by its laws or by the convention itself. If any of those sources recognizes fundamental rights between private parties, that means that the "simple and prompt recourse" could be directed against the private party that has affected the right. We have seen that, at least in the case of the right to reply, the convention enshrines a right creating duties for private parties:

thus, the "recourse" provided by Article 25 paragraph 1 could be employed to sue private parties.[8] Constitutions frequently recognize fundamental rights between private parties and – even more frequently – domestic statutes and laws do so. Thus, in these cases, the legal remedy provided by Article 25 paragraph 1 would be directed against a private party.

The wording of the final part of the section ("even though such violation may have been committed by persons acting in the course of their official duties") suggests that there could possibly be obstacles to taking state officials or the state to court – that may explain the insistence on identifying the state as a potential defendant. By contrast, it seems to assume the lack of obstacles to taking private parties to court.

The Convention on the Rights of the Child imposes several duties on private parties. Some of them read as follows:

Article 3

1. In all actions concerning children, whether undertaken by public or private social welfare institutions, courts of law, administrative authorities or legislative bodies, the best interests of the child shall be a primary consideration.

Article 18

1. States Parties shall use their best efforts to ensure recognition of the principle that both parents have common responsibilities for the upbringing and development of the child. Parents or, as the case may be, legal guardians, have the primary responsibility for the upbringing and development of the child. The best interests of the child will be their basic concern.

Article 27

1. States Parties recognize the right of every child to a standard of living adequate for the child's physical, mental, spiritual, moral and social development.

2. The parent(s) or others responsible for the child have the primary responsibility to secure, within their abilities and financial capacities, the conditions of living necessary for the child's development.

All of these clauses impose duties on private parties. Article 3 makes explicit the extension of the duty to consider the best interest of the child to private social welfare institutions; Article 18 places upon parents or legal guardians the "responsibility" – in proper legal terms, the duty – for the upbringing and the development of the child, and the consideration of the best interests of the child. Article 27.2 refers again to the "responsibility" of parents to secure the conditions of living necessary for the child's development.

State Powers to Impose Duties on Private Parties

In many cases, human rights treaties establish powers for the state to impose duties – burdens such as prohibitions or imperatives – and also liabilities on private parties. That is, in many human rights norms the ultimate passive subject of both duties and sanctions is a private individual.[9] The Convention for the Elimination of All Forms of Discrimination against Women could be read as a complete catalogue of state powers oriented to forbid discrimination against women both in the public *and* in the private spheres. One can quote three examples, among many others:

Article 2

States Parties ... undertake:

(e) To take all appropriate measures to eliminate discrimination against women by any person, organization or enterprise ...

Article 5

States Parties shall take all appropriate measures:

(a) To modify the social and cultural patterns of conduct of men and women, with a view to achieving the elimination of prejudices and customary and all other practices which are based on the idea of the inferiority or the superiority of either of the sexes or on stereotyped roles for men and women ...

Article 11

2. In order to prevent discrimination against women on the grounds of marriage or maternity and to ensure their effective right to work, States Parties shall take appropriate measures:

(a) To prohibit, subject to the imposition of sanctions, dismissal on the grounds of pregnancy or of maternity leave and discrimination in dismissals on the basis of marital status;

(b) To introduce maternity leave with pay or with comparable social benefits without loss of former employment, seniority or social allowances ...

It seems apparent that the three quoted clauses intend to extend their realm to private party relations, and not only to those between private parties and the state. Article 2 para. e explicitly refers to private parties as subjects of state regulation. The modification of "social and cultural patterns of conduct" does not limit itself to state conduct, but basically includes "men and women" of civil society. The imposition of prohibitions (such as of dismissal of women on grounds of pregnancy) and of mandates (such as the introduction of maternity leave) obviously includes private employers, which will be respectively bound by the prohibition and required to pay for the leave. The Committee on the Elimination of Discrimination against Women (1992, para. 9) held, in this regard, that:

It is emphasized, however, that discrimination under the Convention is not restricted to action by or on behalf of Governments (see articles 2 (e), 2 (f) and 5). For example, under article 2 (e) the Convention calls on States parties to take all appropriate measures to eliminate discrimination against women by any person, organization or enterprise.[10]

Another anti-discriminatory instrument, the Convention for the Elimination of All Forms of Racial Discrimination, includes similar clauses. For instance, its Article 2 para. d provides that:

> Each State Party shall prohibit and bring to an end, by all appropriate means, including legislation as required by circumstances, racial discrimination by any persons, group or organization.

This type of clause is not alien to the American Convention on Human Rights. For instance, the convention establishes that:

> Any propaganda for war and any advocacy of national, racial, or religious hatred that constitute incitements to lawless violence or to any other similar action against any person or group of persons on any grounds including those of race, color, religion, language, or national origin shall be considered as offenses punishable by law. (Artlcle 13.5)

> Usury and any other form of exploitation of man by man shall be prohibited by law. (Article 21.3)

State Duties to Prevent Violations by Private Parties

Thirdly, many international human rights treaty clauses explicitly establish state duties to prevent illegal conduct of private parties or impose sanctions when such conduct affects a good protected by a human right – such as life, health, freedom of movement, freedom of expression, bodily integrity, etc. That is, human rights norms authorize the state to act against a private party the conduct of which threatens or assaults that good. This means that human rights norms force such private parties at least to bear the consequences of the state's protective or punitive action. As in these cases there is coincidence between the passive subject of the preventive or punitive action and the author of the conduct deemed to threaten or affect the good protected by a human right, one may go further and say that human rights create a duty on private parties not to affect the good. The Convention on the Rights of the Child includes a long list of examples:

Article 19

1. States Parties shall take all appropriate legislative, administrative, social and educational measures to protect the child from all forms of physical or mental violence, injury or abuse, neglect or negligent treatment, maltreatment or exploitation, including sexual abuse, while in the care of parent(s), legal guardian(s) or any other person who has the care of the child.

2. Such protective measures should, as appropriate, include effective procedures for the establishment of social programmes to provide necessary support for the

child and for those who have the care of the child, as well as for other forms of prevention and for identification, reporting, referral, investigation, treatment and follow-up of instances of child maltreatment described heretofore, and, as appropriate, for judicial involvement.

Article 32

1. States Parties recognize the right of the child to be protected from economic exploitation and from performing any work that is likely to be hazardous or to interfere with the child's education, or to be harmful to the child's health or physical, mental, spiritual, moral or social development.

Article 33

States Parties shall take all appropriate measures, including legislative, administrative, social and educational measures, to protect children from the illicit use of narcotic drugs and psychotropic substances as defined in the relevant international treaties, and to prevent the use of children in the illicit production and trafficking of such substances.

Article 34

States Parties undertake to protect the child from all forms of sexual exploitation and sexual abuse. For these purposes, States Parties shall in particular take all appropriate national, bilateral and multilateral measures to prevent:

(a) The inducement or coercion of a child to engage in any unlawful sexual activity;

(b) The exploitative use of children in prostitution or other unlawful sexual practices;

(c) The exploitative use of children in pornographic performances and materials.

Article 35

States Parties shall take all appropriate national, bilateral and multilateral measures to prevent the abduction of, the sale of or traffic in children for any purpose or in any form.

Article 36

States Parties shall protect the child against all other forms of exploitation prejudicial to any aspects of the child's welfare.

But duties for private parties to respect other individuals' rights are not limited to cases of explicit provisions. Influential human rights scholars have developed an interpretative scheme, consisting in "levels of duties", applicable to every human right – which has actually been adopted by human rights treaty-monitoring bodies.[11] The second "level" of duties consists in those state duties regarding the need to control potential affections of the good protected by a right produced by private parties – these are called "duties to protect". Examples and case law[12] are pervasive: when enshrining legal goods such as life, bodily integrity, freedom of expression, privacy, health or housing, international human rights treaties prescribe their protection, regardless of who threatens them – the state or a private party. Thus, according to this doctrine, every human right is the source of a state duty to protect, and the previously explained argument is applicable to it: private aggressors should bear the protective or punitive action of the state, and have a duty not to affect those goods.[13]

The European Court of Human Rights offers a good illustration of this argument. In the case of *A. v the United Kingdom*, the court found that the beating of a young English boy by his stepfather constituted "inhuman or degrading punishment", and that UK domestic law, which provided the stepfather with the common law defence of "reasonable chastisement", failed to provide adequate protection to the victim. The court held that:

> the obligation on the High Contracting Parties under Article 1 of the Convention to secure to everyone within their jurisdiction the rights and freedoms defined in the Convention, taken together with Article 3, requires States to take measures designed to ensure that individuals within their jurisdiction are not subjected to torture or inhuman or degrading treatment or punishment, *including such ill-treatment administered by private individuals.*[14]

The court concluded (para. 22) that the European Convention on Human Rights required the state to offer the victim "protection, in the form of effective deterrence" against serious breaches of personal integrity, and that the existence of a defence that prevented the state from punishing the stepfather amounted to a breach of Article 3 of the treaty. Thus, under this judgment, the stepfather's beating amounted to "inhuman or degrading punishment" – that is, to a punishable breach of a legal duty; the existence of a legal defence for adults beating children amounted to a state's violation to its duty of protection; and the duty of protection requires the state to carry on procedures to punish the private wrongdoer, and imposes on the private wrongdoer the burden to bear punishment.

To summarize, many human rights treaty clauses which enshrine human rights also involve private party duties and liabilities, and cannot be only understood as limiting their realm to the relations between the bearer of the right and the state.

This panorama seems to raise a certain paradox: what would be the sense of international norms establishing rights that may act as a source of duties upon private parties if private parties are not, by rule, bound to international jurisdiction? If only the state is potentially liable under international law, and only the state is subject to the human rights monitoring bodies: what would be the purpose of inferring private party duties from an international human rights treaty? Why would a treaty mention private party duties if private parties are not generally passive subjects of international sanctions? The next section will be devoted to answering those questions.

INTERNATIONAL HUMAN RIGHTS BECOMING DOMESTIC LAW

These questions point to a classical – and rather obvious – answer in international law. When international law creates duties between private parties, the breach of the duty by the obliged private party, the correlative violation of the bearer's right and the lack of sanctions or any form of reparation are translated into state liability for failure to comply with its duty to protect. International law maintains one of its founding principles: only the state – and not private parties – is liable and subject to its jurisdiction.

This is, however, a partial and incomplete answer, because it fails to acknowledge the potential effects of international law at the domestic level. A first step to recognize this dimension is already reflected in international law: when ratifying a human rights treaty, states undertake to take steps to realize the rights and comply with the duties enshrined in that treaty. This means that states are obliged to develop legally the normative positions that stem from human rights treaties – be they against the state or against private parties.

This remark refers us to the domestic law level, or – to put it in another way – to the "dialogue" between international and domestic law in the human rights field.[15] One of the issues to confront in this regard is that of the system of incorporation of international law into domestic law. Incorporation is rather relevant, because once international norms become part of domestic law, the paradox previously pointed out – the apparent dissonance of establishing duties through international law to private parties that are not liable under its jurisdiction – actually disappears. Once incorporated into domestic law, the international norm, which enshrines human rights and creates legal positions establishing duties to private parties, poses no paradox: private parties are regular active and passive subjects of domestic law.

Let us see the consequences of the choice of different incorporation systems. In systems driven by a dualistic inspiration, typical of the common law tradition, international norms do not become directly part of domestic law. For rights enshrined in an international human rights treaty – along with its respective configuration of normative positions – to become part of domestic law, a domestic piece of legislation – usually an act passed by the congress, parliament or legislature – reproducing the content of those rights is required. In those systems, it is clear that international human rights norms do not directly constitute a source for duties between private parties. However, if the content of international norms is fully reproduced in a domestic piece of legislation, the actual source is irrelevant: the domestic piece of legislation will enshrine human rights which create duties between private parties.

In systems driven by a monistic inspiration – which is the trend in most Latin American countries – the situation is different. Ratification of an international norm *en vigueur* makes it part of domestic law. At the international level, the state is still the only liable subject; however, at the domestic level, things change substantially. If the international norm enshrines rights which create legal positions where private parties are passive subjects, those rights – once they have become domestic law – are a direct source of duties between private parties, and breach of such duties can give rise to liabilities. In this sense, to say that human rights enshrined by international treaties can be invoked between private parties does not pose any major conceptual challenge.

An Argentine example will suffice to prove this point. Until 1984, domestic law did not recognize the right to reply or to make a correction; with the ratification of the American Convention on Human Rights, the right to reply was introduced to the Argentine legal order.[16] Once incorporated into domestic law, private parties can invoke the right of reply against public and private media. That is, a right enshrined in an international human rights norm incorporated into domestic law is the source of duties and liabilities between private parties.

FURTHER THOUGHTS ABOUT THE RELATIONSHIP BETWEEN INTERNATIONAL HUMAN RIGHTS AND DOMESTIC LAW

The previous arguments may require some clarification, taking into consideration another issue, viz. the domestic hierarchy of the piece of legislation which reproduces the provisions of an international norm (in systems driven by a dualistic inspiration) or of the international norm incorporated into the domestic legal order (in systems driven by a monistic inspiration).[17] In the first case, the content of an international norm is reproduced domestically by a legislative act rather than by a constitutional amendment: "human rights" thus enshrined will be weaker than "constitutional" or "fundamental" rights – for instance, they could be abrogated by a subsequent legislative act. In this sense, those rights will bear a lower normative status than those enshrined by the constitution – taking for granted there is a constitution or constitutionally protected rights.

In the second case, if the international norm is granted constitutional hierarchy, "human rights" enshrined by that norm will share the same legal hierarchy as "constitutional" or "fundamental" rights. If, as in many countries, the international norm is under the constitution but above ordinary legislation, the degree of protection of those rights will be intermediate – they may be displaced if there is a conflict with a constitutionally based fundamental right, but they will triumph over an inferior norm. If the international norm stands in the same position as ordinary legislation, human rights enshrined by international treaties will be less protected – their rank will be equal to ordinary legislation, and thus they could be abrogated by a subsequent piece of legislation.

A second – and rather obvious – clarification is linked with the general character of the wording of human rights enshrined in international norms. Regardless of the normative hierarchy of international human right treaties in domestic law – supra-constitutional, constitutional, inferior to the constitution but superior to ordinary legislation, identical to ordinary legislation, among other variants, which may include different hierarchies depending on the type of treaty – from a conceptual viewpoint the degree of generality of international human rights norms is often similar to that of constitutional norms. That is, the detail of the content of human rights enshrined in a human rights treaty is usually similar to the degree of detail of fundamental rights enshrined by a constitution.[18]

Beyond specific differences, the fact is that, regularly, the wording which conveys the content of the rights included both in a constitution and in a human rights treaty is of such a general character that, in order to be concretely enforced, it requires a task of normative specification, defining the passive subjects, the extent of the duties, remedies for non-compliance, etc. This task primarily corresponds – in democratic-republican countries – to the legislative branch,[19] although the executive branch and the judiciary may also play an important role. To a great extent, rights established in a constitution and in human rights treaties require, in order to be enforced, further normative development.

International law scholars used to call this issue the problem of the "self-executing" or "non-self-executing" character of a treaty (see, for example, Buergenthal 1992). This denomination creates unnecessary confusion with the issue of incorporation of treaties into domestic law. The issue of incorporation is a matter to be solved by domestic constitutional law: it is a matter of how a country decides to incorporate into domestic law those international norms by which it has internationally declared to abide. The issue of the so-called "self-executing character" of international treaties is independent of the chosen system of incorporation, and has basically to do with the analysis of the degree of generality of its clauses.[20] While the problem of incorporation refers to a treaty as a whole, the issue of "self-executing" character requires a detailed clause-to-clause analysis: the same treaty could include some "self-executing" clauses, and some others that obviously need further normative specification.[21] This means that the "self-executing" character is a predicate not of a treaty, but of the individual clauses of that treaty.

In the context of the matter of this chapter, this clarification has two relevant consequences.

Firstly, even if a right included in a human rights treaty imposes duties on private parties, and even if that treaty is incorporated – directly or via its reproduction by a domestic piece of legislation – into domestic law, it is very likely that, due to the general character of their wording, those duties would not be directly enforceable by the bearer of the right because the treaty offers no detailed specification of the passive subject and of the content and extent of the duty. To be effective before another private party, that human right would usually need further development by subsequent regulations.

This is not, however, an absolute conclusion: there are cases where the content of the right is described in a relatively detailed fashion in a human rights treaty, and thus it is possible to enforce it directly – at least in some of its features.

In the same line of thought, some inferences from the fact of a human right being enshrined in a human rights treaty cannot be discarded – for example, the possibility of assessing some degree of incompatibility of that right with an inferior norm. But the most frequent case is the need for further regulations for specification of the content of the right. That is, even when an international norm may mention duties for private parties, those duties would need, to a great extent, further normative specification to be enforced.

Secondly, the margin of appreciation or discretion (see, generally, Valiña 1997) that human rights treaties grant the state parties allow them to a great extent to impose duties on private parties, where that imposition is intended to realize the rights enshrined by those treaties. As the ultimate bearers of human rights are human beings, the imposition of duties on private parties to guarantee those rights in practice means, in many cases, the establishment of right/duty relations between private parties, based on regulations explicitly purporting to give concrete effect to a right included in an International human rights treaty. Even where this content is not mandated by a human rights treaty, the fact is that these treaties allow the state parties to impose duties on private parties, and thus, to that extent, the further normative specification operates as a means through which a human right is made enforceable between private parties.[22]

Another Argentine example may illustrate this statement. Before the 1994 constitutional amendment, the Argentine constitution did not enshrine a right to health or to medical services. Even after that amendment, the text of the constitution itself only refers to health in a restricted context – the right of consumers to the protection of health in consumption relations (Article 42). However, the same amendment granted constitutional status to a number of international human rights treaties (Article 75, para. 22). This recognition had the actual effect of expanding the constitutionally protected rights: this was the way in which the right to health – enshrined, among other instruments, by Article 12 of the International Covenant on Economic, Social and Cultural Rights and Article 24 of the Convention on the Rights of the Child – was itself incorporated into the list of constitutionally protected rights.

However, the legislative regulations governing the Argentine health system include duties imposed on non-state actors: social entities, managed by trade unions, and for-profit private health-care providers. Even if none of the international human rights treaties mandates the state to impose duties on private parties to realize the right to health, once these duties have been created, the fact is that private parties – social entities and for-profit private health-care providers – have a duty to guarantee the human right to health, and could be subjected to claims by the bearers of the right in case of non-compliance. Part of the Argentine case law development regarding the right to health has started through litigation against those private parties: in these cases, courts have recognized the constitutional status of the right to health through its enshrinement in international human rights treaties and, simultaneously, have granted remedies to protect that right when the defendant was a private party that had failed to comply with its duties.[23]

SUGGESTING AN INTEGRATED APPROACH BETWEEN INTERNATIONAL AND DOMESTIC LEGAL SOURCES

In those legal systems where international treaties are incorporated into domestic law and rights derived from human rights treaties are granted constitutional status, the relation between "constitutional" or "fundamental" rights based on the constitution and "human rights" based on treaties requires a more detailed analysis. The first point to be made is that the interplay between constitutionally based rights and treaty-based rights forms a sort of block of constitutionally protected rights – paraphrasing here the French notion of *bloc de constitutionalité* – that is, a kind of bill of rights composed by rights derived from different sources. The composition of this "block" generally shows some degree of normative overlapping. We could thus face the following cases:

- There is coincidence between the rights enshrined by both the constitution and international human rights treaties granted constitutional status – that is, rights enshrined in the constitution are also enshrined in international human rights treaties.
- The constitution enshrines rights not enshrined in human rights treaties.
- Human rights treaties enshrine rights not enshrined in the constitution.

Moreover, the first option admits an important variable: sometimes, even when there is coincidence in the rights recognized by both the constitution and international human rights treaties, one instrument specifies with more detail the content of a certain right, or adds features or aspects not included in the supplementary norm.

From a hermeneutical perspective, if interpretive integrity or coherence of norms granted constitutional status is sought, this "block" requires the development of criteria in order to articulate different rights and different components of the rights recognized in various instruments, regardless of the source of those rights – be it the constitution or a treaty. In this sense, the difference between "constitutional" or "fundamental" rights and "human rights" becomes irrelevant: the content of each right may be derived from the constitutional norm, from one or more international norms, or be integrated with features or aspects derived from both types of sources.

One of the most important hermeneutical criteria to articulate constitutionally based rights and treaty-based rights derives precisely from the incorporation of international human rights treaties into domestic law. This refers to the *pro homine* or *pro hominis* principle, which prescribes that, when it is the case that different norms include the same human right, the interpreter shall prefer the norm that treats the right-bearer most favourably (see, for example, Albanese 1996; Pinto 1997). This principle – which is diversely reflected in international human rights treaty clauses (see, for example, American Convention on Human Rights, Article 29; International Covenant on Civil and Political Rights, Article 5; Convention on the Rights of the Child, Article 41) and is considered a fundamental criterion for the interpretation of human rights – allows the interpreter to integrate, under the light of the pre-eminence of the most favourable norm, different aspects of the same right included in diverse normative sources – that is, the constitution or international human rights treaties.

The issue could be clarified with an example. Recognition of the rights to marry and to family protection in the Argentine constitution is short and limited: constitutional clauses only refer to the right of foreigners to "marry in accordance with the laws" (Article 20) and the state duty to establish by law the "full protection of the family", "protection of the welfare of the family" and "economic compensation to families" (Article 14 bis).

When performing the integration of these clauses with the corresponding dispositions of at least eight international human rights instruments granted constitutional status (Universal Declaration, Article 16; American Declaration of the Rights and Duties of Man, Article VI; American Convention on Human Rights, Article 17; ICCPR, Article 23; ICESCR, Article 10; CEDAW, Article 16; CERD, Article 5.d.iv; Convention on the Rights of the Child, Articles 9, 10 and 18–20) the content of the right is significantly expanded.

To narrow the example, this chapter will only focus on one aspect of the right: the right to marry – but the exercise could follow on with every aspect of the right. While the text of the Argentine constitution only refers to the right of foreigners to marry according to the laws, human rights instruments clauses extend the right to every person and specify its content. Thus, "the right of men and women of marriageable age to marry and to found a family shall be recognized" (ICCPR, Article 23(2); American Convention, Article 17(2); Universal Declaration, Article 16.(1)). Laws that regulate marriage, however, are subject to the prohibition of discrimination (Universal Declaration, Article 16(1); American Convention, Article 17(2); specifically to the prohibition of racial discrimination, CERD, Article 5.d.*iv*; and to discrimination against women, CEDAW, Article 16). The laws that regulate marriage are also subject to the mandate of ensuring "equality of rights and responsibilities to the spouses as to marriage, during marriage and at its dissolution" (ICCCPR, Article 23(4); American Convention, Article 17(4); Universal Declaration, Article 16(1); CEDAW, Article 16(1.a–h), regarding equality of rights between men and women, and further specifying the content of the rights and responsibilities to which the mandate of equality applies: the right to enter into marriage, the right to choose a spouse, rights and responsibilities as parents, rights to decide the number and spacing of their children, rights regarding guardianship, wardship, trusteeship and adoption, personal and property rights). Clauses in human rights instruments prohibit marriage "without the free and full consent of the intending spouses" (ICCPR, Article 23(3); ICESCR, Article 10(1); Universal Declaration, Article 16(2); American Convention, Article 17(3); CEDAW, Article 16(1b)). The CEDAW goes even further: it forbids "the betrothal and the marriage of a child", and imposes on the state a duty to "specify a minimum age for marriage and to make the registration of marriages in an official registry compulsory" (CEDAW, Article 16(2)).

Many of these clauses entail effects between private parties: they deprive some private agreements – e.g. betrothal, child marriages, family contracts to marry their children – of any legal effect; they shall be invoked to annul marriage agreements reached without full and free consent of one of the spouses; and they offer the basis to void any private agreement which alters equality of rights and responsibilities between spouses in such areas as parental rights, guardianship, adoption, personal rights or property rights.

Once these provisions become part of the "block" of constitutionally protected rights, there is no conceptual difficulty in designing legal remedies for channelling a claim raised by a private party – for instance, a woman forced into marriage by her family, or a wife whose property rights are affected by her husband – against another private party (her parents or husband or ex-husband) for violation of the prohibitions or the mandates imposed by those provisions.

The discussion above has dealt with the incorporation of international human rights law into domestic law where rights based on constitutional and international sources are supplementary and need integration through the *pro homine* principle. There are some other norms and principles contained both in constitutions and in international human rights treaties which require common consideration and, where needed, integration: norms regarding regulation, limitation or restriction and suspension of rights (see Moncayo 1988). It is not intended to exhaust this topic here – this would require a much more detailed study – but to restrict discussion to underscoring some relevant issues for the matter at hand. Basically, one can point out particular consequences of the interplay between constitutionally based and treaty-based clauses on regulation and restriction of rights.

One could generally say that constitutions establish the basis for the exercise of state power to regulate fundamental rights included in them. Many democratic-republican constitutions include, for example, such guarantees as the requirement of a formal act from the legislative branch to regulate a constitutional or fundamental right, the requirement that regulations be reasonable and proportionate, and the requirement of regulations to respect the substance (or minimum core content) of the right at stake.

International human rights treaties also include clauses regarding the extent of regulations and restrictions of those human rights that they enshrine. One could distinguish between two types of such clauses: generic and specific.

As for generic clauses, the legal wording of many human rights treaties is relatively similar. For example, Article 4 of the ICESCR prescribes that limitations to the rights included in that treaty shall be "determined by law, only in so far as this may be compatible with the nature of these rights and solely for the purpose of promoting the general welfare in a democratic society". The American Convention on Human Rights establishes that restrictions placed on the enjoyment or exercise of rights may not be applied except in accordance with laws enacted for reasons of general interest and in accordance with the purpose for which such restrictions have been established (Article 30); while, according to Article 32, the rights of each person are limited by the rights of others, by the security of all and by the just demands of the general welfare in a democratic society.

Even recognizing their degree of abstraction, one could argue that the legal formulae of generic clauses on regulation and limitations of rights in international human rights treaties are sometimes more specific than some constitutional clauses – this is, for example, the case in Argentina.

While international human rights treaties also require that regulations or restrictions be imposed only by laws, and prohibit the alteration of the substance or nature of the right, they add a qualification to the requirement of "reasonableness": that regulations and limitations are solely justified by the purpose of promoting reasons of general interest and general welfare in a democratic society. This issue requires further elaboration, but at least the reference to a "democratic society" could offer some elements to limit the margin of discretion granted to the state by the "reasonableness" principle – especially when "reasonableness" is subject only to simple judicial scrutiny; that is, to a "mere rationality" standard. If the need to show that the limitation is aimed at promoting the general welfare of a democratic society requires a higher burden of proof from the state, then the application of the *pro homine* principle would incline the balance in favour of the option less restrictive of the right – i.e. less deferential with respect to state powers to limit rights.

However, the field where the principles that limit the state's margin of discretion to regulate and restrict rights are more likely to be meaningful is that of the specific clauses. Specific clauses usually establish a closed list of those criteria to which alone the state may resort to regulate and restrict particular human rights. The application of the *pro homine* principle entails, in these cases, the displacement of the generic clauses which allow regulations and restrictions in favour of the specific clause, where the criteria to which the state could resort to restrict the right are stricter. The American Convention on Human Rights offers a number of examples of specific clauses for the limitation of rights: regarding freedom of conscience and religion (Article 12, para. 4), freedom of thought and expression (Article 13, paras 2–4), the right of assembly (Article 15), freedom of association (Article 16, paras 2 and 3), freedom of movement and residence (Article 22, paras 3 and 4) and political rights (Article 23, para. 2).

In many of these cases, the purpose for which the treaty allows the state to resort to regulation or restriction of a right is the protection of another right or interest. In these cases, the treaty itself becomes a direct source of the possibility of imposing duties between private parties. A good example of this case is Article 13, paragraph 2a, of the American Convention on Human Rights, regarding the possibility of imposing subsequent liabilities for the exercise of freedom of expression. That paragraph allows the state to regulate the imposition of liabilities to the extent necessary to ensure "respect for the rights and reputations of others". Along the same lines, ICCPR Article 20, paragraph 2, mandates the state to forbid "any advocacy of national, racial or religious hatred that constitutes incitement to discrimination, hostility or violence".

There is still another interesting type of case in human rights treaties, conceptually linked but not identical to the issues discussed in the previous paragraph. These are cases where a human rights treaty clause allows the state to impose limits to rights and duties agreed between private parties, with the purpose of protecting a human right. The main difference to the previous examples is that, while clauses allowing limitation or restriction of rights regard the extent of state powers to regulate the content of human rights enshrined by the respective international human rights treaty, in the type of case discussed here, the international instrument, in order to ensure the protection of a human right enshrined in its text, provides a basis for the state to restrict a *different* right, the bearer of which may be a private party.

ICCPR Article 11 a good example of the restriction of a right – and of the duties that may stem from it – justified by the purpose of protecting a human right. It states that "No one shall be imprisoned merely on the ground of inability to fulfill a contractual obligation." In this case, the means to ensure the right of creditors to recover their credit and the duty of the debtor to fulfil her promise are restricted, excluding the potential threat of deprivation of liberty: the justification is the maximum protection of the right to personal freedom and human dignity.

Many of the measures that the state undertakes to take when ratifying the Convention for the Elimination of All Forms of Discrimination against Women – and, in general, any anti-discriminatory instrument – could be read under this light. States undertake to take measures to eradicate discrimination against women "in the political, economic, social, cultural, civil or any other field" (Article 1) by "any person, organization or enterprise" (Article 2, para. e). This entails the possibility of restricting rights of private parties – typically, freedom of contract and property rights – in order to protect women against discrimination, for instance in the economic sphere. Article 13, paragraph b, of that instrument offers a very specific example of this case:

> States Parties shall take all appropriate measures to eliminate discrimination against women in other areas of economic and social life in order to ensure, on a basis of equality of men and women, the same rights, in particular [...] The right to bank loans, mortgages and other forms of financial credit.

The clause offers a basis for the state to restrict the discretion of banking and credit institutions – including private institutions – to choose their customers, prohibiting the possible exclusion of women. This, of course, means a restriction of the freedom of contract of those institutions.

Beyond those national cases where international human rights instruments are granted constitutional status, the arguments made in this section can be adapted to cases where international human rights instruments are part of domestic law and considered to be legally under the constitution, but above ordinary legislation. Two important points could be made in those cases. First, these systems actually add to the assessment of the compatibility of ordinary legislation and state practices with constitutional norms – typical of judicial review schemes – another normative layer, consisting in international human rights instruments. This means that, when such instruments are made part of domestic law and granted higher status than ordinary legislation, ordinary pieces of legislation and state practices are subjected to a second test, besides that of constitutional compatibility: they also have to overcome a test of compatibility with international human rights instruments. This may mean, for example, that where the imperatives or prohibitions regarding a right provided by an international human rights treaty clause are more detailed than a constitutional provision, an ordinary statute may not be substantially unconstitutional, but may be incompatible with an international human rights treaty clause.[24]

Second, even when granted different normative status, some arguments can be also made here in favour of integrating the content of constitutional and international human rights clauses when there is some interpretative leeway for constitutional clauses.[25] As constitutional clauses of higher status, their interpretation could be in these cases either compatible or incompatible with international human rights clauses. However, if they are interpreted in a way which is incompatible with international human rights clauses, even if this would be permissible under domestic law, that interpretation will put the constitution in conflict with international law and make the state liable for breach of international duties. Thus, even if interpretations of constitutional clauses which are incompatible with international human rights norms may be permissible as a matter of domestic constitutional law, there are reasons to prefer interpretations which are compatible with international norms and also permissible under domestic constitutional law. That makes our *pro homine* grounded interpretative integration relevant even for cases where international human rights norms are inferior to the constitution in the domestic normative hierarchy.

SOME REMARKS ON THE RIGHT TO EDUCATION

The human right to education is no exception to the points made so far. The enshrinement of the right to education in international human rights instruments is actually one of the best examples of most of what has been said throughout this chapter. The wording of the right to education when integrating the relevant international human rights instruments – at least, Article 26 of the Universal Declaration of Human Rights, ICESCR Article 13, Articles 28 and 29 of the Convention on the Rights of the Child, the whole text of the Convention against Discrimination in Education, CEDAW Article 10, CERD Article 5 paragraph e.v and, to some extent, ICCPR Articles 20 and 27[26] – clearly confirms the imposition of duties on private parties.

To begin with, the wording of Article 26 of the Universal Declaration of Human Rights, ICESCR Article 13 and Articles 28 and 29 of the Convention on the Right of the Child explicitly designs a complex, multi-party right. Among the active and passive subjects of the rights are every person granted that right – especially children – the state, parents or legal guardians of children and owners or managers of private schools. The respective clauses create both rights and duties for the private actors and duties and regulating powers for the state.

Take, for example, the liberty of parents or legal guardians "to choose for their children schools, other than those established by the public authorities, which conform to such minimum educational standards as may be laid down or approved by the state and to ensure the religious and moral education of their children in conformity with their own convictions" (ICESCR Article 13, para.3). This liberty creates duties to respect for the state, which must not impede the existence of private schools, nor interfere with the choice made by parents or legal guardians to send their children to schools different from state-run schools and in line with their moral or religious orientation. But such a right also has limits, the main one being the respect for the best interest of the child (Convention on the Rights of the Child, Article 3, paras 1 and 2). This may mean that, when parents' choice is deemed to be against the best interest of the child, the state may interfere with this liberty and curtail the parents' possibility of choosing private options for their children. Parents' choice regarding the content of public education and the content of "minimum educational standards" imposed on private schools is also limited.[27]

A private school market is obviously not an unacknowledged issue for these clauses: when enshrining the liberty of other private parties to establish and direct educational institutions (ICESCR Article 13, para. 4), they actually prohibit the state from prohibiting the existence of private educational institutions, or – put in another way – they mandate the state the allow private schools to exist.[28] But, at the same time, they grant the state the possibility of issuing minimum educational standards in allowing private schools to carry on their educational activities (ICESCR Article 13, paras 3 and 4; CRC Article 29, para. 2; Convention against Discrimination in Education, Article 2, para. c), thus limiting the discretion of owners and managers of private schools.

Even more importantly, human rights treaty clauses directly subject owners and managers of private schools to various duties, such as respect for the goals of education set forth by ICESCR Article 13, paragraph 1, and CRC Article 29 paragraph 1; the prohibition of discrimination (Convention against Discrimination in Education, Article 2, para. c; CEDAW Article 10; CERD Article 5, para. e.v); the prohibition of any propaganda for war or advocacy of national, racial or religious hatred which incites discrimination, hostility or violence (ICCPR Article 20); and the mandate that school discipline be administered in a manner consistent with the child's human dignity (CRC Article 28, para. 2).[29]

Even children and other students have duties under these human rights clauses. Access to free primary education is a right the bearer can claim from the state, but its compulsory character (ICESCR Article 13, para. 2.a) is a duty imposed by the state on the bearers of the right, namely children. Granting parents a right to choose educational institutions for their children (ICESCR Article 13, para. 3) also means imposing a duty on their children to accept this choice and limiting children's right to make their own decisions in this area. Granting private parties the right to establish and run educational institutions (ICESCR Article 13, para. 4; CRC Article 29, para. 2) also means granting them the possibility of imposing duties on parents and children in exchange for the delivery of the educational service, given that they comply with state minimum educational standards and other regulations: they typically impose duties such as the payment of tuition or fees and the subjection of students to school discipline and rules. The point has already been made that these duties imposed by private school owners and managers on parents and students are also subject to compliance with limits imposed by state regulations (e.g. educational minimum standards) and respect for students' human rights – human dignity, prohibition of discrimination and consideration of the best interest of the child.

Again, as mentioned before, once these duties imposed by international human rights instrument clauses on private parties become part of domestic law, there are no significant conceptual obstacles against designing legal remedies granting a private party (for instance, parents or legal guardians of a child, or the child itself) a cause of action before domestic courts against another private party – parents or legal guardians, or the owner, manager or directing board of a private school – for failing to comply with his or her duty. It actually seems more convenient to grant a remedy to the bearer of the right, instead of limiting remedies against private party non-compliance to state action.

Imagine, for example, that a private school does not comply with the goals of education imposed by the International Covenant on Economic, Social and Cultural Rights and the Convention on the Rights of the Child. CRC Article 29, paragraph 1.d, establishes, among other goals, that education shall be directed to the "preparation of the child for responsible life in a free society, in the spirit of understanding, peace, tolerance, equality of sexes, and friendship among all peoples, ethnic, national and religious groups and persons of indigenous origin". The inclusion of intolerant or racist education, or the dissemination of war propaganda in a privately owned school, would be a clear case of non-compliance. It would require liabilities to be imposed, and could perfectly give rise to a claim by the child, or by the child's parent or guardians.

Or imagine a case where managers or teachers of a private school administer discipline in a manner which violates the dignity of a child, such as beating or humiliating it.[30] These violations would require the state to impose liabilities, and nothing prevents the creation of civil or criminal legal remedies for the child or its parents to initiate judicial actions.

The same could apply to cases where owners or managers of private schools discriminate or make distinctions on forbidden grounds among students or prospective students. The Convention against Discrimination in Education makes clear that some distinctions shall not be deemed to constitute discrimination – e.g. the establishment or maintenance of separate educational institutions for pupils of the two sexes, or of separate educational institutions based on religious or linguistic reasons (Convention against Discrimination in Education, Article 2, paras a and b). The establishment or maintenance of private educational institutions is, however, only permitted under the conditions that "the object of the institutions is not to secure the exclusion of any group but to provide educational facilities in addition to those provided by the public authorities", that "the institutions are conducted in accordance with that object" and that "the education provided conforms with such standards as may be laid down or approved by the competent authorities, in particular for education of the same level" (Convention against Discrimination in Education, Article 2, para. c). Thus, discrimination by private educational facilities on racial, national or social origin, for example, could constitute violation of international human rights norms by private parties, which could perfectly well be invoked before domestic courts by the offended student or his or her legal representatives. There is even a strong case to argue that distinctions by private schools are only permissible on the explicit grounds of their legal object or mandate – typically, gender in single-sex private schools, or religion in religious private schools – but that their legal object or mandate limits their discretion to discriminate on any other suspect ground not directly connected with it.

Parents could also violate duties established by international human rights clauses, and their violation could constitute the basis for a judicial claim: imagine a case where the kind of education chosen by parents is deemed to be contrary to the best interests of the child. Conflicts of this sort have arisen where, for example, a child of reproductive age wants to access information about sexuality or contraceptive devices. In cases of conflict between the respective choices of parents and child, there are clear indications that access to sexual education is in the best interests of the child, and thus the child's choice should prevail.[31]

CONCLUSION

The author has tried to show throughout this chapter that the idea that it is impossible to invoke human rights among private parties is biased, extremely bound to the commonplaces of traditional international law doctrine, and mistaken in the face of a concrete analysis of the content of human rights treaties and the trend towards growing interaction between international law and domestic law – especially between international human rights law and domestic constitutional law. The observations made do not claim to have exhausted the matter, but offer rather some starting points for a practically oriented research agenda in this field.

In any event, and assuming that someone shares these starting points, more comprehensive research will need to undertake detailed study of each human right which could potentially trigger effects between private parties. The matter is particularly relevant given the fact that many countries in the world have experienced privatization and deregulation processes which put in the hands of private parties functions previously performed by the state – some of them directly sensitive to human rights issues, such as prison, health, education and water services. The issues at stake prompt us to leave aside some outdated dogmas and open our eyes to the new challenges now posed by the protection of human rights.[32]

NOTES

1   This chapter will not address a relatively close problem which has been more thoroughly dealt with in continental constitutional law doctrine: the problem of *Drittwirkung,* or horizontal applicability of constitutional rights between private parties. The intention here is to discuss the applicability of human rights enshrined in international human rights treaties between private parties. There is, however, some overlap between both issues, as will be seen. For a discussion of the *Drittwirkung* doctrine, see Bilbao Ubillos (1997); García Torres and Jiménez-Blanco (1986); Julio Estrada (2000); de la Quadra-Salcedo (1981); Venegas Grau (2004). For a brief account of the problem, see Gomes

Canotilho and Moreira (1993, 144–8); Gomes Canotilho (1998, 1150–60); Sarlet (2000).

2   The statement does not purport to fix the birth of the term, but only to highlight a historical landmark of its generalization. Previous designations of the same concept include "natural rights" and "rights of man". See, in general, Gómez Isa (2003). For a discussion of the use of the "human rights" formula in the context of the drafting of the Universal Declaration of Human Rights, see Glendon (2001); Morsink (1999).

3   In a number of countries, including Australia (Human Rights & Equal Opportunity Commission), El Salvador (Procuraduría para la Defensa de los Derechos Humanos), Guatemala (Procuraduría de los Derechos Humanos), Mexico (Comisión Nacional de los Derechos Humanos) and South Africa (Human Rights Commission), among others, the institution of the *ombudsperson* – which is empowered to monitor the effectiveness of human rights in the local sphere – is identified with the "human rights" label.

4   Given the pre-eminence of treaties as a source of international human rights law, this chapter will focus on human rights treaties and the bodies and mechanisms established thereby. However, the same conclusions could be extended to other human rights bodies, such as those derived from the UN Charter.

5   Some human rights monitoring bodies have also suggested extending the binding character of human rights treaties to international organs and agencies, even if they are not directly subjected to the monitoring mechanism set by those treaties. See, for example, Committee on Economic, Social and Cultural Rights, (1990, paras 2 and 9; 1999, para. 41).

6   See, generally, the ideas deployed by the court regarding the realm of state and private parties' duties, and of state liability when private parties fail to comply with their duties in paras 133–52, especially paras 136, 137 and 147. In the same sense, see the concurring opinions of Judges Cançado Trindade, Salgado Pesante and García Ramírez. Judge Cançado Trindade argues that

> at the operative level, the obligations *erga omnes partes* under a human rights treaty such as the American Convention also assume special importance, in face of the current diversification of the sources of violations of the rights enshrined into the Convention, which requires the clear recognition of the effects of the conventional obligations vis-à-vis third parties (the *Drittwirkung*), including individuals (e.g., in labour relations).

Judge Antonio Cançado Trindade concurs (para. 83). Judge Salgado Pesante underscores that:

> I consider that an extremely important point in this Advisory Opinion is that of establishing clearly the effectiveness of human rights with regard to third parties, in a horizontal conception. These aspects, as is acknowledged, have been amply developed in German legal writings (*Drittwirkung*) and are contained in current constitutionalism.

> It is not only the State that has the obligation to respect human rights, but also individuals in their relationships with other individuals. The environment of free will that prevails in private law cannot become an obstacle that dilutes the binding effectiveness *erga omnes* of human rights.

> The possessors of human rights – in addition to the State (the public sphere) – are also third parties (the private sphere), who may violate such rights in the ambit of individual relationships. For the purposes of this Opinion, we are limiting ourselves basically to the workplace where it has been established that the rights to equality and non-discrimination are being violated.

> Labor rights as a whole acquire real importance in relationships between individuals; consequently, they must be binding with regard to third parties. To this end, all States

must adopt legislative or administrative measures to impede such violations and procedural instruments should be effective and prompt. (Paras 17–20)

Judge García Ramírez basically agrees with these ideas (para. 29).

7 In the same line, see point 5 of the concluding opinion of the court, which states that "the fundamental principle of equality and non-discrimination, which is of a peremptory nature, entails obligations *erga omnes* of protection that bind all States and generate effects with regard to third parties, including individuals". Judge Cançado Trindade's concurring opinion devotes long considerations to the issue (paras 76–85). He argues, for instance, that "The *jus cogens*, in bringing about obligations *erga omnes*, characterizes them as being endowed with a necessarily objective character, and thereby encompassing all the addressees of the legal norms *(omnes)*, both those who integrate the organs of the public power as well as the individuals" (para. 76), and that "In a vertical dimension, the obligations *erga omnes* of protection bind both the organs and agents of (State) public power, and the individuals themselves (in the inter-individual relations)" (para. 77). In the same vein, see Judge García Ramírez's considerations (paras 16, 22 and 26).

8 For considerations about the development of these issues at the domestic level, see Brewer-Carías (1998, 24–5).

9 The European Court of Human Rights has decided in a number of cases that the European Convention on Human Rights and Fundamental Freedoms imposes the state parties with duties which may entail the adoption of measures affecting relationships between private parties. See, for instance, European Court of Human Rights, cases *X & Y v the Netherlands*, para. 23 and *Plattform "Ärzte für das Leben" v Austria*, para. 32.

10 The whole general recommendation reaffirms this idea.

11 The scheme refers to duties "to respect", "to protect" and "to fulfil" and, in some versions, to duties "to promote". See, for example, Eide (1995); van Hoof (1984). For a comprehensive comment on the different versions of the scheme, see Sepúlveda (2003, 157–248).

12 Two cases from different regional human rights systems could illustrate this issue. In its first – and very likely still most important – case, *Velásquez Rodríguez*, the Inter-American Court of Human Rights decided that, regardless of the possibility of proving that forced disappearance was committed by state agents, the state is also liable for deeds committed by private parties or unidentified actors when there is proof of failure to carry on with due diligence the duty to prevent human rights violations (*Velásquez Rodríguez*, paras 172–7). In turn, the European Court of Human Rights decided, in the *Young, Jones & Webster* case, that the state is liable for violation of freedom of association if it tolerates contracting practices between a private enterprise and a trade union forcing a worker to choose between joining a trade union or losing his or her job (*Young, Jones & Webster v United Kingdom*, paras 54 and 56).

13 Again, Advisory Opinion OC-18/03 of the Inter-American Court of Human (2003) offers a good illustration on how state duties of protection may project their effects on third parties (paras 141–9, 152–3). In point 9 of the concluding opinion, the court makes it clear that:

the State has the obligation to respect and guarantee the labor human rights of all workers, irrespective of their status as nationals or aliens, and not to tolerate situations of discrimination that are harmful to the latter in the employment relationships established between private individuals (employer-worker). The State must not allow private employers to violate the rights of workers, or the contractual relationship to violate minimum international standards.

14 See European Court of Human Rights, case *A. v United Kingdom*, para. 22.

15 For some of the problems posed by this relation, see Piza and Trejos (1989, 93–107).

16 See, for instance, Argentine Supreme Court, case *Ekmekdjian, Miguel A. c. Sofovich, Gerardo y otros*, paras 15 and 20–22.

17 See, in general, Sagüés (1998), although the chapter mainly refers to the issue of normative hierarchy of treaties in domestic law.

18 Of course, this is a broad generalization. There are cases where the wording of a constitutional right is more detailed than that of a human rights treaty, and vice versa. However, the generalization is acceptable in terms of the discussion below. For a discussion about problems of indetermination of international human rights treaty clauses, see Haba (1986, 280–314 and 375–412).

19 Examples of this point are the requirement of a formal act by the legislative branch to regulate fundamental rights, and the importance assigned by international human rights treaties to the adoption of legislative measures among the steps taken to ensure the effectiveness of human rights enshrined in those treaties.

20 Regardless of its direct incorporation into domestic law (the need to reproduce its content by a domestic piece of legislation), the "self-executing" character of a treaty clause depends on the detail of its wording – that is, on the degree of "concretion" or "openness" of the duties that stem from it. The issue is not different from that of the "self-executing" character of a constitutional clause.

21 An example taken from the International Covenant on Civil and Political Rights may be useful to illustrate this point: while the duty established in Article 6(5) ("Sentence of death shall not be imposed for crimes committed by persons below eighteen years of age and shall not be carried out on pregnant women") is perfectly applicable without major need for further normative elaboration, the duty established by Article 2(3)(1) ("to develop the possibilities of judicial remedy") obviously requires the adoption of legislative measures to give any effect to such development.

22 See, for example, European Court of Human Rights case law mentioned in note 9.

23 Case law from the Argentine Supreme Court is a good index of this evolution: the diverse precedents which accumulated in the last decade show that the right to health imposes duties to both state and private actors. The following case sequence may help to assess this evolution: Argentine Supreme Court, case *Asociación Benghalensis y otros v Estado Nacional. Ministerio de Salud y Acción Social*, 1 June 2000, para. 10; case *Campodónico de Beviacqua, Ana Carina v Ministerio de Salud y Acción Social. Secretaría de Programas de Salud y Banco de Drogas Neoplásicas*, 24 October 2000, paras 16–21; case *Etcheverry, Roberto Eduardo v Omint Sociedad Anónima y Servicios*, 13 March 2001, General Attorney's brief, para. IV, followed by the majority of the court; case *Hospital Británico de Buenos Aires v Estado Nacional (Ministerio de Salud y Acción Social)*, 13 March 2001, General Attorney's brief, para. VI, and concurring opinion of Judge Vázquez, paras 9–11; case *Monteserin, Marcelino c/ Estado Nacional. Ministerio de Salud y Acción Social. Comisión Nacional Asesora para la Integración de Personas Discapacitadas. Servicio Nacional de Rehabilitación y Promoción de la Persona con Discapacidad*, 16 October 2001, General Attorney's brief, para. VII, and court's opinion, paras 11–13.

24 That would usually make the statute unconstitutional on other grounds: the violation of the normative hierarchy between international instruments and ordinary statutes set by the constitution.

25 This argument would not apply, however, in cases where a constitutional clause is irremediably contrary to an international human rights clause.

26 The normative span is even broader where regional instruments are also applicable. For state parties of the inter-American human rights system, for

example, Article XII of the American Declaration of Rights and Duties of Man, Article 26 of the American Convention on Human Rights in connection with Articles 34(h) and 49 of the Charter of the Organization of American States and Article 13 of the Additional Protocol to the American Convention on Human Rights in the Area of Economic, Social and Cultural Rights (Protocol of San Salvador) may also be relevant. For an insightful and complete elaboration of an integration of (Colombian) constitutional and international components of the right to education, see Góngora Mera (2003).

27 See, for example, European Court of Human Rights, case *Kjeldsen, Busk Madsen and Pedersen v Denmark* (compulsory sex education in state schools when conveyed in an objective, critical and pluralistic manner does not constitute indoctrination or disrespect for parents' religious or philosophical views).

28 Privatization – that is, the transfer of state-owned or state-run schools to the private sector – may pose some additional issues. For an interesting paper examining privatization trends in education, see Coomans and Hallo de Wolf (2005). The authors conclude that "privatisation of education services is not prohibited by international human rights law" (p. 256).

29 At least two cases from the European Court of Human Rights are relevant in this respect. In the case of *Campbell and Cosans v United Kingdom*, the court held that the existence of corporal punishment as a disciplinary measure in the schools attended by the children was a violation of the state's duty to respect the right of parents to ensure such education and teaching in conformity with their own religious and philosophical convictions; and that suspension of a student from school motivated by his and his parents' refusal to accept that he receives or is liable to corporal chastisement amounted to a denial of his right to education. The institutions involved were public schools. The case of *A. v United Kingdom* has already been mentioned, where the court found that the beating of an English boy by his stepfather constituted "inhuman or degrading punishment", and that UK domestic law, which provided the stepfather the common law defence of "reasonable chastisement", failed to provide adequate protection to the victim. Connecting the holdings of the two cases may mean that the existence of beating as a disciplinary measure in private schools would also amount to a violation of the right to education. Cases from the Colombian Constitutional Court go even further in imposing duties on private school owners and managers. In case *T-065/93*, decided on 26 February 1993, the court found that threatening students with expulsion from a private school for failing to follow an order to have a haircut amounted to a violation of the right to the free development of personality. The court said that private school regulations were also subject to the respect of principles and limits established in the constitution, as education is a public service oriented to satisfy a general need. Similar cases include expulsion from private schools grounded on a student's pregnancy.

30 See cases quoted in the previous note.

31 See Committee on the Rights of the Child (2003, para. 24): "In light of articles 3, 17 and 24 of the Convention, States parties should provide adolescents with access to sexual and reproductive information, including on family planning and contraceptives, the dangers of early pregnancy, the prevention of HIV/AIDS and the prevention and treatment of sexually transmitted diseases (STDs)." In addition, "States parties should ensure that they have access to appropriate information, *regardless of their marital status and whether their parents or guardians consent.*" See also City of Buenos Aires Supreme Court, case *Liga de Amas de Casa, Consumidores y Usuarios de la República Argentina y otros c/Gobierno de la Ciudad de Buenos Aires s/acción declarativa de inconstitucionalidad (art. 113 inc. 2º CCBA),*

14 October 2003 (reproductive health law granting children of reproductive age access to information about sexuality and contraception is not unconstitutional, does not violate parents' rights and is in line with the Convention on the Rights of the Child).

32 Along the same lines, Luigi Ferrajoli (2001, 265–6) calls for a "private law constitutionalism", extending the guarantee of fundamental rights before private parties.

REFERENCES

Albanese, S. (1996), "La primacía de la cláusula más favorable a la persona", *Revista La Ley*, Vol. C: 518.

Ambos, K. and Karayan, M. (1999), *Impunidad y Derecho Penal Internacional*, 2nd edition (Buenos Aires: Ad Hoc).

Barberis, J. (1984), *Los sujetos del Derecho Internacional actual* (Madrid: Tecnos).

Bilbao Ubillos, J.M. (1997), *La eficacia de los derechos fundamentales frente a particulares. Análisis de la jurisprudencia del Tribunal Constitucional* (Madrid: Centro de Estudios Constitucionales).

Blanc Altemir, A. (1990), *La violación de los derechos humanos fundamentales como crimen internacional* (Barcelona: Bosch).

Brewer-Carías, A. (1998), "Hacia el fortalecimiento de las instituciones de protección de los derechos humanos en el ámbito interno", in L. González Volio (ed.), *Presente y Futuro de los Derechos Humanos. Ensayos en honor a Fernando Volio Jiménez* (San José: Instituto Interamericano de Derechos Humanos).

Buergenthal, T. (1992), "Self-executing and non self-executing treaties in national and international law", *Recueil des Cours*, 235:IV, 303–400.

Committee on Economic, Social and Cultural Rights (1990), "General Comment No. 2: International technical assistance measures (article 22 of the Covenant)", 2 February, E/1990/23.

_____ (1999), "General Comment No. 11: The right to adequate food (art. 11)", 12 May, E/C.12/1999/5.

Committee on the Elimination of Discrimination against Women (1992), "General Recommendation No. 19, Violence Against Women", 29 January, A/47/38.

Committee on the Rights of the Child (2003), "General Comment No. 4: Adolescent health and development in the context of the Convention on the Rights of the Child", 1 July, CRC/GC/2003/4.

Coomans, Fons and Hallo de Wolf, Antenor (2005), "Privatisation of education and the right to education", in Koen De Feyter and Felipe Gómez Isa (eds), *Privatisation and Human Rights in the Age of Globalisation* (Antwerp: Intersentia), pp. 229–58.

de la Quadra-Salcedo, T. (1981), *El recurso de amparo y los derechos fundamentales en las relaciones entre particulares* (Madrid: Civitas).

Eide, A. (1995), "Economic, social and cultural rights as human rights", in A. Eide, C. Krause and A. Rosas (eds), *Economic, Social and Cultural Rights. A Textbook* (Dordrecht: Martinus Nijhoff), pp. 21–49.

Fernández Flores, J.L. (1991), "La represión de las infracciones del derecho de la guerra cometidas por los individuos", *Revista Internacional de la Cruz Roja*, 105 (May/June).

Ferrajoli, L. (2001), "La democracia constitucional", in C. Courtis (ed.), *Desde otra mirada. Textos de teoría crítica del derecho* (Buenos Aires: EUDEBA), pp. 255–6.

Gómez Guillamón, R. (ed.) (1999), «Derecho penal internacional", in *Jornadas celebradas en el Centro de Estudios Jurídicos de la Administración de Justicia los días 21, 22 y 23 de junio de 1999* (Madrid: Estudios Jurídicos del Ministerio Fiscal).

García Torres, J. and Jiménez-Blanco, A. (1986), *Derechos fundamentales y relaciones entre particulares* (Madrid: Civitas).

Gil-Gil, A. (1999), *Derecho penal internacional. Especial consideración del delito de genocidio* (Madrid: Tecnos).

Glendon, M.A. (2001), *A World Made New. Eleanor Roosevelt and the Universal Declaration of Human Rights* (New York: Random House).

Gomes Canotilho, J.J. (1998), *Direito Constitucional e Teoria da Constituição*, 2nd edition (Coimbra: Almedina).

Gomes Canotilho, J.J. and Moreira, V. (1993), *Constituição da República Portuguesa anotada*, 2nd edition (Coimbra: Coimbra Editora).

Gómez Isa, F. (2003) "La protección internacional de los derechos humanos", in F. Gómez Isa (director) and J.M. Pureza, *La protección internacional de los derechos humanos en los albores del siglo XXI* (Bilbao: Universidad de Deusto), pp. 23–60.

Góngora Mera, M.E. (2003), *El derecho a la educación en la constitución, la jurisprudencia y los instrumentos internacionales* (Bogotá: Defensoría del Pueblo).

Haba, E.P. (1986), *Tratado básico de Derechos Humanos, Tomo I: Conceptos Fundamentales* (San José: Juricentro).

Inter-American Court of Human Rights (2003), "Juridical Condition and Rights of Undocumented Migrants", Advisory Opinion OC-18/03, 17 September.

Julio Estrada, A. (2000), *La eficacia de los derechos fundamentales entre particulares* (Bogotá: Universidad Externado de Colombia).

Kelsen, H. (1979), *Teoría pura del derecho* (Mexico: UNAM).

Moncayo, G.R. (1988), "Suspensión y restricción de derechos y garantías constitucionales (El aporte de las convenciones internacionales al derecho público argentino)", in *Revista Plural* No. 12, "Justicia en democracia" (Buenos Aires) pp. 26–34.

Morsink, J. (1999), *The Universal Declaration of Human Rights. Origins, Drafting and Intent* (Philadelphia, PA: University of Pennsylvania Press).

Pinto, M. (1997), "El principio *pro homine*. Criterios de hermenéutica y pautas para la regulación de los derechos humanos", in M. Abregú and C. Courtis (eds), *La aplicación de los tratados sobre derechos humanos por los tribunales locales* (Buenos Aires: Del Puerto), pp. 163–71.

Piza, R. and Trejos, G. (1989), *Derecho Internacional de los Derechos Humanos: La Convención Americana* (San José: Juricentro).

Sagüés, N.P. (1998), "Mecanismos de incorporación de los tratados internacionales sobre derechos humanos al derecho interno", in L. González Volio (ed.), *Presente y Futuro de los Derechos Humanos. Ensayos en honor a Fernando Volio Jiménez* (San José: Instituto Interamericano de Derechos Humanos), pp. 299–314.

Sarlet, I.W. (2000), "Direitos fundamentais e direito privado: Algumas considerações em torno da vinculação dos particulares aos direitos fundamentais", in I.W. Sarlet (ed.), *A Constituição concretizada. Construindo pontes como o público e o privado* (Porto Alegre: Livraria do Advogado), pp. 107–63.

Sepúlveda, M. (2003), *The Nature of the Obligations under the International Covenant on Economic, Social and Cultural Rights* (Amberes: Intersentia).

Valiña, L. (1997), "El margen de apreciación de los Estados en la aplicación del derecho internacional de los derechos humanos en el ámbito interno", in M. Abregú and C. Courtis (eds), *La aplicación de los tratados sobre derechos humanos por los tribunales locales* (Buenos Aires: Del Puerto), pp. 173–97.

van Hoof, G.H.J. (1984) "The legal nature of economic, social and cultural rights", in P. Alston and K. Tomasevski (eds), *The Right to Food* (Dordrecht: Martinus Nijhoff), pp. 99–105.

Venegas Grau, M. (2004), *Derechos fundamentales y Derecho privado. Los derechos fundamentales en las relaciones entre particulares y el principio de autonomía privada* (Madrid: Marcial Pons).

CASE LAW

City of Buenos Aires Supreme Court, *Liga de Amas de Casa, Consumidores y Usuarios de la República Argentina y otros c/Gobierno de la Ciudad de Buenos Aires s/acción declarativa de inconstitucionalidad (art. 113 inc. 2º CCBA)*, 14 October 2003.

Colombian Constitutional Court, *T-065/93*, decided 26 February 1993.

European Court of Human Rights, *Kjeldsen, Busk Madsen and Pedersen v Denmark*, Eur. Ct. H.R. Ser. A, No. 23, 1 E.H.R.R. 711, 7 December 1976.

European Court of Human Rights, *Campbell and Cosans v United Kingdom*, 48 Eur. Ct. H.R. Ser. A, 25 February 1982.

European Court of Human Rights, *Young, Jones & Webster v United Kingdom*, 13 August 1981, Petitions 7601/76 and 7806/77.

European Court of Human Rights, *X & Y v the Netherlands*, 25 March 1985, Petition 8978/80.

European Court of Human Rights, *Plattform "Ärzte für das Leben" v Austria*, 21 June 1988, Petition 5/1987/128/179.

European Court of Human Rights, *A. v United Kingdom*, Petition 100/1997/884/1096, 23 September 1998.

Inter-American Court of Human Rights, *Velásquez Rodríguez*, 29 July 1988.

Supreme Court of Argentina, *Ekmekdjian, Miguel A. c. Sofovich, Gerardo y otros*, 7 July 1992, majority opinion.

Supreme Court of Argentina, *Asociación Benghalensis y otros v Estado Nacional. Ministerio de Salud y Acción Social*, 1 June 2000.

Supreme Court of Argentina, *Campodónico de Beviacqua, Ana Carina v Ministerio de Salud y Acción Social. Secretaría de Programas de Salud y Banco de Drogas Neoplásicas*, 24 October 2000.

Supreme Court of Argentina, *Etcheverry, Roberto Eduardo v Omint Sociedad Anónima y Servicios*, 13 March 2001.

Supreme Court of Argentina, *Hospital Británico de Buenos Aires v Estado Nacional (Ministerio de Salud y Acción Social)*, 13 March 2001.

Supreme Court of Argentina, *Monteserin, Marcelino c/ Estado Nacional. Ministerio de Salud y Acción Social. Comisión Nacional Asesora para la Integración de Personas Discapacitadas. Servicio Nacional de Rehabilitación y Promoción de la Persona con Discapacidad*, 16 October 2001.

5 Content and Scope of the Right to Education as a Human Right and Obstacles to Its Realization

FONS COOMANS

INTRODUCTION

It is a commonplace to say that everyone has a right to education. However, it is a matter of common knowledge that there is a big gap between the right to education laid down by international texts and the persistence of some disenchanting realities: in 2004 more than 110 million children of primary school age had no access to schooling. In the same year some 800 million adults, almost two-thirds of whom are women, were illiterate. Although girls' education has been expanding all over the world, there are still 60 million girls out of school. In sub-Saharan Africa the number of out-of-school children and illiterate adults even increased between 1990 and 2000 (for detailed data see Education For All 2003, 49–50, 86–7; UNICEF 2005). And for those who do have access to education, it is not self-evident that the education they receive is of good quality. Theory and rhetoric on the one hand and practice and reality on the other are thus poles apart. Practice often shows that education is not seen as a fundamental right which gives rise to governmental obligations, but merely as part of governmental programmes and policy for which expenditure may be shifted or reallocated according to changing governmental priorities and choices. One of the reasons for this situation is that governments insufficiently consider the relevant treaty provisions on the right to education as a touchstone for educational legislation and policy.

Nevertheless, the right to education as a *human right* has a solid basis in international law. It has been laid down in several universal and regional human rights instruments. Examples are the Universal Declaration of Human Rights (Article 26), the UNESCO Convention against Discrimination in Education and the International Covenant on Economic, Social and Cultural Rights (ICESCR) (Articles 13 and 14).[1] The right to education as a human right has been reaffirmed by the UN Commission on Human Rights in resolutions, and a special rapporteur has been appointed to study this right.[2] Over the years a number of studies have been published regarding one important question: what does realization of the right to education entail?[3] However, relatively little international and national case law is available on the various dimensions of the right to education as a human right. This is partly due to the fact that economic, social and cultural rights, the right to education being one of them, have been seen for a long time as "secondary rights" compared to civil and political rights. Their so-called "vague" wording, programmatic nature and problematic justiciability have given them second-rank status among governments and courts. These developments have contributed to a lack of common understanding of these rights in terms of their content and nature of states' obligations. However, these traditional views about the legal nature of economic, social and cultural rights have gradually given way to more recent and modern approaches that depart from the indivisibility of all human rights (civil and political *and* economic, social and cultural). Efforts have been made to strengthen implementation of economic, social and cultural rights by clarifying their normative content in more detail and specifying the nature and content of state obligations. Contributions to this change of perspective and approach have come from academics (Eide et al. 2001; Chapman and Russell 2002), UN special rapporteurs with a mandate in the field of economic, social and cultural rights,[4] and the expert body that monitors implementation of the ICESCR, the UN Committee on Economic, Social and Cultural Rights (CESCR), in particular its general comments.[5] It is interesting to note that the most important developments in the field of economic, social and cultural rights relate to achieving a stronger universal implementation of this particular treaty. Also, the justiciability of economic, social and cultural rights has been recognized progressively in the domestic legal order of a number of countries (Coomans 2006).

The present study aims at clarifying the normative content of the right to education and the corresponding obligations of states. The study also discusses the main obstacles to effective implementation of the right to education from a human rights point of view. The central focus is on the nature, meaning and scope of rights and obligations resulting from Articles 13 and 14 of the International Covenant on Economic, Social and Cultural Rights, which is the main universal treaty including the right to education as a human right.[6] These provisions are of great importance for setting up and maintaining education systems in countries all over the world, because they cover a variety of aspects of the right to education, framed in terms of state obligations. The study typifies the right to education as an empowerment and key right; then deals with the scope of the right as a human right and its special characteristics, in particular with regard to the ICESCR. Next, other relevant universal and regional instruments are discussed briefly. The sixth section deals with the concept of a core content of human rights, with particular attention to the core content of the right to education; this is followed by a discussion of the feasibility of using a typology of state obligations ("to respect", "to protect", "to fulfil") in order to specify the nature of (minimum and core) state obligations resulting from treaty provisions and as a mechanism to determine whether a state is complying with its obligations in relation to the implementation of the right to education. Finally there is an analysis of the main, often non-legal, obstacles to effective implementation of the right to education.

The focus of the study is primarily on the universal human rights instruments, and secondly on the regional instruments adopted in the African and Latin American context. Furthermore, the section on obstacles mainly deals with problems that developing countries face in the process of realizing the right to education, again with a focus on Latin America and Africa.

THE RIGHT TO EDUCATION AS AN "EMPOWERMENT" RIGHT AND "KEY" RIGHT

Education is a social good, because it creates opportunities and provides people with choices. In this sense, education is an end in itself. However, it is also a means to an end, because it helps to achieve economic growth, health, poverty reduction, personal development and democracy (Watkins 2000, 18). Therefore, the right to education as a human right should be characterized an "empowerment" right. Such a right "provides the individual with control over the course of his or her life, and in particular, control over [...] the state" (Donnelly and Howard 1988). In other words, exercising an empowerment right enables a person to experience the benefit of other rights: "the key to social action in defense of rights [...] is an educated citizenry, able to spread its ideas and to organize in defense of rights" (ibid., 234–5). Education enables a person to make a contribution to society as an independent and emancipated citizen. Civil and political rights, such as freedom of expression, freedom of association or the right to political participation, only obtain substance and meaning when a person is educated. J.K. Galbraith (1996) has emphasized that "education not only makes democracy possible; it also makes it essential. Education not only brings into existence a population with an understanding of the public tasks; it also creates their demand to be heard." In this sense, education is a threat to autocratic rule. Governments have used the education system for building a nation, for instance through the introduction of a national language. Often this happened to the detriment of the languages and cultures of ethnic minorities and indigenous groups (Watkins 2000, 44). For such groups, however, the right to education is an essential means to preserve and strengthen their cultural identity.

Education enhances social mobility and helps to people to escape from discrimination based on social status. It enables people to move up the social ladder. Moreover, education promotes the realization of other social, economic and cultural rights, such as the right to work, the right to food or the right to health: an educated person will have a greater chance of finding *v' social definition.*

a job, will be better equipped to secure his or her own food supply and is more aware of public health dangers. In other words, education as a key right unlocks the enjoyment of other human rights. From the perspective of the rights of the child, education contributes to socializing children into understanding and accepting views different from their own (Tomasevski 2001a, paras 11–13). In general, the right to education promotes the fulfilment of the right to an adequate standard of living; it gives people access to the skills and knowledge necessary for full membership of society. In short, the right to education contributes in an important way to the promotion of the essence of human rights, i.e. living in human dignity (Schachter 1983).

Finally, the right to education has a clear overlap with other human rights, such as freedom of religion and the right to privacy: the freedom of parents to determine the (religious) education of their children is part of the freedom of religion, as well as of the freedom of education. It is a matter which belongs to the private life of people, protected by law. Also the freedom of association has a link with the right to education through the freedom to establish private educational institutions. In other words, through its links with other rights, the right to education accentuates the unity and interdependence of all human rights. *+ the full devmt of the person.*

THE SCOPE AND MEANING OF ICESCR ARTICLE 13

why not Art 26CC

The scope and meaning of ICESCR Artcle 13 will be analysed here from the angle of the text of the article itself, its legal history and, in addition, from the general comment on the right to education adopted by the CESCR in December 1999 (Committee on Economic, Social and Cultural Rights 1999c). A general comment is a non-binding but authoritative interpretation of a treaty provision that also gives guidelines for the legislation, policy and practice of state parties. Broadly speaking, Article 13 of the ICESCR was drafted with Article 26 of the Universal Declaration of Human Rights in mind. Three key elements of Article 26 have been included in Article 13: the recognition of a right to education; a guarantee of parental rights in matters of education; and a reference to the aims of education. These three elements are discussed below.

With respect to the right to education as laid down in international documents, two aspects can be distinguished. On the one hand, realization of the right to education demands an effort on the part of the state to make *social* education available and accessible. It implies positive state obligations. This *dimensn* may be defined as the right to receive an education, or the social dimension of the right to education. On the other hand, there is the personal freedom of individuals to choose between state-organized and private education, which can be translated, for example, into parents' freedom to ensure their children's moral and religious education according to their own beliefs. From this stems the freedom of natural persons or legal entities to establish their *freedom* own educational institutions. This is the right to choose an education, or the *dimensn* freedom dimension of the right to education. It requires the state to follow a policy of non-interference in private matters. It implies negative state obligations. Both aspects can be found in ICESCR Articles 13 and 14. Articles 13(2) and 14 cover the social dimension, while Article 13(3)–(4) embodies the freedom dimension.

Speaking in terms of individual rights, the right to education has been defined in the European context as a right of access to educational institutions "existing at a given time" and the right to draw benefit from the education received, which means the right to obtain official recognition of the studies completed (European Court of Human Rights 1968).[7] When ICESCR Article 13 was drafted, the UNESCO representative suggested the following definition of the right to education: "The right of access to the knowledge and training which are necessary to full development as an individual and as a citizen",[8] which is a rather broad and general definition. Both definitions refer to the social dimension of the right to education.

The elements of the freedom of education are well expressed in paragraphs 3 and 4 of Article 13: the freedom of choice and the freedom to establish. This aspect of freedom is typical for a democratic, pluralist society; its origin lies in ideas about respect for individual liberty and freedom of choice.

The aims of education are closely related to education as a human right. It is clear from ICESCR Article 13(1) that education provided for children should aim to teach democratic values and respect for other people. This provision is quite extensive in listing the values to which education should be directed. These include the full development of the human personality and dignity of people, and respect for the human rights of others. In addition, education should contribute to the promotion of understanding, tolerance, friendship and peace among nations and ethnic and religious groups. These values have not only been codified in ICESCR Article 13(1), but are also part of other human rights instruments, such as the Universal Declaration of Human Rights (Article 26(2)) and the Convention on the Rights of the Child (Article 29(1)). The latter convention adds other values to which education should be directed, such as respect for the child's parents and the development of respect for the cultural identity of the child and the natural environment in which it lives. One may agree with the view of one authoritative commentator who concludes that today there is a "broad universal consensus on the major aims and objectives of the right to education", as listed above (Nowak 2001, 251).[9]

The right to education laid down in ICESCR Article 13 is a universal right, granted to every person regardless of age, language, social or ethnic origin or other status. Articles 13 and 14 are rather comprehensive compared to other rights in the covenant. They set out the steps to be taken by states in realizing the right to education. This particularly applies to paragraph 2 of Article 13, which enumerates the separate steps with a view to achieving the full realization of this right. At issue here is the specific obligation of the state to make education available and accessible in a non-discriminatory way. In performing this duty, states have a degree of discretion within the limits of the standards set in Article 13 and the key provisions of Article 2(1). Article 2(1) reads:

> Each State Party to the present Covenant undertakes to take steps, individually and through international assistance and co-operation, especially economic and

technical, to the maximum of its available resources, with a view to achieving progressively the full realization of the rights recognised in the present Covenant by all appropriate means, including particularly the adoption of legislative measures.

An important question here is which obligations may arise from these two provisions. In order to answer this question, an analysis needs to be made of the meaning of the terms "to recognise" and "to respect" which designate the character and scope of the obligations in Article 13.

The Undertaking "To Recognise" the Right to Education

The drafting history of the covenant in general and of Article 13 in particular shows that the use of the term "to recognise" in that provision is closely linked to the idea of progressive realization as provided for in Article 2(1). The opening words of the original draft for paragraph 2 of Article 13 did not contain the term "to recognise", but rather the expression "it is understood". It was subsequently changed into the clause "The States Parties to the Covenant recognise", in order to have a term with a stronger legal meaning.[10] The meaning of the term "to recognise" was expounded by the representative of UNESCO in 1951 during the preparatory work in the Commission on Human Rights as follows:

> recognition meant first and foremost that States should accept the obligation to do all in their power to achieve certain clearly defined aims, without, however, undertaking to attain them in a specified period. Admittedly, they could be achieved only by slow progress, and the time involved would vary according to the relative magnitude of the problems of each country and the means at its disposal.[11]

In order to stress the progressive nature of the obligation to realize the right to primary, secondary and higher education, the clause "with a view to achieving the full realisation of this right" was added. This was believed to be necessary, since it would be unrealistic to expect that states would be capable of realizing these levels of education immediately.[12] In short, the term "to recognise" does not mean the absence or soft character of obligations for states: "Rather recognition triggers the application of general state obligations under Article 2(1)" (Alston and Quinn 1987, 185). It should be stressed, however, that one should differentiate between sub-paragraphs 2(a) (primary education), 2(b) (secondary education) and 2(c) (higher education) of Article 13. The obligation contained in sub-paragraph 2(a) ("Primary education shall be compulsory and available free to all") is unconditional and plainly defined, without a reference to progressiveness. Sub-paragraphs 2(b) and (c) contain conjugations of the verb "to make" and this strengthens their character of progressive realization. That the legal obligation contained in sub-paragraph 2(a) is stronger can also be inferred from Article 14, which is devoted to the implementation of compulsory and free primary education for all for states parties which have not yet reached that goal. The CESCR attaches great value to the guarantee of compulsory and free primary education. When discussing, for example, the report of Zaire, the committee made it clear that charging fees for primary education is contrary to Article 13, paragraph 2(a). A state party cannot justify such a measure by referring to severe economic circumstances: "The provision of such education was an obligation which remained incumbent upon a State Party whatever economic system it had adopted."[13]

In its general comment on Article 13, the Committee on Economic, Social and Cultural Rights (1999c, para. 6) defines Article 13(2) as the right to receive an education. It distinguishes between four interrelated and essential features of education, namely:

- *availability*: functioning educational institutions and programmes have to be available in sufficient numbers in a country, through a public education system and allowing private parties to establish non-public schools;
- *accessibility*: educational institutions and programmes have to be accessible to everyone, without discrimination on any ground, also implying physical and economic accessibility;
- *acceptability*: the form and substance of education, including curricula and teaching methods, have to be relevant, culturally appropriate and of good quality and in accordance with the best interests of the child; this includes a safe and healthy school environment;
- *adaptability*: education has to be flexible, so that it can adapt to the needs of changing societies and communities, and respond to the needs of students within their specific social and cultural context, including the evolving capacities of the child.

This "4-A" scheme is a useful device to analyse the content of the right to receive an education and the general obligations for a state party resulting from it, and measuring the level of its implementation.[14]

The Undertaking "To Respect" the Freedom of Education

According to Article 13(3), states parties undertake to have respect for the liberty of parents to choose other than public schools for their children and to ensure the religious and moral education of their children. The same obligation is encountered in other international instruments, such as the International Covenant on Civil and Political Rights (Article 18(4)), the European Convention on Human Rights (Article 2 of First Protocol) and the UNESCO Convention against Discrimination in Education (Article 5(1b)). At first sight, this obligation only has a negative meaning, i.e. a protection against state interference. From the case law of the Strasbourg supervisory bodies on Article 2 of the First Protocol to the European Convention, however, it can be concluded that the obligation "to respect" should be interpreted in a positive sense as well; it requires a positive, tolerant attitude from the state towards the religious or philosophical convictions of parents when a state wants to introduce subjects into the public school curriculum which may interfere with those convictions (see European Commission 1975, 46; European Court of Human Rights 1982, 18). The European Commission, for example, stated:

> Article 2 not only prohibits the State from *preventing* parents from arranging the education of their children outside the public schools, but also requires the State actively to respect parental convictions within the public schools. This requirement is then obviously not met simply by the observance by the respondent Government of the prohibition, and by the availability of private schools or alternative means of education other than the public schools. (European Commission 1975, 44)

A positive way to respect parental convictions is, for example, the granting of exemption for certain subjects of the curriculum. It is submitted that the term "to respect" in Article 13(3) of the covenant has a similar meaning. The character of the obligation "to respect" is such that it ensures a domain which is free from state interference. This type of obligation fits in well with obligations relating to the implementation of civil and political rights, such as the rights to privacy and to family life. No further measures of implementation are required for it to function in the domestic legal order of state parties. It is of an immediate nature. The term "liberty" in Article 13(3) was expressly chosen over the term "right" in order to ensure that this provision "should not be understood as imposing upon States Parties to the Covenant the obligation to provide religious education in public schools".[15]

Another element of the freedom of education is the liberty of individuals and bodies to establish and direct educational institutions outside the system of state schools. Article 13(4) does not contain the term "to respect", but prohibits the state to interpret Article 13 in such a way that it interferes with this liberty, in other words violates such freedom. The functioning of this liberty within the domestic legal order of a state is subject to such minimum standards as may be laid down by the state. It is evident that such standards may not frustrate this freedom. In addition, non-public schools must comply with the purposes of education laid down in Article 13(1). In fact, this paragraph obliges the state in principle to take a similar course of conduct as in the implementation of the obligation "to respect" of paragraph 3.

OTHER RELEVANT UNIVERSAL INSTRUMENTS

This section highlights briefly a number of universal treaties which contain extensive provisions on the right to education.

The first instrument to be discussed is the Convention against Discrimination in Education, adopted by UNESCO's General Conference in 1960.[16] This convention aims to contribute to the elimination of discrimination in education and the promotion of equality of opportunity and treatment for all in education. The *raison d'être* of this treaty should be understood against the background of discrimination and segregation in education under the apartheid regime in South Africa at that time. This convention is important because it contains an extensive definition of discrimination in education. Article 1 reads:

> For the purposes of this Convention, the term "discrimination" includes any distinction, exclusion, limitation or preference which, being based on race, colour, sex, language, religion, political or other opinion, national or social origin, economic condition or birth, has the purpose or effect of nullifying or impairing equality of treatment in education and in particular:
>
> – Of depriving any person or group of persons of access to education of any type or at any level;
>
> – Of limiting any person or group of persons to education of an inferior standard;
>
> – Subject to the provisions of Article 2 of this Convention, of establishing or maintaining separate educational systems or institutions for persons or groups of persons; or
>
> – Of inflicting on any person or group of persons conditions which are incompatible with the dignity of man.
>
> For the purposes of this Convention, the term "education" refers to all types and levels of education, and includes access to education, the standards and quality of education, and the conditions under which it is given.

Excluded from the scope of the definition of discrimination in education are separate educational institutions for girls and boys, separate education systems for religious or linguistic reasons and private educational institutions (Article 2). Articles 3 and 4 provide for concrete state obligations to eliminate discrimination in education and promote equality of opportunity and treatment for all. Article 5(1)(c) provides for a limited recognition of the right of members of national minorities to carry on their own educational activities and use and teach their own language, but under strict conditions inspired by the fear of autonomy or even secession by national minorities.[17]

The second instrument to be discussed is the Convention on the Elimination of All Forms of Discrimination against Women, adopted in 1979.[18] The first sentence of Article 10 mentions the purpose of this provision, namely an obligation for states parties to eliminate discrimination against women in order to ensure equal rights with men in the field of education. To realize that goal states parties must ensure, among other things, on a basis of equality of men and women, access to the same curricula, the same examinations, teaching staff with qualifications of the same standard and school premises and equipment of the same quality. In addition, states parties are under an obligation to take measures to meet the specific educational needs of girls and women, such as the reduction of female student drop-out rates and the organization of programmes for girls and women who have left school prematurely, and access to specific educational information relating to women's health and family planning. It is interesting to note that this article explicitly requires states to encourage co-education of boys and girls as a means to eliminate stereotyped ideas about the role of men and women in society, while the UNESCO convention discussed above explicitly allowed separate educational institutions for boys and girls. There has been clearly a change of thinking about this issue over the years. It is obvious from Article 10 that states parties have positive obligations which may have drastic effects for those states in which discrimination against girls and women is a structural and systemic characteristic of society and everyday life.

The third instrument to be mentioned here is the Convention on the Rights of the Child, adopted in 1989.[19] The characteristic feature of obligations of states parties resulting from this treaty is the idea that the best interests of the child must be the guiding principle for measures taken for the care and protection of children (Article 3(1)). Articles 28 and 29 deal with education rights of children. These provisions link up with the corresponding articles of the Universal Declaration of Human Rights and the ICESCR. However, compared to these provisions the Convention on the Rights of the Child contains a number of special characteristics which deserve a brief discussion here. At first, Article 28(1a) puts more emphasis on the progressive realization of the right to primary education (use of the verb "to make"), while Articles 13(2a) and 14 of the covenant are more mandatory and strict. Furthermore, Article 28(2) stipulates that states parties shall take all appropriate measures to ensure that school discipline is administered in a manner consistent with the child's human dignity and in conformity with the present convention. Such a provision is lacking in other instruments, with the exception of Article 11(5) of the African Charter on the Rights and Welfare of the Child. Article 28(2) would imply, in the author's view, that corporal punishment at schools is contrary to the rights of the child. Article 28(1e) emphasizes the importance of regular school attendance and the reduction of drop-out rates, aspects which are also lacking in other instruments. Article 29(1) is more extensive and specific with regard to the aims of education in relation to the development of a child's personality. Finally, Article 32(1) provides for protective measures by the state against economic exploitation of children (child labour) which might impede their education. In conclusion, one may say that this convention adds a number of important elements for the protection and education of children which mean a step forward on the way to securing their rights.[20]

The last universal instrument to be mentioned here is ILO Convention No. 169 Concerning Indigenous and Tribal Peoples in Independent Countries.[21] This convention is a revised version of ILO Convention No. 107 on Indigenous and Tribal Populations adopted in 1957. The latter convention aimed at the assimilation of indigenous groups into the non-indigenous community and reflected a paternalistic approach. Criticism by NGOs and indigenous groups led to a revised treaty text, adopted by the International Labour Conference in 1989 (on this process, see Donders 2002, 208–12). The approach that this convention takes towards indigenous peoples is laid down in its preamble. It recognizes:

the aspirations of these peoples to exercise control over their own institutions, ways of life and economic development and to maintain and develop their identities, languages and religions, within the framework of the States in which they live.

The convention recognizes the cultural identity of indigenous groups and subscribes to the need to involve members of indigenous groups in decision-making and policy matters that are of their concern. It seeks to strike a balance between the integration of indigenous groups in society as a whole and their emancipation as distinct groups. This idea is reflected, for example, in one of the treaty provisions on education. Article 29 reads:

> The imparting of general knowledge and skills that will help children belonging to the peoples concerned to participate fully and on an equal footing in their own community and in the national community shall be an aim of education of these peoples.

The other provisions that deal with education issues provide for equal treatment of indigenous peoples with other members of society (Article 26), the involvement of members of indigenous groups in the development of education programmes (Article 27(1)–(2)) and the right of indigenous peoples to establish their own educational institutions with the financial assistance of the state (Article 27(3)). Article 28 deals with the issue of learning the indigenous language for members of these groups, learning the national language and the preservation and promotion of the indigenous languages. Finally, Article 31 aims at the elimination, through education, of prejudice about indigenous groups that exists among people who belong to the majority in a society. Most of these provisions are not framed in terms of rights of indigenous groups, but as obligations for state authorities (compare Article 2), with the exception of the right of indigenous peoples to establish their own educational institutions. The latter is a right that is part of general international law (Permanent Court of International Justice 1935). Although it contains a number of clauses which enable states to escape from certain obligations,[22] the convention as a whole and the education provisions in particular reflect progress compared to the 1957 convention.

I guess just reference this & move on.

REGIONAL INSTRUMENTS

This section will discuss briefly the main instruments adopted in the European, African and Latin American regions.

In Europe, Article 2 of the First Protocol to the European Convention for the Protection of Human Rights and Fundamental Freedoms reads as follows:

> No person shall be denied the right to education. In the exercise of any functions which it assumes in relation to education and to teaching, the State shall respect the right of parents to ensure such education and teaching in conformity with their own religious and philosophical convictions.

(This seems unbalanced.
1st — no-one denied is odd.
2nd — straight into respect for parents. — where are the kids rights?
— what is odd?

This article gives an entitlement to access to public educational institutions without discrimination. It also requires a state party to abstain from interference in the free exercise and free choice of education by pupils and parents. The European Commission and the European Court of Human Rights have interpreted this provision as requiring states only to maintain the level of education services existing at a given time, without imposing an obligation to expand education facilities or to raise disbursements for education.[23] It is thus a rather minimalist provision.

Access to education within the context of labour and other professional activities is covered by the right to vocational training laid down in Article 10 of the European Social Charter (1961). Educational rights of national minorities in the European region were included in Articles 12–14 of the Council of Europe Framework Convention for the Protection of National Minorities (1995). For example, Article 13(1) recognizes the right of persons belonging to a national minority to set up and manage their own (private) educational institutions. However, this right shall not entail any financial obligations for states parties (Article 13(2)). In order to strike a balance between the rights of national minorities on the one hand and territorial integrity and the need for integration of such minorities in society as a whole on the other, Article 14 recognizes that every person belonging to a national minority has the right to learn his or her minority language. However, Article 14 also stipulates that the exercise of this right shall be without prejudice to the learning or teaching of the official language of a country. Other provisions on the protection of regional or minority languages in matters of education have been laid down in Article 8 of the European Charter for Regional or Minority Languages (1992). Finally, within the framework of the European Union a non-binding Charter of Fundamental Rights was adopted in 2000.[24] Article 14 deals with the right to education. It contains the key elements of the European Convention on Human Rights and the European Social Charter relating to education, but it adds that the right to education includes the possibility to receive free compulsory education (Article 14(2)). The latter element is also a key part of ICESCR Article 13.

As for Africa, Article 17(1) of the African Charter on Human and Peoples' Rights[25] provides that "Every individual shall have the right to education." The charter does not contain an elaboration of this brief and general provision. However, in 1990 members of the Organization of African Unity adopted the African Charter on the Rights and Welfare of the Child.[26] This treaty contains a detailed provision on the right to education (Article 11). It is modelled after other universal human rights instruments in which the right to education is incorporated, in particular the ICESCR and the Convention on the Rights of the Child. It also contains some elements that are relevant from an African perspective. These include a clause that education shall be directed to the preservation and strengthening of positive African morals, traditional values and cultures and to the promotion and achievements of African unity and solidarity (Article 11(2)(c) and (f)). Furthermore, Article 11(6) stipulates that states parties shall take all appropriate measures to ensure that children who become pregnant before completing their education shall have an opportunity to continue with their education on the basis of their individual ability. States parties have an additional responsibility to assist parents and, in case of need, provide material assistance and support programmes with regard to nutrition, health, education, clothing and housing (Article 20(2)(a)). The latter provision entails a clear and positive obligation for states parties.

As far as the American continent is concerned, there are several human rights instruments that contain references to the right to education. These are complementary to the protection provided for at the national level. First of all, there is the American Declaration of the Rights and Duties of Man adopted in May 1948, well before the Universal Declaration of Human Rights. Being a declaration, it is a non-binding instrument, but it is applicable to those states that have not ratified the human rights treaties of the Organization of American States (OAS). Article XII deals with the right to education, while Article XXXI provides that it is the duty of every person to acquire at least an elementary education. The American Convention, adopted in 1969, does not contain economic, social and cultural rights, but in Article 26 there is a general obligation for states parties to adopt measures to realize progressively the rights that are implicit in, *inter alia*, the education-related provisions listed in the OAS Charter (Articles 45–49). In 1988 a protocol to the American Convention on Human Rights in the area of economic, social and cultural rights was adopted (Protocol of San Salvador).[27] Article 13 deals with the right to education, and strongly resembles ICESCR Article 13. It includes the right to receive an education and the right to choose an education. Furthermore, in Article 16 about the rights of children, there is another reference to the right to education. What is special about this protocol is that the complaints procedure of the American Convention on Human Rights applies to two provisions of the protocol, namely certain trade union rights (Article 8a) and the right to education (Article 13). That means there is a mechanism open to individuals to enforce this right from the state, in case these rights "are violated by action directly attributable to a State Party to this Protocol".[28] Another instrument that needs to be mentioned here is the Andean Charter for the Promotion and Protection of Human Rights.[29] This is a non-legally binding text adopted by the heads of state of the Andean Community in 2002, comparable to the Charter of Fundamental Rights of the European Union. This instrument proclaimed "the principles, objectives and commitments of the Andean Community regarding the promotion and protection of human rights". Article 24 reaffirms the commitments of states to comply with obligations set forth in the ICESCR, the right to education being one of them. A final instrument is the OAS Draft Declaration on the Rights of Indigenous Peoples, which provides in Article IX a number of education rights of indigenous peoples. States shall take a number of measures to realize these rights. However, the declaration, once adopted, will be of a non-binding nature.[30]

THE CONCEPT OF A CORE CONTENT OF ECONOMIC, SOCIAL AND CULTURAL RIGHTS

The "Core Content" Concept

This section makes some general observations on the concept of a core content of economic, social and cultural rights, and illustrates these observations by identifying some elements of the core content of the right to education.

Generally speaking, proper discussion of the core content of individual rights started only some 15 years ago (for a discussion of these developments see Coomans 2004, 72–8). The term "core content" is to be regarded as a useful means or instrument in helping to analyse and clarify the normative content of economic, social and cultural rights, which are often described as vague and open-ended, with a view to assessing the conduct of states in this field in general and identifying violations in particular. The CESCR referred to the term in its general comment on Article 2(1):

> the Committee is of the view that a minimum core obligation to ensure the satisfaction of, at the very least, minimum essential levels of each of the rights is incumbent upon every State Party. Thus, for example, a State Party in which any significant number of individuals is deprived of essential foodstuffs, or essential primary health care, of basic shelter and housing, or of the most basic forms of education is, prima facie, failing to discharge its obligations under the Covenant. If the Covenant were to be read in such a way as not to establish such a minimum core obligation, it would be largely deprived of its *raison d'être*. (Committee on Economic, Social and Cultural Rights 1990, Annex III, para. 10)

The committee has also started to use the concept in general comments on substantive rights, such as food and education.[31] In the academic literature, Alston (1987, 353) has argued for the use of the term "core content", postulating that "each right must [...] give rise to an absolute minimum entitlement, in the absence of which a State Party is to be considered to be in violation of its obligations". In the author's view, the core content of a right must be understood as meaning its essence, i.e. that essential element without which a right loses its substantive significance as a human right (see Coomans 1992, 38–9; Limburg Principles 1986, No. 56). In fact, therefore, the core content embodies the intrinsic value of each human right. It is a non-variable element of a substantive right.

The core content of a right should be universal; a country-dependent core would undermine the concept of the universality of human rights. The question is, of course, whether the core content of a right should be general and abstract or detailed and concrete. The author's answer would be that a workable definition should be somewhere in between. In general terms the core of a right should be the same everywhere; but it should be "translated" or operationalized at the national or regional level, taking into account national or regional characteristics and circumstances and the specific needs of individuals and groups. However, from a conceptual perspective, the needs of the people and the available opportunities in a state should not determine the core of a right. It should rather be the other way around, starting with the right itself.

In case the core of a right has been realized in a rich state without much difficulty, this would not mean that such a state may lean back and argue that it is complying with its treaty obligations. On the contrary, the task would then be to implement the peripheral part of the scope of a right. In other words, the point of departure for a core content approach would be, in the author's view, the concept of human dignity. The core of a right is to be considered as an expanding floor (not a fixed ceiling), or a bottom from which governments should endeavour to go up, trying to reach higher levels of realization. This also creates a link to the idea of progressive realization contained in ICESCR Article 2(1), which embodies a dynamic element, meaning that realization does not stop when a certain level has been reached.

Complying with obligations which relate to the core of a right should not be dependent upon the availability of resources. In other words, when a government is facing policy dilemmas as a result of limited or insufficient financial resources, priority should be given to the realization of the core of a right. In this respect it is interesting to note that the CESCR has qualified core obligations as non-derogable (Committee on Economic, Social and Cultural Rights 2000, para. 47; 2001, para. 18). In conclusion, the content of a right determines the nature of state obligations, not the other way round. Indeed, the individual right (the norm) should be central. The norm, including its core, gives rise to state obligations, part of them relating to the core (core obligations). Core obligations may be negative as well as positive.

Elements of the Core Content of the Right to Education

First the scope of the right to education needs to be identified as all those elements of the right covered by human rights treaty provisions. That does not only include provisions dealing explicitly with the right to education, such as in the ICESCR and the CRC, but also overlapping elements of other rights. Examples include the right to non-discrimination, rights of the child as a distinct category, freedom of religion (respect for the religious convictions of parents concerning the choice of education for their children), freedom of association (freedom to establish schools), right to privacy (free choice of education, without interference by the state), cultural rights of indigenous groups and the right to work (for teachers and the right to vocational training).

Some of the elements which make up the core content of the right to education are stipulated in ICESCR Articles 13 and 14. Other elements may be inferred from these provisions. There is a clear relationship with elements of the "4-A" scheme identified above.

Access to education on a non-discriminatory basis (accessibility)

First, the essence of the right to education means that no one shall be denied a right to education. In practice this means an individual right of access to the education available, or in more concrete terms the right of access to the existing public educational institutions on a non-discriminatory basis.[32] An example of a violation of this right is restricting access of people belonging to a specific ethnic, linguistic or religious group to the existing public educational institutions, for example the practice in some European countries of discriminating against Roma children in getting access to certain types of education (Coomans 2002). In addition, education provided by the state should be of the same quality for all groups in society; girls, for example, should not be given education of an inferior quality compared to boys (Article 1(1) of the UNESCO Convention against Discrimination in Education (1960) and CEDAW Article 10). Another (extreme) example was the situation in Afghanistan where the Taliban regime banned girls and women from all types of educational institutions (Human Rights Watch 1999).[33] A more subtle case relates to the rule and practice in schools in some African countries to force female students to disclose their pregnancy and to leave the school once the pregnancy has been discovered. This has been found discriminatory against women in a case before the Botswana Court of Appeal (Quansah 1995). Accessibility includes two other dimensions: physical accessibility (education has to be within safe physical reach for children), and economic accessibility (education has to be affordable to all) (Committee on Economic, Social and Cultural Rights 1999c, para. 6).

The right to enjoy free and compulsory primary education (availability)

A second element of the core content of the right to education is the right to enjoy primary education in one form or another, not necessarily in the form of traditional classroom teaching. Primary education is so fundamental for the development of a person's abilities that it can be rightfully defined as a minimum claim. For example, the Supreme Court of India has held the right to (primary) education to be implicit in the right to life because of its inherent fundamental importance.[34] International law on human rights does not define the term "primary education", but guidelines for using this concept and others have been developed within the framework of international organizations such as UNESCO.[35] Primary education relates to the first layer of a formal school system: it usually begins between the ages of five and seven and lasts approximately six years, but in any case no fewer than four years (Tomasevski 1999; Melchiorre 2004). Primary education includes the teaching of basic learning needs and basic education. The term "basic education" is nowadays often used, for example within the framework of international conferences on education, such as the World Declaration on Education for All (Jomtien, Thailand, 1990 and Dakar, 2000), but it is not part of international human rights law. Basic education relates to the content of education, not to the form (formal or non-formal schooling) in which it is presented. As laid down in the Jomtien Declaration: "the focus of basic education must, therefore, be on actual learning acquisition and outcome, rather than exclusively upon enrolment, continued participation in organized programmes and completion of certification requirements" (Article 4). Apart from a school and classroom system, basic education may be given in less traditional forms, such as village- or community-based, or in the open air. This may be necessary owing to shortcomings of the formal school system (lack of adequate buildings, teaching materials or teachers), or because parents are unable to pay for participation in the formal school system. Basic education within the context of the right to primary education as an element of the core content of the right to education would, in the author's view, include literacy, arithmetic, skills relating to one's health, hygiene and personal care, and social skills such as oral expression and problem-solving.[36] In addition, basic education must incorporate some teaching of concepts and values as laid down in Articles 26(2) of the Universal Declaration of Human Rights, ICESCR Article 13(1) and CRC Article 29(1), including respect for human rights. One very important precondition for primary education as a core element is that education should respect the rights of minorities and indigenous populations, in the sense that it should recognize their cultural identity, plight and heritage. An example would be the teaching of literacy in the child's first language (Dall 1995, 153, 158–63).

Usually, basic education is aimed at children within the framework of primary schooling. However, such education is also relevant for other persons who lack basic knowledge and skills. This dimension is called fundamental education in terms of ICESCR Article 13(2d). This type of education is rather broad and would include, *inter alia*, basic literacy and arithmetic, but also basic professional skills which enable people to function as members of society, take part in social and cultural life, generate income, participate in projects aimed at community development and have access to and utilize information from a variety of sources (for example, computer technologies). The enjoyment of this right is not limited by age or gender; it extends to children, youth and adults, including older persons; it is an integral component of adult education and lifelong learning (Committee on Economic, Social and Cultural Rights 1999c, paras 23 and 24). Providing secondary and other forms of education would not belong to the core of the right. These levels of education have less priority from the perspective of the essence of acquiring a basic education.

Primary education as a core element also means that no one, for example parents or employers, can withhold a child from attending primary education (see also Committee on Economic, Social and Cultural Rights 1999a, para. 6). A state has an obligation to protect this right from encroachments by third persons. The obligation of the state to provide for primary education may be characterized both as an obligation of conduct and an obligation of result. When seen from the perspective of ICESCR Article 14 it is an obligation of conduct, because it requires a state to set up and work out a plan of action, within two years after becoming a party to the covenant, for the progressive implementation of compulsory primary education free of charge for all within a reasonable number of years. On the other hand, it is also an obligation of result in terms of meeting basic learning needs, which may be complied with through a variety of delivery systems (e.g. formal or non-formal) and means, providing specific levels of knowledge and skills will be realized.

According to Article 13(2a), primary education shall be compulsory. Usually the starting age for compulsory primary education is six or seven, but the duration of primary education varies considerably between countries. Worldwide there is a trend to lengthen compulsory schooling beyond primary schooling. The rationale for a minimum duration of compulsory schooling beyond 11 years of age is that it should last at least to the minimum age of employment (Tomasevski 2000a, para. 46 and Table 3; Melchiorre 2004). It is obviously not sufficient for primary education to be compulsory by law; what is also necessary is an official state inspection service to supervise and enforce this duty with respect to parents, schools, employers and pupils themselves.

There are a number of factors which may influence actual attendance of children at school.[37] These include inadequacy of school services, such as the distance between a student's home and the school combined with a lack of transport facilities, and lack of running water and sanitation facilities at school. Other factors relate to the socio-economic and cultural status of parents. These include inability to pay for school attendance of their children, traditional attitudes which downgrade education of girls in particular, loss of family income that a child attending classes would otherwise earn, other constraints arising from religion, class, occupation or custom and the inability of parents to help their children in the learning process. Particularly relevant is the physical and mental health condition of children, which may influence school attendance. Other factors which may negatively influence school attendance include teaching given in a language other than the child's mother tongue, a school timetable which is incompatible with seasonal work by children, particularly in rural areas, and the phenomenon that teaching materials and methods do not fit in with the cultural background of children and their parents (adaptability of education).

Article 13(2a) also stipulates that primary education shall be free. The rationale of free primary education should be understood on the basis of entitlement, rather than ability to pay (Tomasevski 2004a, para. 8):

> The human rights obligation of Governments to adequately fund education exists so that children would not have to pay for their schooling or remain deprived of it when they cannot afford the cost. Children cannot wait to grow, hence their prioritized right to education in international human rights law. The damage of denied education while they are growing up cannot be retroactively remedied.

The degree to which primary education is really free is determined by a number of direct and indirect costs,[38] such as school fees,[39] expenses for textbooks and supplies, costs for extra lessons, expenses for meals at school canteens, expenses for school transport, school uniforms or other items of clothing and footwear, medical expenses and boarding fees, where applicable. In some countries it is the practice that the village community or parents provide labour for constructing, running or maintaining the school; this may be seen as a form of indirect costs for those involved. Another form of indirect costs for parents is taxation. Through the fiscal policy of the state, families contribute to the costs of education. Its effects upon the accessibility of education will depend upon the progressiveness of the tax system: do low-income groups pay less, in absolute and relative terms, compared to high-income groups (Tomasevski 1998, para. 12)? One should also look into the effects of IMF and World Bank poverty reduction strategy papers upon the accessibility of education if an increase in education fees is part of the package of measures agreed between the government concerned and the IMF. It is then important to know whether financial or other forms of assistance or compensatory measures are available for underprivileged persons and groups to safeguard continued access to education as a human right (Tomasevski 2000b, paras 29–34).

Primary education must have priority in resource allocation, because it deals with the fundamental basis for a person's development and the development of society as a whole.[40] This would be in line with the idea of a core content of rights which should be seen as a bottom or floor from which states should endeavour to go up. It is the responsibility of the state to provide for primary education and maintain education services. A government cannot waive that responsibility by giving more room to the private sector, or stimulating public-private partnerships for financing the education infrastructure.[41] With respect to the right to education in the European Convention, the Strasbourg court held that a state cannot absolve itself from responsibility by delegating its obligations to private school bodies (European Court of Human Rights 1993, para. 27). UNICEF (Bellamy 1999, 63) has emphasized that "only the State [...] can pull together all the components into a coherent but flexible education system". In its general comment on ICESCR Article 13, the CESCR has stressed that "Article 13 regards States as having principal responsibility for the direct provision of education in most circumstances" (Committee on Economic, Social and Cultural Rights 1999c, para. 48). It has also stressed that states have an immediate duty to provide primary education for all (ibid., para. 51). For those states that have not yet realized compulsory and free primary education, there is an "unequivocal obligation" to adopt and implement a detailed plan of action as provided for in Article 14 (Committee on Economic, Social and Cultural Rights 1999a, para. 9).

Special facilities for persons with an education backlog (availability)

Related to the aspects discussed above is another element of the social dimension of the right to education which, in the author's view, would belong to its core content. This concerns the obligation for the state to take special measures or provide special facilities for those persons who are faced with an education backlog, or who would otherwise have no access to education at all without those special facilities. One can think of girls in rural areas, street and working children, children and adults displaced by war or internal strife and disabled persons.[42] The type of education to be given to these people should be geared to their specific educational needs and will often require specially trained teachers.

Quality of education (adaptability)

Another core element of the right to education, which is less concrete and consequently more difficult to assess, is a certain quality of education for each separate education level. In fact, the right to education implies the right to quality education: education that is available, accessible, acceptable and adaptable to the needs of learners. A state party is under an obligation to provide and maintain this quality level, otherwise attending classes would be meaningless. When assessing this quality, a state should take into account various factors, such as measurable learning outcomes of pupils and students, the efforts and training level of teachers, the availability and quality of teaching materials, the condition of school buildings, a sound school environment, school health, preventive education against HIV/AIDS and drug abuse, science and technology education, etc.[43] The quality level of education should also encompass standards regarding the purposes of education as defined in ICESCR Article 13(1) and CRC Article 29(1). The level of quality is to be determined by the national education authorities and supervised by an independent education inspection unit.

Free choice of education (acceptability)

A further element of the core content of the right to education is free choice of education without interference by the state or a third person, in particular but not exclusively with regard to religious or philosophical convictions. This element would be violated in the case of a state failing to respect the free choice of parents with regard to the religious instruction of their children (Coomans 1992, 39, 238). This means, in practice, that a state must ensure an objective and pluralist curriculum and avoid indoctrination (European Court of Human Rights 1976, 26–7).[44] This is important, because public education entails the danger of political goals, i.e. the most influential "philosophy of life" will be promoted by the state.[45] However, it should be realized that in many countries there is only limited or no opportunity to attend education of one's own choice: either there is only state-controlled education, or, in a mixed system, private education is too expensive for parents.[46] On the basis of international human rights law, there is no obligation for a state to provide financial support to private educational institutions. If it does, however, it should do so on a non-discriminatory basis (see the views of the Human Rights Committee 1999).

These core elements undoubtedly constitute the very essence of the right to education as a human right. Violation of one or more of these elements by the state would mean that the right would lose its material and intrinsic value as a human right.

The right to be educated in the language of one's own choice (acceptability)

A more controversial question is whether the right to be educated in the language of one's own choice is part of the core content of the right to education. In the *Belgian Linguistic* case, the European Court of Human Rights (1968, 31) stated that "the right to education would be meaningless if it did not imply, in favour of its beneficiaries, the right to be educated in the national language or in one of the national languages, as the case may be". This means it is the state that determines whether a specific language is to be a national or official language as a medium of instruction in education.

In addition, the court stressed that an individual cannot claim a right to state-funded education in the language of his own choice. The court rejected positive state action for rewarding such a claim.[47]

On the other hand, it is submitted that a state must respect the freedom of individuals to teach, for instance, a minority language in schools established and directed by members of that minority. This does not imply that a state must allow the use of this language as the only medium of instruction; this would be dependent on the education policy of the state. As a minimum, however, states must not frustrate the right of members of national, ethnic or linguistic minorities to be taught in their mother tongue at institutions outside the official system of public education. However, there is no state obligation to fund these institutions. This right of members of minorities is solidly established in international law.[48] It used to be a cornerstone of the minority protection system established under the auspices of the League of Nations. Moreover, the right of minorities to establish, for their own account, educational institutions in which they are entitled to use their own language was characterized by the Permanent Court of International Justice (1935, text in Hudson 1938, 496, 499) as "indispensable to enable the minority to enjoy the same treatment as the majority, not only in law but also in fact". The court considered these institutions "suitable means for the preservation of their racial peculiarities, their traditions and their national characteristics". It is in this sense that the right to be educated in the language of one's choice belongs to the core content of the right to education. It is one of the elements of a state's obligation to respect that right.

STATE OBLIGATIONS RESULTING FROM THE RIGHT TO EDUCATION

General and Specific Obligations

Obligations of states resulting from ICESCR Articles 13 and 14 may be derived from these treaty provisions themselves, Article 2(1) and General Comments Nos 3, 11 and 13 (Committee on Economic, Social and Cultural Rights 1990, 1999a, 1999c).[49] These may be divided into general obligations and specific obligations. General obligations include an immediate obligation to prohibit discrimination in law and in fact in the area of education. In addition, states have an immediate obligation to begin to take steps, for example, to make primary education compulsory and free. Moreover, states have an obligation not to take retrogressive measures, such as the introduction of school fees where previously education was free. Finally, states have an obligation to protect the most vulnerable groups in society through special programmes, such as schooling for street children. Specific obligations include an obligation to draft, adopt and implement a comprehensive national education strategy; to establish minimum standards for private educational institutions; to develop curricula that conform with the purposes of education; and to set up a school inspection system.[50]

A Typology of Obligations Relating to Implementation of the Right to Education

In order to analyse further and specify the normative content of the right to education and the nature and content of the corresponding obligations of the state, this chapter follows an obligations approach developed in the academic debate. To be more specific, it develops a typology of state obligations as an analytical tool to provide a better understanding of the scope and nature of these obligations in the process of realizing economic, social and cultural rights, and the right to education in particular. Part of the traditional view about implementation of these rights is that they only give rise to positive obligations, while civil and political rights embody only negative obligations for the state. However, it has been recognized increasingly that all human rights give rise to multiple types of duties, or, put differently, to a spectrum of duties. The full protection of a human right, whether civil, political, economic, social or cultural, requires compliance with different duties, both positive and negative.[51] Obligations are interdependent and interrelated, aimed at the full realization of a right. The idea of a typology of obligations was developed by the American political philosopher Henry Shue ([1980] 1996) in his book *Basic Rights*. It was elaborated further by different human rights scholars,[52] one of them being the Norwegian human rights expert Asbjørn Eide. He identified three levels of obligations with respect to the implementation of the right to food (Eide 1987, paras 66–71).[53] He distinguished between the obligations "to respect", "to protect" and "to fulfil" which states parties to the ICESCR have towards individuals under their jurisdiction. This typology of state obligations is also applied in recent general comments of the CESCR, such as the comments on the right to food and the right to education (Committee on Economic, Social and Cultural Rights 1999b, para. 15; 1999c, paras 49–50).

The first level is the "obligation to respect". This obligation prohibits the state itself from acting in contravention of recognized rights and freedoms. This means that the state must refrain from interfering with or constraining the exercise of such rights and freedoms. The second level is the "obligation to protect". This requires the state to take steps – through legislation or by other means – to prevent and prohibit the violation of individual rights and freedoms by third persons. The third level concerns the "obligation to fulfil". This obligation may be characterized as a programme obligation and implies more of a long-term view for its implementation. In general, this will require a financial input which cannot be accomplished by individuals alone.

This typology of obligations is applicable to economic, social and cultural rights as well as to civil and political rights. It demonstrates that the realization of a particular right may require either abstention or intervention on the part of governments. On the basis of Eide's (1987, 29) proposal for a "food security matrix", it is possible to devise a comparable matrix to identify the nature and levels of obligations relating to the implementation of the right to education (Figure 5.1). The matrix distinguishes between the "social" dimension and the "freedom" dimension of the right to education, discussed above. Within each dimension, a further itemization is proposed. The "social" dimension includes the elements of accessibility and availability of education, whereas

personal?

Personal dimension.

Content and Scope of the Right to Education as a Human Right 205

how do these relate to entitlements?

Rights in educat^n

along lines of european model.

I'm not convinced there is an exact correlation bet core content/entitlements & obligations. ALSO his app interactive bits & dift B dift. within that chapter 2 dift to this. Would it be clearer to match entitlement to obligations inclusding categorise obligations?

Dimensions of right to education	Social dimension (right to receive an education)		Freedom dimension (right to choose an education)	
Nature of state obligations	Accessibility	Availability	Liberty to choose	LIBERTY TO ESTABLISH
To respect	Respect free access to public education both in legislation, policy and practice without discrimination (MCO) (1)	Respect existing public education in minority languages	Respect religious and philosophical convictions (granting exemption) Respect freedom of school choice Respect human dignity Respect teaching in minority languages (MCO) (7)	Respect free establishment of private schools (subject to legal minimum standards); Respect (cultural) diversity in education;
To protect	Apply and uphold (3) equal access to education in legislation, policy and practice against violations by third persons (parents, employers) Adopt and implement legislation against child labour	Regulate recognition of private educational institutions and diplomas	Combat indoctrination or coercion by others Protect legally freedom (6) to choose (MCO) Combat discrimination in the admission of students to private institutions Guarantee pluralism in curriculum	Apply and uphold the principle of equality of treatment; Protect legally private teachers' training institutions and diplomas;
To fulfil	Provide special educational facilities for persons with (4) educational back-log (e.g. disabled, girls, drop-outs, street children) (MCO) Eliminate passive discrimination Introduce progressively free secondary and higher education Promote scholarship system	Secure (2) compulsory and free primary education (MCO) Train teachers Make transportation facilities and teaching materials available Combat illiteracy Promote adult education Guarantee (5) quality of education (MCO)	Promote pluralism in the curriculum Promote intercultural education	Provide financial and material support to institutions for private education on a non-discriminatory basis, subject to national standards;

=> put in place too => fulfil

of safe reach? Affordable?

of certain contents.

Figure 5.1   Matrix of state obligations relating to the right to education

Note: MCO = minimum core obligation

the "freedom" dimension refers to the liberty to choose and the liberty to establish. The proposed matrix does not offer an exhaustive list of concrete state action, but merely serves as an illustration of possible options for states. Other forms of conduct or measures can be included, depending on the education situation in each country. The matrix is applicable both to developing countries with an inadequate education system and to countries in which there is a highly developed system of education. It is a device for the elaboration and clarification of the scope and nature of obligations, and it can help to determine whether a state's legislation, policy and practice are in conformity with its obligations under the covenant. The nature of the obligations remains the same; only the measures taken to implement the obligations differ. In rich countries, for example, it is necessary to maintain the existing level of education in a quantitative and qualitative sense, because a drop in services would endanger the accessibility and availability of education.

The following examples illustrate how the matrix can be applied (for other examples see Committee on Economic, Social and Cultural Rights 1999c, para. 50). The obligation "to respect" the right to education requires the state to abstain from interference. It must not prevent children from receiving education, for example by closing educational institutions in times of political tension, in non-conformity with the limitations clause of ICESCR Article 4 (ibid., para. 59). In addition, it requires that the state does not discriminate on the basis of sex or ethnic origin with respect to admission to public schools. Detailed standards for non-discrimination and equal treatment of individuals in education are laid down in the UNESCO Convention against Discrimination in Education (1960), particularly in Articles 1 and 3. The obligation "to respect" can be characterized as an obligation of conduct: it requires the state to follow the course of action specified in the treaty provision (Coomans 1992, 231–2; Nowak 1991, 421–2). The obligation "to protect" requires the state to guarantee the exercise of the right to education in horizontal relations (between private groups or individuals); for example, it must protect against discrimination in admitting students to private schools. Other examples of the obligation to protect are the adoption and enforcement of legislation to combat child or bonded labour in private labour relations, and arrangements for monitoring and enforcing compulsory primary education.

The nature of the right to education is such that positive state action is needed to achieve the full realization of this right. In the opinion of the CESCR, "it is clear that Article 13 regards States as having principal responsibility for the direct provision of education in most circumstances" (Committee on Economic, Social and Cultural Rights 1999c, para. 48), which can be seen as an affirmation of the obligation to fulfil. The obligation "to fulfil" requires states to make the various types of education available and accessible for all and to maintain that level of realization. In order to achieve that aim, states must take a variety of measures. Although legislation may be necessary to provide a legal framework, primarily policy measures, financial and material support are needed to realize this right.[54] The obligation "to fulfil" implies that states have a substantial degree of latitude in complying, depending also upon the specific level of education and taking into account the wording of the treaty obligation (ibid.) – for example, *primary education shall be compulsory and available free to all* (Article 13(2)(a)) versus *the progressive introduction of free secondary education* (Article 13(2)(b)). Implementation of the latter clause gives more latitude to the state than the former. Therefore, the obligation "to fulfil" should be characterized as an obligation of result, leaving the choice of means to the state, providing the result achieved conforms to international standards.

Minimum Core Obligations

It can be seen from the matrix that specific elements of the core content of the right to education give rise to concrete obligations. These obligations may be characterized as minimum core obligations (MCOs), as defined by the CESCR in its general comment on the nature of states parties' obligations (Committee on Economic, Social and Cultural Rights 1990, para. 10). Such obligations are not limited to cost-free (negative) obligations to respect, but also include positive obligations to protect and to fulfil. MCOs resulting from the core content of the right to education apply irrespective of the availability of resources.[55] It is interesting to note that the CESCR also briefly refers to the core content concept in its general comment on Article 13, but framed in terms of core obligations for the state, echoing the wording of General Comment No. 3 on the nature of state obligations. According to the committee, the minimum core obligation with respect to the right to education includes an obligation:

> to ensure the right of access to public educational institutions and programmes on a non-discriminatory basis; to ensure that education conforms to the objectives set out in article 13(1); to provide primary education for all in accordance with article 13(2)(*a*); to adopt and implement a national educational strategy which includes provision for secondary, higher and fundamental education; and to ensure free choice of education without interference from the State or third parties, subject to conformity with 'minimum educational standards' (article 13(3) and (4)). (Committee on Economic, Social and Cultural Rights 1999c, para. 57)

There is clearly overlap with the core elements discussed above, but there are also differences, such as the reference to the objectives of education mentioned in Article 13(1), an element left out here because in the author's view it would be covered by the quality level of education. The CESCR clearly decided to retain the "obligations" language used in General Comment No. 3. In practical terms, however, there seems to be little difference between the core content approach, on the one hand, and the core obligations approach on the other, because core elements of rights of individuals need to be translated into core obligations for the state. However, it may be argued that it is crucial to retain as a point of departure the right of the individual rather than the obligations of the state, because the latter derive from the former, at least from a human rights perspective.

MAIN OBSTACLES TO THE REALIZATION OF THE RIGHT TO EDUCATION

This section focuses on the main obstacles to the realization of the right to education from a human rights perspective. It identifies a number of factors that hinder the implementation of this right in terms of rights of individuals and obligations of duty bearers. These obstacles include, generally speaking, domestic legal and administrative obstacles, financial problems (lack of government resources, school fees), political obstacles (lack of political will and priority at the domestic level, constraints due to developments on the international scene), discrimination against disadvantaged groups, gender-related obstacles, cultural and socio-economic factors (such as child labour) and obstacles relating to the quality of education (substandard education). In a number of situations, several of these obstacles coincide and interrelate. This overview of obstacles is not meant to discuss in detail their impact in specific cases or country situations. Nor does the present section intend to be exhaustive in discussing all relevant factors that have a negative impact on the realization of the right to education.

Domestic Legal and Adminstrative Obstacles

Some countries have a legal system that does not allow the direct application of treaty law on economic, social and cultural rights in the domestic legal order. The relationship between international law and domestic law is of a dualistic nature: treaties are not automatically part of the domestic legal order, but need to be transformed into domestic law. That means that international legal norms do not have an independent status as minimum norms in the domestic legal order. In other countries with a monistic system in which international treaty law does become part of the domestic legal order, judges, law-makers and lawyers are unfamiliar with treaty law on economic, social and cultural rights, although direct applicability of those norms would be possible in principle. This implies that the legal profession of a country may have a poor awareness of and knowledge about treaties and their domestic effect. This is partly due to a lack of attention to and legal training about the meaning of international provisions on economic, social and cultural rights in the curricula of law schools. This shortcoming is crucial in explaining why the legal practitioners in a country may be hesitant to give full domestic force and effect to aspects of the right to education as a human right. Although there are positive developments as far as the domestic justiciability of the right to education is concerned (Tomasevski 2004b), the legal culture of a country is still in many cases a serious obstacle.

In addition, there are administrative obstacles: civil servants in education departments are not familiar with international human rights law. Often they do not know how to implement it. For example, there is a lack of a human rights impact assessment of new legislation and policies in the sphere of education.

Financial Obstacles

Financial obstacles may be approached from two different angles. The first relates to a lack (alleged) of resources available to the government to comply with obligations resulting from the right to education as a human right. The second concerns the existence of school fees as an economic and financial barrier for parents to have their children enrolled in school. Sometimes these aspects interrelate, because the need to charge school fees is caused by an alleged lack of governmental resources.

Governments often argue that they have insufficient resources to justify their inability to make all forms of education available and accessible to all. Indeed, a lack of economic growth or an economic recession, lagging tax revenues and choices made in macroeconomic policies often mean that insufficient resources are available to invest in education. In terms of financial resources available for making primary education compulsory and free, really poor countries are highly dependent on external funds provided by donors to achieve this aim. However, in recent years there has been a decline in bilateral and multilateral aid to education (Education For All 2003, 244). In some countries plans of action, which should be drafted by governments in accordance with ICESCR Article 14, often do not exist, because the government lacks the resources provided by foreign donors to implement the plan.[56] In other countries action plans for education are ready, but there are no resources available to implement them (High-Level Group on Education for All 2003, 20–21). Sometimes the lack of resources is the result of external causes, such as decreasing foreign revenues owing to a fall in the price of agricultural exports or raw materials on the world market, foreign debt repayments or the need to cut the state budget for austerity reasons. However, in many cases chronic under-financing for education is also a product of flawed domestic budgeting, such as insufficient resource mobilization, inequitable patterns of expenditure and misplaced budget priorities (such as excessive funding for military purposes) (Watkins 1999, 136). Also relevant are a lack of coherence in financing and a failure to develop integrated strategies aimed at achieving education for all. For example, the lack of a coherent policy for teacher recruitment and teacher training and an efficient plan for deployment and management of teachers is an important obstacle, in particular when no specific and targeted budget is available to support such a policy. However, part of the problem is indeed financial, because teachers' salaries absorb a huge part of the education budget.

As a reaction to the lack of government resources available for education, a number of African countries decided to embark upon another strategy. In 1998 African ministers of education agreed that the time had come to put an end to the state monopoly of education. Under pressure from and encouraged and supported by the IMF and the World Bank, a strategy of cost-sharing between partners ("public-private partnership") is now promoted (Tomasevski 2003b, 71–7). Partners include the government on the one hand and international donors, the private sector and communities on the other. For African countries this strategy means, for example, that (international) NGOs and local communities (villages) should make up for the state's failings. They have started construction and provision of school facilities in remote areas that have been neglected by the state's education authorities.[57] If such a policy led to financial thresholds for those who are dependent on privately funded schools in certain areas, discrimination against lower income groups and other disadvantaged groups would be the result. Usually, privately funded education benefits the better-off, who can afford it. This trend of excluding disadvantaged groups would be even stronger if the quality level of those privately financed educational institutions was higher, to the detriment of public schools. This example shows that state failure to provide for education might have a negative impact on equality of opportunity for children in all sectors of society (Watkins 2000, 149; see also Coomans and Hallo de Wolf 2005).

School fees are financial obstacles for parents in enrolling their children in education. For many governments in developing countries, school fees are an important source of revenue to fund education. Introducing school fees is part of a policy of cost-sharing in education. The contradictory characteristic of levying fees is that they impose a burden on parents to contribute to the cost of education, while the state has a legal obligation to provide free compulsory primary education for all children. In the view of Oxfam (2001, 2), school fees amount to a tax on school attendance and human development.

Recent studies conclude that the cost of education is the major single reason for parents to keep children who have never attended school at home. This is also applicable to children who have attended school but dropped out, and this trend is stronger in urban areas, where fees are higher, than in rural areas (Education For All 2003, 217). However:

> Any attempt to explain why children either do not attend school or drop out in terms of single causes would be flawed. Different problems interact and become mutually reinforcing. Household demand for education is influenced by cost. But poor households also make judgments about the relationship between cost and the quality of education offered, the distance children have to travel to go to school, and the benefits of education. In each case, gender will be a major factor. Where school quality is deteriorating or costs are rising, as in many low-income countries, it will tend to be girls who are withdrawn first, reflecting a view that the education of girls is less important than those of boys. (Watkins 2000, 117)

In more than 100 countries worldwide there is a practice of levying school fees, despite the fact that many countries have ratified human rights instruments providing for free primary education and the progressive introduction of free secondary and higher education (Education For All 2003, 136). Out of 31 countries in South America and the Caribbean, 12 charge school fees. In five of those 12 countries there is no legal guarantee of free primary education. In sub-Saharan Africa 28 out of 44 countries charge fees for primary education. Fourteen out of those 28 have no legal guarantee of free primary education (Tomasevski 2003c, 68–70).

School fees are not limited to private educational institutions; they are also common practice in many public schools, although public education may nominally be free. This means that parents have no real choice, because both private and public schools are fee-based. For poor families this is a serious problem, because if they cannot afford the payment of the fee, the only option is to keep the child out of school. In particular, flat-rate payments for each child that attends education have a regressive effect, because these will absorb a large part of low incomes. Poor families normally have more children than wealthier families, and richer families usually have more financial room to pay for additional costs of education, such as private tuition and more expensive educational materials (Watkins 2000, 118). Governments present all kinds of reasons as a justification for having or introducing school fees for children of compulsory school age. These include a lack of sufficient public schools compared to the number of private schools that charge fees, lack of government funding of public schools and the need to cut public spending for education as a consequence of structural adjustment programmes (Tomasevski 2003c, 81–2).[58]

Since 1994 a number of sub-Saharan African countries have introduced free primary education with the assistance of external resources provided by donors (for a description and analysis of this development see Riddell 2003; Education For All 2003, 217–21). These countries are Kenya, Malawi, Tanzania, Uganda and Zambia. This development has had major consequences. In addition to a huge increase in the number of pupils enrolled in primary schools, there have been direct effects for the supply side of education. The increase in the number of pupils has meant pressure on classroom facilities (furniture) and educational quality, a rise in the pupil/teacher ratio, an inadequate supply of instructional materials (textbooks) and a shortage in the number of classrooms and schools. Because of the lack of sufficient tax revenues in these countries, dependency on external bilateral and multilateral (World Bank, UNICEF) donor resources to complement national resources will remain. One of the most important effects of making primary education free is the urgent need for additional teachers, their recruitment, training, professional development and guidance while they are at work. A key requirement is to have a well-trained teacher force available *before* free primary education is actually introduced, with a view to guaranteeing educational quality (Riddell 2003, 10–11). A related matter is the need for fair remuneration of teachers. In addition, it should be noted that the HIV/AIDS pandemic has had very serious effects on the teaching force in these countries (Education For All 2003, 221). Although tuition fees have been abolished in these five countries, some costs for parents remain, such as expenses for non-compulsory school uniforms (ibid., 220). Sometimes schools still need additional small contributions from parents, especially when no extra resources from the state become available to pay for school maintenance or school meals (Oxfam 2001, 11). Finally, an important side-effect of making primary education free is that additional capacity is needed in post-primary education to absorb the large numbers of pupils who have concluded their primary schooling. This may give rise to dilemmas about choices for the disbursement of scarce financial resources (Riddell 2003, 8).

Political Obstacles

An important obstacle to the realization of the right to education is of a political nature, rather than a problem of resource mobilization. Implementing the right to education presupposes the recognition of other concomitant rights that are politically sensitive, such as linguistic freedom and educational rights of minorities and the recognition of the cultural identity of indigenous groups. An educated and emancipated citizenry (such as students) may trigger calls for democratic changes, respect for human rights and accountability of those in power, and cause political unrest. Such developments may ultimately lead to a loss of power of the ruling group in a society. Nowadays, therefore, in a number of societies, education fails to receive the priority in budgetary allocation that it should have according to human rights law. There is a lack of governmental economic and fiscal policies that are explicitly based on human rights law, or that have undergone a human rights impact assessment. There are also many countries in which military spending exceeds budget allocations for education by the central government. This shows choices and priorities in government spending which are, for political reasons, not human-rights-based (Tomasevski 2003b, 11–12).

Another serious obstacle that has certain political aspects is the tension between the human rights obligations of governments on the one hand and international financial obligations, such as debt servicing, on the other. Many governments in developing countries are faced with a huge foreign debt and the necessity to pay it back, while human rights obligations require a government to make primary education free and compulsory, which involves large sums of government spending. States are thus faced with a political and legal dilemma. To alleviate unsustainable debt servicing, the international community has facilitated a mechanism that would also allow allocation of extra resources to social sector spending, such as education. Donor countries, the IMF and the World Bank established the Enhanced Heavily Indebted Poor Countries Debt Relief Initiative (HIPC-II). This initiative makes it possible to lay down in poverty reduction strategy papers (PRSPs) arrangements for the transfer of debt-servicing funds to development and poverty eradication purposes, education being one of these (ibid., 133). The problems with this laudable initiative, however, are that the mechanism itself does not consider the human rights effects of the relief measures and that the main actors in the programme – the IMF and World Bank – do not consider themselves bound by human rights instruments. For example, education policies, as part of a PRSP, are not framed in terms of rights of children and obligations of governments; so a human rights impact assessment is lacking (ibid., 136, 138). An analysis of 25 PRSPs showed that 14 explicitly mentioned school fees, while a few limited free education to the poor or to girls (Education for All 2003, 223; Tomasevski 2003c, 53). In this respect, Education for All (2003, 222) concluded that "it is difficult to see how any PRSP can ignore the issue of the affordability of primary education and of the need to eliminate or significantly reduce the charges that households bear in sending children to school".

An additional and related project launched by the World Bank in 2002, the Fast Track Initiative (FTI), provides a number of highly indebted poor countries with the possibility to embark on a fast track to achieve six-year primary school enrolment and completion, provided that they are committed to achieving universal primary education.[59] It is meant to reach the Millennium Development Goal to provide all children with primary schooling by 2015, but it is not framed in terms of realizing the right to education as a human right. The FTI is a recognition that a number of poor countries will not meet the 2015 targets without extra resources and efforts. Honduras is one of the countries that participate in the FTI. However, according to reports, the experience of Honduras with this programme has been disappointing.[60] Owing to the fact that the Honduran government was unable to get a stamp of approval from the IMF for its HIPC performance, it was not able to attract additional IMF funds for debt relief and consequently donors did not provide additional budget support to make education available for all and implement the PRSP. In addition, the IMF and the World Bank, in order to achieve a decrease in government spending, emphasized the need to cut the salaries of teachers, which would undermine the sustainability and quality of education in the longer run. This example shows a lack of impact assessment of the suggested policies from the perspective of the right to education and obligations under human rights treaties. It also shows that although the intentions of the initiative are good, political factors may hinder its implementation and lead to an outcome that is even worse than before.[61]

In more general terms, the FTI has been criticized for the gap between commitments made and actual funding by donors (Education For All 2003, 251), and the lack of civil society involvement in the FTI process has been denounced. More specifically, it has been argued that some needy countries are not able to participate in the FTI because they do not meet the criteria of having a PRSP, such as countries in conflict or post-conflict situations. Also the reduction of teachers' salaries as an element of the FTI has been controversial (ibid., 250). Finally, it has been said that the FTI means a one-sided orientation towards the costs of reaching universal primary education, thus paying little attention to the costs related to reaching gender targets and including vulnerable groups, such as indigenous populations.[62]

A final political obstacle is the fact that international armed conflicts and civil wars have a devastating impact on the realization of the right to education. School buildings and facilities are destroyed and children cannot go to school in conflict areas. Moreover, in a number of African countries where children become child soldiers, this may undermine their future once and for all. Furthermore, pupils are the victims of war traumas which may negatively influence their school performance. Girls may be especially vulnerable to sexual violence once a conflict erupts. Such children may be in need of remedial teaching and psychological help. Teachers are being killed, which makes the period of educational recovery after the end of conflict a very difficult one (ibid., 128–31).

Discrimination Against Vulnerable Groups

In order to analyse the actual situation in countries with respect to obstacles to the realization of the right to education, a non-discrimination test is very important. Which individuals or groups are being denied the right to education or do not have access to education? What are the reasons – legal, structural, financial or other – for such a situation? For example, the CESCR has made it clear that "sharp disparities in spending policies that result in differing qualities of education in different geographic locations may constitute discrimination under the Covenant" (Committee on Economic, Social and Cultural Rights 1999c, para. 35).

Active discrimination in education may occur through intentional acts or failures to act by government authorities or private persons, leading to a discriminatory situation as qualified in Article 1(1) of the UNESCO Convention against Discrimination in Education. The essential characteristic of this provision is that discrimination in education leads to an exclusion of people, based on certain grounds, that obstructs equality of treatment. There are also situations of systemic forms of discrimination in education as a result of more or less structural patterns in society due to financial, social, economic, cultural, historical or geographical reasons. Such situations lead to exclusion, impoverishment or marginalization as a more or less permanent characteristic of the treatment of certain groups in society based on ethnic origin, language, sex or economic condition.[63] An example is the situation in India with respect to child labour and attitudes to primary education. In a study on child labour and education policy, Weiner (1991) concluded that the economic situation in India and its low per capita income are less relevant than one might expect as an explanation for low school enrolments, high drop-out rates and child labour. He argued that a set of beliefs widely shared by state officials, social activists, trade union members and more generally by members of the Indian middle class are more relevant to explain this situation. At the centre of these views are beliefs about the Indian social order and the role of education as a means to maintain differentiations between social classes (the caste system). According to these views, education should be used to preserve this social structure rather than restructure it by providing access to education for the lower castes. Consequently, education policy and practice in India stress education for the better-off and discriminate against educational opportunities for the lower social classes.

Alternatively, while discrimination may be characterized as a social phenomenon that is fed by prejudice and stereotyping, discriminatory treatment of a group of people may also strengthen prejudice (Tomasevski 2002, para. 37). For example, discrimination against children of the Roma minority in the education system of a number of South-East European countries is often interpreted as evidence of their inferiority and backwardness by members of the majority, which further perpetuates negative perceptions and continued discrimination in other spheres of social life (Coomans 2002).

In the sphere of education, disadvantage and marginalization of members of a group due to, for instance, ethnic origin often do not exist in isolation, but interact with other factors, including the disparity between urban and rural regions in the sense that in rural areas there are often fewer schools available than in urban areas. Also, in peripheral and remote areas, school facilities are often of lower quality than in the capital, and teachers are overall less willing to work in remote areas. The school enrolment disparity between boys and girls also interacts with other factors, such as the urban-rural difference, the ethnic factor and the income level of households. In general, poor households in rural areas may find it much more difficult to send their children to school, and this tendency is even stronger when these households belong to an ethnic minority or indigenous group. In particular, girls suffer most in this respect. In addition, deprivation of education perpetuates poverty and thus keeps the cycle unbroken (Watkins 2000, 96–108). Research on this issue relating to the situation in Guatemala, Honduras and Mexico shows that rural and indigenous children are the most excluded from education, either because they have no access at all to school or because they drop out. For example, in Guatemala indigenous people have inadequate access to bilingual intercultural education, and the curriculum offers very little that is relevant for and adapted to the specific situation of indigenous girls (Martinic 2003, 1–2, 8, 11).

The UN Commission on Human Rights has identified additional groups of children who often suffer most from discrimination in education.[64] These include pregnant girls, migrant children, refugee children, internally displaced children, children affected by armed conflicts, children with disabilities, children with HIV/AIDS and imprisoned children. Often those children have no access to education at all, the educational services that are available are not adapted to their specific learning needs or background, or education is not acceptable from a cultural perspective (for example in a language that is not their mother tongue or alien to their indigenous culture). Children of undocumented workers who reside illegally in a country are often deprived of their right to education, not only legally but also in terms of actual access to school.[65] This may imply that they grow up without any form of education, which is fatal for their personal development.

Gender-related Obstacles

Gender-related aspects of education may refer to two different concepts (see, generally, Education For All 2003, Chapter 3; Tomasevski 2003d; Packer 2003). *Gender parity* is a quantitative concept; it refers to the equal enrolment and participation of both girls and boys in different levels of education. *Gender equality* is a qualitative concept; it refers to equal educational outcomes for boys and girls. This latter concept takes into account that girls and boys usually have a different starting position and face different obstacles. Equality in educational outcomes relates to the number of school years attended, learning performance and achievements, academic qualifications and the opportunity to find a job after completing education (Education For All 2003, 116). Both gender parity and gender equality may be studied by using a distinction between rights *to* education, rights *within* education and rights *through* education (ibid., 116–17; Wilson

2003). Rights *to* education relate to equal access for boys and girls to educational institutions. Rights *within* education relate to the possibility to enjoy basic human rights while children are in school. As far as gender is concerned, this dimension concerns situations and instances in which both girls and boys are victims of violence at school, sexism, sexual harassment, intolerance and discrimination. The central issue here is whether more girls tend to be the victim of such practices than boys. Rights *through* education deal with the opportunities pupils have to enjoy other human rights after school completion, such as the rights to work, to an adequate standard of living, to take part in cultural life, to freedom of expression and to political participation. An additional aspect is to measure progress in equality *of* both women and men, rather than merely equality *between* women and men (Tomasevski 2004a, para. 31). This refers, for example, to differences between urban and rural girls in access to education, or differences in drop-out rates between boys from poor families compared to boys from rich families.

Obstacles for girls in exercising their right *to* education relate to school facilities of a lower standard (such as fewer resources for girls' schools in countries with single-sex schooling), fewer or less-qualified teachers, and sometimes forms of overt discrimination, such as the practice in a number of countries to suspend pregnant girls from school. Also restrictions on the courses girls are allowed to take negatively affect their right to education (Chapman and Russell 1998, para. 24). There is information that income inequalities between families also exacerbate gender inequalities. This implies, *inter alia*, that girls will not be enrolled in school when a family gets poorer. In many cases, boys will be given preference over girls in attending school (Watkins 2000, 100; Education For All 2003, 135).

As far as rights *within* education are concerned, girls are often the victims of discrimination, sexual abuse, punishment and intolerance by other pupils and by teachers. This may lead to high drop-out rates and underachievement of girls compared to boys. In other words, schools are not safe havens for girls (ibid., 143–4). Other obstacles that girls face within schools include stereotypes and sexism in textbooks and curricula, a curriculum giving more weight to non-academic subjects such as vocational and home-making skills and science and mathematics courses at a lower level compared to those for boys (Chapman and Russell 1998, para. 24).

As for rights *through* education, the overall picture is that as education systems gradually achieve gender parity and improved quality, girls are likely to perform better than boys (Education For All 2003, 150). However, this does not mean that girls are in a better position to benefit from these qualifications in other spheres of life. Achieving gender equality through education is often still far away. As the UN special rapporteur on the right to education put it:

> Getting girls into schools often founders because education as a single sector does not, on its own, generate sufficiently attractive incentives for girls' parents and the girls themselves if educated girls cannot apply their education to sustaining themselves and/or helping their families. Years of attending school appear

wasted when women do not have access to employment and/or are precluded from becoming self-employed, do not have a choice as to whether to marry and bear children or their opportunities for political representation are foreclosed. (Tomasevski 2002, para. 40)

Socio-economic and Cultural Obstacles

A number of structural socio-economic and cultural factors act as barriers to the realization of the right to education in developing countries (for a discussion of several of these factors see Education For All 2003, 117–25). They are often related to gender aspects. These include traditional customs and social norms and practices within societies and families. They determine the social relationships between women and men and their roles in the family and in society. Such attitudes and views also have an impact on how people assess the value of education and whether children should go to school or stay at home. One of the basic things to take into account in this respect is a traditional division of work within the family: women and girls are supposed to do domestic labour and caring tasks, while men and boys are supposed to go out and earn a living by doing paid work. This division of labour is often characterized by a systemic pattern of discrimination against girls: sons are highly valued, while daughters are often downgraded. The reason for this is that in many societies the idea exists that boys are productive and will contribute later on to the family income, while girls only cost money. These views about the perceived roles of girls and boys to a large extent also determine whether children will go to school. The thinking about the use of child labour is often determined by parents' attitudes about the value of education, their occupation, class, religion, social and cultural traditions and geographical factors. In addition, in some societies female education has a lower value and status that male education (Watkins 2000, 128). One crucial factor is that poor families often need the work of children, both at home and outside, as an additional source of income. If children go to school, parents not only have to pay school fees in many countries, but also lose income they would have had if children had gone out to work. Many children combine going to school with part-time jobs.[66] However, in practice girls are more likely than boys to be at home doing domestic work rather than in school. For example, in Guatemala girls have to help with household tasks and productive work in rural areas, while in urban areas they take care of siblings while the mother goes out to work. In addition, safety reasons and lack of transport are important factors to explain why parents prevent their daughters from attending isolated schools in rural areas (Martinic 2003, 8; Watkins 2000, 127). This also has to do with the role that specific social norms play in family relations. In a number of societies it is quite common for girls to marry at an early age to ensure their future, which implies that they will not go to school or drop out. A girl who has not attended school will attract a higher dowry from the husband's family, because she will supposedly play a traditional role at home and not further develop her personal capacities through education. On the other hand, there are also countries in which an educated girl may yield a higher bride price for the parents. This may be a stimulus for parents to send their daughters to school, not with a view to contributing to their personal development, but as a means of getting a higher price in the marriage market.

Another obstacle related to the incidence of child labour is the legal gap that exists in some countries between the school-leaving age and the official minimum age for employment. For example, in Honduras the school-leaving age is 13, while the minimum age for employment is 14 and the official length of compulsory education is six years. In Burundi the school-leaving age is 12, while the minimum age for employment is 16 and the length of compulsory schooling is six years. In other countries the minimum employment age is lower than the minimum age for the completion of compulsory education. This is the case, for example, in Peru and Niger.[67] Matching is required in order to prevent children starting to work too early.[68] In addition, (legal) enforcement of these standards is lacking in some countries.

An example of a social norm that affects education of girls is that pregnant girls are often suspended from school as a form of punishment for violating school regulations and moral norms prohibiting teenage sexual intercourse. The Supreme Court of Colombia, however, has rejected this form of disciplinary measure and confirmed the girl's right to education:[69]

> Although a suspension from school attendance does not imply a definitive loss of the right to education, it does imply the provision of instruction to the pregnant schoolgirl in conditions which are stigmatizing and discriminatory in comparison with other pupils in her ability to benefit from [the right to education]. Surely, the stigmatization and discrimination implied in the suspension from school attendance have converted this method of instruction [through tutorials] into a disproportionate burden which the pupil has to bear solely because she is pregnant, which in the opinion of the Court, amounts to punishment [...] The conversion of pregnancy – through school regulations – into a ground for punishment violates fundamental rights to equality, privacy, free development of personality, and to education.[70]

In a number of African communities there is still resistance to educating girls. Tradition and community norms prohibit girls from attending school. This was the case in a village in Benin where girls were only allowed to be educated by the local voodoo priest in a secret rite of passage, after which they were supposed to be married. This would ensure their continued protection by the priest (Sengupta 2003).

When education is not adapted to the future of the children, or parents think education will only lead to unemployment, children will be kept out of school or drop out. An example from Burkina Faso may illustrate this:

> People who do not send their kids to school cannot solely be discarded as "ignorant" but might have made a rational choice. Firstly, education is conducted in French, the official language, which is not spoken by most people. When children come to school, they first have to learn French before they may be able to access other subjects. Secondly, unemployment is common among the youth with years in school. The economic incentive to send children to school is thus less convincing today. A main problem is that many children who go to school do not return to farm work any longer. To send children to school might constitute

a double loss: first they cannot participate in farming and herding and thus contribute to subsistence, and, second, they might be able to get a job after school but would be unwilling to accept farming again. (Hasberg 2000, 38, quoted in Tomasevski 2001b, 16)

Children are often the victims of HIV/AIDS in more than one way. They may become infected themselves when the virus is transmitted from mother to child before birth, or they may drop out of school when one parent gets ill or dies and there is no income left to pay the school fees. Furthermore, they may be faced with an education backlog if their teacher is no longer able to work because he/she has fallen ill. It has also been reported that when HIV/AIDS hits a family, girls are often the first to be taken out of school to perform caring tasks (Education For All 2003, 127; Ainsworth et al. 2005). When girls do not attend education, they face a double obstacle:

> Prevented from going to school, [girls] are denied information about how to protect themselves against the virus. Without the benefit of an education, they risk being forced into early sexual relations, and thereby becoming infected. Thus, they pay many times over the deadly price of not going to school.[71]

Obstacles Related to Quality of Education

The quality level of education is difficult to measure (Education For All 2003, 96). In terms of a human rights requirement to make education acceptable for pupils and adaptable to their needs, it is essential that the quality of education be good. However, educational institutions, teachers and children face a number of obstacles in this respect. One general obstacle is the lack of sufficient financial resources to provide for school buildings, facilities and personnel. A consequence may be a poor pupil/teacher ratio: this is highest in sub-Saharan Africa, followed by Asian countries. In Latin America and the Caribbean the number of pupils per teacher is much lower (ibid.). In many low-income countries there has been a tendency to recruit a higher proportion of untrained and poorly qualified teachers, due to a lack of resources (ibid., 99). Resources available for education will be under pressure anyhow: when school fees are abolished, there will be a need for extra government disbursements. Another problem is teacher absenteeism, which is a symptom of the much wider difficulty of low salaries in society, which forces many teachers to have an additional job. The number of unqualified or underqualified teachers is likely to rise when those who are qualified seek a better-paid position elsewhere, preferably in an urban area. Rural areas are not popular among teachers.

As for the school environment, inadequate facilities (poor buildings, lack of furniture, inadequate sanitation, lack of teaching materials, insufficient hours of instruction) seriously hamper a child's ability to concentrate and learn. In addition, corporal punishment, bullying, prejudice and discrimination are barriers to learning and bear the risk of raising the number of pupils who drop out. Such practices are contrary *accepted why*

to a safe school environment (Committee on the Rights of the Child 2001, para. 19).

A school curriculum that is not adapted to the needs of learners and to their cultural identity, diversity and socio-economic background will not help students to acquire knowledge and skills they can use in practice (such as basic knowledge about health and sanitation in primary education, or agriculture or trade-related subjects in secondary or vocational education) (Watkins 2000, 76–7; Martinic 2003, 18). In addition, research results for Latin American countries show low primary education achievement by children from low-income families, while children of high-income families perform well (Schiefelbein 2004, 15–17).[72] This implies that the education system is not adapted to children in different situations, and that the children of low-income groups actually do not learn anything substantial. That is an important reason to drop out and underachieve in the labour market. Consequently, the education system perpetuates inequality in society. One of the reasons for this failure is that the training of teachers does not take into account the different social, economic and cultural backgrounds of children. Nor do teaching and pedagogical methods provide for differentiation (Global Campaign for Education 2002, 5).

Finally, the language of instruction is often a serious barrier to good performance in education (Watkins 2000, 77; Tomasevski 2003b, 176). If the teaching language in the early stages of compulsory or pre-school education is not the mother tongue, there is a risk of pupils falling behind, failing to perform and finally dropping out. Instruction in the indigenous language may contribute to the cultural identity of the people. On the other hand, too much emphasis on instruction in the mother tongue or native language prevents the children from learning the official language. This hampers their opportunities to continue their studies, deploy themselves, find a job and integrate into society. A balance has to be struck between the two methods of instruction, taking into account the fact that language and minority issues, which are very politically sensitive in many countries, may be hard to deal with.

CONCLUDING REMARKS

The aim of the present study was to shed more light, from a human rights perspective, on the normative content of the right to education. On the basis of a legal analysis, entitlements and obligations resulting from the right to education were discussed. Contributions from other disciplines are necessary, because many activities and measures dealing with the implementation of this right will be of an administrative, financial, political or pedagogical nature. This became clear from a discussion of the obstacles impeding realization of this right. Overcoming these obstacles requires political will and a change of views and social norms about the value of education. From a human rights perspective, it is of the utmost importance to clarify (vague) treaty norms in order to explain to governments the precise meaning of treaty obligations that they have accepted voluntarily, and next to scrutinize acts and omissions of governments in terms of observance of these rights and obligations. In addition, it is important to assist monitoring bodies, at both intergovernmental and non-governmental levels, in their work to identify violations and to request governments to redress those violations and change their legislation and policy practice. If states are willing to recognize that education legislation, policy and programmes should be approached from a "human right to education perspective", then obstacles to the realization of the right to education can be tackled in a fair and just manner. This will also help to close the gap between the human rights treaty standards and everyday reality.

NOTES

1   See also the International Convention on the Elimination of All Forms of Racial Discrimination (Article 5(e(v)), the Convention on the Elimination of All Forms of Discrimination against Women (Article10), the Convention on the Rights of the Child (Articles 28 and 29), the African Charter on Human and Peoples' Rights (Article 17), the Protocol of San Salvador to the American Convention on Human Rights (Article 13) and the African Charter on the Rights and Welfare of the Child (Article 11). Some of these provisions are discussed in more detail below.
2   See UN Commission on Human Rights, Resolutions 1998/33, 2001/29 and 2003/19.
3   To mention just a few old and more recent studies within the framework of the United Nations: Ammoun (1957); Tomasevski (1999, 2000a, 2002, 2003a, 2004a).
4   Examples are rapporteurs on the right to food, housing, education and health. For an overview see the website of the UN High Commissioner for Human Rights (www.ohchr.org).
5   These general comments may be consulted at the treaty body database of the Office of the UN High Commissioner for Human Rights (www.unhchr.ch/tbs/doc.nsf).
6   International Covenant on Economic, Social and Cultural Rights, GA Res. 2200 A (XXI), adopted 16 December 1966; entered into force 3 January 1976, 999 *United Nations Treaty Series*, 3.
7   *Belgian Linguistic* case, relating to certain aspects of the laws on the use of languages in education in Belgium (European Court of Human Rights 1968, 31).
8   UN Doc. E/CN.4/SR.226, 4 May 1951, p. 14.
9   See also Batelaan and Coomans (1999). The remainder of the present study will not go into the aims of education laid down in ICESCR Article 13(1).
10   See UN Docs A/C.3/L.621, A/C.3/L.625 and A/3764 (Report of the Third Committee, 1957).
11   UN Doc. E/CN.4/AC.14/SR.1, 17 May 1951, p. 14.
12   UN.Doc. A/3764 and Add. 1, paras 33 and 42.
13   UN Doc. E/C.12/1988/SR.19, para. 10; see also E/C.12/1988/SR.17, paras 27, 40–1 and 48.
14   This scheme was used for the first time by the UN special rapporteur on the right to education in her preliminary report (Tomasevski 1999, Chapter II). See also Tomasevski (2003b, 51–2); Beeckman (2004).
15   UN Doc. A/3764 and Add. 1, Report of the Third Committee of the General Assembly (1957), para. 47.
16   Text in *United Nations Treaty Series*, Vol. 429, p. 93. For a detailed analysis of this convention see Juvigny (1963); McKean (1983); Daudet and Eisemann (2005).

17　Article 5(1)(c) reads in full:

> It is essential to recognize the right of members of national minorities to carry on their own educational activities, including the maintenance of schools and, depending on the educational policy of each State, the use or the teaching of their own language, provided however:
>
> That this right is not exercised in a manner which prevents the members of these minorities from understanding the culture and language of the community as a whole and from participating in its activities, or which prejudices national sovereignty;
>
> That the standard of education is not lower than the general standard laid down or approved by the competent authorities; and
>
> That attendance at such schools is optional.

18　Text in *United Nations Treaty Series*, Vol. 1249, p. 13. For an analysis of this convention see Burrows (1985).

19　Text in *International Legal Materials*, 28 (1989), p. 1448.

20　A comparative analysis of international provisions dealing with the right to education may be found in Gomez del Prado (1998). For a comprehensive and detailed overview and discussion see also Beiter (2006).

21　Text in ILO (1989). On this convention, see Anaya (1996).

22　For example, the clause in Article 28(1) that children belonging to indigenous peoples "shall, *wherever practicable*, be taught to read and write in their own indigenous language ..." (emphasis added).

23　The European Court of Human Rights has interpreted the meaning and scope of Article 2 in three leading judgments (European Court of Human Rights 1968, 1976, 1982).

24　This charter was included in the Draft Treaty Establishing a Constitution for Europe (2004).

25　Text in *International Legal Materials*, 21 (1982), p. 59.

26　Text available at www1.umn.edu/humanrts/africa/afchild.htm.

27　Text in *International Legal Materials*, 28 (1989), p. 156.

28　See Article 19(6) of the Protocol of San Salvador. In the opinion of the Inter-American Commission on Human Rights (IACHR) this could be the case "when a violation occurred because of direct action by the government, that is when the violation might be imputed directly and immediately to the government, and changing the situation would depend on it". See IACHR, *Annual Report 1984–1985*, English translation in Buergenthal and Norris (1986, Part 1, section 3.2, pp. 21–2). See also Melish (2002).

29　Text available at www.comunidadandina.org. Member states of the Andean Community are Bolivia, Colombia, Ecuador, Peru and Venezuela.

30　Text available at www.cidh.org/indigenas.

31　See UN Doc. E/C.12/1999/5 and UN Doc. E/C.12/1999/10. The chapter will deal later with elements of the core content of the right to education as set by the committee in this general comment.

32　Compare ICESCR Articles 2(2) and 3, ICCPR Article 26, CRC Article 2 and Limburg Principles 35 and 37.

33　See the report of the UN Secretary-General on the situation of women and girls in Afghanistan, UN Doc. E/CN.4/Sub.2/2000/18.

34　*Unni Krishnan and Others v State of A.P. and Others*, 4 February (1993) 1 SCC 645.

35　See, for example, UNESCO's Statistical Yearbook and the Revised Recommendation concerning the Standardization of Educational Statistics (1978).

36　An example may illustrate the practice of basic education: in India, the Social Work and Research Centre (SWRC), an Indian NGO, has been working with the poorest of India's rural population. This NGO has set up a number of schools in which:

children are made aware of their rights through songs, puppets and classroom theatre. The curriculum gives them an idea about language and reading and writing in Hindi, as well as the basics of mathematics. Then they make links between letters and words, and between words and phrases. Over the following years, they are taught about social and rural behaviour, how to be self-sufficient, and about the caste system. Then come the theories of social and political thinkers and national heroes, as well as lectures on agriculture and cattle breeding. The focus of the lessons is the environment they live in. The children are taught to make arid land cultivable, and the destructive effect of chopping down trees for firewood. Powerful links are established between the school and everyday working life. (Klotz 1999, 6)

37 These factors are largely drawn from UNESCO's questionnaire for the consultation of member states on the implementation of the Convention against Discrimination in Education, UNESCO Doc. 23 C/72, Annex A (1985). See below for a more detailed discussion of these factors.

38 This paragraph is also based on UNESCO's questionnaire (note 37 above).

39 According to the UN special rapporteur on the right to education, "school fees represent a form of regressive taxation. Their justification routinely points to the inability (or unwillingness) of a Government to generate sufficient revenue through general taxation. Payment for primary schooling ruptures the key principle of taxation whereby people who cannot contribute to public services that are meant for all are not required to do so" (Tomasevski 2000, para. 52). See also Committee on Economic, Social and Cultural Rights (1999a, para. 7).

40 See also. in this respect, Committee on Economic, Social and Cultural Rights, (1999c, para. 51): "States parties are obliged to prioritise the introduction of compulsory, free education."

41 In a number of African countries, state monopoly on education is coming to an end. In addition, there is a tendency to involve the private (business) sector in the funding and building of schools. The privatization of education is supported, and sometimes even imposed, by the IMF and the World Bank within the framework of structural adjustment programmes. See about this development, *UNESCO Sources*, No. 102, June 1998, pp. 12–13; Tomasevski (2003b, Chapter 5).

42 Compare Article 3 of the Jomtien Declaration. See also the Statement to the World Conference on Human Rights on behalf of the Committee on Economic, Social and Cultural Rights, UN Doc. A/CONF.157/PC/62/Add.5, Annex I.

43 See UN Commission on Human Rights, Res. 2003/19, paras 6c and 6d.

44 The court emphasized that Article 2 of the First Protocol should be interpreted in the light of Article 8 (right to privacy), Article 9 (freedom of conscience and religion) and Article 10 (freedom to receive information) of the European Convention on Human Rights.

45 Compare Article 17(3) African Charter on Human and Peoples' Rights, which states: "The promotion and protection of morals and traditional values recognized by the community shall be the duty of the State."

46 Private education means: educational institutions established and run by private individuals or organizations. These private institutions may be partially or fully funded by the state, or alternatively receive no financial contributions from any local, regional or national public authority.

47 Compare the critical observations of the Committee on Economic, Social and Cultural Rights when it discussed the periodic report of Mauritius on the implementation of the ICESCR. The committee noted with concern that Creole and Bhojpuri, the only languages spoken by the large majority of the population, are not used in the Mauritian education system. See UN Doc. E/C.12/1994/8, para. 16.

48 See, for example, ICCPR Article 27, paragraphs 32–4 of the Document of the Copenhagen Meeting of the Conference on the Human Dimension of the CSCE (1990) and Article 4 of the Declaration on the Rights of Persons Belonging to

National or Ethnic, Religious and Linguistic Minorities (UN GA Res. 47/135, 18 December 1992). See also, within the context of the Council of Europe, Article 8 of the European Charter for Regional or Minority Languages (1992) and Articles 12–14 of the Framework Convention for the Protection of National Minorities (1994). However, there is no right to education in a minority language when a state refuses to accept international human rights obligations in this area, such as France; see, for example, the views of the Human Rights Committee (1991).

49 For a detailed discussion of obligations flowing from Article 2(1) see Sepúlveda (2003, Chapter VII).

50 An excellent and very detailed categorization and elaboration of state obligations resulting from the right to education, including an identification of individuals and groups that need special protection, has been developed by the Office of the Ombudsman of Colombia (2004). This document also includes a long list of measurement tools to monitor and evaluate public educational policy from a human rights perspective.

51 For an extensive discussion of the nature of state obligations see Sepúlveda (2003, Chapters IV and V).

52 For an extensive discussion of this development see Sepúlveda (2003, Chapter V).

53 For a more recent version and discussion of the levels of state obligations see Eide (2000, 124–8).

54 See Limburg Principles, No. 17. Legislative measures would be imperative if existing legislation is contrary to the obligations under the covenant; see Limburg Principles, No. 18.

55 "Maastricht Guidelines on Violations of Economic, Social and Cultural Rights", *Human Rights Quarterly*, 20 (1998), pp. 691–704, para. 9. See also Dankwa et al. (1998, 717).

56 Example mentioned by the former UN special rapporteur on the right to education, Katerina Tomasevski in an interview published in *Human Rights Features*, 5–12 April 2004, available at www.right-to-education.org.

57 See Seventh Conference of Ministers of Education of African Member States (MINEDAF VII) (1998), *Final Report*, pp. 16, 31–2 (Durban Statement of Commitment); *UNESCO Sources* No. 102, June 1998, pp. 12–13; *UNESCO Education Today*, No. 5, April–June 2003, pp. 6–7; Kitaev (1999, 136, 139–41).

58 According to Tomasevski, it is difficult to assess whether the failure by governments to make primary education free is caused by inability (which they claim) or unwillingness.

59 For a discussion of the FTI, see Education For All Global (2003, 247–53).

60 See the detailed account of the situation in Honduras in the FOSDEH report, *Honduras Pushed to the Edge*, April 2004, available at www.campaignforeducation.org/resources.

61 The FOSDEH report observes that Honduras' external public debt has increased by 7 per cent from US$4.3 billion in 1999 to US$4.6 billion in September 2003 (p. 4).

62 For a brief overview of some criticisms of the FTI, see the Report of Fourth Meeting of the Working Group on Education for All, UNESCO, Paris, 22–23 July 2003, pp. 13–15.

63 See, on the concept of systemic discrimination, Cunningham (2000).

64 UN Commission on Human Rights, Res. 2001/29, para. 3b.

65 See the concluding observations of the UN Committee on Economic, Social and Cultural Rights on the Dominican Republic, denouncing the situation of black Haitian undocumented workers and their children, UN Doc. E/C.12/1Add. 6, para. 15 and UN Doc. E/C.12/1/Add.16, para. 17. See also the Report of the Inter-

American Commission on Human Rights of 22 February 2001 (Report 28/01), in the case of *Dilcia Yean and Violeta Bosica v the Dominican Republic*, available at www.cidh.org/annualrep/2000eng/. In this case one of the petitioners, of Haitian origin, was not allowed to attend school for lack of a birth certificate, although she was born in the Dominican Republic. The Inter-American Commission adopted precautionary measures to ensure that Violeta Bosica would be able to continue attending school. This measure was carried out by the state. The case is now pending before the American Court of Human Rights.

66 In ILO Convention No. 182 on the Worst Forms of Child Labour (1999) there is much emphasis on the importance of education in eliminating child labour; see in particular Article 7.

67 Detailed data are available in Melchiorre (2004).

68 The need for matching is confirmed in UN Commission on Human Rights, Res. 2001/29, para. 3d.

69 Supreme Court of Colombia/Corte Suprema de Colombia, *Crisanto Arcangel Martinez Martinez y Maria Eglina Suarez Robayo v Collegio Cuidad de Cali*, No. T-177814, 11 November 1998, as quoted by Tomasevski (2003b, 165).

70 For a list of more that 40 countries where early marriage and pregnancy constitute obstacles to girl's education, see Tomasevski (2004a, para. 33).

71 Address by Kofi Annan, UN Secretary-General, launching the Girls' Education Initiative at the World Education Forum on 26 April 2000, quoted in Tomasevski (2001b, 45).

72 This paper also includes references to the situation in other Latin-American countries.

REFERENCES

Ainsworth, M., Beegle, K. and Koda, G. (2005), "The impact of adult mortality and parental deaths on primary schooling in north-western Tanzania", *Journal of Development Studies*, 41: 412–39.

Alston, P. (1987), "Out of the abyss: The challenges confronting the new UN Committee on Economic, Social and Cultural Rights", *Human Rights Quarterly*, 9: 332–81.

Alston, P. and Quinn, G. (1987), "The nature and scope of states parties' obligations under the International Covenant on Economic, Social and Cultural Rights", *Human Rights Quarterly*, 9: 156–229.

Ammoun, C. (1957), *Study of Discrimination in Education* (New York: United Nations).

Anaya, S.J. (1996), *Indigenous Peoples in International Law* (Oxford: Oxford University Press).

Batelaan, P. and Coomans, F. (comps) (1999), *The International Basis for Intercultural Education Including Anti-Racist and Human Rights Education*, 2nd edition (Geneva: International Association for Intercultural Education/UNESCO/Council of Europe), available at http://unesdoc.unesco.org/ulis/cgi-bin/ulis.pl?catno=12483 0&database=ged&gp=0&lin=1.

Beeckman, K. (2004), "Measuring the implementation of the right to education: Educational *versus* human rights indicators", *International Journal of Children's Rights*, 12: 71–84.

Beiter, K.D. (2006), *The Protection of the Right to Education by International Law, Including a Systematic Analysis of Article 13 ICESCR* (Leiden: Martinus Nijhoff).

Bellamy, Carol (1999), *The State of the World's Children 1999* (New York and Geneva: UNICEF).

Buergenthal, T. and Norris, R.E. (eds) (1986), *The Inter-American System*, loose-leaf (Dobs Ferry, NY: Oceana Publications).

Burrows, N. (1985), "The 1979 Convention on the Elimination of All Forms of Discrimination against Women", *Netherlands International Law Review*, 32: 419–60.

Chapman, A. and Russell, S. (1998), *Violations of the Right to Education*, UN Doc. E/C.12/1998/19.

_____ (eds) (2002), *Core Obligations: Building a Framework for Economic, Social and Cultural Rights* (Antwerp: Intersentia).

Committee on Economic, Social and Cultural Rights (1990), "General Comment No. 3: The nature of States' parties obligations (Article 2, paragraph 1 ICESCR)", UN Doc. E/1991/23.

_____ (1999a), "General Comment No. 11: Plans of action for primary education, (Article 14)", UN Doc. E/C.12/1999/4.

_____ (1999b), "General Comment No. 12: The right to adequate food (Art. 11)", 12 May, UN Doc. E/C.12/1999/5.

_____ (1999c), "General Comment No. 13 on the right to education (Article 13 of the Covenant)", CESCR twenty-first session, December, UN Doc. E/C.12/1999/10.

_____ (2000), "General Comment No. 14 on the right to the highest attainable standard of health", UN Doc. E/C.12/2000/4.

_____ (2001), "Statement on poverty and the ICESCR", UN Doc. E/C.12/2001/10.

Committee on the Rights of the Child (2001), "General Comment No. 1 on Article 29(1): The Aims of Education", UN Doc. CRC/GC/2001/1.

Coomans, A.P.M. (1992), "De Internationale Bescherming van het Recht op Onderwijs" ("The international protection of the right to education"), PhD thesis, Maastricht University, Leiden, unpublished.

Coomans, F. (2002), "Discrimination and stigmatisation regarding education: The case of the Romani children in the Czech Republic", in J. Willems (ed.), *Developmental and Autonomy Rights of Children: Empowering Children, Caregivers and Communities* (Antwerp: Intersentia), pp. 225–50.

 _____ (2004), "Exploring the normative content of the right to education as a human right: Recent approaches", *Persona y Derecho*, 50: 61–100.

_____ (2006), *Justiciability of Economic and Social Rights – Experiences from Domestic Systems* (Antwerp: Intersentia).

Coomans, F. and Hallo de Wolf, A. (2005), "Privatisation of education and the right to education", in K. De Feyter and F. Gómez Isa (eds), *Privatisation and Human Rights in the Age of Globalisation* (Antwerp: Intersentia), pp. 229–58.

Cunningham, F. (2000), "Positive action and democracy", in E. Appelt and M. Jarosch (eds), *Combating Racial Discrimination – Affirmative Action as a Model for Europe* (Oxford: Berg), pp. 41–59.

Dall, F.P. (1995), "Children's right to education: Reaching the unreached", in J.R. Himes (ed.), *Implementing the Convention on the Rights of the Child – Resource Mobilization in Low-Income Countries* (The Hague: Martinus Nijhoff/UNICEF), pp. 143–83.

Dankwa, V., Flinterman, C. and Leckie, S. (1998), "Commentary to the Maastricht Guidelines on Economic, Social and Cultural Rights", *Human Rights Quarterly*, 20: 705–30.

Daudet, Y. and Eisemann, P.M. (2005), *Commentary on the Convention Against Discrimination in Education* (Paris: UNESCO).

Donders, Y. (2002) *Towards a Right to Cultural Identity?* (Antwerp: Intersentia).

Donnelly, J. and Howard, R.E. (1988), "Assessing national human rights performance: A theoretical framework", *Human Rights Quarterly*, 10: 214–48.

Education For All (2003), *The Leap to Equality*, Global Monitoring Report 2003–2004 (Paris: UNESCO).

Eide, A. (1987), *The Right to Adequate Food as a Human Right*, UN Doc. E/CN.4/Sub.2/1987/23.

_____ (2000), "Economic and social rights", in J. Symonides (ed.), *Human Rights: Concept and Standards* (Aldershot: Ashgate-Dartmouth/UNESCO), pp. 109–74.

Eide, A., Krause, C. and Rosas, A. (eds) (2001), *Economic, Social and Cultural Rights: A Textbook*, 2nd edition (Dordrecht: Martinus Nijhoff).

European Commission (1975), *Case of Kjeldsen, Busk Madsen and Pedersen*, Report of the Commission, 21 March, Publications of the Court, Series B, Vol. 21.

European Court of Human Rights (1968), *Case relating to certain aspects of the laws on the use of languages in education in Belgium*, Judgment of 23 July, Publications of the Court, Series A, Vol. 6.

_____ (1976), *Case of Kjeldsen, Busk Madsen and Pedersen*, Judgment of 7 December, Publications of the Court, Series A, Vol. 23.

_____ (1982), *Case of Campbell and Cosans*, Judgment of 25 February, Publications of the Court, Series A, Vol. 48.

_____ (1993), *Case of Costello-Roberts v UK*, Judgment of 25 March, Publications of the Court, Series A, Vol. 247-C.

Galbraith, J.K. (1996), *The Good Society: The Humane Agenda* (Boston, MA: Houghton Mifflin).

Global Campaign for Education (2002), *A Quality of Education for All*, briefing paper, May, available at www.campaignforeducation.org.

Gomez del Prado, José L. (1998), UN Doc. E/C.12/1998/23.

Hasberg, S. (2000), *Burkina Faso: Profiles of Poverty* (Stockholm: SIDA).

High-Level Group on Education for All (2003), *Report of the Third Meeting*, Delhi, 10–12 November.

Hudson, Manley O. (1938), *World Court Reports: A Collection of the Judgment Orders and Opinions of the Permanent Court of International Justice, 1932–1935*, Vol. 3, Carnegie Endowment for International Peace, pp. 484–512.

Human Rights Committee (1991), *Herve Barzhig v France*, Communication 327/1988, Views of 11 April 1991.

_____ (1999), *Arieh Hollis Waldman v Canada*, UN Doc. CCPR/C/67/D/1996.

Human Rights Watch (1999), *1999 World Report*, available at www.hrw.org/worldreport99/women/women3html.

ILO (1989), *Official Bulletin*, LXXII: Ser. A, No. 2.

Juvigny, P. (1963), *The Fight Against Discrimination; Towards Equality in Education* (Paris: UNESCO).

Kitaev, I. (1999), *Private Education in Sub-Saharan Africa* (Paris: UNESCO/International Institute for Educational Planning).

Klotz, J.-C. (1999), "India: The children's republic", *UNESCO Sources*, 116 (October): 6–7.

Limburg Principles on the Implementation of the International Covenant on Economic, Social and Cultural Rights (1986), UN Doc. E/CN.4/1987/17; also published in *Human Rights Quarterly*, 9 (1987): 122–35.

Martinic, S. (2003), *Educational Progress and Problems in Guatemala, Honduras and Mexico*, background paper for EFA Global Monitoring Report 2003–2004, November (Paris:UNESCO), available at http://portal.unesco.org/education/fr/ev.php-URL_ID=25755&URL_DO=DO_TOPIC&URL_SECTION=201&URL_PAGINATION=50.html.

McKean, W. (1983), *Equality and Discrimination under International Law* (Oxford: Oxford University Press) pp. 128–35.

Melchiorre, A. (2004), *At What Age … Are School-children Employed, Married and Taken to Court?*, 2nd edition, available at www.right-to-education.org.

Melish, T. (2002), *Protecting Economic, Social and Cultural Rights in the Inter-American Human Rights System: A Manual for Presenting Claims* (New Haven, CT: Orville Schell Center for International Human Rights/Yale University).

Nowak, M. (1991), "The right to education – Its meaning, significance and limitations", *Netherlands Quarterly of Human Rights*, 9: 418–25.

Nowak, M. (2001), "The right to education", in A. Eide, C. Krause and A. Rosas (eds), *Economic, Social and Cultural Rights: A Textbook*, 2nd edition (Dordrecht: Martinus Nijhoff), pp. 245–71.

Office of the Ombudsman of Colombia (2004), *System for Monitoring and Evaluating Public Educational Policy in Furtherance of the Right to Education*, translated from Spanish, available at www.defensoria.org.co.

Oxfam (2001), *Education Charges – A Tax on Human Development*, briefing paper, 12 November (London: Oxfam).

Packer, C. (2003), "Rights-based education to gender equality", in I. Boerefijn, F. Coomans, J. Goldschmidt, R. Holtmaat and R. Wolleswinkel (eds), *Temporary Special Measures – Accelerating de facto Equality of Women under Article 4(1) UN Convention on the Elimination of All Forms of Discrimination against Women*, (Antwerp: Intersentia), pp. 151–79.

Permanent Court of International Justice (1935), *Minority Schools in Albania*, Advisory Opinion, 6 April, Series A/B, No. 64.

Riddell, A. (2003), *The Introduction of Free Primary Education in Sub-Saharan Africa*, background study for EFA Global Monitoring Report 2003–2004, 16 May.

Quansah, E.K. (1995), "Is the right to get pregnant a fundamental right in Botswana?", *Journal of African Law*, 39: 97–102.

Schachter, O. (1983), "Human dignity as a normative concept", *American Journal of international Law*, 77: 848–54.

Schiefelbein, E. (2004), *Education and Employment in Paraguay: Issues and Perspectives*, 12 April (paper on file with author).

Sengupta, S. (2003), "Defying voodoo and statistics, Benin village girls go to school", *International Herald Tribune*, 15 December, p. 2.

Sepúlveda, M. (2003), *The Nature of the Obligations under the International Covenant on Economic, Social and Cultural Rights* (Antwerp: Intersentia).

Shue, H. (1996), *Basic Rights – Subsistence, Affluence and U.S. Foreign Policy*, 2nd edition (Princeton, NJ: Princeton University Press).

Tomasevski, K. (1998), background paper, UN Doc. E/C.12/1998/18.

_____ (1999), *Preliminary Report on the Right to Education*, UN Doc. E/CN.4/1999/49.

_____ (2000a), *Progress Report*, UN Doc. E/CN.4/2000/6.

_____ (2000b), *Report on the Mission to Uganda*, UN Doc. E/CN.4/2000/6/Add.1.

_____ (2001a), *Annual Report of the Special Rapporteur on the Right to Education*, UN Doc. E/CN.4/2001/52.

_____ (2001b), *Removing Obstacles in the Way of the Right to Education*, Right to Education Primers No. 1 (Lund and Stockholm: Raoul Wallenberg Institute/SIDA).

_____ (2002), *Progress Report*, UN Doc. E/CN.4/2002/60.

_____ (2003a), *Progress Report*, UN Doc. E/CN.4/2003/9.

_____ (2003b), *Education Denied – Costs and Remedies* (London and New York: Zed Books).

_____ (2003c), *School Fees as Hindrance to Universalizing Primary Education*, background study for EFA Global Monitoring Report 2003–2004, 27 June.

_____ (2003d), "Rights-based education as pathway to gender equality", in I. Boerefijn, F. Coomans, J. Goldschmidt, R. Holtmaat and R. Wolleswinkel (eds), *Temporary Special Measures – Accelerating de facto Equality of Women under Article 4(1) UN Convention on the Elimination of All Forms of Discrimination against Women* (Antwerp: Intersentia), pp. 151–72.

_____ (2004a), *Final Report*, UN Doc. E/CN.4/2004/45.

_____ (2004b), "Experiences with legal enforcement of the right to education as food-for-thought in exploring models for an optional protocol to the International

Covenant on Economic, Social and Cultural Rights", UN Doc. E/CN.4/2004/ WG.23/CRP.4.
UNICEF (2005), *A Report Card on Gender Parity and Primary Education*, Progress for Children Report, April, available at www.unicef.org/progressforchildren.
Watkins, K. (1999) *Education Now: Break the Cycle of Poverty* (Oxford: Oxfam UK).
_____ (2000) *The Oxfam Education Report* (Oxford: Oxfam UK).
Weiner, M. (1991), *The Child and the State in India* (Princeton, NJ: Princeton University Press).
Wilson, D. (2003), *Human Rights: Promoting Gender Equality in and through Education*, background paper for EFA Global Monitoring Report 2003–2004 (Paris: UNESCO), available at http://portal.unesco.org/education/fr/ev.php-URL_ID=25755&URL_DO=DO_TOPIC&URL_SECTION=201&URL_PAGINATION=50.html.

BIBLIOGRAPHY

Arajärvi, P. (1992), "Article 26", in A. Eide, G. Alfredsson, G. Melander, L. Adam Rehof and A. Rosas (eds), *The Universal Declaration of Human Rights: A Commentary* (Oslo: Scandinavian University Press), pp. 405–28.
Coomans, F. (1998), "Identifying violations of the right to education", in T.C. van Boven, C. Flinterman and I. Westendorp (eds), *The Maastricht Guidelines on Violations of Economic, Social and Cultural Rights*, SIM Special No. 20, Utrecht, pp. 125–46.
Singh, K. (2006), "Right to basic education: International obligations and regional normative action in Africa", *African Yearbook of International Law*, 12: 437–67.
Tomasevski, K. (2006), *The State of the Right to Education Worldwide. Free or Fee: 2006 Global Report*, available at www.katarinatomasevski.com/images/Global_Report.pdf.
Verheyde, M. (2006), *Article 28: The Right to Education – A Commentary on the United Nations Convention on the Rights of the Child* (Leiden: Martinus Nijhoff).
Wildhaber, L. 1986. Artikel 2 Europäische Menschenrechtskonvention/Erstes Zusatzprotokoll. H. Golsong et al. (eds), *Internationaler Kommentar zur Menschenrechtskonvention*, 4th revision, 2000, loose-leaf (Cologne: Carl Heymans Verlag).

6 The Legal Framework of the Right to Take Part in Cultural Life

YVONNE DONDERS

INTRODUCTION

All over the world, peoples, communities, groups and individuals are striving for the preservation and protection of their cultural identity, to which they attach great value because they consider it an important part of their human dignity. Restricting or oppressing the expression and preservation of cultural identities may lead to a sense of confusion, alienation, exclusion and even violent conflict. In order to preserve and develop cultural identities, there is increasing demand for better promotion and protection of cultural rights as an integral part of human rights. These rights have been poorly elaborated in terms of content and scope and often neglected in terms of implementation.

One right which is undeniably part of cultural rights is the right to take part in cultural life, which is laid down in Article 27 of the Universal Declaration on Human Rights (UDHR) and Article 15(1)(a) of the International Covenant on Economic, Social and Cultural Rights (ICESCR). This right seems potentially to play an essential role in the protection of the cultural identities of individuals and communities. However, the normative content and scope of this right and state obligations in respect of it have been little studied.

In the first part of this study, an introduction is given to cultural human rights, in order to situate the right to take part in cultural life. Which human rights could be considered cultural rights, what is the scope of these rights and what role do cultural rights play in the human rights system, including their relationship with other "categories" of human rights? Furthermore, the theory of state obligations with regard to human rights in general and cultural rights in particular is briefly explained. The second part of the study deals with the right to take part in cultural life. Why was such a right included in the international human rights framework and what does this right mean? Its content and scope are examined according to the wording of the text of the provisions adopted and the *travaux préparatoires*, including the drafting process and the intentions of the drafters. Use is also made of interpretative statements by the international body supervising the implementation of this right, as well as studies by academics and specialists. This study will show that the scope and normative content of the right to take part in cultural life have evolved over the years. It has become a broad human right which includes many different aspects, and has a close relationship with other human rights provisions. The right to take part in cultural life implies a broad range of obligations that states may have in implementing it. This study is not meant to be exhaustive, but tries to highlight several elements and issues that may encourage further analysis.

CULTURAL RIGHTS AS THE "CINDERELLA OF THE HUMAN RIGHTS FAMILY"

> … any attempt to talk about cultural issues in terms of rights may be slippery and difficult. (Prott 1988, 94)

The main reason why cultural rights are "slippery and difficult" is that their content and scope are unclear.[1] Although the UN Commission on Human Rights has over recent years confirmed that cultural rights are an integral part of human rights,[2] the category of cultural rights is, compared to civil, political, economic and social rights, conceptually and legally underdeveloped or neglected (Symonides 2000, 175; Hansen 2002, 281). Danilo Türk, in his function as special rapporteur on the realization of economic, social and cultural rights, argued that cultural rights have received "by far the least amount of serious attention" (Türk 1992, 51–2).

The main reason for the underdevelopment of cultural rights is that the term "culture" remains broad and vague, which has led to a lack of consensus on which rights are "cultural" and how to best implement them. Another reason is that relatively few states have been eager to adopt international regulations in relation to cultural rights. Most states have not considered cultural rights to imply positive state obligations. The few regimes that regulated culture did so as part of a more or less totalitarian control over social life as a whole, which often included the denial of other human rights (Donnelly 1989, 154; 1990, 55). States also fear that strengthening cultural rights may lead to tension and instability in society, because giving cultural communities certain rights may empower them, which may endanger national unity (see, *inter alia*, Symonides 2000, 176).

THE NATURE AND SCOPE OF CULTURAL RIGHTS

The nature and scope of cultural rights are closely tied to the term "culture". In simple terms, the idea of culture has over the years evolved from a narrow élitist concept, which mainly referred to fine arts and literature, to a broader concept presenting culture as a process, including components such as language, religion and education. A similar development is visible in the debate on cultural rights.

The first international conference on cultural rights, organized by UNESCO, took place in July 1968. It should be kept in mind that two years earlier, in 1966, the ICESCR had been adopted, which includes the right to take part in cultural life in Article 15(1)(a). The experts at the UNESCO conference discussed the evolution of cultural rights since the adoption of the Universal Declaration, the recognition of cultural rights and the measures to be taken to improve their implementation. According to the final statement of the conference, cultural rights were important because culture enabled persons "to maintain and perpetuate life". Cultural rights were therefore related to the right to life and the right to peace.[3] Other important aspects were communication and education, or "the freedom to know", by which individuals could develop themselves. The statement did not contain references to cultural features, such as religion, language or cultural heritage (UNESCO 1970, 106–7).

There was also discussion on a specific cultural right not provided for in the International Bill of Human Rights: the right to culture (ibid., 3). It was argued that this right meant "every man has the right of access to knowledge, to the arts and literature of all peoples, to take part in scientific advancement and to enjoy its benefits, to make his contribution towards the enrichment of cultural life" (Boutros-Ghali 1970, 73). It was stated that the right to culture implied that a person should have a decent standard of living with regard to food, shelter, health care and education, or else a person would not have the desire or the possibility of participating in culture. It was concluded that a minimum of material well-being would be necessary to give significance to the notion of culture (ibid.).[4]

Over the years there has been a tendency among states and scholars to accept a broader understanding of the concept of culture, which is no longer restricted to fine arts, literature and philosophy, but instead includes distinctive features, ways of thinking and the organization of people's lives. Culture is no longer only seen as a consumer product, but as an expression of the identity of an individual or a community. Cultural rights should accordingly be considered as more than merely rights to enjoy a cultural product. Cultural rights are real human rights aimed at protecting an important part of human dignity (Meyer-Bisch 1993b, 18–20, 23–24; Symonides 2000, 180; Hansen 2002, 285).

Another issue is whether cultural rights belong next to economic and social rights or next to civil and political rights. It has been argued that, in fact, cultural rights are a category connecting or overlapping other categories of human rights and linking individual rights and the rights of peoples and communities. Cultural rights are important not only as a separate category of human rights, but also as a reference to the cultural elements in other human rights. As such, cultural rights embody the indivisibility of all human rights (Meyer-Bisch 1993b, 17–18).[5]

This has also been called the "transversal character" of cultural rights, covering economic, social, civil and political rights. Cultural freedoms, such as freedom of religion, expression and communication, refer to civil rights, while the right to participate in cultural life refers to social and economic rights. The right to education is an example of a mixed right (Meyer-Bisch 1993b, 18–19).[6]

The second part of this transversal character lies in the fact that cultural rights can be considered as being "in between" individual rights and collective rights, as playing an intermediate role between the rights of individuals and the rights of peoples. Cultural rights have an individual as well as a collective dimension, because while legal provisions may be defined as individual rights, their enjoyment is firmly connected to communities. Moreover, apart from individual cultural rights, such as freedom of religion, expression and association, which are essential to the development of cultures, new claims of communities have emerged, such as the collective right to the development and protection of cultural identity and the right not to have an alien culture imposed. Other examples of collective claims concern the right of peoples to their own cultural heritage and to participation in the cultural heritage of the world (Prott 1988, 95–7; Meyer-Bisch 1993b, 18–19, 38–9).[7]

Cultural rights are mainly enjoyed by individuals together, or by individuals in relation to a community. For example, the individual right to participate in cultural life is closely linked to a cultural community. Another approach is that communities as such should enjoy cultural rights, because these rights are meant to give communities the possibility of developing, protecting and preserving their cultural identity. In other words, cultural rights are collective rights (Marie 1993, 203–7, 213; Stavenhagen 2001, 89–92). Individual cultural rights could, to some extent, coincide with collective cultural rights, but the two sets of rights may also be in tension. Individual and community concerns with regard to culture may be different, and cultural rights may lie in between both interests (Eide 2001b, 300–01).

The state approach towards cultural rights has been mainly individual, because the provisions in international human rights instruments have been defined mainly in individuals terms.[8] States generally do not wish to empower communities as such with cultural rights, because they consider such a collective approach to be dangerous for the stability of the society. However, attention is paid to the collective and broad dimension of culture, for example in relation to the rights of minorities and indigenous peoples (Wilhelm 1993, 226–31, 236–7).[9]

Which human rights could be considered to be cultural rights? No international human rights instrument defines cultural rights as such (see also Marks 2003, 295). Again, the list of cultural rights depends on the definition of culture, which may vary from intellectual and artistic achievements to culture in the anthropological sense as the way of life of individuals and communities, including shared beliefs, traditions and customs. In any case, culture is a dynamic concept, which implies that "Cultural rights have an exceptional internal dynamic due to the fact that culture is a living and growing organism, constantly manifesting itself in new ways" (Niec 1998, 181).

Different concepts of culture may lead to different approaches towards cultural rights. If culture, for example, were considered as the accumulated material heritage of humankind, then cultural rights would include the right of equal access to this cultural capital and the right to cultural development. If culture were mainly considered from the creative perspective, meaning the process of artistic and scientific creation, cultural rights would include the right of individuals to create freely and to have free access to these creations in museums, theatres and libraries. Culture could finally be considered a way of life: the sum of its material and spiritual activities and products, including a system of values, symbols and practices, that distinguishes it from another group. Cultural rights would then include the right of a community to maintain and develop its own culture or the right to cultural identity (Stavenhagen 2001, 89–92; Hansen 2002, 283–4; Marks 2003, 295–6).

Different lists have been drawn up of legal provisions in international instruments that could be labelled "cultural rights". A general distinction could be made between cultural rights in the narrow sense and cultural rights in the broad sense. The narrow group contains those rights that explicitly refer to "culture", such as the right to participate in cultural life, as laid down in Article 27 of the Universal Declaration and ICESCR Article 15(1)(a), or the right to enjoy culture for members of minorities, as laid down in ICCPR Article 27. The broad group includes the above-mentioned rights, but further includes other civil, political, social and economic rights that have a link with culture. It might be argued that almost every human right has a link with culture, but the rights specifically meant here are the rights to freedom of religion, freedom of expression and freedom of association and the right to education (Donnelly 1989, 155–6; Meyer-Bisch 1993b, 25; Leuprecht 1993, 76; Eide 2001b, 292; Kartashkin 1982, 127; Marks 2003, 299–300).[10]

The right of self-determination also has an important link with the protection of culture.[11] The right of self-determination, as laid down in ICCPR Article 1 and ICESCR Article 1, provides that "all peoples have the right of self-determination. By virtue of that right they freely determine their political status and freely pursue their economic, social and cultural development." This right has been divided into external and internal self-determination. *External self-determination* means a people's capacity to free itself from colonial or racist rule. This can imply secession and the establishment of a new sovereign and independent state, free association or integration with another independent state, or any other political status freely determined by the people involved. *Internal self-determination* implies the presence of a representative government and a commitment by that government to respect human rights and freedoms, with a special focus on the rights of peoples and communities. Internal self-determination includes the ability to participate in government and in the work of decision-making bodies, without discrimination. It may also refer to some form of self-government or autonomy in the economic, social or cultural field. The internal aspects of the right of self-determination have a direct link with the protection of culture, for example in the form of determining cultural development or granting cultural autonomy.

Patrice Meyer-Bisch, a well-known scholar in the field of cultural rights, has divided cultural rights into three groups, of which the first two are already recognized in international human rights instruments, while the third has been elaborated more recently. These three groups reflect the development of cultural rights from the passive enjoyment of culture, via the active participation in and creation of culture, to the protection of the cultural identity of communities. His scheme of cultural rights is as follows (Meyer-Bisch 1993b, 35–6).

- The right to cultural participation, including the right to participate freely in cultural life (especially freedom of conscience and religion), the right to benefit from scientific and technical progress and the enjoyment of the arts, and the right to intellectual property.
- The right to education, including the right to elementary and functional education and the right to orientation and professional formation.
- The right to cultural identification, including the right to choose a culture and especially a language, the right to cultural heritage and the right to access to communication and expression facilities (the right to communicate).

Cultural rights may also refer to the cultural dimension of human rights. Although some of these rights may have, at first glance, no direct link with culture, they do have important cultural implications. The Committee on Economic, Social and Cultural Rights has acknowledged the cultural elements of, among others, the rights to food, health and housing. It has, for example, determined that the right to adequate housing implies that the construction of houses, the building materials and the supporting policies "must appropriately enable the expression of cultural identity and diversity of housing" (Committee on Economic, Social and Cultural Rights 1991, para. 8g). With regard to the right to health, the committee has, *inter alia*, determined that "all health facilities, goods and services must be … culturally appropriate, *i.e.*, respectful of the culture of individuals, minorities, peoples and communities" (Committee on Economic, Social and Cultural Rights 2000, para. 12c). With regard to the right to adequate food, the committee has stated that the guarantees provided should be culturally appropriate and acceptable (Committee on Economic, Social and Cultural Rights 1999a, paras 7, 8 and 11).

In short, the broad concept of culture, including not only cultural products but also process-oriented aspects such as association, language, religion and education, implies that cultural rights include many different human rights, which may have a civil, cultural, economic, political or social origin. Cultural rights are not only the rights to create and enjoy cultural products: they include rights to have access to and participate in culture, as well as rights that concern the broad concept of culture, including freedoms of association, language and religion and the right to education. Finally, cultural rights refer to the cultural dimension of other human rights, such as the rights to health, housing and food. Cultural rights are consequently more than merely those rights that explicitly refer to culture, but include all human rights that protect or promote components of the cultural identity of individuals and communities as part of their dignity.

STATE OBLIGATIONS WITH REGARD TO CULTURAL RIGHTS

Rights imply a claim by the beneficiary or holder of a right towards the addressee to do something or refrain from doing something. In the case of human rights – as of cultural rights – the main addressee is the state. The UN Commission on Human Rights has confirmed that "States have the primary responsibility for the protection of the full enjoyment of cultural rights by everyone".[12] What is the nature of state obligations with regard to cultural rights?

Negative and Positive Obligations

Generally, state obligations can be divided into negative and positive obligations. Negative obligations imply that the state should refrain from action, whereas positive obligations require state action. Previously, a firm distinction was made between civil and political rights, which demand state abstention or negative obligations, and economic, social and cultural rights, which require an active state policy or positive obligations. Although this argument may still be used, there is general consensus that all human rights are indivisible and interdependent, and that all categories may imply positive as well as negative state obligations.[13] Economic, social and cultural rights are not always merely demanding state action, but may also require non-interference by the state. Examples are trade union freedoms and the right to housing, which also implies that, for example, the shelter of poor people may not be destroyed by the state in order to be replaced by luxury houses without providing alternative housing for the poor.[14]

Accordingly, in principle, cultural rights may imply positive as well as negative obligations. While there is general agreement on the negative obligations of states in relation to cultural rights, the positive obligations are more disputed. For example, in relation to linguistic rights, it is clear that the state has a negative obligation to respect the use of the language of choice in the home. However, does this also mean that the state has a positive obligation to provide language facilities for individuals to use the language of choice in relations with public authorities? Another example concerns the right to education. The state should generally respect a cultural community, small or large, that wishes to organize the teaching of its own values itself. However, the state may limit its support for the development of educational facilities for minority communities according to the resources available to those communities that, for example, have a certain size (Meyer-Bisch 1993b, 29–30).

The "Progressive Realization" of Economic, Social and Cultural Rights

Cultural rights that are part of the ICESCR fall under the regime of that treaty. The key provision in the ICESCR with regard to state obligations is Article 2(1), which lays down that states should undertake to take steps to the maximum of their available resources, "with a view to achieving progressively the full realization of the rights recognized in the present Covenant by all appropriate means, including, in particular, the adoption of legislative measures".

The debate on the meaning of "progressive realization" is ongoing. An important elaboration of the provisions and obligations of the ICESCR are the Limburg Principles on the Implementation of the International Covenant on Economic, Social and Cultural Rights, which were the outcome of a conference of experts organized in Maastricht in 1986.[15] Another important interpretative document relating to ICESCR Article 2(1) is General Comment No. 3 concerning the nature of state obligations (Committee on Economic, Social and Cultural Rights 1990).[16] Many of the Limburg Principles are reflected in this general comment.

In its general comment on Article 2, the committee stated *inter alia* that the obligation to take steps or measures as laid down in Article 2(1) has an immediate character. States should start the implementation immediately and should move as fast as possible towards the objective of total realization. Furthermore, taking the appropriate measures implies not only legislative measures, but also administrative, financial, educational, social and other measures, including judicial remedies (ibid., paras 2, 5 and 9).[17] States are free to determine which measures they consider best to implement the material provisions of the ICESCR; it is for the committee finally to determine whether the state has taken the appropriate steps (ibid., paras 4 and 7; Symonides 2000, 206).[18]

The committee further affirms in its general comment that states should, regardless of their level of economic development, do their utmost to ensure the enjoyment of economic, social and cultural rights and should guarantee "at the very least, minimum essential levels of each of the rights" (Committee on Economic, Social and Cultural Rights 1990, paras 10–11).[19] This phrase points to the so-called "core content" of rights, the essential minimum that states should always guarantee, regardless of the availability of resources or any other difficulties. The issue of core content was first addressed by the committee in 1987, when it was stated that "each right must give rise to a minimum entitlement, in the absence of which a state party is in violation of its obligations" (Alston 1987, 353).[20] Subsequently, the committee has tried to define the core content of specific human rights provisions.[21]

The identification of the core content of a certain right does not imply that the remainder of the right is considered unimportant and therefore to be neglected. States should also take measures concerning the aspects that are not part of the core content. The core content is a *minimum* that states should guarantee, but they are obliged to do as much as possible to realize the *whole* of human rights.

ICESCR Article 2(2) contains a provision that obliges states to take measures to ban immediately *de jure* discrimination in the enjoyment of the rights in the covenant. The idea of progressive realization is not applicable here, since the term "to ensure" is used. Forms of passive discrimination, for example caused by a lack of resources, should be banned as soon as possible. The guarantee of non-discrimination implies a firm legal obligation that is immediately applicable and justiciable for a national court.[22] The principle of non-discrimination may also have implications for the implementation of cultural rights. If, for example, the state finances a cultural institution for one community, it should also take financial measures for the benefit of other communities. This is also spelled out in the International Convention on the Elimination of All Forms of Racial Discrimination (CERD, in force since 4 January 1969), according to which states parties should guarantee the right of everyone, without distinction as to race, colour or national or ethnic origin, to equality before the law, notably in the enjoyment of, *inter alia*, the right to equal participation in cultural activities (Article 5).

The progressive realization principle of ICESCR Article 2 applies only to cultural rights in the ICESCR. Cultural rights in the ICCPR and other relevant human rights instruments may demand immediate steps to be taken by states, irrespective of the availability of resources. Cultural rights in the ICCPR, such as freedom of religion, expression and association, are generally not considered vague and programmatic, but should be guaranteed immediately (ICCPR Article 2; Symonides 2000, 207). The corresponding state obligations can be positive as well as negative. The principle of non-discrimination is also applicable to the provisions in the ICCPR. According to Article 2(1), each state party should respect and ensure the rights of the ICCPR to all individuals "without distinction of any kind, such as race, color, sex, language, religion, political or other opinion, national or social origin, property, birth or other status".

The Tripartite Typology: Obligations to Respect, Protect and Fulfil

An important theory with regard to state obligations is the tripartite typology, developed *inter alia* by Shue and Eide (Shue 1980, 53, 55; Eide 1984, 249–60; 1987). This theory is not based on specific treaty provisions, but instead claims that three types of state obligations, namely the obligation to respect, the obligation to protect and the obligation to fulfil, can, in principle, result from all human rights, whether civil, political, economic, social or cultural in nature. Many scholars have used this theory to clarify the content and scope of economic, social and cultural rights.[23]

The *obligation to respect* means that states should refrain from "anything that violates the integrity of the individual or infringes on his or her freedom, including the freedom to use the material resources available to that individual in the way he or she finds best to satisfy the basic needs" (Eide 1987, para. 67). The *obligation to protect* means that the state should take the necessary measures "to prevent other individuals or groups from violating the integrity, freedom of action, or other human rights of the individual – including the prevention of infringement of the enjoyment of his material resources" (ibid., para. 68).[24] The *obligation to fulfil* means that the state should take measures "to ensure for each person within its jurisdiction has opportunities to obtain satisfaction of those needs, recognized in the human rights instruments, which cannot be secured by personal efforts" (ibid., para. 69). Later, the obligations "to assist", "to ensure" and "to promote" were proposed by scholars (Shue

1984, 86; Eide 2001a, 22; van Hoof 1984, 106). The Committee on Economic, Social and Cultural Rights has used the terms "to facilitate" and "to provide" in its general comments to specify the obligation to fulfil.

The tripartite typology to respect, protect and fulfil has gained international recognition and is used by the Committee on Economic, Social and Cultural Rights (1999a; 1999b; 2000; 2003; 2005b) to clarify state obligations in relation to the provisions in the covenant (Coomans 1992, 233–5; Craven 1995, 109–14; Toebes 1999, 311–38). It demonstrates that states do not just have positive obligations in relation to economic, social and cultural rights, which may have financial implications. States may also have the negative duties to respect and to refrain from action, which do not have financial consequences. The tripartite typology is referred to below to clarify the content and scope of the right to take part in cultural life.

Limits to the Enjoyment of Cultural Rights

It has been often argued that cultural rights could conflict with other human rights and can therefore not be enjoyed unreservedly. This in fact refers to the issue of cultural practices that infringe human rights. It is argued that cultural rights should not support questionable cultural activities, for example the discriminatory treatment of women, reflected in forced marriages, bride price, female circumcision, "widow cleansing" and rights inferior to those of men with regard to land ownership or inheritance. This issue is very sensitive and difficult to answer in general terms. Cultural rights or the right to take part in cultural life should not be categorically rejected solely on the grounds that they might conflict with other human rights. However, the enjoyment of cultural rights may be limited.

First of all, cultural rights could be limited by law. ICESCR Article 4, for example, contains a possibility for states to limit the enjoyment of the rights in the covenant. This provision is, however, conditional. The state may only subject the rights to limitations if these limitations are "determined by law only in so far as this may be compatible with the nature of these rights and solely for the purpose of promoting the general welfare in a democratic society". This limitation clause is not meant to provide states with a simple excuse not to implement the provisions of the ICESCR. Although states are allowed to impose limits on the enjoyment of rights, the possibilities for limitations are restricted by establishing criteria as to the way they may be imposed. The limitations may not be in contradiction with the nature of the rights in the covenant, otherwise the provisions would no longer have value and content. Lack of financial or other resources does not fall under the limitation clause of Article 4 and is therefore not a sufficient ground for limitation (Alston and Quinn 1987, 193–4; Coomans 1992, 38–9).[25]

The question remains how the state should be able to limit cultural rights without making it an excuse for not implementing cultural rights at all. Whether a certain limitation of cultural rights by law is justified depends on the concrete circumstances. The phrase "for the general welfare" may be too broad, and therefore dangerous, if states abuse it to justify certain cutbacks. However, the unlimited exercise of cultural rights may seriously endanger the rights of others or of society. The Committee on Economic, Social and Cultural Rights, for example, has shown that it does not accept the unlimited freedom of creative activity. Creative expressions should not harm the cultural life of society as a whole or of specific groups, such as children. Another example is that the right to take part in cultural life may be limited if cultural activities include discriminatory expressions (Toebes 1999, 297–8; O'Keefe 1998, 911–12; Vlemminx 1992, 325–6; 1994, 117–19.[26]

Secondly, a general rule is that the enjoyment of human rights by one person may not unjustifiably limit or violate the enjoyment of human rights by others. In other words, the enjoyment of cultural rights can be limited by the enjoyment of human rights by others. In fact, many human rights can potentially be in conflict in certain situations.[27] Each of these situations should be evaluated case by case to determine which right prevails over another in a given situation.

The issue remains how to deal with cultural *activities* or *practices* – not to be confused with cultural *rights* – which are in conflict with or limit the enjoyment of human rights. Such practices, it is argued, should not be protected by cultural rights. No general statement can be made on the acceptability of cultural practices and their relation to human rights, since these activities are very diverse and their possible conflict with human rights should be treated on a case-by-case basis. However, in general, cultural practices that are clearly in conflict with international human rights norms cannot be justified by stating that they are protected under the category of "cultural rights". An appropriate criterion could be that cultural practices should not be in conflict with the value of human dignity. This also implies that, for example, cultural communities should guarantee and respect the rights and freedoms of their individual members, including the right to participate in society at large, e.g. through education, the right to take part in the decision-making process that determines and develops the community's cultural life, and the right and freedom to leave the community.

It is clear that changes in these cultural practices should come from the cultural community itself and not be imposed from outside. However, states should try to find ways to promote such changes. In this regard it is interesting to note that, for example, the CERD includes that states parties should adopt immediate and effective measures, particularly in the fields of teaching, education, culture and information, to combat prejudices which lead to racial discrimination and to promote understanding, tolerance and friendship among nations and racial or ethnic groups (Article 7). Furthermore, the Convention on the Elimination of All Forms of Discrimination against Women (in force since 3 September 1981) states in Article 5 that "States Parties shall take all appropriate measures: (a) To modify the social and cultural patterns of conduct of men and women, with a view to achieving the elimination of prejudices and customary and all other practices which are based on the idea of the inferiority or the superiority of either of the sexes or on stereotyped roles for men and women."[28]

THE RIGHT FREELY TO PARTICIPATE IN THE CULTURAL LIFE OF THE COMMUNITY: ARTICLE 27 OF THE UNIVERSAL DECLARATION OF HUMAN RIGHTS

Acting under the supervision of the Economic and Social Council (ECOSOC), the Commission on Human Rights started drafting the Universal Declaration in 1947. The drafting process took place in the Sub-Commission on the Prevention of Discrimination and the Protection of Minorities and in the Third Committee of the General Assembly.[29]

The governments of Chile, Cuba, the United Kingdom and Panama submitted the first formal drafts of a bill of human rights to the General Assembly and the commission. After exhaustive discussions on every provision by the commission, the General Assembly's Third Committee reviewed the draft word by word (United Nations 1950, 12–13; Robinson 1958, 25–7; Kanger 1984, 20). The Universal Declaration on Human Rights was finally adopted by the General Assembly on 10 December 1948.

Article 27 of the Universal Declaration reads as follows:

> 1. Everyone has the right freely to participate in the cultural life of the community, to enjoy the arts and to share in scientific advancement and its benefits.

> 2. Everyone has the right to the protection of the moral and material interests resulting from any scientific, literary or artistic production of which he is the author.

The first paragraph of Article 27 is the only provision of the UDHR that specifically refers to "culture". However, what is meant by "to participate in the cultural life of the community"? What is the definition of "cultural life", and what is meant by "participation"? Which community is meant here?

The Travaux Préparatoires of UDHR Article 27

In one of the first proposals for the Universal Declaration by the Chilean delegation, this provision merely focused on science and did not contain a reference to culture. It was the US delegation that proposed examining the possibility of including the cultural field in this provision. Based on concrete proposals to this end by Saudi Arabia, Bolivia, Brazil, Uruguay and Yugoslavia, the secretariat drafted a provision to be discussed by the commission. The idea was that culture was an important aspect of human life. In its classic form, including arts and literature, culture had to be made more accessible to the masses. The *travaux* show that the first part of paragraph 1 of Article 27 has hardly been negotiated and has not been altered. The first draft by the secretariat turned out to be mainly the same as the final text, except for the term "freely", which was included by the Third Committee of the General Assembly on the suggestion of the Peruvian delegation (Verdoodt 1963, 253; Morsink 1999, 218; United Nations 1950, 70–2). The Peruvian delegation pointed out that the individual should not only have the right to take part in the cultural, artistic and scientific life of the community, but should also have the right to do so in complete freedom. This view was widely supported and was adopted by 38 votes to none, with two abstentions (United Nations 1950, 70–2; Verdoodt 1963, 253–4; Morsink 1999, 218).[30]

The discussion on Article 27 in the commission and the General Assembly mainly focused on the inclusion of a second paragraph on authors' rights (United Nations 1950, 71; Morsink 1999, 220–21).[31] The Mexican delegation submitted a proposal on this issue, which was adopted as the second paragraph of the final provision. Another amendment by the USSR to include a provision that scientific advancement should be in the interest of democracy and the cause of international peace and cooperation was rejected on the basis that science should be free from any interference, especially from the state (United Nations 1950, 71).[32] The final Article 27 was adopted in the commission by 36 votes to none, with four abstentions. The General Assembly adopted it unanimously (ibid.; Verdoodt 1963, 255–6).

The *travaux* show that no discussion took place on the exact content of "free participation in the cultural life of the community". The main idea was to include a reference to culture in the Universal Declaration, without clearly defining the concepts of culture, participation and community. Several authors have, however, elaborated the meaning of Article 27.

Interpretation of UDHR Article 27 by Scholars

Several authors have argued that Article 27(1) implies that every person has the right to participate in every aspect of cultural life. Furthermore, every person has the right to participate actively in scientific progress and passively to enjoy the results of science. The term "freely to participate" means without interference or limitations other than those mentioned in the general limitation clause of UDHR Article 29(2).[33] It is further argued that the reference to arts and scientific advancement in the first paragraph does not necessarily imply a restriction of the expression of culture to these two branches: these aspects of culture were specifically mentioned because they were cultural products that had been almost inaccessible to the average person (Robinson 1958, 139; Verdoodt 1963, 256).

The *travaux préparatoires* show that, with regard to the object of Article 27(1), the drafters had a narrow concept of culture in mind, with an emphasis on arts, literature and education. The background of Article 27(1) was the fact that culture used to be the preserve of a small élite, and large parts of the population did not participate. Article 27(1) was considered to be an encouragement to the state to bring the masses to participate in culture and to make culture available to them. At that time, culture did not refer to a specific lifestyle or to the tradition of a community, or to aspects such as language or religion. As explained above, some authors suggest that Article 27(1) may imply a somewhat broader concept of culture, which means that other expressions of culture could also fall under it. In the author's view, however, the drafters had a narrow concept in mind, which focused on the material aspects of culture. The question is whether the current scope of Article 27 might be broader than just the advancement of the arts and sciences.

Which "community" does Article 27 refer to? Some have argued that the term refers to more than the state. Because of the universality of the rights included in the Universal Declaration, it necessarily comprises "the whole organized human race as well as parts thereof" (Robinson 1958, 139; Verdoodt 1963, 256). Others agree that "the community" refers to the national community and maybe to the world community. In any case, the term "community" did not refer to the situation of minorities, indigenous peoples or other local or regional communities. It is argued that the drafters did not use the formulation of "the culture of his or her community", because that would have referred to the possibility of the culture of one's community differing from the culture of the state in which one lives. In other words, Article 27 "seems to assume that 'the community' one participates in and with which one identifies culturally is the dominant one of the nation-state. There is no hint here of multiculturalism or pluralism" (Morsink 1999, 269).

The subject of Article 27 is the individual, since it refers to "everyone". The addressee is the state, but what obligations does the state have? Some have stated that Article 27(1) concerns a right to freedom as well as a right to service. In general, rights of freedom imply a freedom of action combined with non-interference by others, especially the state. Rights to service imply that the subject of the rights is supposed to be given something. Article 27(1) is a right of freedom to participate in the cultural life of the community and a right of service in the sense that the state should provide the conditions under which both the arts and the scientific benefits can be enjoyed (Kanger 1984, 150–51, 159–60, 163). With regard to the tripartite typology of state obligations, these involve the obligation to respect and to fulfil as well, possibly, as the obligation to protect, in the sense that the state should prevent interference by others.

The precise content of participation in cultural life and the corresponding state obligations remain unclear. The *travaux préparatoires* and the work of scholars do not provide definitive answers in this respect. Case law or statements of a supervisory body could also be helpful in the interpretation of rights provisions with regard to content and state obligations. However, the Universal Declaration is a declaration of principles that were later to be included in a legally binding instrument. Accordingly, states have no clearly defined obligations and do not have reporting obligations on the provisions of the UDHR. Consequently, no clear state practice has developed and the content and scope of UDHR Article 27(1) remain uncertain. At the time of drafting Article 27(1), culture was considered from a narrow perspective, including mainly cultural materials such as arts and literature. Article 27(1) was meant to make the material results of culture available to the masses. However, the question arises as to whether this is still the correct interpretation of this provision.

Perhaps clarification could be found in the ICESCR, adopted two decades later, in which a similar provision on participation in cultural life was included in Article 15(1). The ICESCR has legally binding force and contains a monitoring system which includes a state reporting procedure. Accordingly, states parties and the Committee on Economic, Social and Cultural Rights have developed Article 15(1) and have given an interpretation of the right to participate in cultural life. Article 27 UDHR, however, remains applicable for those states that have not ratified the ICESCR.[34]

THE RIGHT TO TAKE PART IN CULTURAL LIFE: ARTICLE 15(1)(A) OF THE INTERNATIONAL COVENANT ON ECONOMIC, SOCIAL AND CULTURAL RIGHTS

The drafting process of the human rights covenants, including the ICESCR, started in the commission at its fifth session in May and June 1949.[35] During its seventh session in April and May 1951 the commission considered proposals concerning economic, social and cultural rights, drafted by governments and specialized agencies such as the ILO, UNESCO and the WHO.[36] The commission finished its drafting work during its tenth session from February to April 1954. ECOSOC submitted the drafts on economic, social and cultural rights to the General Assembly, which considered them at its ninth session in 1954.[37] The General Assembly worked on the ICCPR and the ICESCR until 1957, then, after a pause of several years, resumed its work in 1966. The ICESCR was finally adopted in 1966[38] and entered into force in 1976.

The ICESCR is a legally binding international human rights instrument that includes a reference to "cultural rights" in the title. However, the only provision explicitly referring to culture is Article 15. This provision is similar, but not identical, to UDHR Article 27 and reads as follows:

1. The States Parties to the present Covenant recognize the right of everyone:

(a) to take part in cultural life;

(b) to enjoy the benefits of scientific progress and its applications;

(c) to benefit from the protection of the moral and material interests resulting from any scientific literary or artistic production of which he is the author.

2. The steps to be taken by the States Parties to the present Covenant to achieve the full realization of this right shall include those necessary for the conservation, the development and the diffusion of science and culture.

3. The States Parties to the present Covenant undertake to respect the freedom indispensable for scientific research and creative activity.

4. The States Parties to the present Covenant recognize the benefits to be derived from the encouragement and development of international contacts and co-operation in the scientific and cultural fields.

Article 15(1)(a) poses several questions. Why was this provision included in the ICESCR? How should Article 15(1)(a) be interpreted? Did the drafters or the states parties at any stage give a description of "cultural life" or "culture"? What is meant by "to take part"? Is there a specific reason why, in comparison with UDHR Article 27, the terms "community" and "freely" are absent in Article 15(1)(a)? Article 15(2) adds a provision on the conservation, development and diffusion of culture. Is culture considered in a broader sense than in the Universal Declaration?

The Travaux Préparatoires of ICESCR Article 15

Commission on Human Rights

The drafting of ICESCR Article 15 by the Commission on Human Rights started during its seventh session in 1951.[39] During the fifth session of the General Assembly in October 1950, several governments had brought up issues related to culture to be included in the covenant. The USSR proposed the right to leisure and culture,[40] Czechoslovakia suggested the right to education and creative expression[41] and Syria wished to include the right to speak one's own language and to study and develop one's own culture.[42]

UNESCO played an important role in the drafting of Article 15. During the seventh session of the commission, the director-general of UNESCO stated that cultural rights and rights to participate in culture could not be omitted from the draft covenant.[43] He presented the following preliminary draft proposal:

> The signatory States undertake to encourage the preservation, development and propagation of science and culture by every appropriate means:
>
> (a) by facilitating for all access to manifestations of national and international cultural life, such as books, publications and works of art [...];
>
> (b) by preserving and protecting the inheritance of books, works of art and other monuments and objects of historic, scientific and cultural interest;
>
> (c) by assuring liberty and security to scholars and artists [...];
>
> (d) by guaranteeing the free cultural development of racial and linguistic minorities.[44]

At the same time, the director-general submitted an alternative text "in case the Commission would prefer a briefer enunciation of cultural rights". The text was as follows:

> The signatory States undertake to encourage by all appropriate means, the conservation, the development and the diffusion of science and culture. They recognize that it is one of their principal aims to ensure conditions which will permit everyone:
>
> 1. to take part in cultural life;
>
> 2. to enjoy the benefits of scientific progress and its applications;

3. to obtain protection for his moral and material interests resulting from any scientific or artistic production of which he is the author.[45]

Chile formally submitted this preliminary UNESCO draft provision to the commission.[46] Draft Article 30,[47] adopted by the commission at its seventh session, was similar to the brief version proposed by the director-general of UNESCO. However, the third sub-paragraph on authors' rights was rejected.[48]

During the eighth session of the commission in 1952, several amendments to this proposal were submitted. In paragraph 1, after "science and culture", the USSR wished to insert the words "and to ensure the development of science and education in the interests of progress and democracy and of the maintenance of peace and co-operation between peoples", similar to the proposals made during the drafting of the Universal Declaration.[49] The French delegation proposed to reinsert a third sub-paragraph on authors' rights.[50] The United States submitted a proposal to reformulate the provision in a more direct way:

States Parties to the present Covenant recognize the right of everyone:

(a) to take part in cultural life;

(b) to enjoy freedom necessary for scientific research and creation.[51]

Paragraph (b) was later revised by the United States on the initiative of Lebanon into "to enjoy the benefits of scientific progress and its applications".[52]

No thorough discussion took place on the first part of the provision concerning the right to take part in cultural life. The US proposal to include a specific recognition of what was called "the right to culture", instead of ensuring conditions for the development of cultural life, was widely supported, and adopted by 14 votes to none with three abstentions.[53] Apart from some general statements on the importance of the inclusion of such a provision on culture, the meaning of the term "cultural life" and the scope of the provision were not discussed. The negotiations in the commission on this provision mainly focused on the proposals of the USSR to include a reference to democracy and peace, and on the French proposal concerning authors' rights. Most delegations were opposed to including a reference that the development of science and culture should be in the interest of peace, democracy and cooperation, because it could be a pretext for state control. It was argued that scientific research and creative activity should be independent of any external criteria. The French proposal on authors' rights was also rejected, because most delegations found the issue too complex to be dealt with in a human rights covenant. Moreover, it was argued that this matter was properly being dealt with by UNESCO.[54] At its eighth session in 1952 the commission adopted the final draft provision, which was similar to the final ICESCR Article 15, except for paragraph 1(c) on authors' rights and paragraph 4 on international cooperation, which were added by the General Assembly.[55]

General Assembly

The General Assembly had been working on the ICESCR since 1950, when several states submitted the first proposals to the commission. Over the years, the General Assembly closely followed the work of the commission and several delegations expressed their opinions on drafts circulating in the commission. States generally supported the draft provision on participation in cultural life. In general, the same issues as discussed in the commission were brought up during the negotiations in the General Assembly. The USSR still wished to include a reference to the fact that science and culture should serve the interests of peace and democracy,[56] while France expressed the need for the inclusion of authors' rights.[57]

In October and November 1957, five years after the adoption of the draft in the commission, the main negotiations on the drafting of Article 15[58] took place in the General Assembly. Czechoslovakia submitted an amendment to add the issue of peace and cooperation to the second paragraph and add a fourth paragraph on international cooperation in the field of science and culture.[59] Saudi Arabia issued a proposal, similar to the Czechoslovak proposal, to include the interests of progress and democracy.[60] Uruguay proposed to include a paragraph on authors' rights, similar to that in UDHR Article 27.[61]

In general, the negotiations in the General Assembly on the various amendments were similar to those in the commission several years before. Many states found a reference to peace and cooperation unnecessary and undesirable, because such a reference would give states an opportunity to exert their influence on science and culture.[62] Limited debate took place on the precise content of the right to take part in cultural life. One of the interesting issues was a proposal by UNESCO that Article 15 make a reference to *communities* involved in the participation in cultural life. It was argued that the individual normally participates in the cultural life of various communities. According to UNESCO, states should not only recognize the right of everyone to participate in his or her national cultural life, but also respect the right of a person to have access to foreign cultures or the cultural life of smaller communities within the state. UNESCO accordingly proposed to change the first paragraph into "to take part in the cultural life of the communities to which he belongs".[63]

The final outcome of the negotiations in the General Assembly was the adoption of the Czech amendment on an extra paragraph on international cooperation and the adoption of a paragraph on authors' rights. The other amendments and the proposal of UNESCO concerning communities were rejected or withdrawn. The General Assembly adopted the final draft during its twelfth session in 1957.[64] The ICESCR, however, was not adopted until 1966. Between 1957 and 1966 the text of Article 15 was not changed.

ICESCR Article 15(1) is similar to Article 27 of the Universal Declaration. However, the negotiations, especially in the General Assembly, show that some states, under the influence of UNESCO, were willing to consider the provision in a somewhat broader context. UNESCO, in particular, brought up new issues, such as the role of cultural communities. It pointed out that apart from the national culture, other cultural communities could also be important to individuals. However, states did not extensively discuss the scope of the provision and gave no interpretation of the concept of "culture" or "cultural life". At the time of its adoption, Article 15(1) was still mainly meant to make the "high" material aspects of culture more broadly available. No reference was made to any community, which shows that the emphasis still lay in participation in the *national* cultural life. Moreover, the drafters did not have in mind the "popularization" of culture. The right to take part in cultural life did not imply the right of all people to enjoy those cultural activities that they *themselves* found worthwhile. Cultural access did not mean that the masses could rule on *which* cultural activities should be available and accessible. The intention was to increase access mainly to aspects of "high" culture (see also O'Keefe 1998, 912–13).

The question is to what extent the intention of the drafters is still the valid interpretation of Article 15(1)(a). How has the supervisory body of the covenant, the Committee on Economic, Social and Cultural Rights, dealt with the implementation of Article 15(1)(a)?

Guidelines for the Reporting Procedure under the ICESCR

In 1990 the Committee on Economic, Social and Cultural Rights adopted revised guidelines for the reporting procedure.[65] These guidelines provide states parties with directions on how to report on the implementation of the ICESCR. With regard to Article 15(1), states parties should describe the legislative and other measures adopted to fulfil the right of everyone to take part in cultural life and manifest their culture. According to the guidelines, the committee wants to know which funds are available for the promotion of cultural development, what institutional infrastructure has been established, what role the mass media play in this process and how mankind's cultural heritage is preserved and presented. The committee also asks states to provide information on the steps taken for the conservation, development and diffusion of science and culture, through the educational system, the media and communication. It requests information on the "promotion of awareness and enjoyment of the cultural heritage of national ethnic groups and minorities and of indigenous peoples". Finally, the committee requests information on the "promotion of cultural identity as a factor of mutual appreciation among individuals, groups, nations and regions".[66]

In the guidelines, no definition of culture or cultural life is given. It is interesting that the concept of cultural identity is used in the guidelines, and thereby brought into a direct relationship with ICESCR Article 15(1). The use of the term "cultural identity" can be a sign of the (silent) acceptance of a broader concept of culture than the drafters of Article 15(1) had in mind. Cultural identity "as a factor of mutual appreciation", as described in the guidelines, is more than merely the material aspects of culture. Special attention is further given to minorities and other communities, and to the protection of their cultural heritage. With the revised guidelines, the committee seems to broaden the scope of Article 15(1) to include more than mere access to culture and cultural products, and recognizes the collective dimension of culture.

According to the guidelines, the role of the state is not only a passive one, but also active. Article 15(1) may require positive obligations, such as funds to be made available, the establishment of institutions and the involvement of the media and communication. While the drafters considered the state to be the proper body to determine which cultural activities should be supported, in the guidelines the committee argues that Article 15(1) contains the right to take part in the cultural life "which he or she considers pertinent" (see also O'Keefe 1998, 913). It appears that the ideas of UNESCO concerning the role of cultural communities other than and beyond the national community, which had been rejected during the drafting of Article 15, were now endorsed by the committee.

State Reports and Concluding Observations by the Committee

The supervisory role of the committee in its consideration of periodic state reports is important to clarify the scope of provisions in the covenant, including Article 15.[67] In their reports, states describe how they have implemented the provisions of the covenant. The committee then engages in a dialogue with the state, after which it provides comments in the form of so-called concluding observations. During the first 25 years of the covenant, Article 15 was hardly given any attention by either the committee or states parties in their periodic reports (O'Keefe 1998, 904–5). A short analysis of the latest reports shows that, in recent years, states have generally followed the guidelines as adopted by the committee in reporting on Article 15(1)(a). They include information on laws and cultural policies adopted, as well as general figures concerning funds made available for the implementation of the right to take part in cultural life. States report on a broad range of issues, including measures taken to make culture available to as many people as possible, to facilitate freedom of cultural expression and promote creativity and to conserve cultural heritage.

The state reports show that cultural life is considered a broad concept. As indicated in the guidelines, states refer to, for example, visual arts, performing arts, traditional folk arts, crafts and literature. They also provide information on cultural industries and institutions, such as cinemas, theatres, libraries and museums. Measures taken concern the protection of the artist, freedom of creation and the dissemination of creative results. Another topic addressed is the protection of cultural heritage, including monuments and archaeological sites. States mention the role of education, which includes not only cultural education but also the dissemination of information on different cultures, including the promotion of an intercultural dialogue. The role of the mass media in promoting the right to take part in cultural life is discussed. In their cultural policies, states parties recognize the special needs of person with disabilities, children and the elderly to enable them to take part in cultural life.[68] Finally, states pay attention to the protection of the culture of minorities and indigenous peoples, including measures taken in relation to the protection of different languages. In their reports, states generally use concepts such as multiculturalism and cultural pluralism.[69]

The committee in its concluding observations also deals with a wide variety of topics relating to the implementation of the right to take part in cultural life. In its comments, concerns, suggestions and recommendations, the committee does not refer to specific provisions of the covenant but deals with issues related to its implementation. In its concluding observations in recent years, the committee has dealt with the narrow as well as the broad scope of cultural life. It has commented on policies and funds related to cultural associations and institutions, cultural performances and arts – in other words, culture in the more classic sense of the term.[70] The committee has also paid attention to the situation of specific groups, such as indigenous peoples, minorities and the Roma, including their rights to housing, health, education and employment, as well as the protection of their language, intellectual property and the issue of access and ownership of to natural resources and land.[71] Language rights have recently been specifically referred to by the committee as part of the right to take part in cultural life. These include the use of minority languages in private, for example names, and in public, for example in the media and in relation to the administration.[72] The committee, for example, recommended that Morocco and the Libyan Arab Jamahiriya legally recognize Amazighe as a minority language, and that Slovenia take measures to guarantee that education is provided also in the mother tongue of minorities.[73] The committee has in the case of Morocco argued that, since the minority forms a large part of the population, such as *in casu* the Amazighe community, it has the right to exercise its own cultural identity in conformity with ICESCR Article 15(1)(a).[74]

The committee also deals with the issue of cultural practices that may be harmful to the enjoyment of human rights. In several concluding observations it expresses its concern about the "prevalence of customs, traditions and cultural practices, which lead to substantial discrimination against women and girls" or which impede "the full enjoyment by women and girls of their rights".[75] For example, it mentions polygamy as a violation of the dignity of women and discrimination against them.[76] The committee also urges states to overcome barriers and obstacles based on cultural and religious traditions that prevent women from fully participating in cultural life.[77]

From the concluding observations, it appears that the committee adheres to a broad interpretation of Article 15(1)(a), in accordance with its guidelines. In its concluding observations the committee does not specifically refer to Article 15(1) or any other provision. Instead, it deals with issues that may concern various provisions, including Article 2 on non-discrimination and Article 3 on the equal right of men and women to enjoy economic, social and cultural rights. The committee furthermore speaks of the situation of minorities and indigenous peoples in relation to culture, housing, health etc. The committee has even referred to rights in the ICCPR, such as freedom of expression and freedom of information,[78] or ILO Convention 169 on Indigenous and Tribal Peoples.[79] It is clear that the narrow scope, as understood by the drafters of the covenant, has been abandoned, and that the right to take part in cultural life has been given a broader scope over the years by the states parties and the committee.

General Discussion on Article 15 by the Committee on Economic, Social and Cultural Rights

The committee further clarifies the scope of the covenant by adopting general comments on specific provisions. These general comments are usually preceded by so-called "days of general discussion" on such provisions. The committee held such a day of general discussion on Article 15(1) during its session in December 1992. Attention was not only paid to the right to participate in culture, but also to the "right to culture" and other cultural rights. In aid of this debate, one of the committee members, S.R. Konaté (Senegal), prepared a working paper on these matters. A general comment on Article 15(1) was not adopted, however.

Committee working paper on cultural rights (December 1992)

In his working paper, Konaté emphasized that cultural rights are generally underdeveloped because of a lack of clarity about the content and legal implications for states. Konaté made a clear distinction between the right to take part in cultural life and the right to culture. He argued that these rights are often confused, including by the committee in its guidelines, but do not have the same meaning and implications. The right to culture, although acknowledged as relevant, for example by UNESCO, is not included in international law and is more than the right to take part in cultural life. It implies that the individual plays an active role in the development of this culture and can identify him/herself as part of it. The right to take part in cultural life presupposes the recognition of the right to culture of the community to which the individual belongs. Consequently, the right to take part in cultural life is considered to be an individual right, while the right to culture may be regarded as a collective right.[80]

Konaté maintained that Article 15(1) does not refer to specific terms, but to a general concept of "cultural life". He confirmed that the drafters of the ICESCR had a limited conception of culture in mind, focusing on the external manifestations of culture, such as libraries, museums and works of art. In general, Konaté advised the committee to widen the scope of the concept of cultural life, including its individual and collective dimension. "Culture is no longer an expression of knowledge or demand for recreational activities as consumer goods, but reflects a way of being and feeling, in short, the community's way of life and thought."[81]

Konaté further asserted that the right to take part in cultural life includes the right to have access to culture, to enjoy the benefits and demand their protection and to contribute freely to its development. He also argued that the right to have access to culture includes the right to choose a culture, and implies equal opportunities and non-discrimination in this respect. The right of access to culture entails the freedom to engage in creative activity, access to the means of dissemination and protection of the cultural and artistic heritage as an important aspect of cultural identity.[82]

In the working paper, special attention was paid to the situation of minorities in relation to culture, referring to ICCPR Article 27, which lays down the right to enjoy culture for members of minorities. Konaté argued that both the right to take part in cultural life and the right to enjoy culture embody the idea of the autonomy and identity of the individual. The individual must have the possibility of identifying with the cultural community of her/his choice and of establishing relations with it. In his view, minorities are justified in demanding not only recognition of but also respect for their cultural values. The committee should thus give priority to the protection of the cultural rights of minorities.[83]

Finally, Konaté described several difficulties in the implementation of cultural rights. He argued that the progress achieved by states parties in implementing cultural rights largely depends on the level of implementation of other rights, such as the right to education and the right to an adequate standard of living. Konaté argued that access to culture is largely dependent on the economic and social development of a particular society. A minimum of physical well-being is necessary to give the idea of culture any significance.[84]

Konaté's working paper offers an interesting elaboration of cultural rights in general and ICESCR Article 15(1) in particular. For example, the link between cultural rights and other human rights, such as the right to education, the right to freedom of expression and rights related to cultural heritage, is noteworthy. In the present author's view, it is important to connect different human rights to the concept of culture, thereby reaffirming the principles of indivisibility, interrelatedness and interdependence of human rights.

The link between the promotion and protection of cultural rights and economic and social development is also important. In Konaté's view, a minimum of development is necessary to give culture any meaning. However, one can also argue that if culture is considered in a broad sense, as a "way of life", it is to some extent independent of the level of development. Aspects of culture such as language, religion and traditions, as well as creativity, also exist in the economically most underdeveloped parts of the world. Some other aspects of culture, such as museums, the protection of cultural heritage and education, might demand more economic and social development. However, a minimum of cultural rights, or the core of the right to take part in cultural life, should always be protected by states, irrespective of their economic and social development.[85]

With regard to the object, subject and addressee of Article 15(1)(a), Konaté made several interesting remarks. The object of cultural life should be considered in a broader perspective than was envisaged by the drafters, including material as well as intangible aspects. The subject of Article 15(1)(a) is the individual. However, the collective dimension of the right to take part in cultural life should also be recognized. The collective dimension also comes forward in the recognition that special attention should be paid to the cultural rights of minorities. Finally, the addressee is the state, which has negative as well as positive obligations. The concrete content of these obligations, however, remains broad and vague.

Day of general discussion in the committee

In December 1992 the committee held a day of general discussion on Article 15(1), in the course of which the Konaté report was the main point of reference. Apart from the committee members, several external experts were invited to take part in the debate, including representatives of UNESCO and several NGOs. In general, committee members stated that the lack of reporting by governments on cultural rights in general, and Article 15 in particular, showed the need to clarify this provision. They generally expressed their agreement on the ideas in the working paper and endorsed the broad vision on Article 15(1) as formulated by Konaté.[86]

While the discussion was too short to draw firm conclusions, the contributions of individual members of the committee show a possible development of Article 15(1). Several members explicitly expressed their willingness to adopt a broad concept of culture as being more than cultural manifestations, and to include language, literature, clothing, shelter, arts, customs and traditions. The scope of Article 15(1)(a) should accordingly be broadened to include not only access to cultural materials but also active engagement in culture and participation in the decision-making process. Several components of the right to take part in cultural life were formulated, such as participation, access, policy-making and artistic freedom. Especially for minorities, participation in policy-making was considered to be of importance to prevent a certain culture from being turned into a mere tourist attraction, or being "museumized". States should not consider cultural rights a luxury, but instead should do as much as possible to allow the greatest number of people to participate.[87]

Another important point was that several members indicated the individual as well as the collective dimension of the right to take part in cultural life. While it was emphasized that Article 15(1) contains an individual right, the community aspect of it was firmly acknowledged. The collective dimension of Article 15(1) lies in the fact that communities often provide cultural values.[88]

Few committee members paid attention to state obligations with regard to Article 15(1). The emphasis was laid on negative obligations such as the obligation to respect. Positive obligations following from the obligations to protect and to fulfil were not explicitly discussed. States should mainly respect the development and preservation of cultures and should, as far as possible, refrain from interference.[89] The formulation of a core content of Article 15(1) as a minimum to be guaranteed by states was not discussed.

One of the problems identified by several members was that cultures *of* states and cultures *within* states may differ, which would make a general approach towards the monitoring of Article 15(1) very difficult. It was proposed to ask states parties themselves to describe their cultural indicators, which could be compared with the committee's indicators.[90] In the author's view, besides the fact that it remains unclear what these "indicators" are, inviting states parties to decide on the description of the cultural life and the communities involved might give them an opportunity to restrict the application of Article 15(1). On the other hand, the involvement of states parties provided information on the specific situations and, if it were tested against the committee's own indicators, it would be interesting to involve states in the whole process of developing cultural rights in general and the right to take part in cultural life in particular.

NGO representatives touched upon the sensitive issue of cultural expressions that violate human rights. It was argued that cultural practices which are damaging to health or to the enjoyment of other human rights should not be regarded as part of the right to take part in cultural life.[91] Unfortunately, none of the committee members expressed an opinion on this matter.

The value of the discussion in the committee is that it shows the potential of Article 15(1). As stated above, the right to take part in cultural life is one of the most important cultural rights, and Article 15(1)(a) is the only provision in the ICESCR that directly refers to culture. The debate showed that the members of the committee struggled with well-known issues, such as the definition of culture, the individual and collective dimensions of this right and the corresponding state obligations.

At the end, the committee expressed the wish to continue the discussion in order to come to a clarification of the obligations of states with regard to cultural rights in general and Article 15(1) in particular.[92] However, it is only recently that the committee has followed up the work on the right to take part in cultural life. It has been involved in several meetings concerning the elaboration of this right. A round-table discussion was organized in Quezon City (Philippines) in February 2002 and the Conference on the Right to Take Part in Cultural Life was held in Barcelona (Spain) in November 2002, where committee members exchanged views with experts in the field of cultural rights. Within the framework of the World Forum of Cultures in Barcelona in 2004, several regional meetings were organized to elaborate the normative content of the right to take part in cultural life. While the broad range of issues related to this right were discussed extensively during these meetings, limited progress has been made in relation to the concrete drafting of a general comment.[93]

THE DEVELOPMENT OF THE RIGHT TO TAKE PART IN CULTURAL LIFE

While at the time of adopting UDHR Article 27 and ICESCR Article 15, the right to participate/take part in cultural life was supposed to make the material aspects of culture available and accessible to larger parts of the population, it now has a broader content and scope. What could nowadays be considered the object and subject of the right to take part in cultural life? And which obligations do states parties have in implementing this right?

The Object and Subject of the Right to Take Part in Cultural Life

To determine the object of the right to take part in cultural life, one needs to clarify the content and scope of the concepts of "to take part" and "cultural life". The concept of "cultural life" has evolved in accordance with the development of the concept of culture. As described above, three concepts of culture in relation to cultural rights can be distinguished. The first is the classic concept of culture as including arts, literature, theatre and museums. The second concept is culture in a plural form including all manifestations and expressions – for example, folk music, handicrafts, popular press, television and radio. The third concept of culture is the way of life of a society, in other words the society's underlying and characteristic pattern of thought (O'Keefe 1998, 905; see also Stavenhagen 2001, 87–91). It seems that the content of Article 15(1)(a) on the right to take part in cultural life has followed these three stages. While the drafters still focused on the first concept of "high" culture, the guidelines of the committee suggest a move to the second concept, which includes popular forms of culture. Finally, during the day of general discussion in 1992, as well as in its more recent dealing with state reports, the committee has considered culture in its broad form as a way of life.

As regards the concept of "to take part", it has become clear from the above that it has a passive and an active side. On the passive side, to take part means to have access to cultural life and enjoy its benefits, without any form of discrimination. It also means to have access to information concerning cultural life. Taking part in cultural life implies that cultural life should be protected and preserved, in particular its cultural and artistic heritage.

On the more active side, taking part in cultural life implies the right and freedom to choose and to change a cultural affiliation and to contribute freely to cultural life and its development by means of creative or other activities. Such freedom implies a right to self-identification, which is essential to the dignity of the individual. Taking an active part in cultural life also implies the right to take part in the decision-making process in relation to it.

Language is not only a means of communication, but also an essential element of cultural life, as it forms thoughts, perceptions and emotions. To take part in cultural life therefore also implies the freedom to use and express oneself in the language(s) of one's choice, in private and, as much as possible, in public, as well as to disseminate cultural information freely in the preferred language(s).

As stated earlier, the right to take part in cultural life is closely related to other human rights, such as freedom of thought and religion, freedom of association and the right to education. In the various aspects of participation, especially the active ones, the concept of freedom is a central element. The emphasis on *freedoms* next to rights reflects the dynamic character of culture as a changeable and adaptable process. It is therefore unfortunate that the term "freely" was left out of Article 15(1)(a) in comparison with Article 27 of the Universal Declaration.

With regard to the subject, Article 15(1)(a) speaks of the right of "everyone" to take part in cultural life. It thereby shows clearly that the subject of the right to take part in cultural life is the individual. However, participation in cultural life has a strong collective connotation. Taking part in cultural life implies the existence of a cultural life linked to a cultural community. In other words, the right to take part in cultural life can only be enjoyed in the context of a cultural collectivity. It is unfortunate that no reference was made in Article 15(1) to a collective dimension, as is done in ICCPR Article 27, which states that members of minorities have the right, *in community with other members of their group*, to enjoy their culture, practise their religion and speak their language.

In relation to the right to take part in cultural life, particular attention is paid to cultural communities such as minorities or indigenous peoples. The committee's debates on state reports show that it regards Article 15(1)(a) as guaranteeing for both minorities and indigenous peoples the freedom to practise their culture as well as the opportunity to promote awareness of it, including a degree of autonomy. By encouraging states to protect distinct cultures and communities, the committee touches upon the collective dimension of this right, without giving it the status of a collective right as such (see also O'Keefe 1998, 916–18).

State Obligations with Regard to the Right to Take Part in Cultural Life

The right to take part in cultural life implies negative as well as positive state obligations. The state party has the passive duty to respect participation, but it also should take active measures to develop and enlarge participation in cultural life. A state party does not fulfil its obligations under Article 15(1)(a) by merely removing formal obstacles to equal participation in culture. It is expected to do more than simply allow individuals and communities to practise their cultures without hindrance; it should take active measures to preserve and foster cultures. In other words, Article 15(1)(a) is more than a non-discrimination provision; the state party should provide *substantive* ability to participate in culture, which implies negative as well as positive obligations (ibid., 905–6, 916–18; Vlemminx 1992, 197, 207, 239; Marks 2003, 304–6).

The obligation to respect

The obligation to respect implies, in general, that the state party is obliged to respect the freedom of the individual to choose, develop, assert and change a preferred cultural orientation. It implies that states parties recognize the existence of different cultures within their territory and that they value them as part of a national and global culture.

States parties should further refrain from action that might obstruct the individual from taking part in cultural life. Obligations in this regard could entail state party respect for the freedom to provide, collect and pass on cultural information and cultural ideas in a preferred form and language. Such respect should always be guaranteed; practical circumstances, such as a shortage of resources, could not be an excuse for a state party not to respect these cultural freedoms. Respect for cultural freedoms is closely linked to respect for other fundamental freedoms, such as freedom of expression, religion and assembly, which are central components of cultural life, as well as to the right to non-discrimination (Vlemminx 1992, 231–3; 1994, 115, 138; Eide 2001b, 293–5; Symonides 2000, 206; Hansen 2002, 300–01; Marks 2003, 305).

The obligation to protect

The obligation to protect implies that the state party should protect the right to take part in cultural life from unwanted interference by public or private bodies, and also by foreign cultural influences unwanted by the community involved. Examples in this regard may be strong interference in cultural life by religious institutions and the possible standardization or homogenization of cultures through interference by third parties (O'Keefe 1998, 911, 919). Moreover, the state party should protect the individual's right to take part in cultural life against third parties who, by the assertion of their cultural identity or engagement in cultural activities, disrupt the enjoyment of this right. For example, the cultural expressions of one community may not be unjustifiably offensive to other communities. This issue is closely related to the limits to the enjoyment of cultural rights, as discussed above (Eide, 2001b, 293–5; Symonides 2000, 206).

The obligation to fulfil

Several positive measures are described in the second paragraph of Article 15, which lays down various steps to be taken by states parties to achieve cultural participation, including the conservation, development and diffusion of culture. States parties should not only promote popular participation in culture in general, but should also actively support the accessibility of cultural activities to the widest possible audience. The means of support may include financial means (O'Keefe 1998, 905–6, 908, 911).

The state should further take measures to improve the conditions under which the right to take part in cultural life can be enjoyed. It should, for example, encourage the spread of culture(s) among the population and promote the development of culture(s) for the future. Concrete measures may, for example, include improving access to cultural life through funds or the establishment of an institutional infrastructure to promote popular participation in cultural life. In this regard, the state has a special responsibility with regard to marginalized or disadvantaged groups in society (Eide 2001b, 293–5; Symonides 2000, 206; Vlemminx 1992, 199–200, 231–3; 1994, 115, 138). The committee has, for example, recognized in its General Comment No. 5 on persons with disabilities that states should promote access to places of cultural performances and services, and eliminate communication barriers by using books and information materials in simple language and special devices for deaf or blind persons. Finally, the committee maintains that "in order to facilitate the equal participation in cultural life of persons with disabilities, Governments should inform and educate the general public about disability".[94]

The obligation to conserve, develop and disseminate culture also entails state protection of culture and cultural heritage for generations to come. This implies, for example, the protection of monuments, sites, cultural property and museums. The protection of cultural heritage is guaranteed in a number of instruments, including the UNESCO conventions on world natural, cultural and intangible heritage, and the Hague Convention on the Protection of Cultural Property in Armed Conflict.[95] It also implies protection of traditional culture and folklore or crafts, including active support for the study, promotion and diffusion of these activities – for example, the circulation of educational and cultural materials (see Marks 2003, 307–10). Other specific measures could be exemptions from laws that penalize cultural practices, for example special hunting and usufruct laws, or specific measures, such as motorcycle helmet laws for Sikhs, the funding of ethnic associations or multilingual ballots or special voting measures, or the protection of symbolic claims, such as religious holidays (see, for example, Levy 1997, 25; Hansen 2002, 301).

Since the right to take part in cultural life includes not only access to culture but also active participation in the decision-making process on cultural matters, the state should ensure that individuals can take part in the general political process. States should, for example, ensure representation of different communities in relevant decision-making bodies, or at least consult them or have them participate actively in matters of their concern, such as cultural development.

As regards positive measures to be taken by states, some inspiration could be drawn from the Convention on the Protection and Promotion of the Diversity of Cultural Expressions, adopted by the General Conference of UNESCO in October 2005. Although the convention does not contain substantive rights of individuals or communities, but mainly rights of states, several provisions speak of measures that *may* be taken by states to protect cultural diversity. These measures have a clear link with the measures that states could take to implement the right to take part in cultural life. For example, according to the convention, states may take measures that "provide opportunities for […] the creation, production, dissemination, distribution and enjoyment of such domestic cultural activities, goods and services, including provisions relating to the language used for such activities, goods and services" (Article 6(b)). This provision furthermore speaks of measures to establish and support public institutions, to support artists and others involved in the creation of cultural expressions, and to enhance the diversity of the media, including through public service broadcasting (Article 6(f)–(h)). Such measures could include public financial assistance (Article 6(d)). States should furthermore encourage individuals and groups to create, produce, disseminate, distribute and have access to their own cultural expressions, "paying due attention to the special circumstances and needs of women as well as various social groups, including persons belonging to minorities and indigenous peoples" (Article 7(a)). Although under this convention states may decide what kind of measures to take, by becoming parties to the convention they accept a responsibility to take positive measures in relation to the promotion and protection of cultural diversity.[96] This is closely linked to the promotion of access to and participation in cultural life.

CONCLUDING REMARKS

The scope of the right to take part in cultural life has evolved over the years. At the time of the adoption of the UDHR, the right to participate freely in the cultural life of the community in Article 27 aimed at making culture available and accessible to all people, whereby culture was considered in its narrow scope as involving material aspects, such as arts and literature. The term "community" referred to the national community.

The right to take part in cultural life, as laid down in ICESCR Article 15(1)(a), has the same background. It was meant to make cultural life accessible and available to the whole population. At the time of drafting Article 15(1), culture mainly referred to *national* culture and was approached in a narrow sense as equivalent to cultural material(s). Other aspects of a broader concept of culture, such as language, religion and education, were dealt with in separate provisions in the ICESCR and the ICCPR. Moreover, Article 15(1) was drafted as an individual right; no reference was made to its possible collective dimension.

In 1990 the committee adopted the revised guidelines for the reporting procedure, in which it broadened the scope of Article 15(1). In these guidelines the committee used new concepts, such as cultural identity, cultural development and the right to manifest one's culture. The committee also asked states parties to report on how they promote the cultural heritage of national ethnic groups, minorities and indigenous peoples. Article 15(1)(a) no longer merely refers to national culture; rather states are also considered to have a responsibility for the preservation of cultures of other communities.

The committee made a further attempt to clarify the content and scope of ICESCR Article 15(1)(a) during its general discussion on this provision in 1992. While the committee as such did not draw general conclusions, the interventions by the various committee members showed the possible development of the right to take part in cultural life. Most members endorsed the broad concept of culture going beyond its practical results, and including non-material aspects such as traditions, language, religion, etc. Furthermore, participation in culture was considered to be more than having access to it: it includes being able to contribute actively to culture and to participate actively in the decision-making process. With regard to state obligations, the committee members tended to stress negative obligations, such as the obligation to respect. States should not interfere with the free development and expression of culture. The obligations to protect and to fulfil were not particularly discussed by the committee.

Nowadays, it seems that the right to take part in cultural life entails a whole range of issues, some of which are closely linked to other human rights. It concerns rights of creators and transmitters of culture and the right of individuals to contribute and have access to culture, as well as rights related to the promotion and preservation of cultural identity, including education, language and religion. It also concerns the protection of cultural heritage and the establishment and consolidation of cultural institutions, such as museums, libraries and archives. These issues are closely linked to the rights to education and self-determination, as well as the rights to freedom of thought, religion, expression and assembly.

This broad approach towards the right to take part in cultural life consequently poses questions about the exact scope and normative content of this right. Because of the broad scope of "cultural life", it would be difficult to elaborate a core content of the right specifying the essential minimum without which it would lose its *raison d'être*. It would be equally difficult to determine the scope of all the corresponding state obligations. Only a few have been touched upon above, but much more analysis and clarification is needed. If "to take part" and "cultural life" are considered in a broad perspective, many different state obligations might be enumerated, negative as well as positive. Many of these obligations have a link with other rights in the covenants. Again, this study is not exhaustive and more research is needed to draw a clearer picture of the normative content and scope of the right to take part in cultural life and of the state obligations it entails.

It is important to address, albeit with caution, the relation between cultural freedoms and cultural practices that may be considered to infringe human rights. Cultural rights in general and the right to take part in cultural life in particular may not be used to limit the rights and freedoms of others or to impose a culture upon individuals. The promotion and protection of cultural rights should not imply the uncritical acceptance of harmful cultural practices: cultural practices should not conflict with the core value of human rights, namely human dignity. On the other hand, while an attitude of concern towards certain cultural practices may be necessary to protect human dignity, such an attitude should not lead to a rejection of cultural rights or of the right to take part in cultural life as a whole. Cultural human rights are essential to protect an important part of the dignity of human beings. Many individuals and communities need such protection, and measures need to be taken in order for them to be able to take part in cultural life. Cultural rights and the right to take part in cultural life should be the basis for ending policies of forced assimilation and discrimination against individuals and communities, as well as for respect for the right to be different, which is based on the human rights principle of equality. The right to be different, as described in the preamble of the UNESCO Declaration on Race and Racial Prejudice (1978), implies the right not to be excluded, humiliated, exploited or forcibly assimilated. It is in this spirit that cultural rights and the right to take part in cultural life should be respected, protected, promoted and fulfilled.

NOTES

1 Cultural rights have been described as a "Cinderella" to show that, from a legal standpoint, they are the least developed rights within the human rights spectrum; see Niec (1997, 3; 1998, 176).

2 Commission on Human Rights, Resolutions 2002/26 (22 April 2002), 2003/26 (22 April 2003), 2004/20 (16 April 2004) and 2005/20 (15 April 2005), all entitled "Promotion of the enjoyment of the cultural rights of everyone and respect for different cultural identities", para. 1.

3 Other authors have argued that the Convention on the Prevention and the Punishment of the Crime of Genocide (in force since January 1951) contains one of the most fundamental cultural rights, namely the right of groups to exist. According to Article 2 of the Genocide Convention, genocide includes, among others, acts causing serious bodily or mental harm to members of the group and forcibly transferring children of a group to another group. See Stavenhagen (2001, 87, 103).

4 The right to culture is often confused with the right to take part in cultural life, although they do not have the same meaning. In fact, only the latter is codified in international instruments. This issue was also dealt with by the Committee on Economic, Social and Cultural Rights – see later in this study.

5 See also the reports of Special Rapporteur Türk, who agrees that many human rights have an important cultural dimension. The protection for example offered to indigenous peoples, minorities or other communities by human rights would be meaningless if their cultural rights, such as the right not to be assimilated and the right to cultural autonomy, are not respected. See Türk (1992, 51–2).

6 See also, on the issue of cultural liberty, UNDP (2004).

7 See also the Universal Declaration of the Rights of Peoples, Algiers, 4 July 1976, in which several cultural rights of peoples are laid down. This declaration was not adopted by states, however, but by civil society organizations.

8 Only the right to self-determination, as included in the ICESCR and the ICCPR (both Article 1), is a right of "all peoples". This right includes the right to "… freely pursue their economic, social and cultural development". This right is briefly dealt with below.

9 These developments include the adoption of the UN Declaration on the Protection of National or Ethnic, Religious and Linguistic Minorities (1992) and the work on the UN Draft Declaration on the Protection of Rights of Indigenous Peoples, adopted by the Human Rights Council on 29 June 2006. The collective dimension is also visible in the state reports to the Committee on Economic, Social and Cultural Rights under the ICESCR, especially concerning the implementation of Article 15(1)(a) – see below.

10 Several monitoring bodies, such as the European Court of Human Rights and the Inter-American Commission on Human Rights, have also used other provisions to protect culture, such as the right to life, the right to health and the right to family life and home: see Donders (2002, 231–41, 269–300).

11 An in-depth analysis of the right of self-determination falls outside the scope of this study. See on this right, among others, Aikio and Scheinin (2000); Henrard (2000); Hannum (1996); Cassese (1995).

12 See Commission on Human Rights, Res. 2005/20, *Promotion of the enjoyment of the cultural rights of everyone and respect for different cultural identities*, 14 April 2005, para. 5. Other addressees may be identified, such as other individuals and communities. See, for example, Article 29 of the Universal Declaration on Human Rights, which says that all members of society share a responsibility in the realization of human rights, and the preambles of the ICCPR and the ICESCR,

which also refer to the obligations of individuals towards other individuals and the community. See also Clapham (2006). The focus in this study will, however, be on the obligations of states.

13 Vienna Declaration and Programme of Action, World Conference on Human Rights 1993, UN Doc. A/Conf.157/23, para. 5.

14 See, *inter alia*, van Hoof (1984, 107). This position is also taken by the Committee on Economic, Social and Cultural Rights (1997).

15 UN Doc. E/CN.4/1987/17, "The Limburg Principles on the Implementation of the International Covenant on Economic, Social and Cultural Rights", also published in *Human Rights Quarterly*, 9 (1987): 122–5; See, further, one of the working papers of the conference (Alston and Quinn 1987).

16 Although this is an authoritative text, the general comment is not legally binding.

17 See also Limburg Principles, Nos 16 and 21, 1987.

18 See also Limburg Principles, Nos 17, 18 and 20, 1987.

19 See also Limburg Principles, No. 25, 1987.

20 See also Commission on Human Rights, Res. 1993/14 on economic, social and cultural rights, para. 7.

21 See, for an elaboration of the core content of the right to education, the contribution of Coomans in this volume. See also Toebes (1999, 281–3) on the core content of the right to health. The CESCR has used the concept of core content and core obligations in several general comments: see Committee on Economic, Social and Cultural Rights (1990, para. 10; 1999a, para. 8; 1999b, para. 57; 2000, paras 43–5; 2003, paras 17–38; 2005a, paras 18–31; 2005b, paras 25–40; 2005c, paras 19–31. See also Maastricht Guidelines, guideline 9 (van Boven et al. 1998, 1–12).

22 Limburg Principles, Nos 35–9; see also Coomans (1992, 36); Committee on Economic, Social and Cultural Rights (1998, para. 9).

23 See, on the obligation theory, Alston and Tomasevski (1984), especially the contributions of Alston, Shue, van Hoof and Tomasevski. See also Limburg Principles; van Boven et al. (1998).

24 See also Maastricht Guidelines, guideline 6 (van Boven et al. 1998, 4).

25 Limburg Principles, Nos 52, 56.

26 See the *travaux préparatoires*, UN Doc. E/CN.4/SR.235, p. 6.

27 One can think of the "Danish cartoon affair", which reflected tension between freedom of religion and freedom of expression. The answer is not to reject either one of these rights, or to privilege a priori one over the other. "A human rights approach requires ... to seek harmony between these freedoms in practice ...", see Boyle (2006, 188).

28 The Protocol to the African Charter on Human and Peoples' Rights on the Rights of Women in Africa (in force since 25 November 2005) includes a similar provision in Article 2(2) that "States Parties shall commit themselves to modify the social and cultural patterns of conduct of women and men ... with a view to achieving the elimination of harmful cultural and traditional practices and all other practices which are based on the idea of the inferiority or the superiority of either of the sexes ..." See also Hansen (2002, 288–9).

29 For more details on the background and drafting process of the Universal Declaration on Human Rights see Verdoodt (1963); Humphrey (1984); Robinson (1958); Kanger (1984); United Nations (1950). The sub-commission has been renamed Sub-Commission on the Promotion and Protection of Human Rights.

30 UN Doc. A/C.3/SR. 150, 1948, pp. 619 and 634.

31 UN Doc. A/C.3/SR. 150, 1948, p. 617.

32 UN Doc. A/C.3/SR. 150, 1948, pp. 633–4.

33 In UDHR Article 29(2) it is laid down that limitations should be based on law in order to protect the rights of others or to protect morality, public order or the general interest of a democratic society.

34 Currently, 157 states have ratified the ICESCR. For the other states, Article 27 is the valid provision with regard to participation in cultural life (August 2006).

35 See UN Doc. E/CN.4/364, May 1950, and UN Doc. A/2929, July 1955, paras 1–20, pp. 2–4.

36 See, on the seventh session of the commission, UN Doc. E/1992 (E/CN.4/640), 24 May 1951, pp. 23–4.

37 UN Doc. A/2929, July 1955, paras 21–50, pp. 4–6.

38 General Assembly, Res. 2200A (XXI), 16 December 1966.

39 See UN Doc. E/1992 (E/CN.4/640), 24 May 1951.

40 UN Doc. A/C.3/SR. 289, September–December 1950, para. 32, p. 114.

41 UN Doc. A/C.3/SR. 299, September–December 1950, para. 33, p. 188.

42 UN Doc. A/C.3/SR. 299, September–December 1950, para. 55, p. 189. See UN Doc. E/CN.4/513, 2 March 1951, para. 20, p. 14; UN Doc. E/CN.4/529, 29 March 1951, para. xiv, p. 9.

43 UN Doc. E/CN.4/AC.14/SR.1, 17 May 1951, pp. 13, 16, 21. The UNESCO General Conference in February 1952 adopted Resolution 9.1, in which it was laid down that UNESCO was prepared to take the responsibilities involved in the implementation of the right to education and the right to culture; see UN Doc. E/CN.4/655/Add.4, 17 April 1952, p. 2.

44 UN Doc. E/CN.4/ 541, 18 April 1951.

45 UN Doc. E/CN.4/541 Rev.1, p. 3.

46 UN Doc. E/CN.4/613 and E/CN.4/613 Rev.1, May 1951.

47 The first drafts were part of a single human rights covenant. When separating the various provisions into two separate covenants, Article 30 first became ICESCR Article 16 and later Article 15.

48 See UN Doc. E/1992 (E/CN.4/640), 24 May 1951, p. 34 and Annex I, p. 72.

49 UN Doc. E/CN.4/L.52, 25 April 1952.

50 UN Doc. E/CN.4/L.75, France: Draft amendment to Article 30, 29 April 1952.

51 UN Doc. E/CN.4/L.81, United States of America: Draft amendment to Article 30, 2 May 1952.

52 UN Docs E/CN.4/L.105 and E/CN.4/L.105 Rev.1, Lebanon: amendment to the amendment submitted by the United States of America (E/CN.4/L.81), 13 May 1952; UN Doc. E/CN.4/L.81/Rev. 1, United States of America: Draft amendment to Article 30, 14 May 1952.

53 UN Doc. E/2256, April–June 1952, p. 19; E/CN.4/SR.294, 27 May 1952, p. 5.

54 UN Doc. E/2256, April–June 1952, p. 19; E/CN.4/SR.292, 27 May 1952, pp. 5–15; E/CN.4/SR.293, 27 May 1952; E/CN.4/SR.294, 27 May 1952, pp. 3–5.

55 UN Doc. E/CN.4/666/Add.5, 14 May 1952; see also UN Doc. E/2573, Annex I, Draft International Covenants on Human Rights, Article 16.

56 UN Doc. A/C.3/SR.565, October 1954, para. 32.

57 UN Doc. A/C.3/SR.566, October 1954, paras 16 and 22.

58 At that time it was Article 16, but, for the sake of clarity, from here it will be referred to as Article 15.

59 UN Doc. A/C.3/L.633, Czechoslovakia: amendment to Article 16 of the draft Covenant on Economic, Social and Cultural Rights (E/2573, Annex IA).

60 UN Doc. A/C.3/L.634, Saudi Arabia: amendment to document A/C.3/L.633, October–November 1957.

61 UN Doc. A/C.3/L.636 and Add.1, Costa Rica and Uruguay: amendment to Article 16 of the draft Covenant on Economic, Social and Cultural Rights (E/2573, Annex IA), October–November 1957.

62 UN Doc. A/C.3/SR. 796, October 1957, pp. 173–4; see also A/OR/12 Annexes, agenda item 33, 1957.
63 UN Doc. A/C.3/SR. 797, October 1957, p. 178; see also A/OR/12 Annexes, agenda item 33, 1957.
64 UN Doc. A/C.3/SR. 799, October 1957, pp. 190–91; see also A/OR/12 Annexes, agenda item 33, 1957.
65 The reporting procedure under the ICESCR is laid down in Article 16 of the covenant.
66 UN Doc. E/C.12/1991/1, 17 June 1991, revised general guidelines regarding the form and content of reports to be submitted by states parties under Articles 16 and 17 of the International Covenant on Economic, Social and Cultural Rights.
67 Another supervisory role could be the consideration of complaints. However, no such procedure for state or individual complaints has been established under the ICESCR. See, for an extensive analysis of an individual complaint procedure under the ICESCR, Arambulo (1999). The debate on establishing a procedure is ongoing: see the work of the open-ended working group to consider options regarding the elaboration of an optional protocol to the ICESCR, available at www.ohchr.org/english/issues/escr/group3.htm.
68 This is in conformity with General Comment No. 5 on Persons with Disabilities, para. 36 (1994), and General Comment No. 6 on Economic, Social and Cultural Rights of Older Persons, paras 39–40 (1995).
69 See, for example, the state reports of Slovakia (11 July 2001), Poland (13 July 2001), United Kingdom (10 August 2001), Georgia (10 August 2001), Benin (5 September 2001), Luxembourg (28 September 2001), Estonia (2 October 2001), New Zealand (16 October 2001), Israel (16 October 2001), Russian Federation (17 November 2001), Democratic People's Republic of Korea (15 May 2002), Yemen (17 May 2002), Guatemala (26 July 2002), Greece (23 October 2003), Lithuania (9 December 2002), Ecuador (20 December 2002), Spain (14 January 2003), Moldova (14 April 2003), Denmark (28 April 2003), Italy (24 May 2003), Malta (26 May 2003), Chile (14 June 2003), Kuwait (20 November 2003), China (4 March 2004), Slovenia (26 May 2004), Uzbekistan (24 June 2004), Norway (6 July 2004), Canada (28 October 2004 and 30 August 2005) and Bosnia and Herzegovina (3 February 2005).
70 See, for example, the concluding observations of the committee on Estonia (E/C.12/1/Add.85, December 2002) and Luxembourg (E/C.12/1/Add.86, May 2003).
71 See, for example, the concluding observations of the committee on Venezuela (E/C.12/1/Add.56, May 2001), Bolivia (E/C.12/1/Add.60, May 2001), Syrian Arab Republic (E/C.12/1/Add.63, September 2001), Panama (E/C.12/1/Add.64, September 2001), Croatia (E/C.12/1/Add.73, November 2001), France (E/C.12/1/Add.72, November 2001), Sweden (E/C.12/1/Add.70, November 2001), Colombia (E/C.12/1/Add.74, November 2001), Czech Republic (E/C.12/1/Add.76, June 2002), Japan (E/C.12/2002/12, November 2002), Slovakia (E/C.12/1/Add.81, December 2002), Estonia (E/C.12/1/Add.85, December 2002), Brazil (E/C.12/1/Add.87, May 2003), Guatemala (E/C.12/1/Add.93, December 2003), Ecuador (E/C.12/1/Add.100, June 2004), Chile (E/C.12/1/Add.105, November 2004), China (E/C.12/1/Add.107), Serbia and Montenegro (E/C.12/1/Add.108, 23 June 2005), Libyan Arab Jamahiriya (E/CN.12/LYB/CO/2, 25 January 2006), Slovenia (E/C.12/SVN/CO/1, 25 January 2006), Mexico (E/CN.12/CO/MEX/4, 17 May 2006), Morocco (E/CN.12/MAR/CO.3, 19 May 2006) and Canada (E/CN.12/CAN/CO/4 and 5, 19 May 2006).
72 See, for example, the concluding observations of the committee on Slovenia (E/C.12/SVN/CO/1, 25 January 2006), Morocco (E/CN.12/MAR/CO/3, 19 May 2006) and Canada (E/CN.12/CAN/CO/4 and 5, 19 May 2006).

73 See the concluding observations on Slovenia (E/C.12/SVN/CO/1, 25 January 2006), Morocco (E/CN.12/MAR/CO/3, 19 May 2006) and Libyan Arab Jamahiriya (E/CN.212/LYB/CO/2, 25 January 2006).
74 See the concluding observations on Morocco (E/CN.12/MAR/CO/3, 19 May 2006), para. 63 (original in French).
75 See, for example, the concluding observations of the committee on Nepal (E/C.12/1/Add.66, September 2001), Syrian Arab Republic (E/C.12/1/Add.63, September 2001), Jamaica (E/C.12/1/Add.75, November 2001), Algeria (E/C.12/1/Add.71, November 2001), Benin (E/C.12/1/Add.78, June 2002), Yemen (E/C.12/1/Add.92, December 2003), Zambia (E/C.12/1/Add.106, 23 June 2005), Libyan Arab Jamahiriya (E/CN.212/LYB/CO/2, 25 January 2006) and Morocco (E/CN.12/MAR/CO/3, 19 May 2006).
76 Concluding observations of the committee on Morocco (E/CN.12/MAR/CO/3, 19 May 2006), para. 14.
77 See General Comment No. 16 on Article 3 of the ICESCR: The equal right of men and women to the enjoyment of all economic, social and cultural rights, E/C.12/2005/4, 11 August 2005, para. 31.
78 Concluding observations of the committee on Libyan Arab Jamahiriya (E/CN.212/LYB/CO/2, 25 January 2006).
79 Concluding observations of the committee on Mexico (E/CN.12/CO/MEX/4, 17 May 2006), para. 28.
80 UN Doc. E/C.12/1992/WP.4, Konaté, 25 November 1992, p. 4.
81 UN Doc. E/C.12/1992/WP.4, Konaté, 25 November 1992, pp. 2–3, 15–16.
82 UN Doc. E/C.12/1992/WP.4, Konaté, 25 November 1992, pp. 5–8.
83 UN Doc. E/C.12/1992/WP.4, Konaté, 25 November 1992, pp. 8–9.
84 UN Doc. E/C.12/1992/WP.4, Konaté, 25 November 1992, pp. 12–14.
85 The UNDP Human Development Report 2004 emphasizes that cultural liberty is in fact a vital part of human development.
86 UN Doc. E/C.12/1992/SR.17, 11 December 1992, pp. 9–11.
87 See, for example, the contributions of Mrs Bonoan-Dandan (Philippines), Ms Hausermann of Rights and Humanity and Mr Texier (France), UN Doc. E/C.12/1992/SR.17, 11 December 1992, pp. 4–7 and 12.
88 See, for example, the contributions of Mrs Bonoan-Dandan (Philippines) and Mr Mratchkov (Bulgaria), UN Doc. E/C.12/1992/SR.17, 11 December 1992, pp. 4–5 and 8.
89 See, for example, the contribution of Mr Wimer-Zambrano (Mexico), UN Doc. E/C.12/1992/SR.17, 11 December 1992, p. 5.
90 See, for example, the contribution of Mrs Bonoan-Dandan (Philippines), UN Doc. E/C.12/1992/SR.17, 11 December 1992, pp. 4–5.
91 See the contribution of Ms Hausermann of Rights and Humanity, UN Doc. E/C.12/1992/SR.17, 11 December 1992, pp. 6–7.
92 UN Doc. E/C.12/1992/SR.18, 11 December 1992, p. 2.
93 Academic institutions and NGOs have also undertaken several initiatives, though without direct involvement of the committee: see, for example, Helsinki Roundtable on the Right to Take Part in Cultural Life (1994); Meyer-Bisch (1993a). The University of Fribourg has a research programme on cultural rights and has created an observatory on diversity and cultural rights in cooperation with a platform of NGOs, within which a declaration on cultural rights is being prepared – see www.unifr.ch/iiedh.
94 See General Comment No. 5: "Persons with Disabilities", 9 December 1994.
95 The Hague Convention for the Protection of Cultural Property in the Event of Armed Conflict, adopted 14 May 1954, entered into force 7 August 1956; UNESCO Convention concerning the Protection of the World Cultural and Natural Heritage,

adopted 18 November 1972, entered into force 17 December 1975; UNESCO Convention for the Safeguarding of the Intangible Cultural Heritage, adopted 17 October 2003.

96 On 15 October 2007 sixty-nine states were party to the convention. The convention entered into force on 18 March 2007.

REFERENCES

Aikio, P. and Scheinin, M. (eds) (2000), *Operationalising the Right of Indigenous Peoples to Self-Determination* (Abo/Turku: Institute for Human Rights, Åbo Akademi University).

Alston, P. (1984), "International law and the human right to food", in P. Alston and K. Tomasevski (eds), *The Right to Food* (Utrecht: Martinus Nijhoff/SIM), pp. 9–68.

_____ (1987), "Out of the abyss: The challenges confronting the new UN Committee on Economic, Social and Cultural Rights", *Human Rights Quarterly*, 9: 332–81.

Alston, P. and Quinn, G. (1987), "The nature and scope of states parties' obligations under the International Covenant on Economic, Social and Cultural Rights", *Human Rights Quarterly*, 9: 156–229.

Alston, P. and Tomasevski, K. (eds) (1984), *The Right to Food* (Utrecht: Martinus Nijhoff/SIM).

Arambulo, M. (1999), *Strengthening the Supervision of the International Covenant on Economic, Social and Cultural Rights – Theoretical and Procedural Aspects*, School of Human Rights Research Series No. 3 (Antwerp: Intersentia/Hart).

Boutros-Ghali, B. (1970), "The right to culture and the Universal Declaration of Human Rights", in UNESCO, *Cultural Rights as Human Rights* (Paris: UNESCO), pp. 73–5.

Boyle, K. (2006), "The Danish cartoons", *Netherlands Quarterly on Human Rights*, 24:2, 185–91.

Cassese, A. (1995), *Self-determination of Peoples: A Legal Reappraisal* (Cambridge: Cambridge University Press).

Clapham, A. (2006), *Human Rights Obligations of Non-State Actors* (Oxford: Oxford University Press).

Committee on Economic, Social and Cultural Rights (1990), "General Comment No. 3: The nature of States parties' obligations (Art. 2, para. 1 of the Covenant)", fifth session, 14 December, contained in document E/1991/23.

_____ (1991), "General Comment No. 4: The right to adequate housing (Art. 11(1) of the Covenant)", sixth session, 13 December, contained in document E/1992/23.

_____ (1997), "General Comment No. 7: The right to adequate housing (Art. 11(1) of the Covenant) – Forced evictions", sixteenth session, 20 May, contained in document E/1998/22, annex IV.

_____ (1998), "General Comment No. 9: The domestic application of the Covenant", nineteenth session, 3 December, E/C.12/1998/24.

_____ (1999a), "General Comment No. 12: The right to adequate food (Article 11)", twentieth session, 12 May, E/C.12/1999/5.

_____ (1999b), "General Comment No. 13: The right to education (Article 13)", twenty-first session, 8 December, E/C.12/1999/10.

_____ (2000), "General Comment No. 14: The right to the highest attainable standard of health (Article 12)", twenty-second session, 11 August, E/C.12/2000/4.

_____ (2003), "General Comment No. 15: The right to water", twenty-ninth session, 20 January, E/C.12/2002/11.

_____ (2005a), "General Comment No. 16: The equal right of men and women to the enjoyment of economic, social and cultural rights (Article 3)", thirty-forth session, 11 August, E/C.12/2005/4.

_____ (2005b), "General Comment No. 17: The right of everyone to benefit from the protection of the moral and material interests resulting from any scientific, literary or artistic production of which he is the author (Article 15, paragraph 1(c))", thirty-fifth session, 12 January 2006, E/C.12/GC/17.

_____ (2005c), "General Comment No. 18: The right to work", thirty-fifth session, 6 February 2006, E/C.12/GC/18.

Coomans, A.P.M. (1992), *De Internationale Bescherming van het Recht op Onderwijs* [*The International Protection of the Right to Education*] (Leiden/Maastricht: Stichting NJCM Boekerij 20).

Craven, M. (1998), "The protection of economic, social and cultural rights under the inter-American system of human rights", in D.J. Harris and S. Livingstone (eds), *The Inter-American System of Human Rights* (Oxford: Clarendon Press), pp. 289–322.

Donders, Yvonne M. (2002), *Towards a Right to Cultural Identity?*, School of Human Rights Research Series Vol. 15 (Antwerp: Intersentia).

Donnelly, J. (1989), *Universal Human Rights in Theory and Practice* (London: Cornell University Press).

_____ (1990), "Human rights, individual rights and collective rights", in J. Berting, P. Baehr, J. Herman Burgers, Cees Flinterman, Barbara de Klerk, Rob Kroes, Cornelis van Minnen and Ko Vander Wal (eds), *Human Rights in a Pluralist World* (Westport/London: Meckler), pp. 39–62.

Eide, A. (1984), *Food as a Human Right* (Tokyo: United Nations University).

_____ (1987), *Final Report of the Special Rapporteur on the Right to Food*, UN Doc. E/CN.4/Sub.2/1987/23.

_____ (2001a), "Economic, social and cultural rights as human rights", in A. Eide, C. Krause and A. Rosas (eds), *Economic, Social and Cultural Rights – A Textbook*, 2nd edition (Dordrecht: Martinus Nijhoff), pp. 9–28.

_____ (2001b), "Cultural rights as individual human rights", in A. Eide, C. Krause and A. Rosas (eds), *Economic, Social and Cultural Rights – A Textbook*, 2nd edition (Dordrecht: Martinus Nijhoff), pp. 289–302.

Hannum, H. (1996), *Autonomy, Sovereignty and Self-Determination* (Philadelphia, PA: University of Pennsylvania Press).

Hansen, S.A. (2002), "The right to take part in cultural life: Toward defining minimum core obligations related to Article 15(1)(A) of the International Covenant on Economic, Social and Cultural Rights", in A. Chapman and S. Russell (eds), *Core Obligations: Building a Framework for Economic, Social and Cultural Rights* (Antwerp: Intersentia), pp. 279–304.

Helsinki Roundtable on the Right to Take Part in Cultural Life (1994), *Report of the Helsinki Roundtable on the Right to Take Part in Cultural Life*, 30 April – 2 May 1993, Circle Publication No. 6 (Helsinki: Arts Council of Finland).

Henrard, K. (2000), *Devising an Adequate System of Minority Protection: Individual Human Rights, Minority Rights and the Right to Self-Determination* (The Hague: Martinus Nijhoff).

Humphrey, J.P. (1984), *Human Rights and the United Nations: A Great Adventure* (New York: Transnational Publishers).

Kanger, H. (1984), *Human Rights in the UN Declaration* (Upsala/Stockholm: Almqvist & Wiksell International).

Kartashkin, V. (1982), "Cultural rights", in K. Vasak and P. Alston (eds), *The International Dimensions of Human Rights* (Paris: UNESCO), pp. 127–30.

Leuprecht, P. (1993), "Le sous-développement des droits culturels, vu depuis le Conseil de l'Europe", in P. Meyer-Bisch (ed.), *Les droits culturels, une catégorie sous-*

développée de droits de l'Homme, Actes du VIIIe Colloque interdisciplinaire sur les droits de l'Homme (Fribourg: Editions Universitaires Fribourg), pp. 73–97.

Levy, J.T. (1997), "Classifying cultural rights", in W. Kymlicka and I. Shapiro (eds), *Ethnicity and Group Rights* (New York and London: New York University Press), pp. 22–66.

Marie, J.-B. (1993), "Les droits culturels: Interface entre les droits de l'individu et les droits des communautés", in P. Meyer-Bisch (ed.), *Les droits culturels, une catégorie sous-développée de droits de l'Homme*, Actes du VIIIe Colloque interdisciplinaire sur les droits de l'Homme (Fribourg: Editions Universitaires Fribourg), pp. 197–213.

Marks, S. (2003), "Defining cultural rights", in M. Bergsmo (ed.), *Human Rights and Criminal Justice for the Downtrodden – Essays in Honour of Asbjorn Eide* (Leiden: Martinus Nijhoff), pp. 293–324.

Meyer-Bisch, P. (ed.) (1993a), *Les droits culturels, une catégorie sous-développée de droits de l'Homme*, Actes du VIIIe Colloque interdisciplinaire sur les droits de l'Homme (Fribourg: Editions Universitaires Fribourg).

——— (1993b), "Les droits culturels forment-ils une catégorie spécifique de droits de l'Homme?", in P. Meyer-Bisch (ed.), *Les droits culturels, une catégorie sous-développée de droits de l'Homme*, Actes du VIIIe Colloque interdisciplinaire sur les droits de l'Homme (Fribourg: Editions Universitaires Fribourg), pp. 279–90.

Morsink, J. (1999), *The Universal Declaration of Human Rights – Origins, Drafting and Intent* (Philadelphia, PA: University of Pennsylvania Press).

Niec, H. (1997), "Cultural rights: At the end of the World Decade for Cultural Development", paper presented at Intergovernmental Conference on Cultural Policies for Development, Stockholm, 30 March – 2 April 1998, UNESCO Doc. CLT-98/Conf.210/Ref.2.

——— (1998), "Casting the foundation for the implementation of cultural rights", in H. Niec (ed.), *Cultural Rights and Wrongs – A Collection of Essays in Commemoration of the 50th Anniversary of the Universal Declaration of Human Rights* (Paris: UNESCO), pp. 176–90.

O'Keefe, R. (1998), "The right to take part in cultural life under Article 15 of the ICESCR", *International and Comparative Law Quarterly*, 47:3/4, 904–23.

Prott, L. (1988), "Cultural rights as peoples' rights in international law", in J. Crawford (ed.), *The Rights of Peoples* (Oxford: Clarendon Press), pp. 161–75.

Robinson, N. (1958), *The Universal Declaration of Human Rights – Its Origin, Significance, Application and Interpretation* (New York: Institute of Jewish Affairs).

Shue, H. (1980), *Basic Rights: Subsistence, Affluence and US Foreign Policy* (Princeton, NJ: Princeton University Press).

——— (1984), "The interdependence of duties", in P. Alston and K. Tomasevski (eds), *The Right to Food* (Utrecht: Martinus Nijhoff/SIM), pp. 83–95.

Stavenhagen, R. (2001), "Cultural rights: A social perspective", in A. Eide, C. Krause and A. Rosas (eds), *Economic, Social and Cultural Rights – A Textbook*, 2nd edition, (Dordrecht: Martinus Nijhoff), pp. 85–110.

Symonides, J. (2000), "Cultural rights", in J. Symonides (ed.), *Human Rights, Concept and Standards* (Paris: UNESCO), pp. 175–227.

Toebes, B. (1999), *The Right to Health as a Human Right in International Law*, School of Human Rights Research Series No. 1 (Antwerp: Intersentia/Hart).

Tomasevski, K. (1984), "Human rights indicators: The right to food as a test case", in P. Alston and K. Tomasevski (eds), *The Right to Food* (Utrecht: Martinus Nijhoff/SIM), pp. 135–67.

Türk, Danilo (1992), UN Doc. E/CN.4/Sub.2/1992/16, 3 July 1992.

UNDP (2004), *Cultural Liberty in Today's Diverse World*, Human Development Report 2004, available at www.UNDP.org.

UNESCO (1970), *Cultural Rights as Human Rights* (Paris: UNESCO).

United Nations (1950), *These Rights and Freedoms* (New York: UN Publications).

van Boven, T., Flinterman, C. and Westendorp, I. (eds) (1998), *The Maastricht Guidelines on Violations of Economic, Social and Cultural Rights*, SIM Special No. 20 (Utrecht: SIM).

van Hoof, G.J.H. (1984), "The legal nature of economic, social and cultural rights: A rebuttal of some traditional views", in P. Alston and K. Tomasevski (eds), *The Right to Food* (Utrecht: Martinus Nijhoff/SIM), pp. 97–110.

Verdoodt, A. (1963), *Naissance et signification de la Déclaration universelle des droits de l'Homme* (Paris: Louvain-Paris).

Vlemminx, F. (1992), *Grondrechten en moderne beeldende kunst [Basic Rights and Modern Plastic Art]* (Zwolle: W.E.J. Tjeenk Willink).

_____ (1994), *Het profiel van de sociale grondrechten [The Profile of Basic Social Rights]* (Zwolle: W.E.J. Tjeenk Willink).

_____ (1998), *Een nieuw profiel van de grondrechten – een analyse van de prestatieplichten ingevolge klassieke en sociale grondrechten [A New Profile of Basic Rights – An Analysis of the Obligations of Conduct of Classic and Social Rights]* (Zwolle: W.E.J. Tjeenk Willink).

Wilhelm, M. (1993), "L'étendue des droits à l'identité à la lumière des droits autochtones", in P. Meyer-Bisch (ed.), *Les droits culturels, une catégorie sous-développée de droits de l'Homme*, Actes du VIIIe Colloque interdisciplinaire sur les droits de l'Homme (Fribourg: Editions Universitaires Fribourg), pp. 212–44.

UN Documents (in Chronological Order)

Note: All these documents and other UN documents mentioned in this chapter can be found on the website of the Office of the UN High Commissioner for Human Rights (www.ohchr.org) under "treaty bodies".

A/C.3/SR.150, Summary record of the third session of the General Assembly, 1948.

A/C.3/SR. 289, Draft first international covenant on human rights and measures of implementation, fifth session, 19 September – 15 December 1950.

E/CN.4/364, Report by the Secretary-General on the activities of the United Nations organs and specialized agencies in matters within the scope of articles 22–27 of the Universal Declaration of Human Rights, May 1950.

E/CN.4/513, Commission on Human Rights Seventh Session, Agenda Item 3, Memorandum by the Secretary-General, 2 March 1951.

E/CN.4/529, Commission on Human Rights Seventh Session, Agenda Item 3, Memorandum by the Secretary-General, 29 March 1951.

E/CN.4/541, Commission on Human Rights Seventh Session, Agenda Item 3, suggestions submitted by the Director-General of UNESCO, 18 April 1951.

E/CN.4/613 and E/CN.4/613 Rev.1, Commission on Human Rights Seventh Session. Chile: proposal on the Right to Education and Cultural Rights based on suggestions of UNESCO, 5 and 7 May 1951.

E/CN.4/AC.14/SR.1, Commission on Human Rights Seventh Session, Working Group in Economic, Social and Cultural Rights, summary record of the first meeting, 17 May 1951.

E/1992 (E/CN.4/640), Report of the seventh session of the Commission on Human Rights, 24 May 1951.

E/CN.4/655/Add.4, Commission on Human Rights Eighth Session, Observations submitted by Specialized Agencies on the Proposed Covenant on Economic, Social and Cultural Rights in pursuance of Resolution 543 (VI) of the General Assembly, 17 April 1952.

E/CN.4/L.52, Commission on Human Rights Eighth Session, Union of Soviet Socialist Republics: Draft amendment to Article 30, 25 April 1952.

E/CN.4/541 Rev.1, Commission on Human Rights Seventh Session, Agenda Item 3, Draft Articles on Educational and Cultural Rights submitted by the Director-General of UNESCO, 27 April 1952.

E/CN.4/L.75, Commission on Human Rights Eighth Session, France: Draft amendment to Article 30, 29 April 1952.

E/CN.4/L.81, Commission on Human Rights Eighth Session, United States of America: Draft amendment to Article 30, 2 May 1952.

E/CN.4/L.105 and E/CN.4/L.105 Rev.1, Commission on Human Rights Eighth Session, Lebanon: amendment to the amendment submitted by the United States of America (E/CN.4/L.81), 13 May 1952.

E/CN.4/L.81/Rev. 1, Commission on Human Rights Eighth Session, United States of America: Draft amendment to Article 30, 14 May 1952.

E/CN.4/666/Add.5, Commission on Human Rights Eighth Session, Article 30 of the Draft Covenant on Economic, Social and Cultural Rights, text adopted by the Commission at its 294th meeting on 14 May 1952.

E/CN.4/SR.292, Commission on Human Rights Eighth Session, Summary Record of the Two Hundred and Ninety Second meeting, 27 May 1952.

E/CN.4/SR.293, Commission on Human Rights Eighth Session, Summary Record of the Two Hundred and Ninety Third meeting, 27 May 1952.

E/CN.4/SR.294, Commission on Human Rights Eighth Session, Summary Record of the Two Hundred and Ninety Fourth meeting, 27 May 1952.

E/2256, Report of the Eighth session of the Human Rights Commission, April–June 1952.

E/2573, Annex I, Draft International Covenants on Human Rights, 1954.

A/C.3/SR.565, Draft international covenant on human rights and measures of implementation, October 1954.

A/2929, Annotations on the text of the draft International Covenants on Human Rights, New York, 1 July 1955.

A/C.3/L.633, Czechoslovakia: amendment to Article 16 of the draft Covenant on Economic, Social and Cultural Rights (E/2573, Annex IA). To be found in A/OR/12 Annexes, General Assembly, Twelfth session, Third Committee, 795–799th meeting, October–November 1957.

A/C.3/L.634, Saudi Arabia: amendment to document A/C.3/L.633. To be found in A/OR/12 Annexes, General Assembly, Twelfth session, Third Committee, 795–799th meeting, October–November 1957.

A/C.3/L.636 and Add.1, Costa Rica and Uruguay: amendment to Article 16 of the draft Covenant on Economic, Social and Cultural Rights (E/2573, Annex IA). To be found in A/OR/12 Annexes, General Assembly, Twelfth session, Third Committee, 795–799th meeting, October–November 1957.

A/C.3/SR. 796, Summary Record of the General Assembly, Third Committee Twelfth session, October 1957.

A/C.3/SR. 797, Summary Record of the General Assembly, Third Committee Twelfth session, October 1957.

A/C.3/SR. 799, Summary Record of the General Assembly, Third Committee Twelfth session, October 1957.

E/CN.4/Sub.2/1987/23, The Right to Adequate Food as a Human Right, Report prepared by Mr A. Eide, 1987.

E/CN.4/Sub.2/1989/19, Realization of Economic, Social and Cultural Rights, Preliminary Report prepared by Mr Danilo Türk, Special Rapporteur, 28 June 1989.

E/CN.4/Sub.2/1990/19, Realization of Economic, Social and Cultural Rights, Progress Report prepared by Mr Danilo Türk, Special Rapporteur, 6 July 1990.

E/C.12/1991/1, Revised General Guidelines regarding the form and content of reports to be submitted by States Parties under Articles 16 and 17 of the International Covenant on Economic, Social and Cultural Rights, 17 June 1991.

E/CN.4/Sub.2/1991/17, The Realization of Economic, Social and Cultural Rights, Second Progress Report prepared by Mr Danilo Türk, Special Rapporteur, 18 July 1991.

E/CN.4/Sub.2/1992/16, The Realization of Economic, Social and Cultural Rights, Final Report prepared by Mr Danilo Türk, Special Rapporteur, 3 July 1992.

E/C.12/1992/WP.4, Implementation of Cultural Rights, analytical study of article 15 of the International Covenant on Economic, Social and Cultural Rights, by Mr S.R. Konaté, 25 November 1992.

E/C.12/1992/SR.17, General Discussion on the Right to Take Part in Cultural Life as recognized in Article 15 of the Covenant, 11 December 1992.

7 Study of the Right to Enjoy the Benefits of Scientific and Technological Progress and Its Applications

WILLIAM A. SCHABAS

Progress, man's distinctive mark alone,
Not God's, and not the beasts.
                              Robert Browning, "A Death in the Desert" (1864)

INTRODUCTION

Tucked away at the tail end of the Universal Declaration of Human Rights, in what is for all intents and purposes its final substantive provision, is the right of "everyone" to "share in scientific advancement and its benefits".[1] This norm is couched within a somewhat larger "cultural rights" provision, one of two in the declaration. It is also set out in the International Covenant on Economic, Social and Cultural Rights, where it occupies a similarly neglected and obscure position. There it is formulated slightly differently as the right of "everyone" to "enjoy the benefits of scientific progress and its applications".[2] In recent years the right to enjoy the benefits of scientific progress has taken on a renewed importance because of the apparent tension that exists between it and the protection of intellectual property. More generally, this debate makes a significant contribution to attempts by human rights law to address the phenomenon known as "globalization".

Neither the Universal Declaration of Human Rights nor the International Covenant on Economic, Social and Cultural Rights suggest any normative hierarchy. In practice, however, economic, social and above all cultural rights have to a large extent been treated as subordinate or secondary. Some of this is a legacy of attempts that date to the early years of the Cold War, aimed at eliminating them altogether from human rights treaty law on the grounds that they were inappropriate in a binding text. The legal instruments themselves do not assist in righting the balance. Although debate continues, there is still no consensus, let alone a treaty provision, authorizing a right of individual petition with respect to violations of economic, social and cultural rights, even though this possibility has been unquestioned for several decades with respect to civil and political rights. All of this continues, despite appeals to the contrary, such as the call in the Vienna Declaration and Programme of Action that "All human rights are universal, indivisible and interdependent and interrelated."[3] But not only does the question of the right to enjoy the benefits of scientific progress and its applications suffer from the more general marginalization of economic, social and cultural rights: within that category of human rights it has received little attention. To borrow a concept from Hersch Lauterpacht (1952), if economic, social and cultural rights lie at the vanishing point of international human rights law, then the question of the right to enjoy the benefits of scientific and technological progress and its applications lies at the vanishing point of economic, social and cultural rights.

Neither of the two provisions, Article 27(1) of the Universal Declaration and Article 15(1) of the covenant, is referenced in subsequent resolutions of the General Assembly. The issue has been barely addressed in the academic literature. Special rapporteurs consider matters concerning scientific research in a variety of contexts, but it is only rarely that they refer to the positive legal right to enjoy the benefit of scientific progress. States parties to the covenant, in their initial and periodic reports to the Committee on Economic, Social and Cultural Rights, have provided only the most summary information, with rare exceptions treating Article 15(1)(b) as an opportunity to boast about how well the state promotes scientific research. The committee, for its part, has offered little guidance with respect to application and interpretation of the norm. As Audrey Chapman (2000, para. 25) observed quite bluntly in her research paper for the Committee on Economic, Social and Cultural Rights, "The human rights community has neglected Article 27 of the UDHR and Article 15 of the Covenant."

Thus a contemporary study of the right to enjoy the benefits of scientific and technological progress and its applications has precious little authority on which to rely. This state of affairs may seem frustrating at the outset. Yet it provides an opportunity to propose and develop a content of the norm that is consistent with the realities of the human condition at the dawn of the twenty-first century. Nor could it be otherwise. How could a norm concerned with "progress" be confined to interpretative approaches dating to the early years of the development of international human rights law? Nevertheless, as with all international norms, the starting point of the enquiry must be their drafting by international institutions. The *travaux préparatoires* are relevant perhaps not so much for any contribution they may make to legal interpretation – after all, the Vienna Convention on the Law of Treaties suggests they have a subordinate role; moreover, human rights instruments should be applied in an "evolutive" and dynamic manner[4] – as for their intrinsic historical interest.

FORMULATION OF THE RIGHT IN INTERNATIONAL LEGAL INSTRUMENTS

The principal universal instruments to recognize the right to enjoy the benefits of scientific progress and its accomplishments are the Universal Declaration of Human Rights and the International Covenant on Economic, Social and Cultural Rights. It is also recognized in the main instruments of the inter-American system for the protection of human rights, but not in the other regional systems. Certain instruments adopted under the aegis of UNESCO are also relevant to the right.

Article 27(1) of the Universal Declaration of Human Rights

Article 27 of the Universal Declaration of Human Rights reads as follows:

> (1) Everyone has the right freely to participate in the cultural life of the community, to enjoy the arts and to share in scientific advancement and its benefits.

> (2) Everyone has the right to the protection of the moral and material interests resulting from any scientific, literary or artistic production of which he is the author.

Drafting of UDHR Article 27(1)

The right "to share in scientific advancement and its benefits" appeared in the initial draft of the declaration, which was prepared by John P. Humphrey of the UN Secretariat for the Commission on Human Rights in early 1947. Humphrey's text read: "Everyone has the right to participate [freely] in the cultural life of the community, to enjoy the arts and to share in scientific advancement and its benefits."[5] Humphrey was placing art before science, perhaps reflecting a personal idiosyncrasy, as Johannes Morsink (2000, 218) has suggested. In preparing his initial draft, Humphrey had drawn upon national constitutions, as well as various drafts submitted by international organizations and non-governmental organizations.

The actual source of the provision was a text submitted by Chile which had been prepared by the Inter-American Juridical Committee as part of the drafting process of the American Declaration on the Rights and Duties of Man, which was going on in parallel. The American Declaration was adopted in May 1948, more than six months before the Universal Declaration. Article 13(1) of the American Declaration of the Rights and Duties of Man states: "Every person has the right to take part in the cultural life of the community, to enjoy the arts, and to participate in the benefits that result from intellectual progress, especially scientific discoveries."[6]

Humphrey's 48-article document was initially considered by the Drafting Committee of the Commission on Human Rights. When its report was being considered, the Soviet delegate questioned what was meant by "sharing in the benefits that resulted from scientific discoveries". Eleanor Roosevelt, who was chairing the proceedings, replied that "as regards sharing in the benefits that resulted from scientific discoveries, the idea of the Drafting Committee had been to stress the universality of such sharing". Then the Soviet delegate, Bogomolov, suggested that "this phrase appeared to imply the obligation to reveal the patents of scientific discoveries". Roosevelt answered that "it would be possible to insert a comment to the effect that the Article did not imply the obligation to reveal the secret of scientific discoveries that had been patented".[7] This initial exchange is the first recorded discussion of the norm in international human rights law. It reveals that from the very beginning there was a tension between the right to enjoy the benefits of scientific progress and the protection of intellectual property.

The text underwent minor changes within the Commission on Human Rights. The version submitted to its third session, in June 1948, referred to everyone's right to participate "in the benefits that result from scientific discoveries". Here it was again modified, on the proposal of the Chinese expert, Peng Chun Chang, who said the text should be changed to "share in scientific advancement", adding enigmatically that "the phrase was derived from Bacon".[8] The Soviet delegate, Pavlov, spoke in favour of the provision, noting that "the benefits of science were not the property of a chosen few, but the heritage of mankind". He stressed that "the task of science was to work for the advancement of peaceful aims and to make human life better".[9] The Chinese proposal was accepted by a vote of eight to three with five abstentions, but the word "benefits" was removed, for no apparent reason.[10]

The draft then proceeded to the General Assembly, where it was studied in detail by the Third Committee. Perez Cisneros, the Cuban delegate, urged that the word "benefits" be restored, because "not everyone was sufficiently gifted to play a part in scientific advancement". He said the text should say that everyone has the right "to share in the benefits that result from scientific advancement".[11] René Cassin agreed, stating that "even if all persons could not play an equal part in scientific progress, they should indisputably be able to participate in the benefits derived from it".[12] The Cuban text, with the reference to "and its benefits", was accepted by the Third Committee[13] and included in the final version of the Universal Declaration adopted by the General Assembly on 10 December 1948.

Interpretation of Article 27(1)

One observer has questioned whether it was "just accidental" that the drafters of the Universal Declaration of Human Rights linked intellectual property rights with the right to enjoy the benefits of scientific progress and its applications, or did they understand them "to be intrinsically interconnected" (Chapman 2000)? What was to become Article 27 of the Universal Declaration was originally contemplated as a "cultural rights" provision, and John Humphrey's initial draft did not even address the issue of intellectual property. This was proposed by René Cassin,[14] but with opposition from Eleanor Roosevelt, who did not see that the issue belonged in the instrument at all.[15] The Drafting Committee of the Commission on Human Rights disagreed on whether to include an intellectual property provision, although it submitted the matter with a note saying it "should receive consideration for treatment on an international basis".[16] The Conference on the Berne International Copyright Convention, held in June 1948, probably influenced the discussions in the Commission on Human Rights, which was meeting at the same time. Inclusion of the issue within Article 13 of the American Declaration of the Rights and Duties of Man was also influential.

The Commission on Human Rights rejected the proposed provision on intellectual property, although its decision was subsequently reversed by the Third Committee (Morsink 2000, 220–22). Despite the fact that the possible conflict between the right to benefit from scientific progress and the protection of intellectual property was only addressed directly in the early exchange between Roosevelt and Bogomolov, the context of the drafting of Article 27 suggests the delegates understood that the relationship between the two norms was not inadvertent, and that one could not be interpreted without reference to the other (Adalsteinsson and Thorhallson 1993, 578).

Article 27(1) of the Universal Declaration is not cited in subsequent resolutions of the General Assembly dealing with scientific and technological progress, so it is not necessarily appropriate to speak of authoritative interpretation. Nevertheless, it seems valid – *cum grano salis* – to treat General Assembly resolutions and declarations dealing with the subject of scientific progress as relevant to the interpretation of UDHR Article 27(1). The Declaration on Social Progress and Development, adopted by the UN General Assembly in 1969, includes in its preamble: "Conscious of the contribution that science and technology can render towards meeting the needs common to all humanity …"[17] The Charter of Economic Rights and Duties of States, adopted in 1974, has a more substantial reference, and one that seems focused on the right to benefit from scientific progress, although it presents this as a right of states rather than belonging to individuals:

> 1. Every State has the right to benefit from the advances and development in science and technology for the acceleration of its economic and social development.

> 2. All States should promote international scientific and technological co-operation and the transfer of technology, with proper regard for all legitimate interests including, *inter alia*, the rights and duties of holders, suppliers and recipients of technology. In particular, all States should facilitate the access of developing countries to the achievements of modern science and technology, the transfer of technology and the creation of indigenous technology for the benefit of the developing countries in forms and in accordance with procedures which are suited to their economies and their needs.

> 3. Accordingly, developed countries should co-operate with the developing countries in the establishment, strengthening and development of their scientific and technological infrastructures and their scientific research and technological

activities so as to help to expand and transform the economies of developing countries.

4. All States should co-operate in research with a view to evolving further internationally accepted guidelines or regulations for the transfer of technology, taking fully into account the interest of developing countries.[18]

The 1975 Declaration on the Use of Scientific and Technological Progress in the Interest of Peace and for the Benefit of Mankind is also of interest.[19] Its preamble notes that "while scientific and technological developments provide ever increasing opportunities to better the conditions of life of peoples and nations, in a number of instances they can give rise to social problems, as well as threaten the human rights and fundamental freedoms of the individual". The declaration is largely focused on the possible abusive use of science and technology in a way contrary to the protection of human rights. It calls upon states to promote international cooperation to ensure that the results of scientific and technological developments are used in the interests of strengthening international peace and security, freedom and independence, and also for the purpose of the economic and social development of peoples and the realization of human rights and freedoms in accordance with the UN Charter. The declaration affirms that "All States shall take measures to ensure that scientific and technological achievements satisfy the material and spiritual needs for all sectors of the population." Furthermore:

> All States shall take measures to extend the benefits of science and technology to all strata of the population and to protect them, both socially and materially, from possible harmful effects of the misuse of scientific and technological developments, including their misuse to infringe upon the rights of the individual or of the group, particularly with regard to respect for privacy and the protection of the human personality and its physical and intellectual integrity.

Another useful indicator of the evolving content of the norm protecting the right to enjoy the benefits of scientific progress and its applications appears in the Proclamation of Tehran, adopted by the 1968 International Conference on Human Rights.[20] The preamble of that document has "regard to the new opportunities made available by the rapid progress of science and technology". Paragraph 18 declares: "While recent scientific discoveries and technological advances have opened vast prospects for economic, social and cultural progress, such developments may nevertheless endanger the rights and freedoms of individuals and will require continuing attention." It is worth recalling that the document is rather laconic, consisting of only 20 paragraphs, and this enhances the importance of the reference to scientific discoveries and technological advances. The subsequent paragraph in the proclamation, which addresses disarmament, deals with scientific "progress" indirectly. It says that disarmament "would release immense human and material resources now devoted to military purposes. These resources should be used for the promotion of human rights and fundamental freedoms."

The Vienna Declaration and Programme of Action, adopted at the 1993 Vienna Conference, refers quite directly to the right:

Everyone has the right to enjoy the benefits of scientific progress and its applications. The World Conference on Human Rights notes that certain advances, notably in the biomedical and life sciences as well as in information technology, may have potentially adverse consequences for the integrity, dignity and human rights of the individual, and calls for international cooperation to ensure that human rights and dignity are fully respected in this area of universal concern.

The provision in the Vienna Convention seems almost disappointing compared with the reference in the Proclamation of Tehran. It manifests shifting priorities in international human rights, away from a focus on disarmament and the harmful uses of scientific progress and towards concerns about biotechnology.

Article 15(1) of the International Covenant on Economic, Social and Cultural Rights

Article 15 of the International Covenant on Economic, Social and Cultural Rights states:

1. The States Parties to the present Covenant recognize the right of everyone:

(a) To take part in cultural life;

(b) To enjoy the benefits of scientific progress and its applications;

(c) To benefit from the protection of the moral and material interests resulting from any scientific, literary or artistic production of which he is the author.

2. The steps to be taken by the States Parties to the present Covenant to achieve the full realization of this right shall include those necessary for the conservation, the development and the diffusion of science and culture.

3. The States Parties to the present Covenant undertake to respect the freedom indispensable for scientific research and creative activity.

4. The States Parties to the present Covenant recognize the benefits to be derived from the encouragement and development of international contacts and co-operation in the scientific and cultural fields.

The International Covenant on Economic, Social and Cultural Rights, and its companion, the International Covenant on Civil and Political Rights, were intended to provide a binding legal regime for the "common standard of achievement" that was outlined in the Universal Declaration of Human Rights. The two instruments were based largely on the Universal Declaration, but there are significant differences. For example, although the protection of intellectual property, as presented in Article 27 of the declaration, is reaffirmed in Article 15 of the covenant, the more general provision on the right to property, set out in Article 17 of the declaration, finds no parallel in either of the covenants.[21] The reference in Article 15(1)(b) of the International Covenant on Economic, Social and Cultural Rights to "enjoy[ment of] the benefits of scientific progress and its applications" is somewhat different to the formulation of Article 27(1) of the Universal Declaration, which speaks of "shar[ing] in scientific advancement and its benefits". In contrast with other provisions of the covenant, where the rights stated in the declaration were developed in some detail, in the case of the right to enjoy the benefits of scientific progress there is no further elaboration.

Drafting of ICESCR Article 15(1)

The initial draft of the International Covenant on Economic, Social and Cultural Rights was prepared by the Commission on Human Rights. It was submitted to the General Assembly in 1954, and subsequently debated within the Third Committee before final adoption in 1966. In addition to the Universal Declaration of Human Rights, the commission had several other relevant sources to draw upon. In May 1951 UNESCO made submissions on the cultural rights provisions which were based on an expert consultation it had organized.[22] The UNESCO proposal included a text that significantly expanded upon the principles set out in Article 27(1) of the Universal Declaration:

> The Signatory States undertake to encourage the preservation, development and propagation of science and culture by every appropriate means:
>
> (a) By facilitating for all access to manifestations of national and international cultural life, such as books, publications and works of art, and also the enjoyment of the benefits resulting from scientific progress and its application;
>
> (b) By preserving and protecting the inheritance of books, works of art and other monuments and objects of historic, scientific and cultural interest;
>
> (c) By assuring liberty and security to scholars and artists in their work and seeing that they enjoy material conditions necessary for research and creation;
>
> (d) By guaranteeing the free cultural development of racial and linguistic minorities.[23]

A companion provision dealt with the issue of intellectual property.[24] An alternative proposal from UNESCO reads as follows:

> The Signatory States undertake to encourage by all appropriate means, the conservation, the development and the diffusion of science and culture.
>
> They recognize that it is one of their principal aims to ensure conditions which will permit every one:
>
> 1. To take part in cultural life;
>
> 2. To enjoy the benefits resulting from scientific progress and its applications;
>
> 3. To obtain protection for his moral and material interests resulting from any literary, artistic or scientific work of which he is the author.

Each signatory State pledges itself to undertake progressively, with due regard to its organisation and resources, and in accordance with the principle of non-discrimination enunciated in paragraph 1, article 1 of the present Covenant, the measures necessary to attain these objectives in the territories within its jurisdiction.[25]

It was the second of the UNESCO proposals that the Commission on Human Rights took as a basis for discussion during its seventh session. Havet, speaking on behalf of UNESCO, said that "The right of everyone to enjoy his share of the benefits of science was to a great extent the determining factor for the exercise by mankind as a whole of many other rights."[26] He explained that:

Enjoyment of the benefits of scientific progress implied the dissemination of basic scientific knowledge, especially knowledge best calculated to enlighten men's minds and combat prejudices, coordinated efforts on the part of States, in conjunction with the competent specialized agencies, to raise standards of living, and a wider dissemination of culture through the processes and apparatus created by science.[27]

The commission adopted the following text, which was based upon a draft submitted by the United States,[28] by 15 votes with three abstentions.

They recognize that it is one of their principal aims to ensure conditions which will permit every one:

1. To take part in cultural life;

2. To enjoy the benefits resulting from scientific progress and its applications.[29]

The provision on intellectual property proved more controversial,[30] and was actually rejected by the commission, by seven votes to seven with four abstentions.[31] A year later, when the item returned to the agenda, the commission again voted not to include a text on intellectual property in the draft covenant.[32] The commission's report to the Economic and Social Council summarized the discussions on the provision concerning culture and science:

Members generally favoured the inclusion of a provision preserving the freedom of scientific research and creation. Some members deemed it essential to complete the article by adding a provision to the effect that States undertook to ensure the development of science and culture in the interests of progress and democracy and in the interests of ensuring peace and co-operation among nations. Most members, however, were opposed to including a statement of the ends which scientific research should serve, on the grounds that scientific research by its nature was independent of any external criterion and that a statement of aims such as that envisaged might provide a pretext for State control of scientific research and creative activity. A proposal for the addition of a provision for the protection of rights deriving from scientific, literary or artistic productions was opposed by a majority of members, and it was pointed out that the matter was properly being dealt with by UNESCO, that it could not adequately be treated in a short provision and that authors' rights had to be considered in the light of the claims of the community and of the world at large.[33]

The reference to the aims of scientific research concerned a proposal from the Soviet Union.[34] The final version of the provision adopted by the Commission on Human Rights, entitled "Rights relating to culture and science", read:

1. The States Parties to the Covenant recognize the right of everyone:

(a) To take part in cultural life;

(b) To enjoy the benefits of scientific progress and its applications.

2. The steps to be taken by the States Parties to this Covenant to achieve the full realisation of this right shall include those necessary for the conservation, the development and the diffusion of science and culture.

3. The States Parties to the Covenant undertake to respect the freedom indispensable for scientific research and creative activity.[35]

Article 15 of the International Covenant on Economic, Social and Cultural Rights was considered by the Third Committee of the General Assembly at its twelfth session, in 1957. The issues were largely the same as those in the Commission on Human Rights. There was general agreement on recognition of the right to enjoy the benefits of scientific progress and its applications, but controversy, as there had been earlier, about the Soviet bloc proposal to add a reference to the aims of science,[36] as well as the recognition of intellectual property rights. In one of the very rare comments on paragraph 1(b) of the draft, D'Souza of India noted that the right to enjoy the benefits of scientific progress and its applications was "an essentially practical matter. Undoubtedly, scientific discoveries should benefit not only all individuals but also nations, regardless of their degree of development."[37] In the lengthy debate on Article 15, nothing further was said on the subject of the right to enjoy the benefits of scientific progress and its applications. Article 15(1) was adopted by the Third Committee by 68 votes with two abstentions.[38] A Czechoslovak proposal on the objectives of scientific research was partially successful, as was the text on intellectual property, although by a somewhat unconvincing vote of 39 states, with nine opposed and 24 abstaining.[39] The entire article was then adopted by 71 votes with one abstention.[40]

Interpretation of ICESCR Article 15(1)

As a treaty provision, in principle Article 15 of the International Covenant on Economic, Social and Cultural Rights should be interpreted according to the norms set out in the Vienna Convention on the Law of Treaties.[41] But although the Vienna Convention proposes that the drafting history of a treaty be only a "supplementary means of interpretation", in practice both scholars and judges often stress its importance. The drafting history provides a useful indication as to the balance to be struck among the competing elements of

Article 15. According to Audrey Chapman (2000, para. 23), the drafting history of Article 15

> underscores that the three provisions of Article 15 in the ICESCR were viewed by drafters as intrinsically interrelated to one another. Three major human rights instruments – the American Declaration, the UDHR, and the Covenant – enumerate these rights as components of a single article. The rights of authors and creators are not just good in themselves but were understood as essential preconditions for cultural freedom and participation and scientific progress.

Another writer has referred to the "tension" that results from the juxtaposition of the right to scientific progress alongside the protection of intellectual property in Article 15 (Green 2000, para. 46).

International human rights organs have urged a dynamic or "evolutive", as it is sometimes called, approach to interpretation. Accordingly, construction of human rights treaties should not be constrained by the intent of the drafters. In one sense, dynamic interpretation is justified by a claim that this is what the drafters intended anyway. They understood that circumstances would change over time, and that it would be wrong to limit the scope of human rights treaties to the situation availing at the time of adoption. As Maria Green (ibid., para. 45) observed in her study for the Committee on Economic, Social and Cultural Rights:

> In the context of modern human rights issues, articles 15 (1) (b) and 15 (1) (c) of the ICESCR raise very real questions of interpretation and implementation. We face a world with issues that the drafters of the ICESCR could never have envisaged, from an AIDS epidemic reigning in one part of the world while the drugs that could help are largely owned in another, to scientifically engineered non-reproducing crops, to scientists "bio-prospecting" for traditional knowledge whose ownership does not fit into existing patent definitions. Then, too, with the recent tying of intellectual property to trade law, international intellectual property rights have undergone a sea-change, becoming universal, compulsory, and enforceable in ways that were never dreamt of in the middle of the last century.

According to Green, the drafters of the covenant, working in the 1950s and early 1960s, "did not seem to deeply consider the difficult balance between public needs and private rights when it comes to intellectual property. When the question was raised, they tended to dismiss it almost out of hand." She concludes that the drafters assumed that the goals of Article 15(1)(b) were "obvious and beyond discussion", and that the benefits of science were considered to be a fundamental human right that belongs to everyone. From their standpoint, Article 15(1)(c) contemplated the issue of intellectual property "almost exclusively of authors as individuals". She explains that the drafters probably did not consider such modern phenomena as the "corporation-held patent, or the situation where the creator is simply an employee of the entity that holds the patent or the copyright" (ibid.).

The Committee on Economic, Social and Cultural Rights – the primary body responsible for interpretation and implementation of the covenant – has been working on a general comment on the subject of intellectual property

CHK

for several years, but nothing has yet been issued. General Comment No. 6, entitled "The economic, social and cultural rights of older persons", is the only general comment of the committee to speak directly to the right to enjoy the benefits of scientific progress and its applications:

> With regard to the right to enjoy the benefits of scientific progress and its applications, States parties should take account of recommendations 60, 61 and 62 of the Vienna International Plan of Action and make efforts to promote research on the biological, mental and social aspects of ageing and ways of maintaining functional capacities and preventing and delaying the start of chronic illnesses and disabilities. In this connection, it is recommended that States, intergovernmental organisations and non-governmental organisations should establish institutions specialising in the teaching of gerontology, geriatrics and geriatric psychology in countries where such institutions do not exist.[42]

General Comment No. 5, on "persons with disabilities", has several paragraphs on the right to take part in cultural life, but makes no observations whatsoever on the right to enjoy the benefits of scientific progress.[43] It seems that there is much to be said on how scientific progress may enhance equality for disabled persons, and the silence of the committee on this subject is disappointing.

On 27 November 2000, in cooperation with the World Intellectual Property Organization, the committee organized a day of discussion on the "right of everyone to benefit from the protection of the moral and material interests resulting from any scientific, literary or artistic production of which he is the author". A discussion paper prepared by Dr Audrey Chapman (2000), as well as several background papers (Green 2000; Bidault 2000; Dommen 2000; ECOSOC 2000a, 2000b), highlighted the significance of the right to enjoy the benefits of scientific progress within the context of the protection of intellectual property. The committee had already manifested its concern for these issues in a statement issued for the Third Ministerial Conference of the World Trade Organization, held in Seattle in November 1999.

The committee said it was aware of the impending further rounds of trade liberalization negotiations, and that new areas such as investments might be included in the WTO system. For the committee, it was "even more urgent that a comprehensive review also be undertaken to assess the impact that trade liberalization may have on the effective enjoyment of human rights, especially the rights enshrined in the Covenant". The committee said that the UNDP *Human Development Report 1999* (UNDP 1999) signalled a strong warning against the negative consequences of the Agreement on Trade-Related Aspects of Intellectual Property Rights (TRIPS), particularly on food security, indigenous knowledge, bio-safety and access to health care, which it noted were major concerns in its implementation of Articles 11–15 of the covenant:

> The wave of economic and corporate restructurings undertaken to respond to an increasingly competitive global market and the widespread dismantling of social security systems have resulted in unemployment, work insecurity and worsening labour conditions giving rise to violations of core economic and social rights set forth in articles 6 to 9 of the Covenant.[44]

At the conclusion of the day of discussion, the committee took the unusual step of issuing a "statement" on the subject, which explored the conflict in the relationship between the right to enjoy the benefits of scientific progress and the protection of intellectual property. The committee stated that "intellectual property rights must be balanced with the right to take part in cultural life and to enjoy the benefits of scientific progress and its applications". According to the committee, a human-rights-based approach to intellectual property dictated respect for the other elements of Article 15. As a result, the committee encouraged "the development of intellectual property systems and the use of intellectual property rights in a balanced manner that meets the objective of providing protection for the moral and material interests of authors, and at the same time promotes the enjoyment of these and other human rights". It noted that "intellectual property is a social product and has a social function". Therefore, intellectual property protection should serve "the objective of human well-being, to which international human rights instruments give legal expression".[45]

The statement added that "It is essential that intellectual property regimes facilitate and promote development cooperation, technology transfer and scientific and cultural collaboration."[46] Under the subheading "Balance", the committee insisted upon the need to reconcile the protection of public and private interests in knowledge: in providing incentives for creation and innovation, states should not provide undue advantages for private interests at the expense of the public interest in enjoying broad access to new knowledge. The committee said that an example of such balancing could be found in the recent WTO Declaration on the TRIPS Agreement and Public Health,[47] which acknowledged that intellectual property protection is important for the development of new medicines, but at the same time also recognized the concerns about its effect on prices.[48]

The 1991 guidelines prepared by the Committee on Economic, Social and Cultural Rights for states parties to the covenant, to be considered in the fulfilment of their reporting obligations under Articles 16 and 17, indicate several dimensions of Article 15 that it considers to be pertinent:

2. Please describe the legislative and other measures taken to realize the right of everyone to enjoy the benefits of scientific progress and its applications, including those aimed at the conservation, development and diffusion of science. In particular, provide information on the following:

(a) Measures taken to ensure the application of scientific progress for the benefit of everyone, including measures aimed at the preservation of mankind's natural heritage and at promoting a healthy and pure environment and information on the institutional infrastructures established for that purpose.

(b) Measures taken to promote the diffusion of information on scientific progress.

(c) Measures taken to prevent the use of scientific and technical progress for purposes which are contrary to the enjoyment of all human rights, including the rights to life, health, personal freedom, privacy and the like.

(d) Any restrictions which are placed upon the exercise of this right, with details of the legal provisions prescribing such restrictions.[49]

By and large, in their reports to the committee states parties offer summary professions of their commitment to scientific research.[50] More unusually, they present a detailed account of the organization and funding of scientific research.[51] Sometimes they explain that the right is enshrined in the constitution.[52] On occasion the reports also review measures for the dissemination of scientific knowledge.[53] Other states make no comments whatsoever on the right, and refer to science in a perfunctory and inadequate manner.[54]

There are no reservations or declarations by states parties that have any bearing on the right to enjoy the benefits of scientific progress or its applications.

UNESCO Instruments

As the UN specialized agency with responsibility for scientific matters, UNESCO's principal references within international human rights law include the two provisions under consideration in this chapter, namely Article 27 of the Universal Declaration of Human Rights and Article 15 of the International Covenant on Economic, Social and Cultural Rights. In its relatively developed body of law, however, there is little of direct relevance to the right to enjoy the benefits of scientific progress and its applications.

The UNESCO General Conference in 1974 adopted a recommendation on the status of scientific researchers. Its main interest is in providing definitions of some of the terminology, specifically "science" and "technology":

> The word "science" signifies the enterprise whereby mankind, acting individually or in small or large groups, makes an organised attempt, by means of the objective study of observed phenomena, to discover and master the chain of causalities; bring together in a co-ordinated form the resultant sub-systems of knowledge by means of systematic reflection and conceptualisation, often largely expressed in the symbols of mathematics; and thereby furnishes itself with the opportunity of using, to its own advantage, understanding of the processes and phenomena occurring in nature and society.

> The word "technology" signifies such knowledge as relates directly to the production or improvement of goods or services.[55]

More recently, the Declaration on Science and the Use of Scientific Knowledge, adopted in 1999 by the World Congress on Science in Budapest, develops in detail the issues touched upon by the Committee on Economic, Social and Cultural Rights with respect to the relationship between the right to enjoy the benefits of scientific progress and the protection of intellectual property. For example, the declaration states:

> Measures should be taken to enhance those relationships between the protection of intellectual property rights and the dissemination of scientific knowledge

that are mutually supportive. There is a need to consider the scope, extent and application of intellectual property rights in relation to the equitable production, distribution and use of knowledge. There is also a need to further develop appropriate national legal frameworks to accommodate the specific requirements of developing countries and traditional knowledge and its sources and products, to ensure their recognition and adequate protection on the basis of the informed consent of the customary or traditional owners of this knowledge.

Also of some relevance is the Universal Declaration on the Human Genome and Human Rights, adopted by the UNESCO General Conference in 1997 and endorsed by the UN General Assembly the following year.[56] It is not, however, focused so much on the benefits as on the potential abuses of science. Article 13, which falls under the subhead "Conditions for the exercise of scientific activity", states:

> The responsibilities inherent in the activities of researchers, including meticulousness, caution, intellectual honesty and integrity in carrying out their research as well as in the presentation and utilization of their findings, should be the subject of particular attention in the framework of research on the human genome, because of its ethical and social implications. Public and private science policy-makers also have particular responsibilities in this respect.

The declaration urges states to foster the international dissemination of scientific knowledge concerning the human genome, human diversity and genetic research, particularly between industrialized and developing countries. Developing countries are to benefit from the achievements of scientific and technological research so that their use in favour of economic and social progress can be for the benefit of all.

Two subsequent UNESCO instruments address the right to benefit more directly. In 2003 the UNESCO General Conference adopted the International Declaration on Human Genetic Data. It contains the following provision:

> Article 19 – Sharing of benefits
>
> (a) In accordance with domestic law or policy and international agreements, benefits resulting from the use of human genetic data, human proteomic data or biological samples collected for medical and scientific research should be shared with the society as a whole and the international community. In giving effect to this principle, benefits may take any of the following forms:
>
> (i) special assistance to the persons and groups that have taken part in the research;
>
> (ii) access to medical care;
>
> (iii) provision of new diagnostics, facilities for new treatments or drugs stemming from the research;
>
> (iv) support for health services;
>
> (v) capacity-building facilities for research purposes;

(vi) development and strengthening of the capacity of developing countries to collect and process human genetic data, taking into consideration their specific problems;

(vii) any other form consistent with the principles set out in this Declaration.

(b) Limitations in this respect could be provided by domestic law and international agreements.

On 19 October 2005 the UNESCO General Conference adopted the Universal Declaration on Bioethics and Human Rights. Article 15 of that instrument, entitled "Sharing of benefits", is drawn from the earlier declaration, although it is formulated so as to be of more general scope. It declares:

1. Benefits resulting from any scientific research and its applications should be shared with society as a whole and within the international community, in particular with developing countries. In giving effect to this principle, benefits may take any of the following forms:

(a) special and sustainable assistance to, and acknowledgement of, the persons and groups that have taken part in the research;

(b) access to quality health care;

(c) provision of new diagnostic and therapeutic modalities or products stemming from research;

(d) support for health services;

(e) access to scientific and technological knowledge;

(f) capacity-building facilities for research purposes;

(g) other forms of benefit consistent with the principles set out in this Declaration.

2. Benefits should not constitute improper inducements to participate in research.

Both declarations appear to be an attempt at specific and detailed formulation of the rights set out in the more general provisions of the Universal Declaration of Human Rights and the International Covenant on Economic, Social and Cultural Rights.

Regional Systems

As already mentioned, the right to enjoy the benefits of scientific progress and its applications was set out in the American Declaration of the Rights and Duties of Man even before its appearance in the Universal Declaration of Human Rights. In principle, the right can be invoked in individual petitions to the Inter-American Commission on Human Rights, but it does not appear to have generated any case law. A similar provision, broadly comparable to ICESCR Article 15(1), appears in the principal normative instrument of the inter-American system concerning cultural rights, the Additional Protocol to the American Convention on Human Rights in the Area of Economic, Social and Cultural Rights (Protocol of San Salvador). Article 14 of the text states:

Right to the Benefits of Culture

1. The States Parties to this Protocol recognize the right of everyone:

a. To take part in the cultural and artistic life of the community;

b. To enjoy the benefits of scientific and technological progress;

c. To benefit from the protection of moral and material interests deriving from any scientific, literary or artistic production of which he is the author.[57]

The Council of Europe instruments dealing with economic, social and cultural rights do not echo in any way Article 27(1) of the Universal Declaration of Human Rights. In fact, the Council of Europe instruments seem to effect a separation between social rights and cultural rights, with the latter being addressed in relatively recent specialized documents concerning, for example, national minorities and regional and minority languages. The right to enjoy the benefits of scientific progress appears to have been lost in the process. Nevertheless, relevant issues are addressed indirectly by the Council of Europe. The Convention on Human Rights and Biomedicine is focused principally on protecting the individual from scientific experimentation. Article 2 states: "The interests and welfare of the human being shall prevail over the sole interest of society or science."[58] Other provisions deal with specific issues concerning the rights of the individual and the potential abuse of scientific research.

The African Charter on Human and Peoples' Rights does not have any provision relevant to the subject. The recent Protocol to the African Charter on Human and Peoples' Rights on the Rights of Women in Africa,[59] in a provision entitled "Right to a Healthy and Sustainable Environment", requires states parties to take all appropriate measures to "promote research and investment in new and renewable energy sources and appropriate technologies, including information technologies and facilitate women's access to, and participation in their control".

CONTENT OF THE NORM AND SCOPE OF STATE OBLIGATIONS

By virtue of the recognition of the right to enjoy the benefits of scientific progress within the ICESCR, the general provisions of that instrument are applicable. Specifically, the right to enjoy the benefits of scientific progress and its applications must be "exercised without discrimination of any kind as to race, colour, sex, language, religion, political or other opinion, national or social origin, property, birth or other status".[60] Moreover, it may be subject "only to such limitations as are determined by law only in so far as this may be compatible with the nature of these rights and solely for the purpose of promoting the general welfare in a democratic society".[61]

The right to enjoy the benefits of scientific progress interacts with several other categories of rights, including the cultural right to protection of intellectual property and many of the economic and social rights, such as the right to health and the right to food. It is also relevant to the civil and political right to receive and impart information.

Relationship with Protection of Intellectual Property

Lawrence Helfer has explained that there are two valid approaches to the relationship between human rights and intellectual property. The first treats the two as being in fundamental conflict. The second "sees both areas of law as concerned with the same fundamental question: defining the appropriate scope of private monopoly power that gives authors and inventors a sufficient incentive to create and innovate, while ensuring that the consuming public has adequate access to the fruits of their efforts" (Helfer 2004a, 168). The right to enjoy the benefits of scientific progress and its applications and the right to protection of intellectual property are joined at the hip, so to speak, by virtue of their inclusion within the same general provision. The drafting history of the two major texts shows that this was more than just accidental, although there is no evidence of any serious debate at the time about the tension between the two rights, in contrast with the current situation. It appears that they were assumed to be fundamentally compatible. Moreover, it seems clear that all the attention was focused on the quite controversial issue of whether to recognize a right to protection of intellectual property at all. Many who participated in the debates did not consider that intellectual property had any place within a human rights declaration. By contrast, recognition of the right to enjoy the benefits of scientific progress did not elicit any objections. The brevity of the discussions at the time, though frustrating in terms of their guidance for detailed interpretation of the relevant provisions, confirms the broad consensus for their inclusion within the Universal Declaration and the ICESCR.

Within the past decade, the relationship between intellectual property and the right to enjoy the benefits of scientific progress has taken on considerable importance. The debate has been spurred by the "globalization" of intellectual property protection in the WTO TRIPS agreement (Helfer 2004b). As referred to earlier, these issues were identified in both the UNESCO-sponsored Declaration on Science of 1999 and the statement issued in 2001 by the Committee on Economic, Social and Cultural Rights. Substantial initiatives in this area have also been undertaken by the UN Sub-Commission on the Promotion and Protection of Human Rights and the Commission on Human Rights itself.

In 2000 the Sub-Commission on the Promotion and Protection of Human Rights adopted, by consensus, a resolution entitled "Intellectual property rights and human rights".[62] The resolution resulted from a preliminary report prepared by J. Oloka-Onyango and D. Udagama on globalization and its impact on the full enjoyment of human rights.[63] It was also prompted by an NGO initiative from the Lutheran World Federation, the Habitat International Coalition and the International NGO Committee on Human Rights in Trade and Investment, which had submitted a statement to the sub-commission entitled "The WTO TRIPS Agreement and Human Rights". It urged the sub-commission to "reassert the primacy of human rights obligations over the commercial and profit-driven motives upon which agreements such as TRIPs are based".[64] During debate on the resolution, members of the sub-commission noted that trade-related questions of intellectual property rights threatened the realization of economic, social and cultural rights.[65]

The sub-commission resolution specifically states that "the implementation of the TRIPS Agreement does not adequately reflect the fundamental nature and indivisibility of all human rights, including the right of everyone to enjoy the benefits of scientific progress and its applications". It refers to "the balance of rights and duties inherent in the protection of intellectual property rights, and its provisions relating to, inter alia, the safeguarding of biological diversity and indigenous knowledge relating to biological diversity, and the promotion of the transfer of environmentally sustainable technologies". It affirms that the right to protection of intellectual property is "subject to limitations in the public interest", and refers to "the social function of intellectual property". The resolution also invokes the rights to health, to food and to self-determination as raising issues of conflict with the TRIPS agreement. The sub-commission resolution identifies a number of areas where difficulties arise, including impediments to the transfer of technology to developing countries, the consequences for the enjoyment of the right to food of plant variety rights and the patenting of genetically modified organisms, "bio-piracy" and the reduction of communities' (especially indigenous communities') control over their own genetic and natural resources and cultural values, and restrictions on access to patented pharmaceuticals and the implications for the enjoyment of the right to health. A second resolution, to much the same effect, was adopted the following year by the sub-commission.[66]

Resolutions by the Commission on Human Rights, also contesting the human rights consequences of the TRIPS agreement, were soon to follow.[67] These resolutions "sparked substantial controversy among the Commission members ... because [they] called into question the impact" of TRIPS (Dennis 2000, 191). Within the commission the United States said that by questioning "the validity of internationally agreed protections of intellectual property rights" the text was "bad public health policy" (ibid.). The European Union expressed its understanding that "no provisions in this resolution can be interpreted as undermining or limiting existing international agreements, including in the field of intellectual property" (ibid.).

There are some quite sophisticated arguments that attempt to find some common ground between the TRIPS agreement and the right to enjoy the benefits of scientific progress. Hoe Lim (2001), in a paper prepared for the Committee on Economic, Social and Cultural Rights, noted that the TRIPS agreement attempts to strike the desired balance between public and private interest. Article 7 of the TRIPS agreement emphasizes the role of promotion of the public interest in the protection of intellectual property. Entitled "Objectives", it states: "the protection and enforcement of intellectual property rights should contribute to the promotion of technological innovation and to the transfer and dissemination of technology, to the mutual advantage of producers and users of technological knowledge and in a manner conducive to social and economic welfare, and to a balance of rights and obligations". Lim makes an interesting comparison between Article 7 of the TRIPS agreement and the intellectual property provisions of the human rights instruments (Lim, 2001):

> Interestingly, while the expressly stated objectives of the TRIPS Agreement lay emphasis on promoting social and economic welfare, such objectives are not explicit in Articles 27.2 of the UDHR and Article 15.1(c) of the ICESCR. These articles seek to protect the interests of authors and inventors not so much for the sake of the broader public interest but because they are recognized as worthy of protection as such.

One of the by-products of the sub-commission resolutions was a report by the UN High Commissioner for Human Rights saying that the "balance between public and private interests found under article 15 – and article 27 of the Universal Declaration – is one familiar to intellectual property law", and adding that it appeared to "bind States to design IP systems that strike a balance between promoting general public interests in accessing new knowledge as easily as possible and in protecting the interests of authors and inventors in such knowledge".[68] The High Commissioner for Human Rights noted that "recognising the links between the standards in the TRIPS Agreement and the promotion and protection of human rights is not the same as saying that the TRIPS Agreement takes a human rights approach to intellectual property protection".[69] She pointed out that the *raison d'être* of TRIPS was essentially commercial, and that while commercial objectives were not necessarily incompatible with the promotion of human rights, "if we truly wish to factor the promotion and protection of human rights into the objectives of the TRIPS Agreement, different ways and strategies of promoting and protecting scientific progress and its results should be explored in particular cases".[70] She explained further:

> the Agreement only alludes to the *responsibilities* of IP holders that should balance those rights in accordance with its own objectives. The prevention of anti-competitive practices and the abuse of rights, the promotion of technology transfer, special and differential treatment for least developed countries are merely referred to – but unlike the rights it sets out, the Agreement does not establish the content of these responsibilities, or how they should be implemented. To illustrate the difference, a human rights approach might set out the minimum standards required for protection against anti-competitive practices or for the promotion of technology transfer to developing countries in much the same way as the Agreement now sets out minimum standards for the protection of patents or trademarks. Consequently, the balance identified in the TRIPS Agreement might not equate with the balance required under article 15 of ICESCR.[71]

Under "Conclusions and Recommendations", the High Commissioner referred specifically to the right to enjoy the benefits of scientific progress. She said that in implementing systems for intellectual property protection, states should ensure that they balance the right of everyone to take part in cultural life and to enjoy the benefits of scientific progress and its applications and, on the other hand, the right of an individual to benefit from the protection of the moral and material interests resulting from any scientific, literary or artistic production of which he or she is the author. The High Commissioner said that implementation of the TRIPS agreement should be monitored so as to ensure that its minimum standards achieve such a balance between the interests of the general public and those of the authors. The High Commissioner supported the WHO statement that "countries are advised to carefully monitor the implementation of the TRIPS Agreement in order to formulate comprehensive proposals for the future review of the TRIPS Agreement".[72]

The High Commissioner continued, directly addressing the promotion of the right of all to enjoy the benefits of scientific progress and its applications:

> The design of IP systems should take into account the fact that the grant of overly broad patents can be used to block future medical research. The design of IP systems should, in calculating the difficult trade-off between public and private interests, take into consideration that the increasing tendency to grant patents for "me-too" drugs may run counter to the primary objective of IP systems to promote innovation, and focus too heavily on promoting private commercial interests. The requirements under the TRIPS Agreement for the grant of patents – novelty, inventive step and industrial applicability – are open to interpretation under national legislation and each country can decide according to local conditions. Consequently, the High Commissioner encourages interpretations of these requirements that do not lose sight of the public interest in the wide dissemination of knowledge under article 15.[73]

The report of the UN High Commissioner provides some useful guidance in determining how the nebulous requirement of "balance" between the right to enjoy the benefits of scientific progress and the protection of intellectual property is to be struck. Part of the difficulty here is that in another area, far from the murky waters of international trade, human rights law has developed a discourse that relies on the protection of intellectual property. This is the cluster of issues that concerns the protection of traditional knowledge belonging to indigenous peoples.

Scientific Knowledge of Indigenous Peoples

The Declaration on the Rights of Indigenous Peoples, adopted by the United Nations General Assembly in September 2007, states:

Article 31

1. Indigenous peoples have the right to maintain, control, protect and develop their cultural heritage, traditional knowledge and traditional cultural expressions, as

well as the manifestations of their sciences, technologies and cultures, including human and genetic resources, seeds, medicines, knowledge of the properties of fauna and flora, oral traditions, literatures, designs, sports and traditional games and visual and performing arts. They also have the right to maintain, control, protect and develop their intellectual property over such cultural heritage, traditional knowledge, and traditional cultural expressions.

2. In conjunction with indigenous peoples, States shall take effective measures to recognize and protect the exercise of these rights.[74]

An earlier draft, adopted by the sub-commission in 1999, went slightly further, recognizing the right of indigenous peoples to "the full ownership, control and protection of their cultural and intellectual property".[75] It said they were entitled to restitution of cultural and intellectual property "taken without their free and informed consent or in violation of their laws, traditions and customs".[76] According to at least one observer, these rights are in opposition with existing approaches to intellectual property, including the TRIPS regime (Coombe 1998, 71). But they are also, potentially, in conflict with the right of *everyone* to enjoy the benefits of scientific progress and its applications.

The Principles and Guidelines for the Protection of the Heritage of Indigenous People, prepared by Erica-Irene Daes,[77] special rapporteur of the Sub-Commission on the Promotion and Protection of Human Rights, do not directly address the issue of intellectual property. Nevertheless, she has said that the "heritage of indigenous peoples" includes "cultural property" and "all kinds of scientific, agricultural, medicinal, biodiversity-related and ecological knowledge, including innovations based upon that knowledge".[78] Accordingly, the special rapporteur has considered that national laws should authorize indigenous peoples to prevent "the acquisition, documentation or use of their heritage without proper authorisation of the traditional owners".[79] Laws should deny third parties the right to obtain "patent, copyright or other legal protection for any element of indigenous peoples' heritage" that does not also provide for "sharing of ownership, control, use and benefits" with "traditional owners".[80]

Aside from the general recognition of intellectual property rights in the Universal Declaration and the covenant, it has been argued that the intellectual property rights of indigenous peoples are also protected by other instruments. The main specialized treaty in this area is ILO Convention No. 169 concerning Indigenous and Tribal Peoples in Independent Countries.[81] Although it does not directly address the issue of intellectual property, Article 13(1) requires governments to "respect the special importance for the cultures and spiritual values of the peoples concerned of their relationship with the lands or territories, or both as applicable, which they occupy or otherwise use, and in particular the collective aspects of this relationship". Also, the Convention on Biodiversity[82] acknowledges the contribution of knowledge and innovation made by indigenous peoples, in particular their right to give or withhold their consent before their natural resources are used, and also to participate in the benefits derived from such use. Article 8(j) says that:

> Each Contracting Party shall, as far as possible and as appropriate … subject to its national legislation, respect, preserve and maintain the knowledge, innovations and practices of indigenous and local communities embodying traditional lifestyles relevant for the conservation and sustainable use of biological diversity and promote their wider application with the approval and involvement of the holders of such knowledge, innovations and practices and encourage the equitable sharing of the benefits arising from the utilisation of such knowledge, innovations and practices.

Indigenous peoples provide many examples of the "bio-piracy" of "inventions" and "discoveries" that had long been part of their traditions. For example, in the 1990s the US International Plant Medicine Corporation obtained a patent for ayahuasca or yagé, which is a sacred plant of the indigenous peoples of Amazonia. The so-called "invention" was a variety of the ayahuasca, *Banisteriopsis* Caapi, which had been domesticated by indigenous peoples hundreds of years ago. The "inventor", Loren Miller, admitted having collected the sample from the farmstead of an indigenous family of the Ecuadorian Amazon. Antonio Jacanimijoy (1998) observes that "On the one hand it is scandalous that it should be possible for a person to acquire a patent for a plant that we have known and made use of for many years, and on the other hand it has to be admitted that it is a serious affront to our peoples for a person to appropriate a sacred symbol that belongs to us all."

Jacanimijoy provides as another example a patent awarded to the French Institute of Scientific Research for Development in Cooperation, for the "discovery" of a natural product to combat the disease known as leishmaniasis. Leishmaniasis occurs in tropical areas, where it is transmitted by mosquitoes. In the late 1980s French and Bolivian researchers, relying upon ethno-botanical studies in the Chimane tribe, an indigenous people living in the areas in which the disease is endemic, "discovered" a plant called evanta. The scientists named the active principle "chimanines", in honour of the indigenous people who disclosed their traditional knowledge. They went on to patent their "discovery", in effect depriving the Chimane of the right to decide how this product may be used and to derive some profit from its commercial use (ibid.).

In addressing the "balancing" between intellectual property rights and the right to enjoy the benefits of scientific progress, the Sub-Commission on the Promotion and Protection of Human Rights has acknowledged the importance of protecting the intellectual property of indigenous peoples. The preamble to its 2000 resolution notes a panel discussion organized by the World Intellectual Property Organization on 9 November 1998 on "Intellectual property and human rights".[83] In her report on TRIPS, the High Commissioner for Human Rights said that she "encourage[d] the adaptation of IP systems so that they fully take into account cultural and other rights of indigenous and local communities".[84]

One observer has noted that "Most indigenous peoples do not seek protection for their cultural heritage in order to commercialise it, but rather to prevent outsiders from exploiting it."[85] In this context, a helpful paradigm for the protection of the rights of indigenous peoples may be the body of legal norms concerning cultural diversity. For example, the action plan annexed to the Universal Declaration on Cultural Diversity, adopted by the UNESCO General Conference in November 2001, urges "Respecting and protecting traditional knowledge, in particular that of indigenous peoples; recognising the contribution of traditional knowledge, particularly with regard to environmental protection and the management of natural resources, and fostering synergies between modern and local knowledge" (UNESCO 2002). UNESCO proceeded with the preparation of an international treaty dealing with cultural diversity. The Convention on the Protection and Promotion of the Diversity of Cultural Expressions was adopted by the UNESCO General Conference in October 2005. The preamble to that instrument recognizes "the importance of the vitality of cultures, including for persons belonging to minorities and indigenous peoples, as manifested in their freedom to create, disseminate and distribute their traditional cultural expressions and to have access thereto, so as to benefit them for their own development". Under the heading "Measures to promote cultural expressions", Article 7 of the convention requires states parties "to create in their territory an environment which encourages individuals and social groups ... to create, produce, disseminate, distribute and have access to their own cultural expressions, paying due attention to the special circumstances and needs of women as well as various social groups, including persons belonging to minorities and indigenous peoples".[86] It has been noted that the UNESCO approach to cultural heritage and diversity is fundamentally "conservationist", whereas the World Trade Organization approach is essentially "protectionist".[87]

Scientific Progress and Economic and Social Rights

Aside from the reference to "scientific progress" in ICESCR Article 15(1), the term "progress" ("progressively", "progressive") is employed in a more general manner to describe the standard for implementation of all of the rights set out in the instrument. For example, Article 2(1) states that "Each State Party to the present Covenant undertakes to take steps, individually and through international assistance and co-operation, especially economic and technical, to the maximum of its available resources, with a view to achieving progressively the full realisation of the rights recognized in the present Covenant by all appropriate means ..."[88] The use of the word "progress" in these two contexts may be more than a mere semantic coincidence. Although "progressive" implementation of the covenant is stated to be dependent upon such factors as international assistance and cooperation, especially economic and technical, human experience teaches us that a very significant factor in the progressive improvement of such areas as availability and quality of food, housing and health is our ability to enjoy the benefits of scientific progress and its applications. Or in other words, the right set out in Article 15(1) has a direct bearing on the obligation contained in Article 2(1). In turn, this means that Article 15(1) is related to each of the other individual rights set out in the covenant. This is especially apparent with regard to the rights to health and to food, although it is also not without its connections with the rights to housing, to "the continuous improvement of living conditions" and to education.

Article 12 of the covenant sets out in detail the right to health, noting in particular the reduction of the stillbirth rate and infant mortality, the healthy development of the child, the improvement of all aspects of environmental and industrial hygiene and the prevention, treatment and control of epidemic, endemic, occupational and other diseases. Obviously the progressive realization of these rights involves enjoyment of the benefits of scientific progress. But it is a fact that not *everyone* enjoys the benefits of scientific progress in this respect. It is beyond the scope of this chapter to provide a detailed critique of the health-care business, dominated by transnational corporations headquartered in developed countries. It should suffice to recall that the vindication of this fundamental human right is dependent upon investment policy, profits and other factors that obey agendas other than the progressive realization of the right for *everyone*. Scientific progress in this area is distorted and often perverted by crass financial considerations. For example, somewhere in the world – mainly in Africa – one child dies every 30 seconds of malaria. Some 1.5–2.7 million people are killed by malaria each year. But multinational pharmaceutical companies devote their research efforts to developing drugs for "erectile dysfunction" and similar real or imagined maladies of the rich, rather than to eliminating the scourge of malaria among the world's poor. The term "neglected diseases" is used to describe phenomena like malaria and tuberculosis, which the World Health Organization says can be characterized as diseases that "affect almost exclusively poor and powerless people living in rural parts of low-income countries".[89] An academic writer has said that "gross disparities in access to treatment, which stem from the same 'pathologies of power' – to use Farmer's term – that are at the root of so much suffering in the world, are starkly inconsistent with the notion of a universal right to benefit from scientific progress" (Yamin 2002).

The drafters of the relevant norms in the Universal Declaration and the covenant resisted attempts to incorporate references to the objectives of scientific research. There was a strong feeling that research priorities were in some sense related to the free intellectual choice of scientists. This concern is reflected in Article 15(3) of the covenant: "The States Parties to the present Covenant undertake to respect the freedom indispensable for scientific research and creative activity." Some recent statements suggest a greater willingness of human rights institutions to attempt to orient scientific research for the greater good. In 2003 the Commission on Human Rights adopted a resolution entitled "Access to medication in the context of pandemics such as HIV/AIDS, tuberculosis and malaria".[90] The resolution included a call to states "to take all appropriate measures, nationally and through cooperation, to promote research and development of new and more effective preventive, curative or palliative pharmaceutical products and diagnostic tools". The Committee on the Rights of the Child, in its General Comment No. 3 on HIV/AIDS and the rights of the child, said that "States parties must ensure that HIV/AIDS research programmes include specific studies that contribute to effective prevention, care, treatment and impact reduction for children."[91] The Declaration of the World Conference against Racism, Racial Discrimination, Xenophobia and Related Intolerance, adopted in Durban in September 2001, urged states, non-governmental organizations and the private sector to "work with health professionals, scientific researchers and international and regional health organizations to study the differential impact of medical treatments and health strategies on various communities".

Given the inherent concerns about the influence of commercial factors on research priorities, the pronounced trend in developed countries to link publicly funded scientific research with the private sector raises questions. This development is reflected in legislative measures such as the Bayh-Dole Act in the United States, which is aimed at "technology transfer" from university-based research to the private sector. Obviously it is a phenomenon with both positive and negative aspects. That publicly funded research conducted in a university environment is then exploited commercially may be decisive to promoting the enjoyment of scientific progress. On the other hand, there is the danger that pure research, motivated by a combination of intellectual curiosity and general social interests and funded from public sources, may become perverted when it is associated with commercial priorities.

Access to existing medications is also fundamental to enjoyment of the benefits of scientific progress. The Commission on Human Rights resolution noted that "access to medication in the context of pandemics such as HIV/AIDS, tuberculosis and malaria is one fundamental element for achieving progressively the full realisation of the right of everyone to the enjoyment of the highest attainable standard of physical and mental health".[92] The Committee on the Rights of the Child has said that "States parties should negotiate with the pharmaceutical industry in order to make the necessary medicines locally available at the lowest costs possible."[93] Issues concerning intellectual property are of especial importance with regard to the right to health. Pharmaceutical manufacturers argue that high prices for medication, which are a result of the temporary monopolistic situation deriving from patent protection, are a necessary element in funding research and development. But they have the inevitable consequence of making the most technically advanced medications inaccessible to the sick and dying in developing countries. The special rapporteur on the right to health has warned that "the commercial motivation of intellectual property rights encourages research, first and foremost, towards 'profitable' diseases, while diseases that predominantly affect people in poor countries – such as river blindness – remain under-researched".[94]

Joseph Stiglitz (2003) has argued that TRIPS

> deprived millions in the developing world of access to life-saving drugs. As a chorus of researchers has pointed out, the provisions, pushed by the pharmaceutical companies, were so unbalanced that they were bad for scientific progress. Here, there has been some progress – but not enough. Provisions demanded by the US would have made it difficult for small countries to gain affordable access. Developing countries also continue to worry about bio-piracy – the patenting by western firms of traditional foods and drugs.

Concerns that the TRIPS agreement might result in effective denial of the right to health led to some important adjustments, agreed in August 2003 in accordance with the earlier Doha Declaration on the TRIPS Agreement and Public Health. This will allow countries to produce generic copies of patented drugs under compulsory licence to export drugs to countries with no or little drug-manufacturing capacity. As the special rapporteur on health noted, "the protracted negotiations that led to this Decision should have been informed by the human rights responsibility of rich States to engage in international assistance and cooperation in relation to the right to health". He cautioned that "the effectiveness of the Decision will depend on the extent to which it actually does lead to increased access to medicines for the poor".[95]

The right to food, expressed in the covenant as the right to be "free from hunger", is directly connected to scientific progress by the text of Article 11. It declares that states shall take measures needed to "improve methods of production, conservation and distribution of food by making full use of technical and scientific knowledge". But scientific research with respect to food suffers from many of the same problems as medical and pharmaceutical research. It is driven by profit, and generally neglects those who are the hungriest. The special rapporteur on food has complained of a total lack of serious investment in any of the five most important crops of the poorest arid countries: sorghum, millet, pigeon pea, chickpea and groundnut. "Only 1 per cent of research and development budgets of multinational corporations is spent on crops that might be useful in the developing world", he observed. Research and design of genetically modified seeds has been largely directed towards creating a form of vertical integration between seed, pesticides and production, all to increase corporate profits. Special Rapporteur Ziegler noted that "A marked paradigm shift has occurred from a system seeking to foster food security on the basis of the free exchange of knowledge, to a system seeking to achieve the same goal on the basis of the private appropriation of knowledge."[96]

Scientific Progress and Civil and Political Rights

The relationship between scientific progress and the implementation of civil and political rights may not be so obvious, although it should not be forgotten that the Universal Declaration of Human Rights, which first recognizes the right to enjoy the benefits of scientific progress, makes no distinction between different categories of rights. When the draft international covenant was split in half, in 1951, it was not obvious which way certain rights should go, and there is no doubt that some rights had a claim to both categories. Arguably, this is the case with the right to enjoy the benefits of scientific progress.

The category of civil and political rights where this is perhaps most apparent is the freedom "to seek, receive and impart information and ideas of all kinds, regardless of frontiers, either orally, in writing or in print, in the form of art, or through any other media".[97] We live in an age of rapidly evolving science and technology in terms of access to information. Our lives have all been transformed by developments like mobile telephones, the

Internet and satellite television. Here the benefits have been enormous, and have particular potential for developing countries. For example, in the past, education and research at university-level institutions was stymied by poor library resources. The cost of developing adequate research collections of books, periodicals and documents was simply prohibitive. This undoubtedly contributed to a "brain drain" in developing countries.

Technological developments have to some extent levelled the playing field. A great deal of academic research, in both the pure sciences and the humanities and social sciences, is now available on the Internet. Access to these materials is possible from countries that could not and cannot aspire to have mature research libraries. It is one of science's great ironies that Internet technology was initially developed by the military establishment in the United States with a view to communication in the event of nuclear war. In fact, the Internet has become a profoundly democratic and egalitarian factor in access to information. The special rapporteur on freedom of opinion and expression has said "the new technologies and, in particular, the Internet are inherently democratic, provide the public and individuals with access to information sources and enable all to participate actively in the communication process".[98] According to the special rapporteur, "the Internet is a unique opportunity for opening all peoples to an increasing exchange of information, opinions and ideas. Moreover, the worldwide availability of Internet resources might greatly contribute to economic, social and cultural progress, particularly in developing countries."[99] A recent resolution of the Commission on Human Rights calls upon states to "facilitate equal participation in, access to and use of, information and communications technology such as the Internet, applying a gender perspective, and to encourage international cooperation aimed at the development of media and information and communication facilities in all countries".[100]

Protection from the Abuse of Scientific Progress

Despite the rejection of attempts to include language concerning the purposes of scientific research within the normative provisions concerning the right to enjoy the benefits of scientific progress, there is now much authority for the view that there must be protection against the abusive use of scientific research. It is worth recalling that the only reference to science in the International Covenant on Civil and Political Rights occurs in the provision concerning torture, which declares: "In particular, no one shall be subjected without his free consent to medical or scientific experimentation."[101] It recalls – indeed, its adoption was driven by – the abuse of scientific research conducted by Nazi doctors in extermination camps such as Auschwitz (Lifton 1986). According to Audrey Chapman (2000):

> A human rights approach further establishes a requirement for the state to protect its citizens from the negative effects of intellectual property. To do so, governments need to undertake a very rigorous and disaggregated analysis of the likely impact of specific innovations, as well as an evaluation of proposed changes in intellectual property paradigms, and to utilize these data to assure

non-discrimination in the end result. When making choices and decisions, it calls for particular sensitivity to the effect on those groups whose welfare tends to be absent from the calculus of decision-making about intellectual property: the poor, the disadvantaged, racial, ethnic and linguistic minorities, women, rural residents.

The High Commissioner for Human Rights has also addressed the issue of abuse of scientific research, warning of the danger that patent regimes be used to actually block scientific research.[102] In asking states parties to the International Covenant on Economic, Social and Cultural Rights to indicate, in their initial and periodic report, "Measures taken to prevent the use of scientific and technical progress for purposes which are contrary to the enjoyment of all human rights, including the rights to life, health, personal freedom, privacy and the like", the Committee on Economic, Social and Cultural Rights confirms that it shares this interpretation of Article 15.[103]

A great deal of scientific research is devoted to objectives that are inherently evil and harmful. The foremost examples in this respect concern the development of weapons which are inherently illegal – that is, they are either indiscriminate in that they fail to distinguish adequately between combatants and non-combatants or they cause unnecessary suffering.[104] Yet enormous resources in developed countries continue to be devoted to research on such illegal weaponry. In a bizarre way, by mandating the use of weapons that limit the potential for harm to what military exigencies strictly require, international humanitarian law seems to suggest that it is appropriate for scientific research to be devoted to "better" and more "humane" weaponry. In effect, victims of armed conflict thereby enjoy the benefits of scientific progress and its applications, to the extent that they are maimed or burned by weapons that are a technologically advanced as possible. So-called "precision-guided munitions" or "smart bombs" permit combatants to reduce "collateral damage". Weapons that are targeted using global positioning satellites are another example of technological progress being employed to reduce undesired civilian casualties. Regrettably, in the real world of contemporary armed conflict, combatant forces do not necessarily use such state-of-the-art weaponry even if it is available to them, at least in the early stages of war, because they are required to consume stocks of older weapons before these become totally obsolete, much as a merchant sells off the earliest stocks before they reach their "sell-by" date. It is only when the older weapons are exhausted that the smartest of the smart bombs will be employed. Thus, even in warfare, the right to enjoy the benefits from scientific progress is engaged – and violated – in the choice of weapons.

Other forms of research also have the potential for great harm. Technology involving the production of toxic chemical substances, for example, as well as research in the area of genetics, is of concern in this respect. The 1975 UN Declaration on the Use of Scientific and Technological Progress in the Interests of Peace and for the Benefit of Mankind recommended that:

> All States shall take appropriate measures to prevent the use of scientific and technological developments, particularly by the State organs, to limit or interfere with the enjoyment of the human rights and fundamental freedoms

of the individual as enshrined in the Universal Declaration of Human Rights, the International Covenants on Human Rights and other relevant international instruments.[105]

Furthermore:

> All States shall take measures to extend the benefits of science and technology to all strata of the population and to protect them, both socially and materially, from possible harmful effects of the misuse of scientific and technological developments, including their misuse to infringe upon the rights of the individual or of the group, particularly with regard to respect for privacy and the protection of the human personality and its physical and intellectual integrity. (Chapman 2000, para. 34)

CONCLUSIONS

The right of everyone to enjoy the benefits of scientific progress and its applications, set out in Article 27(1) of the Universal Declaration of Human Rights and Article 15(1) of the International Covenant on Economic, Social and Cultural Rights, has been relatively neglected. Its adoption was uncontroversial, and the *travaux préparatoires* of both instruments offer little to guide the contemporary interpreter of the norm. They do reveal that there was an inherent tension, from the beginning, between enjoyment of the benefits of scientific progress and the protection of intellectual property. This issue has taken on great importance in recent years with the globalization of intellectual property regimes, as expressed in mechanisms like the TRIPS agreement of the World Trade Organization. Throughout the human rights systems, great concerns have been expressed about such issues as the development of medications for "neglected diseases", the virtual unavailability of the most modern medications because of the high prices associated with patent monopolies and the perversion of biomedical and biotechnology research agendas in the interests of the bottom line of transnational corporations. The relationship between the right to enjoy the benefits of scientific research and the protection of intellectual property has become a touchstone within the larger debate about the effects of globalization on the promotion and protection of human rights.

The norm set out in Article 27(1) of the Universal Declaration and Article 15(1) of the covenant has a great deal of unexploited potential. Its universal acceptance, as reflected in the drafting history of the two provisions, makes it especially useful and promises great effectiveness. Moreover, on reflection, it seems to be intricately linked with the entire philosophy that underlies the rights enshrined in the covenant, namely progressive realization of the rights to food, medical care, education, housing and so on. Freedom from want will be achieved in part by a fairer distribution of resources and by international cooperation, but it will also result from scientific progress. Given its obvious significance, it is quite striking how rarely the norm is actually invoked. The reports of the relevant special rapporteurs, and the resolutions of such bodies as the Commission on Human Rights, the General Assembly and the Sub-Commission on the Promotion and Protection of Human Rights, only make rare references to the provisions protecting the right to enjoy the benefits of scientific progress. Perhaps greater attention will also enhance, more generally, the role of the much-neglected fifth category, "cultural rights", within the overall scheme of protection of international human rights.

ACKNOWLEDGEMENTS

Nicolas Rouleau and Edel Hughes assisted in the research on this chapter.

NOTES

1   Universal Declaration of Human Rights, GA Res. 217 A (III), UN Doc. A/810 (1948), Article 27(1).
2   International Covenant on Economic, Social and Cultural Rights (1976) 993 UNTS 3, Article 15(1)(b).
3   Vienna Declaration and Programme of Action, UN Doc. A/CONF.157/24 (1993), para. 5.
4   *The right to information on consular assistance in the context of the guarantees of due process of law*, Inter-American Court of Human Rights, Advisory Opinion OC-16/99, 1 October 1999, para. 114.
5   UN Doc. E/CN.4/AC.1/3, p. 14. It was Article 35 of the original 48-article draft prepared by Humphrey.
6   OAS Doc. OEA/Ser.L/V/II.23, doc. 21, rev. 6.
7   UN Doc. E/CN.4/AC.2/SR.9, pp. 3-4.
8   UN Doc. A/C.2/SR.70, p. 4.
9   UN Doc. A/C.2/SR.70, p. 5.
10   UN Doc. A/C.2/SR.70, p. 6.
11   UN Doc. A/C.3/261.
12   UN Doc. A/C.3/261, p. 619.
13   UN Doc. A/C.3/261, p. 634.
14   UN Doc. E/CN.4/AC.1/W.2/Rev.2.
15   UN Doc. E/CN.4/SR.15, p. 5.
16   UN Doc. E/CN.4/SR.15, p. 15.
17   GA Res. 2542 (XXIV).
18   GA Res. 3253 (XXIX), para. 13.
19   GA Res. 3384 (XXX).
20   Proclaimed by the International Conference on Human Rights at Teheran on 13 May 1968. See www.unhchr.ch/html/menu3/b/b_tehern.htm.
21   On the omission of the right to property, see Schabas (1991).
22   The UNESCO draft suggestions were submitted in UN Doc. E/CN.4/541/Rev.1.
23   UN Doc. E/CN.4/AC.14/2, p. 3, art. (d).
24   UN Doc. E/CN.4/AC.14/2, p. 3, art. (e).
25   UN Doc. E/CN.4/AC.14/2, p. 4.
26   UN Doc. E/CN.4/SR.228, p. 11.
27   UN Doc. E/CN.4/SR.228, p. 12.
28   UN Doc. E/CN.4/L.81/Rev.1.
29   UN Doc. E/CN.4/SR.230, p. 7.

30 UN Doc. E/CN.4/L.104. It was submitted by France, which had consistently taken the lead on this issue.
31 UN Doc. E/CN.4/SR.230, p. 7.
32 UN Doc. E/CN.4/SR.294, p. 4.
33 UN Doc. E/CN.4/669, UN Doc. E/2256, para. 126.
34 UN Doc. E/CN.4/L.52.
35 UN Doc. A/2929, p. 329.
36 See UN Doc. A/C.3/L.633, proposed by Czechoslovakia.
37 UN Doc. A/C.3/SR.796, para. 20.
38 UN Doc. A/C.3/SR.799, para. 35.
39 UN Doc. A/C.3/SR.799, para. 35.
40 UN Doc. A/C.3/SR.799, para. 36.
41 Vienna Convention on the Law of Treaties (1979) 1155 UNTS 331, Articles 31–3.
42 "General Comment No. 6", UN Doc. HRI/GEN/1/Rev. 6, para. 42.
43 "General Comment No. 5", UN Doc. E/1995/22, paras 36–8.
44 "Statement of the United Nations Committee on Economic, Social and Cultural Rights to the Third Ministerial Conference of the World Trade Organization (Seattle, 30 November to 3 December 1999)", UN Doc. E/C.12/1999/9, para. 4.
45 "Follow-up to the day of general discussion on article 15.1(c), Monday, 26 November 2001, Human rights and intellectual property, Statement by the Committee on Economic Social and Cultural Rights", UN Doc. E/C.12/2001/15, para. 4.
46 UN Doc. E/C.12/2001/15, para. 15.
47 "World Trade Organization, Declaration on the TRIPS Agreement and Public Health, Ministerial Conference, Fourth Session, Doha, Qatar, adopted on 14 November 2001", WT/MIN(01)/DEC/2, para. 3.
48 WT/MIN(01)/DEC/2, para. 17.
49 "Revised General Guidelines Regarding the Form and Contents of Reports to be Submitted by States Parties Under Articles 16 and 17 of the International Covenant on Economic, Social and Cultural Rights", UN Doc. E/C.12/1991/1.
50 For example, "Second periodic report of Israel", UN Doc. E/1990/6/Add.32, paras 531–40; "Initial report of Brazil", UN Doc. E/1990/5/Add.53, para. 873; "Fourth periodic report of Italy", UN Doc. E/C.12/4/Add.13.
51 "Second report of New Zealand", UN Doc. E/1990/6/Add.33, paras 651–75; "Fourth report of Canada", UN Doc. E/C.12/4/Add.15, paras 549–63.
52 "Initial report of Moldova", UN Doc. E/1990/5/Add.52, paras 593, 595; "Fourth periodic report of Denmark", UN Doc. E/C.12/4/Add.12, para. 481; "Initial report of China", UN Doc. E/1900/5/add.59, p. 233.
53 "Fourth periodic report of Denmark", UN Doc. E/C.12/4/Add.12, paras 485–6.
54 "Fourth periodic report of Italy", UN Doc. E/C.12/4/Add.13.
55 "Recommendation on the Status of Scientific Researchers, 1974, adopted on 20 November 1974 by the General Conference of UNESCO at its eighteenth session, held in Paris", in Symonides and Volodin (1999, 218).
56 UN Doc. A/RES/53/152.
57 Additional Protocol to the American Convention on Economic, Social and Cultural Rights, O.A.S. T.S. No. 69, (1989) 28 I.L.M. 156, entered into force 16 November 1999 (San Salvador Protocol).
58 Council of Europe Convention for the Protection of Human Rights and Dignity of the Human Being with Regard to the Application of Biology and Medicine (Convention on Human Rights and Biomedicine), ETS. 164, Oviedo, 4 April 1997.
59 Organization of African Unity, African Charter on Human and Peoples' Rights, adopted on 27 June 1981; Protocol to the African Charter on Human and Peoples'

Rights on the Rights of Women in Africa, adopted by the Second Ordinary Session of the Assembly of the Union, Maputo, 11 July 2003.

60 ICESCR, Article 2(2).

61 ICESCR, Article 4.

62 UN Doc. E/CN.4/Sub.2/RES/2000/7. For the draft resolution see UN Doc. E/CN.4/Sub.2/2000/L.20.

63 UN Doc. E/CN.4/Sub.2/2000/13.

64 UN Doc. E/CN.4/Sub.2/2000/NGO/14.

65 Eide (UN. Doc. E/CN.4/Sub.2/2000/SR.11, para. 27; UN. Doc. E/CN.4/Sub.2/2000/SR.24, para. 51; UN. Doc. E/CN.4/Sub.2/2000/SR.25, para. 82); Rodriguez Cuadros (UN. Doc. E/CN.4/Sub.2/2000/SR.12, para. 60); Oloka-Onyango (UN. Doc. E/CN.4/Sub.2/2000/SR.25, para. 89).

66 "Intellectual property and human rights", UN Doc. E/CN.4/Sub.2/RES/2001/21.

67 "Access to Medication in the Context of Pandemics such as HIV/AIDS", UN Doc. E/CN.4/RES/2001/33; "Access to Medication in the Context of Pandemics such as HIV/AIDS", UN Doc. E/CN.4/RES/2002/32; "Access to Medication in the Context of Pandemics such as HIV/AIDS, Tuberculosis and Malaria", UN Doc. E/CN.4/RES/2003/29.

68 "The Impact of the Agreement on Trade-Related Aspects of Intellectual Property Rights on human rights", UN Doc. E/CN.4/Sub.2/2001/13, paras 10–11.

69 UN Doc. E/CN.4/Sub.2/2001/13, para. 21. On this see also Helfer (2004b, 168).

70 UN Doc. E/CN.4/Sub.2/2001/13, para. 22.

71 UN Doc. E/CN.4/Sub.2/2001/13, para. 23.

72 UN Doc. E/CN.4/Sub.2/2001/13, paras 61–2 (references omitted). The reference is to "Globalisation, TRIPS and access to pharmaceuticals", *WHO Policy Perspectives on Medicines: WHO Medicines Strategy 2000–2003*, No. 3, March 2001 (WHO/EDM/2001.2), p. 6.

73 UN Doc. E/CN.4/Sub.2/2001/13, para. 62 (references omitted).

74 United Nations Declaration on the Rights of Indigenous Peoples, UN General Assembly Resolution 62/295 of 13 September 2007.

75 "Draft United Nations Declaration on the rights of indigenous peoples", UN Doc. E/CN.4/Sub2/RES/1994/45, Article 29. See also "Technical Review of the United Nations Draft Declaration on the Rights of Indigenous Peoples", UN Doc. E/CN.4/Sub.2/1994/2/Add.1.

76 UN Doc. E/CN.4/Sub2/RES/1994/45, Article 12.

77 "Draft Principles and Guidelines for the Protection of the Heritage of Indigenous People, Final Report of the Special Rapporteur", UN Doc. E/CN.4/Sub.2/1995/26; "Report of the Seminar on the Draft Principles and Guidelines for the Protection of the Heritage of Indigenous People", UN Doc. E/CN.4/Sub.2/2000/26. The draft principles and guidelines were adopted by the sub-commission: UN Doc. E/CN.4/Sub.2/DEC/107/2000/107.

78 UN Doc. E/CN.4/Sub.2/1995/26, para. 51.

79 UN Doc. E/CN.4/Sub.2/1995/26, para. 23(b).

80 UN Doc. E/CN.4/Sub.2/1995/26, para. 23(c).

81 "Convention (No. 169) concerning Indigenous and Tribal Peoples in Independent Countries", adopted on 27 June 1989 by the General Conference of the International Labour Organization at its seventy-sixth session.

82 "The Convention on Biological Diversity", adopted on 5 June 1992 by the UN Conference on Environment and Development (UNCED), Rio de Janeiro, Brazil.

83 Papers presented at this meeting are available at www.wipo.int/documents/en/meetings/1998/indip/.

84 UN Doc. E/CN.4/Sub.2/2001/13, para. 65.

85   "Guideline for the review of the draft principles and guidelines on the heritage of indigenous, Working paper submitted by Yozo Yokota and the Saami Council", UN Doc. E/CN.4/Sub.2/AC.4/2004/5, para. 26.
86   Convention on the Protection and Promotion of the Diversity of Cultural Expression, CLT-2005/CONVENTION DIVERSITE-CULT REV.
87   UN Doc. E/CN.4/Sub.2/AC.4/2004/5, paras 8–9.
88   See also Articles 13(2)(b) and (c), 14, 16(1), 18, 21 and 22.
89   UN Doc. E/CN.4/2003/58, para. 81. On "neglected diseases", see the 2004 report of Special Rapporteur Paul Hunt: UN Doc. E/CN.4/2004/49.
90   UN Doc. E/CN.4/RES/2003/29; also UN Doc. E/CN.4/RES/2004/26.
91   "General Comment No. 3", UN Doc. CRC/GC/2003/3, para. 29.
92   UN Doc. E/CN.4/RES/2003/29.
93   UN Doc. CRC/GC/2003/3.
94   UN Doc. E/CN.4/2004/49, para. 42.
95   "Report of the Special Rapporteur, Paul Hunt; Mission to the World Trade Organization", UN Doc. E/CN.4/2004/49/Add.1, para. 44.
96   "Report submitted by the Special Rapporteur on the right to food, Jean Ziegler, in accordance with Commission on Human Rights resolution 2003/25", UN Doc. E/CN.4/2004/10, para. 37.
97   International Covenant on Civil and Political Rights, (1976) 999 UNTS 171, Article 19(2).
98   "Report of the Special Rapporteur on the promotion and protection of the right to freedom of opinion and expression, Mr Abid Hussain, submitted in accordance with Commission resolution 2001/47", UN Doc. E/CN.4/2002/75, para. 67. But on the negative aspects of the Internet, see e.g. "Uniting Against Terrorism", UN Doc. A/60/825, paras 58–61, 85.
99   "Report of the Special Rapporteur on the promotion and protection of the right to freedom of opinion and expression, Ambeyi Ligabo", UN Doc. E/CN.4/2006/55, para. 37.
100 "The right to freedom of opinion and expression", UN Doc. E/CN.4/RES/2004/42, para. 4(a); also "The right to freedom of opinion and expression", UN Doc. E/CN.4/RES/2003/42, para. 5.
101 International Covenant on Civil and Political Rights, Article 7(2).
102 UN Doc. E/CN.4/Sub.2/2001/13. See Heller and Eisenberg (1998).
103 UN Doc. E/C.12/1991/1.
104 *Legality of the Threat or Use of Nuclear Weapons*, International Court of Justice, Advisory Opinion, 8 July 1996, para. 78.
105 GA Res. 3384 (XXX), Article 2.

REFERENCES

Adalsteinsson, Ragnar and Thorhallson, Pall (1993), "Article 27", in G. Alfredsson, A. Eide and G. Melander (eds), *The Universal Declaration of Human Rights, A Common Standard of Achievement* (The Hague: Kluwer Law), pp. 575–96.
Bidault, Mylène (2000), "La protection des droits culturels par le Comité des droits économiques, sociaux et culturels", UN Doc. E/C.12/2000/14.
Chapman, Audrey R. (2000), "Approaching intellectual property as a human right: Obligations related to Article 15(1)(c)", UN Doc. E/C.12/2000/12.
Coombe, Rosemarie J. (1998), "Intellectual property, human rights and sovereignty: New dilemmas in international law posed by the recognition of indigenous knowledge and the conversation of biodiversity", *Indiana Global Legal Studies Journal*, 6: 59–115.

Dennis, Michael J. (2000), "The Fifty-fifth Session of the UN Commission on Human Rights", *American Journal of International Law*, 94:1, 189–97.

Dommen, Caroline (2000), "Economic, social and cultural rights and WTO work on intellectual property rights – Current processes and opportunities", UN Doc. E/C.12/2000/20.

ECOSOC (2000a), "Protecting the rights of Aboriginal and Torres Strait Islander traditional knowledge", UN Economic and Social Council, UN Doc. E/C.12/2000/17.

ECOSOC (2000b), "Protection of Intellectual Property under the TRIPS Agreement", UN Economic and Social Council, UN Doc. E/C.12/2000/18.

Green, Maria (2000), "Drafting history of Article 15(1)(c) of the International Covenant on Economic, Social and Cultural Rights", UN Doc. E/C.12/2000/15.

Helfer, Laurence R. (2004a), "Human rights and intellectual property: Conflict or co-existence?", *Netherlands Quarterly of Human Rights*, 22: 167–79.

_____ (2004b), "Regime shifting: The TRIPs agreement and new dynamics of international intellectual property lawmaking", *Yale Journal of International Law*, 29: 1–83.

Heller, Michael A. and Eisenberg, Rebecca S. (1998), "Can patents deter innovation? The anticommons in biomedical research", *Science*, 280 (1 May): 698–700.

Jacanimijoy, Antonio (1998), "Initiatives for protection of rights of holders of traditional knowledge, indigenous peoples and local communities", WIPO/INDIP/RT/98/4E, 15 July.

Lauterpacht, H. (1952), "The problem of the revision of the law of war", *British Yearbook of International Law*, 39: 360–82.

Lifton, Robert J. (1986), *The Nazi Doctors: Medical Killing and the Psychology of Genocide* (New York: Basic Books).

Lim, Hoe (2001), "Trade and human rights: What's at issue?", UN Doc. E/C.12/2001/WP.2.

Morsink, Johannes (2000), *The Universal Declaration of Human Rights: Origins, Drafting, and Intent* (Philadelphia, PA: University of Pennsylvania Press).

Schabas, William A. (1991), "The omission of the right to property in the international covenants", *Hague Yearbook of International Law*, 4: 135–60.

Stiglitz, Joseph (2003), "Trade imbalances", *The Guardian*, 15 August.

Symonides, J. and Volodin, V. (1999), *UNESCO and Human Rights, Standard-Setting Instruments, Major Meetings, Publications* (Paris: UNESCO).

UNDP (1999), *Human Development Report 1999* (New York: Oxford University Press).

UNESCO (2002), *Main Lines of an Action Plan for Implementation of the UNESCO Universal Declaration on Cultural Diversity* (Paris: UNESCO).

Yamin, Alicia Ely (2002), "Not just a tragedy: Access to medications as a right under international law", *Boston University International Law Journal*, 21: 325–70.

8 Conclusion

VLADIMIR VOLODIN AND YVONNE DONDERS

"A new era in the human rights work of the United Nations has been proclaimed." With these words, Kofi Annan opened the first session of the Human Rights Council in June 2006. A year before, in his report *In Larger Freedom*, Annan had maintained that human rights, development and security form a three-pillar unity. He argued that no society can develop without peace and security, no state can be secure if its people are condemned to poverty and no nation can be secure or prosperous for long if the basic rights of its members are not protected.

The Secretary-General reiterated that the promotion and protection of *all* human rights, whether civil, cultural, economic, political or social, are necessary for a life in dignity. He thereby reaffirmed the principles of indivisibility, interrelatedness and interdependence of all human rights. These principles have been confirmed on several occasions, for example at the World Conference on Human Rights in Vienna in 1993, as well as more recently in the resolution of the General Assembly establishing the Human Rights Council.

Daily practice reveals, however, differential attitudes towards civil and political rights, on the one hand, and economic, social and cultural rights on the other. States tend to take more seriously civil and political rights. There is often a sense of intolerance towards violations of civil and political rights as opposed to violations of economic, social and cultural rights. At the same time, an increasing number of situations where human rights are not respected are conditioned upon economic, social and cultural factors. To mention the most eloquent example, widespread poverty, which continues to be one of the most serious challenges in today's world, is linked to shortcomings in education, especially lack of quality education, as well as lack of adequate food and proper health care. All these problems, as recognized in the various international instruments, have inherent human rights dimensions. The implementation of human rights clearly requires a holistic approach. All the different categories of human rights, laid down in the Universal Declaration, were meant to be achieved for all human beings. The particular attention paid to certain rights or to specific groups does not change the principle that all human rights are equally important and that many rights cannot be implemented without others; this principle preserves all its pertinence despite the particular attention that could be paid to certain rights at certain times.

Respect for human rights and fundamental freedoms remains a main purpose of the United Nations. This is a shared goal of all the different bodies, programmes and specialized agencies, each one of which should contribute to the realization of human rights within its fields of competence. UNESCO as a specialized agency was assigned the task of promoting collaboration among states through education, science and culture in order to further universal respect for justice, for the rule of law and for the human rights and fundamental freedoms. UNESCO's actions in the promotion of human rights focus on advancing mutual understanding among peoples, promoting education and maintaining, increasing and diffusing knowledge.

In accordance with its mandate, UNESCO advances all human rights by means of education and research. The organization, for example, encourages research cooperation, conducts studies, organizes seminars and conferences and disseminates the results. UNESCO has a special responsibility for human rights relating to education, science, culture and information. The studies in this book were commissioned as part of its efforts to increase knowledge on the rights within its competence. This knowledge should not only benefit academic and research institutions but should become an instrument in the hands of policy-makers in their action to improve implementation. This publication serves to uphold the principles of indivisibility, interrelatedness and interdependence of all human rights. It also addresses various issues of general character linked to economic, social and cultural rights. Several of the rights within the mandate of UNESCO are analysed in order to elaborate further on their nature, content and corresponding state obligations.

Clearly, the issues at stake are not the same for each of these rights. While much work within the UN system, as well as within the academic community, has been done on the right to education, the same cannot be said for the right to take part in cultural life and the right to enjoy the benefits of scientific progress and its applications. At the same time, the picture of our world today obliges us to look with increasing attention into these issues. Violations of cultural rights have been the underlying cause of tensions within and between societies, and have even led to violent conflicts. Furthermore, while scientific and technological progress has brought prosperity and opportunities for some, it has been out of reach for most others, for example in the field of information technology and health facilities, including medicine. Even with regard to the right to education many questions are still unsettled. The debate has moved from "education for all" to "quality education for all". Education should not only be available and accessible for all children, but it should also have a quality and relevance that makes it useful for their future.

Much remains to be done at the conceptual level. More clarity concerning the scope and content of these rights is needed for them to be better implemented by states. The international human rights law is designed to protect human beings against the abuses of states. International human rights standards and mechanisms for their protection provide states with guidance on how to implement human rights in their territories. They indicate what action states should refrain from so as not to interfere with or constrain the exercise of human rights. They also establish what states should do in order to fulfil human rights and prevent and prohibit their violation by third parties.

A fundamental element of human rights protection is the existence of a judicial remedy. This implies that, apart from monitoring through the various reporting procedures, courts or other adjudicating institutions should be able to handle cases of alleged violations of human rights. While for civil and political rights there is a general consensus on their justiciability at both national and international levels, for most economic, social and cultural rights international or national judicial scrutiny is disputed. These rights are said to be unsuitable for handling by a court or similar body. However, jurisprudence in a number of countries with different judicial systems shows otherwise. Economic, social and cultural rights are justiciable to the extent that they give rise to obligations to respect and protect. Moreover, national courts have managed to address issues relating to the more problematic obligation to fulfil. The "insuperable" character of the obstacles to the justiciability of these rights is more perceived than real. The fact that the mandate of the working group dealing with the elaboration of an optional protocol to the International Covenant on Economic, Social and Cultural Rights has been prolonged by the Human Rights Council is a sign of the increasing consensus on the need to place all categories of rights on an equal footing. The clarification of the content of these rights, as well as the corresponding state obligations, continues to be vital.

Further elucidation of their content would also greatly contribute to the elaboration of indicators to assess the level of their implementation. By developing indicators, legal human rights norms are translated into operational standards allowing for the establishment of measurable goals and benchmarks. Indicators would thus increase the capacity for monitoring the performance of states and serve for the identification of problematic areas where additional efforts are required. A major step towards the realization of economic, social and cultural rights would be the development of a set of indicators specific to each right. Some progress has been made in relation to the right to education, but much more work remains to be done with regard to the right to take part in cultural life and cultural rights in general and the right to enjoy the benefits of scientific and technological progress.

The well-known phrase that "human rights can only be enjoyed if they are known" preserves all its pertinence. This is why human rights education is an integral part of the right to education and is considered itself as a human right. UNESCO has done much work to integrate human rights firmly in education, in the curricula as well as in the educational processes, the pedagogical methods and the environment in which education takes place.

Human rights should be integrated in research as well. This implies not only that continued research is needed on human rights issues. It means that a human-rights-based approach should be applied to all research undertaken.

Moreover, the conduct of research and the sharing of information on human rights issues, especially in the fields of education, culture, science and communication, should not only serve academic and research institutions. It should also equip policy-makers all over the world with knowledge which allows them to advance human rights.

REFERENCE

Annan, Kofi (2005), *In Larger Freedom: Towards Development, Security and Human Rights for All*, Report of the UN Secretary-General, UN Doc. GA A/59/2005, 21 March.

Index